DAZZLING DEBUTS

FIRST AT-BAT HOME RUNS

Edited by Giselle Stancic, Bill Nowlin,
and Jacob Pomrenke

Associate editors: Len Levin and Carl Riechers

Society for American Baseball Research, Inc.
Phoenix, AZ

Dazzling Debuts: Home Runs in First At-Bat

Edited by Giselle Stancic, Bill Nowlin, and Jacob Pomrenke
Associate editors Len Levin and Carl Riechers

Design: Gilly Rosenthol

Front cover photograph: Joleneloeber / Dreamstime.com

978-1-960819-31-4 (paperback)
978-1-960819-30-7 (ebook)
Library of Congress Control Number: 2024920579

Cronkite School at ASU
555 N. Central Ave. #406-C
Phoenix, AZ 85004
Phone: (602) 496-1460
Web: www.sabr.org
Facebook: Society for American Baseball Research
Twitter: @SABR

DAZZLING DEBUTS

FIRST AT-BAT HOME RUNS

CONTENTS

INTRODUCTION

Every baseball player experiences a series of *firsts* when they step onto the field: the nervous excitement of entering the locker room, the pride of putting on the team uniform, the awe-inspiring moment of exiting the dugout and crossing the white lines. But when a player walks up to the plate and hits a home run in his first major-league at-bat, he creates a wave of excitement among the fans, achieves a rare feat for the record books — and experiences the thrill of a lifetime in his professional career.

Dazzling Debuts: First At-Bat Home Runs is a celebration of these unforgettable moments, a tribute to the players who swung for the fences and, against the odds, connected with destiny. From the earliest days of the game to the modern era, the lore of the first at-bat home run has captivated fans and players alike. Through the end of the 2024 season, the number of major-league first at-bat home runs stands at 141. This book highlights a player from every current major-league team except the Milwaukee Brewers, who are still awaiting their entry into this exclusive group. However, we are including a first at-bat home run from the city's former team, the Milwaukee Braves, and look forward to the day that Brewers fans can celebrate their first.

For teams represented by players who are retired from the game, we're featuring a SABR biography that highlights his electrifying first at-bat homer. For teams represented only by active players, like the Texas Rangers and Washington Nationals, we're offering game recaps of their momentous days. And speaking of active players, let's not forget New York Yankees star Aaron Judge, who hit a home run in his first at-bat – just four pitches after teammate Tyler Austin hit his own first at-bat home run.

Stories of triumph

Within these following pages, you'll encounter players as diverse and captivating as the game they play:

- **Meet Daniel Nava** of the Boston Red Sox, who, on the very first pitch he saw, launched a grand slam and sent Fenway Park into a frenzy.
- **Witness the determination of Paul Gillespie**, the only AL/NL player to hit home runs in both his first and last at-bats, both times with the Chicago Cubs.
- **Relive the legendary home run of Pete Hill**, Negro National League star and future Hall of Famer, over the center-field fence at Detroit's Mack Field.
- **Marvel at the speed of Johnnie LeMaster**, San Francisco Giants shortstop who hit an inside-the-park home run off the Astroturf at Candlestick Park.

- **Feel the power of Mark Worrell**, a right-handed pitcher who defied expectations by slugging a three-run homer in his first at-bat as a St. Louis Cardinal.
- **Share in the awe of Marcus Thames' dazzling debut** when he hit his first home run as a Yankee against future Hall of Famer Randy Johnson.
- **Experience the fleeting triumph of John Hester**, the Arizona Diamondbacks catcher whose first homer would be the only one of his four years in the majors.
- **Be there for the start of Gary Gaetti's All-Star career**, when his first home run would foreshadow 359 more during his 20 years as a big-leaguer.
- **Cheer for Jon Nunnally**, the only player to achieve the feat of a first at-bat home run in both the US major leagues and Japan's Nippon Professional Baseball.

From Hall of Famers like Earl Averill, whose first at-bat home run led to a legendary career, to journeymen like Dave Machemer, whose long-awaited first at-bat proved that dreams can sometimes take years to achieve, each story tells the tale of a professional baseball player's resilience, accomplishment, and pure enjoyment in playing the game.

Beyond the major leagues

Dazzling Debuts also celebrates the global reach of baseball, and with the generous assistance from our colleagues in SABR chapters worldwide, we're honored to include players who hit first at-bat home runs in these national leagues:

- Nippon Professional Baseball – Japan
- Korea Baseball Organization – Korea
- Liga Mexicana del Pacífico – Mexico
- Liga de Béisbol Profesional Roberto Clemente – Puerto Rico

We welcome further information from countries such as the Dominican Republic, Venezuela, and other baseball leagues. These records, and the diligence it takes to preserve them, illustrate the universal appeal of a first at-bat home run and the shared thrill of achieving this remarkable event.

In addition, with research support from our colleagues at the All-American Girls Professional Baseball League Players Association, we explored the records for first at-bat home runs in the AAGPBL. While we did not locate a documented example, we have included an article about on-the-field innovations adopted by the AAGPBL to encourage more home-run hitting during the league's tenure (1943 to 1954), to better showcase the power and athleticism of women baseball players.

Explore more online

Every first at-bat home run tells a story, and while this book includes a selection of these once-in-a-lifetime memories, you can visit **SABR.org/dazzling-debuts** to immerse yourself in the interactive world of first at-bat home runs. Explore our full collection of player biographies, including:

- George Tebeau and Mike Griffin, nineteenth-century pioneers who were the first known major-leaguers to homer in their first at-bats – and both did so on the very same day.
- Hoyt Wilhelm, the Hall of Fame pitcher whose first at-bat home run at the Polo Grounds would be the only one of his 21-year career.
- Bill White, eight-time All-Star first baseman, who after hitting his first at-bat home run, added a single and double to his debut-game total.
- Dave Eiland, the only player in major-league history to give up a home run to the first batter he faced and hit a home run off the first pitcher he faced.
- Jay Bell, who hit his first home run the first time he ever stepped foot inside a major-league ballpark.
- Dan Bankhead, the first Black pitcher in the National League, who introduced himself to the Ebbets Field crowd with a blast to deep center field.
- Norihiro Komada, Japan's "Mr. Grand Slam" who played for 18 years in Nippon Professional Baseball and kicked off his career in style.

You can also discover online:

- Thrilling game recaps with play-by-play accounts.
- Player photographs and videos of their memorable swings.
- Audio recordings of players reliving their first at-bat homers.
- Links to more SABR resources like the Biography Project, Games Project, and Ballparks Project.

A shared passion

Dazzling Debuts: First At-Bat Home Runs is a celebration of the past and a look to the future of the game that we love. Baseball reminds us that anything is possible, that dreams can come true, and that with hard work and dedication, even the rarest of feats can be accomplished.

The *Dazzling Debuts* project team extends our deepest gratitude to the authors, editors, players, and research colleagues who shared their expertise and passion for baseball to make this publication possible.

And to every player who has ever stepped up to the plate for the first time and hit a home run: Congratulations on your achievement! We are so appreciative of the joy you bring to the game.

To the next generation of players: May your first home runs be just the beginning. We can't wait to see what you will do.

Giselle Stancic
September 2024

Scan here to find our full collection of Dazzling Debuts biographies, game recaps, exclusive audio interviews, and video highlights online at SABR.org!

JOHN HESTER

BY BILL PRUDEN

On August 28, 2009, John Hester made his major-league debut in a way kids can only dream of, hitting a home run in his first major-league at-bat. Hester became, according to MLB.com, the 102nd player to start his batting career that way.[1] But despite the dreamlike quality of his debut, his first home run was a culmination of years of hard work and dedication to a game he loved. His first at-bat was only part of a 10-year baseball odyssey that had its share of ups and downs but which, Hester said, left him with no regrets, winding up, in his view, "exactly the way it was supposed to."[2]

John Graves Hester was born on September 14, 1983, in Atlanta, the son of John Hester, a salesman, and Jo Hester, a schoolteacher who later became a photographer. He had two older sisters.[3] Hester attended Marist School, a private Catholic high school where he starred in football and baseball. While there was some interest from college football recruiters, baseball was his true love.[4]

Hester began playing baseball when he was seven years old. Originally a first baseman, he volunteered to be the catcher on a day when the team's regular catcher did not show up, and he found that he loved it. He "loved being involved" and he "loved getting dirty." While there was a little back and forth between first base and catching, for all intents and purposes by the end of that season he was a catcher, and he would be one until the end of this professional career. As the catcher at Marist, he earned all-state honors in 2002, after a season in which the right-handed-hitting backstop hit .400 with 8 home runs and 50 runs batted in. He then headed to Stanford University in California, where he continued his baseball career while pursuing a degree in economics.[5]

At Stanford, Hester played sparingly in his freshman and sophomore seasons, although he did have the unwanted distinction as a freshman of grounding to third for the final out as Rice defeated Stanford to win the College World Series in June 2003.[6] But for the most part, Hester rode the bench his first two years at Stanford. He watched and learned while Donny Lucy, who later played in parts of three seasons for the Chicago White Sox, handled most of the Cardinals' catching chores.[7] However, in 2005 Hester assumed the role of starting catcher when Lucy, who subsequently graduated, left school after being drafted by the White Sox, starting and playing every inning in 58 of the team's 59 games on a Stanford team that included future major leaguers Jed Lowrie and Greg Reynolds.[8] As a junior Hester hit .282 with a .358 on-base percentage and a .414 slugging average. He hit five home runs and had 41 RBIs. He also distinguished himself behind the plate with a .991 fielding average, while allowing only four passed balls, tied for

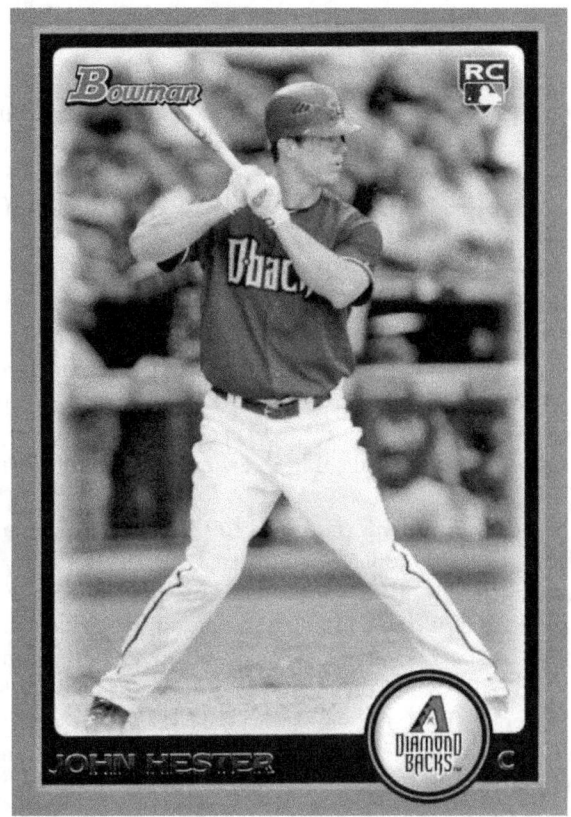

John Hester, Arizona Diamondbacks – Courtesy of Trading Card Database

the fewest among those who qualified in the Pac-10. He threw out just under 29 percent of would-be basestealers. In the postseason, Hester hit .278 with a stolen base in the NCAA Waco Regional and earned All-Regional honors. At season's end he was named the co-winner of Stanford's Most Improved Player Award and was an honorable mention All-Pac-10. He was also an honorable mention Pac-10 All-Academic choice, validating his belief that Stanford offered him the best combination of athletics and academics.[9]

At the end of his junior year at Stanford, Hester was drafted by the Boston Red Sox in the 33rd round of the 2005 amateur draft. But after heading off to Alaska to play summer ball, he never heard from the Red Sox.[10] Their reaction made Hester realize that for all his years in the game and the dreams he had long harbored, the "best thing for [him] was to play as a senior and then graduate."[11] And that he did. While working toward his degree in economics, he turned in another stellar performance behind the plate for the Cardinals. While his offensive numbers dropped off a little from the previous season, he remained a central cog on a Stanford team that exceeded expectations by defeating Texas in the Austin Regional.[12] Indeed, Hester's grand slam in the second game of the tourney was a key to the victory. While the team's season ended with losses to Oregon State, Hester had a memorable season and collegiate career, one that was capped by his selection by the Arizona Diamondbacks in the 13th round of the 2006 draft.[13]

With his Stanford degree in hand, Hester began his professional career after signing a contract with Arizona on June 15, 2006. Assigned to Missoula (Montana), the Diamondbacks' entry in the Rookie-level Pioneer League, the young catcher hit .271 in 56 games. He had 41 RBIs and scored 36 runs; 26 of his 52 hits went for extra bases. He boasted a .997 fielding average, had seven passed balls, and threw out 22 percent of the runners who attempted to steal on him.

Hester spent the 2007 season with the Visalia (California) Rawhide of the Class-A California League. The 6-foot-4 backstop batted .263 in 79 games with 43 RBIs. His fielding average dropped slightly, as he committed a career high 10 errors while allowing nine passed balls. He threw out 35 percent of those who attempted to steal.

In 2008, Hester was promoted to the Mobile (Alabama) BayBears of the Double-A Southern League. As the team's primary catcher, he played in 92 games, hitting .268 with 49 RBIs and 11 home runs. He continued to develop his skills behind the plate, raising his fielding average and reducing the number of passed balls, while throwing out 30 percent of would-be basestealers. After a short stint with the Phoenix Desert Dogs in the Arizona Fall League, Hester started the 2009 season on the Triple-A Reno Aces.

With the majors within reach, Hester turned in a fine performance with the Aces, hitting .328 with 66 RBIs and 61 runs scored in 92 games. His effort earned him an unexpectedly early promotion when on August 27 he was called up by the Diamondbacks.[14] Accompanied by his girlfriend (later his wife), Kristina, he headed to Phoenix.[15]

Arriving in time for the Friday, August 28, game against the Houston Astros, Hester was told he would start behind the plate in Sunday's game, but that he would get a chance to pinch-hit that night. With the team tired from the road trip that ended with a night game, which did not allow for their customary early morning return to Arizona, manager A.J. Hinch told Hester he planned to have him pinch-hit for starting pitcher Max Scherzer when the hard-throwing right-hander reached his pitch limit.[16] Hester's moment came in the bottom of the sixth.

With the Diamondbacks leading 11-6 and Scherzer having given up five earned runs while throwing 107 pitches, Hester got the nod from the skipper. Before he got his chance, the Diamondbacks scored another run when Miguel Montero hit a home run off Wilton López, a rookie who was also making his major-league debut. After Montero's homer, López got Gerardo Parra to fly to center, walked Brandon Allen, and struck out

Álex Romero. That brought Hester, hitting for Scherzer, to the plate with two outs.

In the matchup of two players both making their major-league debuts, Hester came out ahead. He hit López's 2-and-2 delivery 420 feet over the center-field wall to become the 102nd player to homer in his first major-league at-bat. For Hester it was a dream come true. Looking back, he said, "[A]s soon as I hit it I knew it was going to go out." His first reaction was "no way." It was, he recalled, "so surreal ... you work your entire life for this moment and it happens." He added there were "no words to describe it," and it was "such a fun moment." Contributing to the fun were his teammates' excited reactions. They enthusiastically applauded their new teammate and encouraged him to take a curtain call before the cheering crowd. Hester's good fortune on that memorable night also included his mother arriving in Phoenix in time to witness the big event, and the home-run ball caroming back onto the field and subsequently being given to the excited rookie who hit it.[17]

Hester unsurprisingly was thrilled with the way his debut went, commenting, "To have a start like this, it's something I could only have wished for, and it came true."[18] But his first major-league at-bat was only the beginning. He played in 14 more games over the rest of the 2009 season. He finished with a batting average of .250. His first-at-bat home run was his only homer that year, but he drove in two more runs and also counted two doubles among his seven hits. While almost half of his game appearances were as a pinch-hitter, Hester caught in eight games, six of which he started. Despite the small sample size, by throwing out two of the eight runners who attempted to steal, and allowing no passed balls, the 25-year-old Hester gave every indication he could be a big-league catcher.

Diamondbacks manager Hinch offered early praise, observing that Hester was "very solid behind the plate, a very bright guy who knows how to call games. He's handled the role which is a difficult role pretty well. ... I think he handles the staff well."[19] For Hester it was a big learning experience, and he said he tried to absorb as much as he could "from pretty much whoever's willing to give it to [him]."[20]

Having gotten a taste of the big leagues, Hester was ready for more when he reported to spring training in February 2010. His performance during his late-season call-up was cause for optimism, but when the Diamondbacks broke from spring training, Hester was sent back to Reno. The team decided to go with Montero, who had been the primary backstop in 2009, and Chris Snyder, who was eventually sent to the Pittsburgh Pirates at the trading deadline. Hester was not that surprised and he used his playing time with the Aces to further hone his skills. He ended up playing in 37 games. He hit .370 with 51 hits, 23 of them for extra bases. He drove in 29 runs and did a solid job behind the plate.

Before long Hester got a second shot at the big leagues when he was called up by the Diamondbacks in April, making his first appearance on April 11. He ultimately played in 38 games for a team that finished 65-97, having fired Hinch in midseason before turning to Kirk Gibson with little discernible change. Hester's season in some respects mirrored the team's. Hitting .211, he had 20 hits, adding two home runs to the auspicious debut blast.

Seeking to catch on with the Diamondbacks for good, over the winter of 2010-2011, Hester played in 10 games for the Gigantes del Cibao in the Dominican Republic Winter League. He hit .265, but his nine hits were matched by nine strikeouts. The start of the 2011 season saw Hester again in Reno. He hit .263 in 10 games before becoming the "player to be named later" in a trade the Diamondbacks had made with the Baltimore Orioles before the season.

That transaction represented another chapter in the continuing education the Stanford-educated Hester received in professional baseball. In looking back, he recalled how the call-ups and resulting spring hopes translated to only another season in Triple A. He "recognize[d] how easy it was to view players as assets." He came to understand the precarious nature of his own baseball situation. Years later, he recalled that when he was traded to the Orioles, he saw it as a "new start," but while he was excited about the opportunity, it was still "jarring."

Hester continued working to establish himself as solid backup major-league catcher, but after his career was over, he thought back to the time he was the proverbial "player who was named later." He ruefully observed that with the deal he "had checked almost every box on the transaction sheet." But he also acknowledged that he still got to "experience it all."

The Orioles sent Hester to the Norfolk Tides of the Triple-A International League. He played in 82 games for Norfolk, batting .251, but unlike the previous two years, when September rolled around, there was no call-up to the majors.

Hester started the 2012 season back with the Tides, but on April 12 he was released. He was not unemployed for long. While driving from Norfolk back home to Phoenix, he got a call from the Los Angeles Angels. Looking for catching insurance, the Angels signed him on April 22.[21] Going to the Angels was, Hester said, a very "lucky" move. His experience with the Angels "was great" from the outset, as they "made [him] feel a part of the organization."

The Angels assigned Hester to the Triple-A Salt Lake Bees, where he played in 26 games and hit .217. But as the Angels' need for catching depth became evident, Hester was called up. The move proved to be fortuitous, for not long after, starting catcher Chris Iannetta broke his wrist. Hester helped fill the gap, appearing in 39 games, 27 of which he started. He hit only .212, however, as the Angels finished the season with a record of 89-73.

Reflective of the roller-coaster his baseball life had become, Hester began the 2013 season back in Salt Lake City. While he got another late-season call-up after hitting .237 for the Bees, September 16, 2013, marked his final major-league appearance. He pinch-hit in the eighth inning of an Angels' 12-1 blowout of the Oakland A's and drew a walk. He caught the bottom of the ninth for his last major-league stint behind the plate.

The 2014 season saw Hester again with the Salt Lake Bees. He appeared in 71 games, starting in 65, and batted .261, his best minor-league season average since his effort with Reno in 2009. But unlike the season preceding his magical first-at-bat homer, when the 2014 minor-league season ended, Hester was not recalled by the Angels. On September 30 the 31-year-old catcher was released.

Again he was not without a team for long. The Philadelphia Phillies, looking for depth at catcher, signed Hester to a minor-league deal with a spring-training invitation.[22]

Unhappily for Hester, while in spring training he tore the medial meniscus in his left knee, and the required surgery left him sidelined for a crucial six weeks.[23] While, in his own words, he "bounced back quickly" from the surgery, he missed most of spring training, losing the opportunity to truly compete for a roster spot. Instead, after appearing in nine games with the Triple-A Lehigh Valley Iron Pigs and a single appearance with Double-A Reading, on June 3, 2015, John Hester was released by the Phillies.

Notwithstanding the Phillies' decision, Hester recovered from the injury and still had the option of trying to sign with another team. He would most likely return to the minors and have to work his way back to the big leagues. Adding to his decision-making process was that his wife, Kristina, whom Hester married in 2013, was 8½ months pregnant with their first child. Although it was a challenging time, he said his decision was not all that hard to make. The situation was very different from when he was released by the Orioles and signed by the Angels. That time, he recalled, he "was not ready for my career to end, I was not ready to stop playing." But after that first experience, he had come to accept that it was all "part of the game," and he was "not going to play forever." Hester had "scratched the itch" and had the satisfaction of achieving his dream of being a big-league baseball player. He walked away from the game he loved after playing professional baseball for 10 seasons. Hester said he "did not regret a thing," and he believed that it all went "exactly the way it was supposed to." Looking back, he said, "I did not want to bounce around or play Triple A just to have a job."

But with a baby on the way, he did not rule out being involved in baseball in another capacity. After talking with veterans and front-office types who cautioned that it could be hard to reconnect with the game after being away, Hester took a job as a scout for the Seattle Mariners.[24] At the same time, he also looked ahead and earned his license as an investment adviser.[25] After three years as a baseball scout, a job that often kept him on the road and away from his growing family (a second daughter was born in 2017), Hester left baseball behind – at least directly. He joined Pacific Capital Resource Group in Scottsdale, Arizona, as a financial adviser.[26]

John worked for Pacific Capital until the fall of 2021, when he joined the Baseball Division of BIP Wealth, one of the Southeast's leading wealth-management firms, of which he was a one-time client. Based in Scottsdale, Hester as of 2024 worked with draft-eligible, current, and retired baseball players and their families. BIP's Baseball Division includes other former players who, like Hester, can bring their own experience to the process.[27] Hester said that "as a former player I have walked in their shoes and that helps build trust." Some of the agents he deals with are people he knows from his playing days, so his baseball background complements his financial expertise and experience.[28]

Meanwhile, although he no longer has to endure the travel burdens of professional baseball, Hester stayed involved with sports and fatherhood. His older girls are involved in swimming and volleyball. A third daughter was born in December 2023.[29]

SOURCES

In addition to the sources cited in the Notes, the author consulted Baseball-Reference.com and Baseball-Almanac.com.

NOTES

1   Ed Eagle, "Players with Home Run in First At Bat," MLB.com, https://www.mlb.com/news/home-run-in-first-at-bat-c265623820.

2   Author telephone interview with John Hester, March 7, 2024. Unless otherwise indicated, all direct quotations attributed to Hester come from this interview.

3   Hester interview.

4   Hester interview.

5   John Hester, 2005 Baseball Roster, Stanford University Athletics, https://gostanford.com/sports/baseball/roster/john-hester/7329.

6   Pat Borzi, "With First Trophy in Hand, Rice Starts Quest for More," *New York Times*, June 25, 2003.

7   Hester interview.

8   DBacksEurope, "Your Random D-Back: John Hester," AZ Snake Pit, May 18, 2023, https://www.azsnakepit.com/2023/5/18/23727508/your-random-d-back-john-hester.

9   Hester, 2005 Baseball Roster.

10 Mark Whicker, "Hester Ends Up Being Angels' Catch of the Day," *Orange County Register* (Orange, California), May 12, 2012, https://

www.ocregister.com/2012/05/12/hester-ends-up-being-angels-catch-of-the-day/.

11 Whicker.

12 DBacksEurope, "Your Random D-Back: John Hester."

13 Associated Press, "Hester's Grand Slam Gives Stanford Edge Over Texas," ESPN, June 4, 2006, https://www.espn.com/college-sports/news/story?id=2469723.

14 Hester interview.

15 Hester interview.

16 Hester interview.

17 "Your Random D-Back: John Hester; Hester interview; Bob McManaman, "View from the Press Box," *Arizona Republic* (Phoenix), August 29, 2009.

18 Bob McManaman, "D-Backs bust out bats, rout Astros," *Arizona Republic*, August 29, 2009. ester Homers in First MLB At-Bat as D-Backs Roll."

19 Jim Gintonio, "Hester Feeling 'More Comfortable," *Arizona Republic*, September 9, 2009.

20 Gintonio.

21 Whicker.

22 "Report: Phillies to Sign Catcher John Hester," Sports Talk Philly, October 23, 2014, https://www.sportstalkphilly.com/news/report-phillies-to-sign-catcher-john-hester.

23 Shawn Krest, "Phillies' John Hester Out Six Weeks After Knee Surgery," CBS Sports, March 10, 2015, https://www.cbssports.com/mlb/news/phillies-john-hester-out-six-weeks-after-knee-surgery/.

24 Hester interview.

25 DBacksEurope, "Your Random D-Back: John Hester."

26 Hester interview; "John Hester Joins BIP Wealth's Baseball Division," PR Newswire, October 12, 2021, https://www.prnewswire.com/news-releases/john-hester-joins-bip-wealths-baseball-division-301397245.html.

27 "John Hester Joins BIP Wealth's Baseball Division."

28 Hester interview.

29 Hester interview; "John Hester, CFP," BIP Wealth, https://bip-wealth.com/team/john-hester-cfp/.

JERMAINE DYE

BY SEAN KOLODZIEJ

For a professional athlete, it takes perseverance and courage to come back from an injury and play again at an elite level. Jermaine Dye had to do this many times during his baseball career. Despite having to overcome injuries at almost every stop during his 14 years in the majors, the 6-foot-4, 210-pound right fielder with a powerful bat and a great arm succeeded when most others would have failed. Beginning with a home run in his first major-league at-bat, he was able to add a Silver Slugger Award, a Gold Glove Award, and a World Series MVP Award to his résumé before retiring.

Jermaine Trevell Dye was born on January 28, 1974, in Oakland, California, to Bill and Neda (Morgan) Dye. He grew up in San Pablo, 14 miles north of Oakland, where his father drove a bus for the city. On some summer mornings, Jermaine and his sister Angie would be dropped off by their father at Candlestick Park in San Francisco. They watched the Giants take batting practice from the bleacher seats, and would be joined later on by their father after he completed his route.

Dye's father was also his coach in various youth leagues throughout his childhood. After he made it to the big leagues, Dye's father was still there for him. "He calls when he sees something wrong, and I call him when I need to tell him what I think," Jermaine told the *San Francisco Chronicle*. "He's been my coach all my life."[1]

Dye went to Will C. Wood High School in Vacaville, California. He was the quarterback for the football team and a small forward for the basketball team, and pitched for the baseball team. He received scholarship offers to play football (from Brigham Young) and basketball (from the University of Nevada at Las Vegas)), but ultimately chose to pursue baseball. "He was a good all-around player, a good student, everything," said Don Trolinger, Dye's high-school batting coach. "We knew he had (talent). We just didn't know where he would go with it."[2]

Dye was drafted by the Texas Rangers in the 43rd round (1,210th overall) of the June 1992 amateur draft. Opting to not sign with the Rangers, he chose to go to Cosumnes River College in Sacramento, California, to play for coach Rod Beilby. Instead of pitching, Beilby recommended that Jermaine become a hitter. The coach's suggestion turned out to be good advice. Dye finished his freshman year leading the team with a .397 batting average with a .480 on-base percentage and a .744 slugging percentage. He was second on the team in runs scored (29). He had nine assists as an outfielder. He was named Bay Valley Conference Most Valuable Player for the 1993 season.

Dye was drafted again, this time by the Atlanta Braves in the 17th round (488th overall) of the June 1993 draft. Brave scout Dave Wilder signed him on June 6.

Jermaine Dye, Atlanta Braves – Courtesy of Trading Card Database

Dye, 19 years old, started the 1993 season playing for the Braves affiliate in the Rookie-level Gulf Coast League (later known as the Florida Complex League). After batting .347 in 31 games, he was moved up to the Danville (Virginia) Braves of the Appalachian League. Dye hit his first professional home run at Danville. He finished the season batting .277 in 25 games.

After making a good impression playing rookie ball, Dye was promoted to the Macon (Georgia) Braves of the Class-A South Atlantic League for 1994 and continued to hit well, clocking 15 home runs with 98 RBIs while batting .298 in 135 games with a league record 41 doubles.

Another year brought another promotion, and Dye opened the '95 season playing for the Double-A Greenville Braves (Southern League). He again proved he was capable of hitting professional pitching, turning in 15 home runs with 71 RBIs while batting .285 in 104 games. He had an impressive 22 assists playing the outfield.

Once the season ended in Greenville, Dye played in the Arizona Fall League for the Sun Cities Solar Sox. The Braves sent Hall of Famer Willie Stargell, a special assistant, to Arizona to work with Dye. He hit well again, leading the league with 41 RBIs. The Braves added Dye to their 40-man major-league roster to prevent their losing him in the Rule 5 draft. The move gave Dye an automatic invite to spring training for the 1996 season.

After batting .364 with 12 RBIs in 25 spring-training games, Dye started the 1996 season with Richmond Braves of the Triple-A International League. This was not a controversial move, as the Braves already had three very good outfielders in Ryan Klesko, Marquis Grissom, and David Justice. "This spring Dye showed the kind of all-around natural ability that he had shown in previous years in the minors," Braves assistant general manager Dean Taylor said. "We feel he has a solid future as an everyday outfielder at the major-league level."[3]

Justice dislocated his left shoulder on May 15. The Braves needed an outfielder to replace him on the roster, and Dye was called up. Dye made his major-league debut on May 17. On a 1-and-0 count, he homered in his first at-bat off Reds pitcher Marcus Moore. He was the first Atlanta player to accomplish the feat, and the first Brave to do so since Chuck Tanner did it for Milwaukee in 1955.

Dye went on to win the starting right fielder job for the rest of the season, hitting .281/.304/.459 with 12 home runs in 98 games. Justice continued to travel with the team as he recovered from his injury, and he formed a bond with Dye. Said Justice, "I didn't have anybody to show me what I needed to do to be successful when I first came into the majors. That's why I'm going to do my best to help Jermaine become the best player that he can be."[4]

The Braves went 96-66 that season, finishing first in the NL East Division, and swept the Los Angeles Dodgers in the best-of-three Division Series. Dye only had two hits in 11 at-bats in the series, but one of the hits was a seventh-inning home run in Game Two that broke a 2-2 tie. After beating the St. Louis Cardinals in the Championship Series four games to three (Dye was 6-for-28), the Braves faced the New York Yankees in the World Series. After winning the first two games, the favored Braves lost the next four. Dye struggled in the series, going 2 for 17 (.118) with one RBI.

After losing the World Series, the Braves looked to revamp their outfield for the 1997 season. They traded Justice and Grissom to Cleveland for Kenny Lofton. They also traded Dye, along with pitcher Jamie Walker, to the Royals for outfielder Michael Tucker and infielder Keith Lockhart. The Royals were looking for a right-handed outfielder, and Dye fit the role perfectly. The trade was not received well in Kansas City, however, as Tucker was viewed as an up-and-coming prospect.

The 1997 season turned out to be a disaster for the Royals. Manager Bob Boone was fired in July and the club finished 67-94, in last place in the AL Central Division. Dye was plagued by injury. He ended up playing only 75 games, as he dealt with a severe bone bruise in his left foot. Later he suffered a strain in his right quadriceps. His offense declined, too, and at one point in the season, he was sent down to Triple-A Omaha to work on his hitting.

The Royals (72-89) moved up to third place in 1998. Dye played in only 60 games for the Royals. He had played poorly in spring training, largely because of his still sore right quadriceps, and he started the year at Omaha. He was recalled by the Royals in early May, but was again demoted to Omaha on June 29. He returned to the majors on August 11 when the Royals traded Jermaine Allensworth to the New York Mets. After seeming to get into a hitting groove, Dye tore cartilage in his right knee while getting into his car on September 1. The injury put an end to his season. In KC, he hit just .234, with 5 homers and 23 RBIs.

Because Dye was struggling at the plate and was injury-prone, expectations were probably low for his 1999 season. But he arrived fully healthy for spring training, although without a guarantee of making the big-league roster. He played well enough in spring training that when the Royals traded outfielder Jeff Conine to the Baltimore Orioles, Dye was named the starting right fielder to begin the season. He made the most of the opportunity. Finally playing fully healthy, he hit .294 with 27 home runs and 119 RBIs. The fans took to him, too, chanting "Dye-no-mite!" when he made a good play.

Dye continued his excellent hitting in 2000, establishing career highs in batting average (.321) and home runs (33), to go along with 118 RBIs. The numbers were good enough for him to be voted to start the All-Star Game. Dye's fielding was outstanding too; he won the AL Gold Glove for right fielders. He was the first Royals outfielder to win the award since Willie Wilson in 1980. Alongside teammates Johnny Damon and Carlos Beltrán, the Royals outfield seemed destined for great things.

That outfield was soon broken up. Damon, in the last year of his contract, was traded to the Oakland A's on January 8, 2001. Kansas City, a small-market team, had many players due for contract extensions, including Dye, whose contact was expiring at the end of 2002.

The 2001 season started out strong for Dye. He continued his solid hitting and great defense. Then, on July 25, he was traded to the Oakland A's in a three-team trade that sent Neifi Pérez to the Royals. As part of the trade, the Colorado Rockies received José Ortiz, Mario Encarnación, and Todd Belitz. Joe Posnanski, a columnist for the *Kansas City Star*, wrote, "Dye is everything that we want Kansas City baseball to be about. He's modest, works hard, keeps to himself, plays well, and now he's gone because the Royals simply can't afford him. Or won't afford him. Only (Royals owner) David Glass knows for sure."[5]

With the addition of Dye, the Athletics were sending a message that they were going all in on reaching the playoffs. With the help of Dye's bat (.297 batting average, 13 home runs, and 59 RBIs in 61 games), the A's finished the season with a record of 102-60, in second place in the AL West (the Seattle Mariners finished with a historic 116-46 record), and earned a wild-card spot in the postseason. In the AL Division Series,

Dye fractured his tibia by fouling a ball off his left leg in Game Four. The A's lost that game, and the series.

Dye signed a three-year, $32 million extension to stay with the A's on January 16, 2002. The deal was the richest in team history at the time. The contract also included a $14 million team option for the 2005 season. Dye started the season on the injured list, still recovering from his broken leg. He made his season debut on April 26. He ended up batting .252 with 24 home runs and 86 RBIs in 131 games. The A's finished in first place in the AL West with a record of 103-59. But like the year before, they lost in the AL Division Series, this time to the Minnesota Twins, three games to two. Dye hit .400 for the series but had only one RBI.

Dye struggled with injuries for most of the 2003 season. He landed on the injured list twice. On April 24 he slipped and injured his knee while fielding a ball. On July 6 he separated his right shoulder in a home-plate collision with Anaheim catcher Bengie Molina. He played in only 65 games, hitting an abysmal .172 with 4 home runs and 20 RBIs. The A's again finished in first place in the AL West with a record of 96-66, and again lost the Division Series in five games, this time to the Boston Red Sox. Dye was 3-for-13 in the series with a home run and 3 RBIs.

Coming into the 2004 season, Dye was in the last year of his three-year contract with the A's. He was set to make over $11 million, and the A's had a $14 million option for 2005. He needed a great season for the team to justify the team's picking up that option. He started the year off strong. At the All-Star break, he was batting .285 with 16 home runs and 54 RBIs. In early August, Dye sprained his thumb while trying to make a sliding catch on the artificial turf in Minneapolis. Instead of taking time off, he insisted on playing through the pain. But the injury clearly affected his swing, and he cooled off in the second half of the season. He finished the year batting .265 with 23 home runs and 80 RBIs. The A's declined to exercise Dye's $14 million option. He became a free agent for the first time in his career.

Dye signed with the Chicago White Sox on December 9, 2004. The two-year deal was for $10.15 million, with a $6.75 million option for 2007. Dye turned down more lucrative offers to play for the White Sox, saying, "I felt Chicago was going in a good direction and with the pitching staff, I felt I had a better chance of helping the team out and getting into the playoffs. . . . I just wanted to be somewhere I could be happy."[6]

Dye replaced Magglio Ordóñez for the 2005 season. Ordóñez had spent the first eight seasons of his career with the White Sox, making the All-Star team four times and putting up power numbers. Dye matched that performance, hitting .274 with 31 homers and 86 RBIs in the regular season. The postseason, though, was when Dye truly earned his contract.

The 2005 White Sox finished in first place in the AL Central Division with a record of 99-63. They bulldozed their way through the postseason, sweeping the Red Sox in the Division Series, ousting the Angels, four games to one in the Championship Series, then sweeping the Houston Astros in the World Series. Dye was named the World Series MVP after hitting .438 with a home run and 3 RBIs, including the game-winning RBI in the deciding Game Four.

The next year, 2006, proved to be the monster year for Dye. He hit .315 with 44 home runs (second only to David Ortiz in the AL) and 120 RBIs. He made his second All-Star Game and won a Silver Slugger Award. He finished fifth in AL MVP voting. The White Sox, however, could not make it back to the World Series. They finished with a record of 90-72 and were third in the AL Central Division. On October 30 they exercised their $6.75 million option for Dye's 2007 season.

The 33-year-old Dye struggled in the first half of the season. He came back stronger in the second half, finishing the year with a respectable 28 home runs and 78 RBIs. His name came up in trade rumors all season, but on August 18 he signed a two-year extension with the White Sox worth $22 million, with a mutual option for 2010. Chicago struggled as a team and finished the year in fourth place in the division with a 72-90 record.

Dye returned to form in 2008, hitting .292 with 34 home runs and 96 RBIs. He tied for second in the AL with 77 extra-base hits. He finished second in the All-Star final vote to Evan Longoria, who made the last spot on the team. The White Sox returned to their winning ways and finished in first place in the AL Central Division, but lost in the Division Series to the Tampa Bay Rays three games to one. Dye batted .375 in the series, including a home run in Game Four.

Dye hit his 300th career home run on April 13, 2009. Making it extra special, the next batter, Paul Konerko, also hit his 300th home run. Dye hit well in the first half of the season. At the All-Star break, he had a .302 average with 20 home runs and 55 RBIs. However, his output severely declined after the break: just .179 with 7 home runs and 26 RBIs. According to Dye, the problem was that "he received less regular playing time after the White Sox's outfield became more 'crowded.'"[7] Left fielder Carlos Quentin returned from plantar fasciitis on July 20 and center fielder Alex Ríos was claimed off waivers on August 10. From then on, Dye got fewer at-bats and his slump continued into September. "Having everyone rotate between the outfield and DH, doing all that, I think it made it that much tougher than being in the lineup every day, trying to work your way out of a slump," he said. "It just kind of piled up and piled up."[8] On November 6 the White Sox bought out his $12 million mutual option for $950,000, making him a free agent again.

Dye entered the 2009-2010 offseason as a 35-year-old, two-time All-Star veteran with a World Series MVP to his name. Expectations were that he would have to take a pay cut from his previous year's $11.5 million salary. However, the offers that came in were surprisingly low. The Chicago Cubs offered him a one-year, $3 million contract. "No doubt, I've probably slowed down a little bit (defensively), but not enough to not be getting (attractive) offers," Dye said. "I just want to be treated fairly. I know the market is down, but there are still guys getting money that I feel I'm better than."[9] Dye decided to turn down all the low offers and wait until a good situation arose. He stayed in shape all season and set his sights on signing with a team for the 2011 season.

In 2010 Dye was inducted into the Cosumnes River College Hall of Fame. He said that being inducted was "one of the top three awards I have received. I played baseball in high school, but CRC is where I learned how and what it would take to play professional baseball."[10]

As the 2011 major-league season approached, Dye still had not received an offer he liked, and he was not interested in signing a minor-league contract. On March 31, 2011, he announced his retirement from baseball.

Retiring from baseball allowed Dye to spend more time with his wife, Tricia, and take a more active role in raising his three children, Devin, Tiara, and Jalen. Because he no longer had to travel during the baseball season, he was able to watch his kids play youth sports. He became an avid golfer, appearing in many pro-am tournaments. He began hosting an annual golf tournament benefiting Fresh Start, which provides surgeries and medical care to children in need. "Every year we come together and see what we are able to provide for these children through this one event, which is happiness, it's incredible," said Dye. "I'm very grateful to be a part of Fresh Start for so many years, providing life-changing work to so many."[11]

SOURCES

Unless otherwise indicated, all statistics and team records were taken from baseball-reference.com.

NOTES

1   Michelle Smith, "Dad Still Coaching Dye/Muni Driver Helped Steer His Career," *San Francisco Chronicle*, June 20, 2004: 31.

2   Tim Casey, "Everybody Loves Jermaine, a Nice Guy Who Finished First," *Sacramento Bee*, October 28, 2005: 17.

3   Bill Zack, "Braves Happy to Leave Florida, Spring Training," *Anderson* (South Carolina) *Independent Mail*, March 29, 1996: 27.

4   Terrence Moore, "Dye May Make Tutor Justice Expendable," *Atlanta Constitution*, May 18, 1996: 49.

5   Joe Posnanski, "Reality Is, Royals Can't Afford Anyone," *Kansas City Star*, July 25, 2001: 34.

6   Dave Van Dyck, "Dye the Kind of Guy Sox GM Wants," *Chicago Tribune*, December 10, 2004: 4-3.

7   "Why Is Jermaine Dye Looking for Work?" FoxSports, published February 11, 2010, updated January 8, 2015. https://www.foxnews.com/sports/why-is-jermaine-dye-looking-for-work, accessed May 15, 2024.

8   "Why Is Jermaine Dye Looking for Work?"

9   "Why Is Jermaine Dye Looking for Work?"

10 Jermaine Dye bio, California Community College Athletic Association, CCCAA (cccaasports.org), accessed May 15, 2024.

11 "Fresh Start Swings into Action, Presenting 8th Annual Celebrity Gold Classic Hosted by Jermaine Dye in Chicago. https://www.freshstart.org/news/fresh-start-swings-into-action-presenting-8th-annual-celebrity-golf-classic-hosted-by-jermaine-dye-in-chicago/, accessed May 15, 2024.

LUIS MONTAÑEZ

BY MALCOLM ALLEN

Less than one percent of players hit a home run in their first major-league at-bat. Achieving the hitting Triple Crown – leading a league in batting average, homers, and RBIs – in the minors is similarly unlikely.[1] Through 2023, an exclusive fraternity of just three members have achieved both of those feats: Gene Hasson, Bob Nieman, and the lone batsman to do them in the same year – Luis Montañez.[2]

Montañez, a right-handed-hitting outfielder, spent 15 years in professional baseball, including parts of four seasons in the majors with the Baltimore Orioles (2008-2010) and Chicago Cubs (2011).

On December 15, 1981, Luis Anibal Montañez García was born in Bayamón, Puerto Rico. He had an older sister. Their mother, Yolanda García Montañez, was a teacher, educating students from elementary through high-school levels. IBM employed her as a computer instructor, and she taught her own children to be bilingual from an early age. Luis's father, also named Luis Montañez, was a computer programmer and analyst. Before his career in tech, he pitched for neighborhood and town semipro teams, but his baseball ambitions were derailed by two tours in Vietnam after he was drafted into the US Army.

In Puerto Rico, the younger Luis was introduced to baseball by playing street games with broomsticks and bottle caps, and from batting against his father in the backyard. But an early experience discouraged him. "He hit me with a baseball when I was small, in the mouth, and it kind of scared me," he recalled. "I didn't want to play at all."[3]

Meanwhile, his dad became involved with upgrading the computer systems for one of the United States' largest medical centers, Jackson Memorial Hospital, affiliated with the University of Miami. Consequently, the Montañez family moved back and forth between Puerto Rico and Florida several times. Luis was about 11 when his father signed him up for his first organized baseball team, in Miami, to combat summer boredom. "My first year I was horrible," Montañez said. "I had two hits the entire season." He avoided the sport for a year, but things changed when he tried again. "All of a sudden I was good. I don't know how," he said. "A miracle from God. A divine providence."[4]

Despite Montañez's late start, his evident potential convinced his father to settle the family permanently in Miami, where strong high-school baseball programs would aid his son's development. Luis attended Coral Park High School, the same institution the Canseco twins – 1988 AL MVP José Canseco, and his brother Ozzie – graduated from in the early 1980s. "The road in front of the school was called Canseco Way," Montañez noted.[5] When the brothers appeared at an alumni game while he was a student, Montañez recalled, José arrived in a Ferrari,

Luis Montañez, Baltimore Orioles – Courtesy of Baltimore Orioles

sporting stylish Oakley sunglasses, with a supply of brand-new baseballs.

At Coral Park, Montañez maintained an excellent 3.8 grade-point average.[6] Then 6-feet tall and 170 pounds (he was listed at 6-feet-1, 195 as a professional), he attracted scouts with his shortstop play, particularly after one diving stop up the middle in a critical, sophomore-year district contest. "The ball jumped up and I kind of reacted to it, caught it, came up with the throw, got the out and saved a couple runs," he explained. "It was like an Ozzie Smith-type play. From that day, I started to get a lot of attention."[7]

Nicknamed Monty, the strong-armed Montañez honed his skills with a Police Athletic League team during summers.[8] As a high-school senior, he earned All-State recognition by batting .431 with 7 homers and 14 steals in 33 games.[9] With his June 2000 graduation approaching, he and his friend, Gulliver Preparatory School shortstop David Espinoza, were shaping up as Dade County's first first-round selections in baseball's amateur draft since Álex Rodríguez in 1994. Before 2000 was over, Rodríguez signed a record 10-year, $252 million free-agent deal negotiated by Scott Boras, the agent who also secured the first $50 million and $100 million baseball contracts for other clients. Boras wound up representing Espinoza, too, who peaked in Triple A after the Cincinnati Reds selected him 23rd overall, but Montañez, his family, and advisers declined the agent's overtures.[10]

On draft day, Montañez was drafted third overall by the Chicago Cubs. Shortly thereafter, he signed through scout Mike Soper for terms including a $2.75 million bonus.[11] "We thought Montañez was the best player for us in the country," explained Cubs scouting director Jim Hendry. "He's a lot like the [Alex] Gonzalez kid who plays for Toronto. His bat at 18 is probably farther along."[12]

"That week was hectic to say the least. The whole school kind of knew I was going to get drafted high because all the publications had said a lot of teams were interested in me," Montañez reflected in 2006.[13] The following year, he recalled, "There was a lot of pressure because I was 18 and coming out of high school. … My expectations were, yeah, I want to be in the major leagues in three years, and maybe that wasn't realistic."[14]

In the summer of 2000 Montañez's professional career had an outstanding beginning: 10 hits in his first 18 at-bats for the Cubs' rookie-level Arizona League affiliate.[15] He wound up earning the circuit's Most Valuable Player honors after producing a .344/.438/.531 slash line in 50 games. At the conclusion of the campaign, he was promoted to the Class-A Midwest League, where he appeared in eight contests for the Lansing (Michigan) Lugnuts.

Heading into 2001, Montañez was number 73 on *Baseball America*'s list of top 100 prospects. He was named to the Midwest League's midseason all-star team.[16] Although he batted .255 with five homers, he had 121 strikeouts in 124 games. His 33 doubles tied for seventh in the league.

In 2002 Montañez moved to the Daytona Cubs, in the advanced Class-A Florida State League. He batted .265, but with just four homers in 124 games. On defense, his error total increased from 32 to 38. He also made 22 of his appearances at second base instead of shortstop. At least partly due to Montañez's lack of progress, the Cubs dismissed Daytona manager Dave Trembley after the season. "There are a lot of people that were held accountable for this kid [Montañez]," Trembley remarked seven years later. "He didn't meet his obligation to the Chicago Cubs because, quite honestly, he wasn't mature enough."[17]

"I was real immature," Montañez said in 2007. "I have a relaxed personality. Dave's a little more tense and wanted me to get after it a little more. There was a little bit of frustration, like, 'Why doesn't this kid really care?' That's probably the perception I gave off. It's not that I didn't want to do well. I cared a lot."[18]

When Montañez returned to Daytona in 2003, his offensive numbers regressed (.253/.305/.333). He played more second base than shortstop (82 games to 33) while a younger prospect, Ronny Cedeño, took over the latter position. In 2004 Montañez was back at Daytona for the third consecutive year – but not for long. After just 20 appearances, he agreed to learn a new position in the Low-A Northwest League. "I was having a lot of defensive problems with throwing accuracy from the infield,

so I decided to go to the outfield and see if I could relieve the pressure off my defense and do a little more offensively," he said. "It got in my head that I didn't want to throw the ball away, and I'd throw the ball away."[19]

Later, Montañez acknowledged that the demotion represented a crossroads of sorts. "Sometimes you question whether you're good enough, but mostly I questioned whether I really wanted to do it. I was considering moving on with my life in another direction," he said. "But I sat down, thought about it, and said: 'Forget about that. This is a privilege. Everybody wants to do this.'"[20]

After joining the Boise Hawks, Montañez batted .297 with 8 homers and 48 RBIs in 72 games. He made the All-Star team and helped Boise win the Northwest League championship.[21] Next, he gained more outfield experience with the Gigantes de Carolina of the Puerto Rican Winter League, where his offense continued to improve from facing pitchers who had already reached the majors or Triple A.[22]

Montañez was back in the Midwest League to begin 2005. He played left field and batted .305 with 28 doubles and 12 homers in 82 games with the Peoria (Illinois) Chiefs. Still just 23, he was the lone Puerto Rican player to see action in that summer's Futures Game, the showcase of minor-league all-stars. "I am proud, it is the first time that I can represent Puerto Rico, that I have the flag on my uniform," he said. Montañez went 1-for-3 in the contest.[23] "Now that I made the change to the outfield, it's a little different, but I've been adjusting and things are going well," he said. "I have a lot of discipline, I have been maturing as a hitter."[24] That summer, Montañez ascended to the Double-A Southern League for the first time. In 45 games with the West Tenn Diamond Jaxx, he batted .268. The team finished with the circuit's best regular-season record before falling in the best-of-five finals.

Although Montañez hit .369 in 38 games with West Tenn in 2006, he batted just .225 in his first taste of Triple A, 82 games with Iowa Cubs of the Pacific Coast League. "I knew it was a hard road. I knew there was a lot of competition," he reflected that June. "But being young you think nothing's against you and that you can take on the world. I quickly realized that the competition was a little bit harder than I thought coming in."[25]

With outfielders Matt Murton and Ángel Pagán having cracked Chicago's big-league outfield corps in the previous two seasons – and top prospect Félix Pie on the verge of doing the same – the Cubs released Montañez in October. In November, he signed with the Baltimore Orioles. Baltimore's director of scouting, John Stockstill, who held the same position with the Cubs until the end of the 2005 campaign, opined, "[Montañez] might have had too high expectations on himself and the club pushed him a little too hard as well."[26]

During his first spring training with the Baltimore organization, Montañez described how the pressure he used to feel as a first-round draft pick had subsided. "As the years went on and more first-rounders show up in camps, I don't feel it anymore. I'm just one of the guys," he said. "I've made a lot of

All-Star teams, I went to the Futures Game two years ago. I've had some good years. So I'm happy with it. I'm still young. I don't feel like I need to start rushing."[27]

Yet Montañez's initial year in the Orioles' chain saw him moving backward, again. After hitting .259 in 69 Triple-A International League games with the Norfolk (Virginia) Tides to begin 2007, he was sent down to the Double-A Eastern League, where he batted .339 in 31 contests with the Bowie (Maryland) Baysox.

When Montañez, 26, found himself back at Bowie to begin 2008, he responded with the best season of his professional career. In 116 games, he batted .335 with 26 homers, 97 RBIs, and a .601 slugging percentage – all league-leading figures. He was named the Orioles organization's Player of the Month for both May and July.[28] He just missed winning the home-run derby at the Eastern League All-Star Game (Travis Snider prevailed, 7-6).[29] Against the Altoona Curve on August 1, Montañez hit for the cycle in a 5-for-6, 8-RBI performance.[30] In the *Baltimore Sun* two days later, Orioles manager Dave Trembley – Montañez's former Class-A skipper – said, "He's a guy that's drawing some attention to himself with the type of season he's having."[31]

"I had to have a breakout year," Montañez said. "Not necessarily what I did, but I felt I had to have a really outstanding season to make a push because there were a lot of young prospects that recently signed for a lot of money that they were going to want to give opportunities to. If someone all of a sudden puts up numbers that are over the top, then they have to give them an opportunity."[32]

Montañez's chance arrived shortly after he achieved the cycle. The following night in Seattle, Orioles center fielder Adam Jones fouled a pitch from the Mariners' Félix Hernández off his foot. Although Jones finished that game, it soon became apparent he had broken a bone in his foot and would be sidelined for more than four weeks. Montañez was called up to the majors and debuted at Angel Stadium on August 5. He played the final inning of a Baltimore victory in left field and caught the only ball hit his way, a fly out off the bat of Mark Teixeira.

The next day, Trembley put Montañez in the starting lineup, batting eighth. Baltimore trailed 4-0 before Montañez's first big-league at-bat, leading off the top of the third inning. Facing right-hander Ervin Santana, a 2008 All-Star who ranked third in the American League in strikeouts entering the contest, Montañez blasted the second pitch he saw, sailing the ball over the center-field wall for a home run.

Through 2023, Montañez and Buster Narum (in 1963) remained the only Orioles to go deep in their first major-league at-bat in the American League franchise's first 70 seasons in Baltimore. (In 1887 Mike Griffin of the Baltimore Orioles in the American Association – then a major league – also earned the distinction.) Narum, a pitcher, was a career .059 hitter, though three of his seven hits were round-trippers.

In his next at-bat after the homer, Montañez pulled a line-drive single off Santana. He finished 2-for-4 with two runs scored. The Orioles lost, however, 9-4, and he was charged with an error on his only defensive chance, misplaying a Teixeira double into an extra base.

Five days after his debut, Montañez enjoyed his first three-hit game in the majors, against the Texas Rangers at Oriole Park at Camden Yards. When he had another three-hit night four days later in Cleveland, two of the knocks drove in runs during Baltimore's eight-run eighth inning. "Everything is icing on the cake," he said. "Whenever they want to put me in, I'm just going to try to do my best. It's been a complete whirlwind. I've gone from the West Coast to the East Coast, from Double A to the big leagues. I'm trying to take it all in. It's been absolutely outstanding. A great week."[33]

One oddity concerning Montañez's rookie campaign was that despite not being called up until August, he was credited with the game-winning hit in the Orioles' April 28 victory over the Chicago White Sox at US Cellular Field. The game had been suspended in the top of the 12th inning, and Montañez's decisive 14th-inning RBI single came on August 25, when the contest was completed in Baltimore. Officially, the game went down in the books as having been played on April 28.

When Double-A Bowie's season ended in early September, Montañez learned that he had finished with the Eastern League's batting and home-run crowns, and shared the RBI lead with Akron's Wes Hodges, making him the circuit's first Triple Crown winner since Danny Thomas did it in 1976.[34] "It's been the perfect season, so far," Montañez said, confessing that he had been checking the box scores and teasing a former Baysox teammate who failed to score from first base on one of his doubles.[35]

Although the last-place Orioles went just 14-35 after Montañez joined the team, he appeared in 38 games – 27 starts – and batted .295 with 3 homers and 14 RBIs. Mostly, he played left field (20 starts), but Trembley also used him at designated hitter (3), right field (2), and center field (2). When asked what Montañez needed to improve to establish himself as a big-leaguer, Trembley focused on defense. "Better routes in the outfield number one. Two, better accuracy throwing the ball. Three, better positioning. I think he plays too deep," the skipper observed. "Guys that play deep are afraid of the ball going over their head."[36]

During spring training 2009, Trembley noted Montañez's progress. "Last year, he looked very unsure in the outfield. This year, he looks much more comfortable, and his throwing has really improved."[37] Recalling their difficult 2002 season together in Class A, Trembley said, "I wish him well. I'm glad the lights have gone on. I feel good for him."[38]

But during the offseason the Orioles traded for two new outfielders, Ryan Freel and ex-Cub Félix Pie, to supplement their established starters – Jones, Nick Markakis, and Luke Scott. Montañez noted that competition for big-league spots was something he expected, and said, "[Trembley's] fair with everybody. If I don't earn it, I'd go as happy as I can be to Triple A."[39] Despite hitting .340 in exhibition play, Montañez began the season at Norfolk.[40]

On April 21, 2009, Montañez returned to the majors after Freel went on the 15-day disabled list. Montañez shared left field with lefty hitters Pie and Scott, but he tore a ligament in his right thumb while attempting a diving catch in Toronto on May 2. For nearly three weeks, Montañez tried to play through the pain, but the limitations caused by the injury worsened and he underwent surgery.[41] Following a brief rehabilitation assignment to the minors, he returned to the Orioles in September, but he finished the largely lost season with a .183 average in just 82 at-bats at the top level.

That winter, Montañez returned to the Puerto Rican league and produced a .324/.367/.514 slash line in 28 games for the Criollos de Caguas. The Criollos' manager, Carmelo Martínez, had also been Montañez's first skipper in rookie ball. In 1983, Martínez had become one of just two Puerto Ricans to homer in their first big-league at-bat before Montañez. (Benny Ayala, in 1974, was the other.) "We did talk about it once, and we thought it was unique," Montañez said.

Montañez started in Triple A again in 2010, but for the second consecutive season, he joined the Orioles before April was over to replace an injured outfielder (Pie). Montañez did not hit well initially, however, and he wound up starting just 11 games – only three after May 12, when a superior defender, Corey Patterson, joined the club after signing a free-agent deal. Then on June 23 – three weeks after Trembley was fired – Montañez tore his oblique muscle during batting practice. At the time, he was hitting .140 in 57 at-bats. "This has been the worst year of my career. It's like everything has gone completely backward," he said. "The hits haven't fallen, the at-bats haven't been there; now I get injured. It seems like I can't catch a break this year."[42]

Later that summer, Montañez played some rehabilitation games in the minors, but he never made it back to Baltimore and the organization released him after the season. "My injuries came at the most inopportune time," he said in 2024.

In January 2011 Montañez returned to the franchise where he started his professional career. "There were mixed emotions, but it was something I wanted to do," he explained. "I was proactive in going to the Cubs and saying I wanted to be back in their organization, because I loved that organization. They gave me the opportunity, and I felt I had something to prove or something left to do in that organization."[43]

Before spring training, he represented Puerto Rico in the Caribbean Series as a member of Caguas' championship club. Next, he joined the Triple-A Iowa Cubs and batted .369 with 5 homers and 43 RBIs in his first 42 games. After Chicago's Marlon Byrd suffered broken facial bones on May 21 when he was hit by a pitch and went on the disabled list, Montañez finally became a big-league Cub. "It's been a long journey, but actually, it goes by fairly quick when you're enjoying yourself playing ball," he said. "I'm happy to be here. It's one of the top achievements of my career."[44]

Montañez remained in the majors through the end of June and came back again in September. Overall, he batted .222 in 36 games for Chicago, including a homer off former Cy Young Award winner Barry Zito at Wrigley Field. Although he was released that fall, Montañez characterized his time with the Cubs as "like closure for me in a sense."[45]

In 2012 Montañez went to spring training with the Philadelphia Phillies, but that franchise's Triple-A Lehigh Valley (Pennsylvania) affiliate released him in early May. He caught on with the St. Louis Cardinals' Triple-A Memphis club and finished the year with a .241 average with just two homers in 101 games between the two teams.

When the best offers he could find for 2013 involved returning to Double A, Montañez recalled, "I said, 'No way.'" Instead, he signed with the Somerset (New Jersey) Patriots of the independent Atlantic League, which turned out to be a fun experience and atmosphere. "I had some reservations about coming to independent ball but it was so many times better than what I thought I was getting into," Montañez said.[46] He performed so well that the Los Angeles Angels of Anaheim offered him a chance with their Double-A Texas League club, the Arkansas Travelers, which he accepted hoping it would lead to better opportunities.

That did not happen as it turned out, but Montañez wound up representing Puerto Rico again that winter in the 2014 Caribbean Series, following a winter-ball trade to the champion Indios de Mayagüez. He then returned to the Somerset Patriots and batted .289 with 17 homers and 74 RBIs. That winter, Montañez, 33, finished his 15-year professional career with Mayagüez. In 129 major-league games over parts of four seasons, he hit .223 with 5 homers.

"I probably hung up my spikes too early, out of frustration," Montañez said in 2024. "But I was always looking forward to other endeavors, so there were no regrets."

After baseball, Montañez returned to Florida and spent four years as a full-time insurance agent. But aviation was always his passion – as a child he dreamed he would be a fighter pilot – so he hit the books, began taking classes, and became a professional pilot in 2020. He explained that the fields of aviation and baseball are not as different as they appear. "Ballplayers always say they miss the competition and camaraderie. But flying is also competitive," he said. "Versus the elements, the plane, your brain. And the pilot community is small, with a clubhouse feel."

As of 2024, Montañez was certified to fly multi-engine planes – "like Cessnas"– and he was getting into flight instruction. He hoped to fly bigger aircraft in the future. "Baseball happily got in the way of my dream," he said. "I wish I had started sooner." A divorced, single dad with two daughters and a son – ages 13, 11, and 8 – he resided in Parkland, Florida, where he also provided personal hitting instruction and appeared at baseball clinics.

After the Minnesota Twins' Eddie Rosario in 2015 became the fourth Puerto Rican to homer in his first big-league at-bat, Montañez confessed that his feelings were bittersweet after his former winter league teammate achieved the feat: "You don't want too many members in the exclusive club." But as Montañez said after he, too, went deep in his first chance, "It means my name's going to be in the record books for as long as baseball exists, so it's real neat."[47]

ACKNOWLEDGMENTS

Special thanks to Luis Montañez. Telephone interview with author on April 16, 2024.

The author would like to thank Josie Conway from Major League Baseball Players Alumni; and SABR colleagues Bob Bogart, Bob LeMoine, Wayne McElreavy, John C. Olsen, and Jacob Pomrenke for research assistance.

SOURCES

In addition to the sources cited in the Notes, the author consulted www.ancestry.com, www.baseball-reference.com, www.retrosheet.org, and https://sabr.org/bioproject.

NOTES

1   Baseball-Reference recognized 23,114 unique major leaguers through the end of the 2023 season. While different sources differ on the exact number of players who homered in their first at-bat, the Yankees' Jasson Domínguez became the 136th player to do it on September 1, 2023, according to MLB.com. Ed Eagle, "Players with Home Run in First At-Bat," MLB.com, September 1, 2023, https://www.mlb.com/news/home-run-in-first-at-bat-c265623820 (accessed April 27, 2024).

2   In 1948 Hasson (Canadian-American League) and Nieman (Ohio-Indiana League) each won minor-league Triple Crowns. More than a decade earlier, Hasson homered in his first major-league at bat, for the Philadelphia Athletics, on September 9, 1937. Nieman went deep in his first two big-league at-bats, for the St. Louis Browns, on September 14, 1951. Overall, Baseball-Reference listed 27 major-league (American League, National League, nineteenth-century American Association, and major Negro Leagues) Triple Crown winners through 2023, none of them players who also homered in their first big-league at-bats. The same source recorded 146 minor-league Triple Crown winners during that same period. "Triple Crown," https://www.baseball-reference.com/bullpen/Triple_Crown (accessed April 27, 2024). For perspective consider that, entering 2024, 321 official no-hitters had been pitched in the majors – more than the number of first-at-bat homers (136) and major- and minor-league Triple Crowns (173) combined.

3   Roch Kubatko, "Q&A/Luis Montañez," Baltimore Sun, March 4, 2007: D5.

4   Jorge Arangure Jr., "O's Take Flier on Two Former First-Round Picks," Washington Post, February 26, 2007: E8.

5   Unless otherwise cited, all Luis Montañez quotes are from a telephone interview with the author on April 16, 2024. Hereafter cited as Montañez interview.

6   Luis Montañez, 2001 Bowman baseball card.

7   Arangure, "O's Take Flier on Two Former First-Round Picks."

8   Luis Montañez, Howe Sportsdata questionnaire, July 24, 2000.

9   Phil Rogers, "Cubs Take a Shortstop; Sox a QB," Chicago Tribune, June 6, 2000, https://www.chicagotribune.com/news/ct-xpm-2000-06-06-0006060135-story.html (accessed January 2, 2024).

10   Montañez interview.

11   "News," Cape Cod Times (Hyannis, Massachusetts), July 30, 2000, https://www.capecodtimes.com/story/news/2001/01/27/july-30-2000/50992244007/ (accessed March 17, 2024).

12   Rogers, "Cubs Take a Shortstop; Sox a QB."

13   Kevin Baxter, "Top Baseball Draft Picks Hitting a Wall," Barre-Montpelier (Vermont) Times Argus, June 11, 2006, https://www.timesargus.com/news/top-baseball-draft-picks-hitting-a-wall/article_bb87e805-8024-5e79-9626-bba75faa546c.html (accessed January 2, 2024).

14   Kubatko, "Q&A/Luis Montañez."

15   Luis Montañez, 2001 Bowman's Best baseball card.

16   Orioles 2009 Media Guide, 74.

17   Jeff Zrebiec, "O's Montañez Squares Himself with Trembley," Baltimore Sun, March 28, 2009: 1D.

18   "O's Montañez Squares Himself with Trembley."

19   Kubatko, "Q&A/Luis Montañez."

20   Zrebiec, "O's Montañez Squares Himself with Trembley."

21   Orioles 2009 Media Guide, 74.

22   Ricardo Zúñiga, "MLB: Montañez, Único Jugador Boricua en Estrellas del Futuro," Laredo (Texas) Morning Times, July 9, 2005, https://www.lmtonline.com/lmtenespanol/article/MLB-Monta-ez-nico-jugador-boricua-en-10355774.php (accessed March 17, 2024).

23   Orioles 2009 Media Guide, 74.

24   Zúñiga, "MLB: Montañez, Único Jugador Boricua en Estrellas del Futuro."

25   Baxter, "Top Baseball Draft Picks Hitting a Wall."

26   Arangure, "O's Take Flier on Two Former First-Round Picks."

27   Kubatko, "Q&A/Luis Montañez."

28   Orioles 2009 Media Guide, 74.

29   Dan Hickling, "Home Run Lifts North All-Stars," Binghamton (New York) Press & Sun Bulletin, July 17, 2008: 5C.

30   "Montañez Hits for Cycle as Bowie Pounds Curve, 19-3," Indiana (Pennsylvania) Gazette, August 2, 2008: 17.

31   Jeff Zrebiec, "Getting Their Attention," Baltimore Sun, August 3, 2008: 6D.

32   Mike Ashmore, "Montañez Happy to Get a Shot with Somerset Patriots," Hunterdon County Democrat (Raritan, New Jersey), April 26, 2013, https://www.nj.com/hunterdon-county-democrat/2013/04/Montañez_happy_to_get_a_shot_w.html (accessed March 26, 2024).

33   Jeff Zrebiec, "Eight Is Enough," Baltimore Sun, August 15, 2008: 16Z.

34   Before Thomas, the other Eastern League Triple Crown winners were Joe Munson (1925), Bob Chance (1963), and George Scott (1965). Orioles 2009 Media Guide, 74.

35   Jeff Zrebiec, "Montañez Rules Minors from Majors," Baltimore Sun, September 2, 2008: 5A.

36   Don Markus, "No Winter Vacation," Baltimore Sun, September 11, 2008: 5A.

37   Associated Press, "O's Promising Left Fielder Left Out," Wilmington (Delaware) News Journal, March 22, 2009: 55.

38   Zrebiec, "O's Montañez Squares Himself with Trembley."

39   "O's Montañez Squares Himself with Trembley."

40 *2010 Orioles Media Guide,* 122.

41 Jeff Zrebiec, "Montañez May Be Out Awhile with Bad Thumb," *Baltimore Sun,* May 24, 2009: 3F.

42 Jeff Zrebiec, "Oblique Injury to Put Montañez on DL," *Baltimore Sun,* June 25, 2010.

43 Ashmore, "Montañez Happy to Get a Shot with Somerset Patriots."

44 Paul Sullivan, "Montañez Fills Roster Spot," *Chicago Tribune,* May 25, 2011: 6A.

45 Mike Ashmore, "Montañez Happy to Get a Shot with Somerset Patriots."

46 Ryan Dunleavy, "Montañez Returns to Double-A Ball," *Home News Tribune* (Somerville, New Jersey), June 21, 2013: 15.

47 Jeff Zrebiec, "Trip Ends in Fall," *Baltimore Sun,* August 7, 2008: 3Z.

DANIEL NAVA

BY BILL NOWLIN

From 2010 through 2017, Daniel Nava played in 589 major-league games (for five different teams), but the high point of his entire career came on the very first pitch he saw. He hit it for a grand slam, only the second player in major-league history to accomplish such a memorable feat.[1]

By the time his 2010 debut season was over, Nava had logged 188 plate appearances, with a .242 batting average and a .351 on-base percentage. He'd driven in 26 runs in 60 games, but still had just that one home run to his credit.

Nava's signing to the Boston Red Sox was something else that was quite unusual at the time. There was no multimillion-dollar signing bonus. His bonus was $1.00. He was a player who had failed to make his college baseball team and instead became the team's equipment manager. It's probably safe to say that his love of the game and his determination – with encouraging support along the way – led him to persevere and forge a career in baseball.

Daniel James Nava was a switch-hitting outfielder, occasional first baseman, and sometimes designated hitter who played for five major-league teams. He was a member of the 2013 World Series champion Boston Red Sox. He was born to Don and Becky Nava in Redwood City, California, on February 22, 1983. Don Nava was – and as of 2024 remained – in the fitness industry. Becky Nava raised Daniel and his two younger siblings, one brother and one sister.

Daniel attended St. Francis High School in Mountain View, California, about 15 miles southeast of Redwood City. For college, he went to Santa Clara University in the city of the same name, about another 10 miles farther east.

Nava took his time to develop into the 5-foot-10, 195-pound player he became in the majors. He was a youngster "who clawed and clawed just to stay relevant in his sport."[2] Even in Little League, he was told he was too small to play.[3] He explained, "I entered high school at a robust 4-foot-8, 70 pounds, and was basically just struggling to make the team my freshman year. I ended up making the team all four years, but never played very much. When I did play, I was just so small, so I didn't do very well. I was more of a defensive guy. I mainly played center field because I was light as a feather, meaning that I could cover a lot of ground. But I never really was any type of prospect."[4]

When it came to college, Nava tried out for the baseball team at Santa Clara, but did not succeed. Instead, he joined as the team's equipment manager. He found himself washing uniforms and taking care of the bats and balls. He also had other responsibilities that connected more to his future career in player development. Using the relatively simpler technology of

Daniel Nava, Boston Red Sox – Courtesy of Boston Red Sox

the day, he worked with video and data. "I kind of logged a lot of stuff that was going on. I got to watch the game from a different perspective. My brain was turned on and engaged in the game."[5]

Santa Clara cost too much for his parents, however, and after one year he transferred to junior college at the College of San Mateo. He made the baseball team and succeeded in becoming a Junior College All-American.[6] Coach Doug Williams at San Mateo was also an important influence. That he even tried out for the team at San Mateo was the result of a chance encounter at an area gym, when Daniel ran into an old friend he'd known back in Little League days, Chris Mezzavilla. "All the players then are pretty much the same stature. I was one of the better players in the league, but then everyone else grew and I didn't. When I ran into him in the gym, I'm sure he had these memories of me. He said, 'Hey, what are you doing? You should come and try out at the junior college.'" Daniel figured, "Why not?" But there was a moment when he sat down with Coach Williams, who asked him, "When was the last time you played?" – and Daniel's response was, "Almost three years ago, in high school." He says he remembers the coach's jaw kind of dropped.[7]

Still, Coach Williams gave him a shot and Nava joined in a scrimmage against another team. "I hadn't seen live pitching for three years, since the tryout at Santa Clara. I struck out my first at-bat. I didn't even swing. I remember walking back to the dugout and thinking I could smash this guy. He dotted some pitches. I felt like I shouldn't have swung because they weren't good pitches for me to hit, but I told myself I'd be ready in my next at-bat. This guy's going to make a mistake. I hit a home run. I destroyed it. I have never hit a ball that far in my life." He went on to hit for the cycle that day.[8] Coach Williams believed in him and encouraged him, and that support carried him going forward.

Nava had considerable success for San Mateo, batting over .400. Santa Clara took notice and invited the former equipment manager to return there for his senior year, on a full baseball scholarship. With just the one year of eligibility left, Daniel got in 200 at-bats, and hit a West Coast Conference-leading .395 with an on-base percentage of .494. He also earned his degree in psychology.

Nava's playing stats didn't get him any offers from big-league teams, so he joined the Chico (California) Outlaws of the independent Golden Baseball League – twice. In 2006, he says, "I tried out for the Chico Outlaws and actually got cut by them. So I didn't play for a whole year. I was trying to get picked up, trying anything to play somewhere. But every door got shut. Basically, about a year after I got cut from Chico, they called me up and told me that one of their players wasn't able to make it out, so if I wanted a chance to play – I wasn't even guaranteed a shot – that I could cruise on up there and try out for the team." (Chico is in Northern California, about 90 miles north of Sacramento.)[9]

He made the Outlaws in 2007 and hit .371 (OBP .475), for which he credited manager Mark Parent. Mike Andrews of SoxProspects.com wrote, "*Baseball America* ranked Nava the top indy league prospect, just a year after he didn't even make the team. The caveat, of course, is that this is independent ball, not a major-league affiliate. That didn't stop Boston's Jared Porter, now director of professional scouting [for the Red Sox] but then the assistant director, from signing Nava following the season."[10]

It cost the Red Sox just one dollar to sign Nava. But the dollar didn't go to him, it went to the Outlaws. The deal included an additional $1,499 that would be paid if he made it through spring training. He did. He never received the one-dollar bill, though. It does not hang framed in his home. That first dollar and the rest of the $1,500 went to Chico, as the price for selling his contract to the Red Sox.

Nava's first assignment was to the Lancaster JetHawks in the Advanced-A California League. There his manager in 2008 was Chad Epperson, another important influence. Nava ranked high in most batting categories, with a .341 batting average and 59 RBIs in 85 games.[11]

Nava took another couple of steps up the ladder in 2009, playing (also under Epperson) in Salem, Virginia, in the Advanced-A Carolina League. He hit .339 in 29 games for the Salem Red Sox. Of Epperson, Nava said, "He went to bat for me with the front office and more or less said, 'This kid can play. This kid can hit. I don't care what you guys have seen, but this kid can play.' He said that to me: 'You can play' – and that goes a long way, at any time, but when you're up against it."[12]

When he was called up to the Double-A (Eastern League) Portland Sea Dogs, he did even better, driving in 23 runs in 32 games and batting .364.

Nava started the 2010 season with Triple-A Pawtucket. The Red Sox had a need to develop young talent, however, and he was called up to the big leagues soon after. The Red Sox had two outfielders on the disabled list – Jacoby Ellsbury with a fractured rib since May 24 and Jeremy Hermida with an injured but not broken rib. Hermida's last game was June 9. After Boston's June 11 game, they sent Josh Reddick, batting just .176, down to Pawtucket. They decided to give Nava a shot. The *Boston Globe* called him "Pawtucket's best outfielder, with a .294 average, 8 homers, and 38 RBIs."[13]

The next day's newspapers had a lot more to say about Nava. His debut came on Saturday afternoon, June 12, 2010. Nava was playing left field and batting ninth in the Boston lineup, in an interleague game at Fenway Park against the visiting Philadelphia Phillies. He'd done a pregame interview with Red Sox radio broadcaster Joe Castiglione, who told him a story he himself had been told by the former Milwaukee Braves outfielder Chuck Tanner, who had homered in his first at-bat in April 1955. Castiglione passed on Tanner's simple advice: "Swing at the first pitch, because you'll never get it back."[14]

Joe Blanton was the starting pitcher for the Phillies. Right fielder J.D. Drew led off the bottom of the second with a solo home run. With a single from each of the next three Boston batters, the Red Sox loaded the bases and Nava stepped into the batter's box, batting left-handed.

He swung at the first pitch – Blanton later said it was a sinker that didn't sink – and hit the ball deep into the Red Sox bullpen in right-center field, where teammate Manny Delcarmen leapt and snared it. "I was just looking for something to drive," Nava said after the game. As he rounded the bases, he said, he thought, "Oh, man, I just hit a grand slam."[15] Both of his parents were at the game.

Only three other ballplayers have hit a grand slam in their first major-league at-bat: Bill Duggleby, for the Philadelphia Phillies on April 22, 1898; the aforementioned Jeremy Hermida (whose rib injury had given Nava the opportunity) for the Florida Marlins on August 31, 2005; and Kevin Kouzmanoff, for the Cleveland Indians on September 2, 2006. Kouzmanoff was the only other one to do so on the first pitch.[16]

The very next inning, Nava was presented with an opportunity to do it all over again. The bases were loaded and Blanton still on the mound. On the fourth pitch, Nava struck out on a half-swing. He had been well aware the bases were loaded once more "and some thought crossed through my head that it would be ridiculous" should he replicate the feat.[17] The Red Sox went on to win the game, 10-2. Nava had one more hit in the game, a double to the gap in left-center field in the sixth. His homer provided the winning runs and the reliever who caught the ball in the bullpen – Manny Delcarmen – had come into the game, was the pitcher of record at the end of the fifth, and got the win.

Nava picked up another RBI the next afternoon, on a ninth-inning single in a losing effort.

By the end of June, he'd played in 15 games, with 11 RBIs, and was batting .291. Notably, he reached base one way or another in his first 12 games, and 17 of his first 18.

There were a couple of returns to Pawtucket before the season was over, but when it was all said and done, Nava appeared in 60 major-league games, with a more modest .242 batting average, but a decent .351 on-base percentage. He had driven in 26 runs and scored 23. The grand slam was the only home run he hit all season long.

Only one other Red Sox player had hit a homer on the first pitch thrown to him – Bill "Lefty" Lefebvre, a pitcher who had never played in the minors, but homered in his big-league debut on June 10, 1938. In all, there were nine Red Sox players before Nava who had homered in their first at-bat for Boston. Among them was Nava's teammate Darnell McDonald, who had done so less than eight weeks earlier, on April 20.[18]

During 2011, the regular Red Sox outfielders stayed healthy for most part and Nava spent the entire season with the Triple-A PawSox, despite having been designated for assignment in May. (He was hitting .192 at the time.) He was not claimed off waivers and thus was able to remain in the organization. Two days after he'd been sent down in March, the *Boston Globe* ran an editorial – not in the sports section but on its editorial page – characterizing him as "Cinderella, after the ball" but saying he'd be back: "The real Daniel Nava story should not be about dreams coming true, but about how people with true desire and character keep on working, making their own fortunes."[19] With Pawtucket, Nava hit .268 in 121 games, with 10 homers and 48 RBIs.

Nava began the 2012 season with the PawSox but was called up in early May, doubling and driving in a run on May 10. He got his second major-league homer on May 14. By the end of June, he was batting .302. He began to tail off but remained with the team until near the end of July, when an injured wrist dictated a disabled list stay for a few weeks. By season's end, he was batting .243.

Nava was married in the early offseason of 2012. As of early 2024, he and his wife, Rachel (née Parker), lived in the Greater Nashville area and have two children, their daughter, Faith (born August 5, 2013), and son, Zeke (born September 2, 2016).

The year 2013 saw the Red Sox go from worst to first – last place in the AL East in 2012 to winning the World Series in 2013. On April 8, Nava's seventh-inning three-run homer in the Fenway Park home opener provided all the runs in a 3-1 win over the visiting Orioles. Then on April 15, two bombs exploded near the finish line of the Boston Marathon just after the end of that day's Red Sox game. The team was on their way out of town immediately after the game. Their first day back in Boston was a highly emotional one, on April 20. The Red Sox were losing 2-1 when Nava stepped to the plate with two on and two outs in the bottom of the eighth. He hit a three-run homer into the Red Sox bullpen and won the game, with the final score of 4-2.

Nava was a major contributor to Boston's resurgence that season, playing in 134 games and batting .303 (eighth in the league), and his .385 ranked fifth in on-base percentage. "More playing time unlocked his potential," wrote Peter Abraham.[20] Among his teammates, only David Ortiz topped him in batting average (.309) and OBP (.395).[21]

In postseason play, manager John Farrell – citing intangibles – opted for Jonny Gomes in left more often than Nava, who played in just two ALDS games and two ALCS games (in Game One, he had the only hit for Boston, a ninth-inning single).[22] Throughout his career, though a switch-hitter, Nava hit much better against right-handers than left-handers. In 2013 he hit .322 against righties, compared with .252 against lefties.[23]

But it did help that Nava could hit from both sides of the plate. Back with Lancaster, he was told that part of the reason he made the team out of spring training was that he could switch-hit.[24]

Nava played in the first five of the six World Series games, starting in right field in two of them. He was 2-for-14 with two RBIs, both in the 5-4 loss to the Cardinals in Game Three. The Red Sox won the Series and Daniel Nava received a World Series championship ring.

Nava got off to a slow start in 2014, starting in 17 of the first 20 games but batting only .149. He was sent to Pawtucket for a month, but took a while to get going. He hit just .253 at Triple A. By season's end, back with the Red Sox he bumped his average up to .270. In 408 plate appearances, he drove in only 37 runs.

Nava's 2015 season started slowly as well. Penciled in as more of a reserve player,[25] he still appeared in 27 of Boston's first 45 games, but hit just .159. A left thumb strain saw him rehab in 10 games with Pawtucket, but he hit only .250 and was designated

Daniel Nava, Boston Red Sox – Courtesy of Boston Red Sox

for assignment just before the end of July. About a week later, he was claimed by Tampa Bay. He appeared in 31 games for the Rays, batting .233 with only 3 RBIs. In November, his contract expired and the following month he signed a one-year deal as a free agent with the Los Angeles Angels of Anaheim.

Nava hit .288 over his first eight games in 2016 but left-knee tendinitis cost him three weeks. When he came back, his hitting declined. He was batting .222 by the end of May, the same mark at the end of June, and just .235 at the end of July. He'd hit one home run. At the end of August, the Kansas City Royals arranged to acquire his contract. He got into nine September games with KC, but had only 12 plate appearances and one base hit.

Nava enjoyed a bit of a resurgence in 2017. He signed with the Philadelphia Phillies, made the team in spring training, and played in 80 games, often as a pinch-hitter. He homered in each of his first two at-bats, but added only two more during the rest of the year. He hit for a solid .301 average, but drove in only 21 runs.

The next year, 2018, Nava went to spring training with the Pittsburgh Pirates as a nonroster invitee. But before he could really get started, he required back surgery on February 27. He was expected to be out 10 to 12 weeks; instead, he did not play pro ball that year. Pain had prompted him to go in for a discectomy, for a "quick cleanup." Relief was immediate, but he contracted an infection and the situation became so bad he had to be wheeled into the ICU, unable to walk. The doctors were able to clear it up, but Nava "had to learn to walk again. That whole year was just gone."[26]

Nava wasn't ready to give up yet. In June 2019 he signed up to play independent baseball with the American Association's Kansas City T-Bones. He wanted to prove he was healthy and could still play, hopefully to catch on with an affiliated team. At age 36, he was the oldest player on the team but got into 71 games, primarily at first base. He hit for a .288 average and his 46 RBIs were second-best on the team. The T-Bones won their division but lost out in the playoff semifinals. No minor-league teams stepped forward to pick up Nava.

That winter Nava played in seven Mexican Pacific League games in Sinaloa for the Algodoneros de Guasave. He had four base hits – all singles – batting .148. Teams in other countries are sometimes quick to cut "import players" and his playing career was over.

The 2017 season was the last Nava played in the major leagues. His career stats show just 12 errors in 1,015 chances (.988), and a .266 batting average with a .357 on-base percentage. He drove in 206 runs in 1,977 plate appearances.

The pandemic year of 2020 saw minor-league baseball close for the season. Nava thought about training at a remote site to perhaps be called up if a major-league team had a sudden need, but nothing came of it.

"Then 2021 rolled around and it kind of felt it was time to move in a different direction. Through some contacts with the Dodgers, I finally got hooked up with them. My first position was in Arizona and I was an assistant hitting coach in the Arizona Complex League. From there I went to Low-A Rancho Cucamonga and I was the bench coach there."[27]

In 2023 Nava was named manager of the Great Lakes Loons, the Dodgers' club in the High-A Midwest League, based in Midland, Michigan. The Loons finished 76-55, first in the East Division, but lost out in the single-game playoff for the league championship.

Nava talked with the *Boston Globe*'s Peter Abraham about transitioning from playing to coaching. "The biggest adjustment is the mind-set. You go to the park as an observer of everyone else. When you're playing, you're focused on yourself and what you're doing and how your body's feeling. As a coach, nobody cares about you.… It's more about [getting other players] ready for the next level. That's why I want to coach at the highest level, because contributing to a win at the big leagues is completely different than the impact of a win in the minors." He added, "I would love to be a manager. A lot of things I learned at the end of my career really opened my eyes to things I overlooked as a younger player." He looked forward to being able to offer support and encouragement to others.[28]

In 2024, Daniel Nava was named the outfield coordinator for the Dodgers' minor-league system, a roving position that saw him travel to the various teams and work with young prospects in the system. Working in player development, perhaps he would be able to encourage others as he, in earlier days, had been encouraged.

SOURCES

In addition to the sources cited in the Notes, the author consulted Baseball-Reference.com and Retrosheet.org. Video of Nava's first three at-bats in the game, including the first-pitch grand slam, are available on YouTube at: https://www.youtube.com/watch?v=yf4k8hr1sv4

NOTES

1   Kevin Kouzmanoff had hit a grand slam on the first pitch he had been thrown, on September 2, 2006. See Andrew Harner's Games Project account of that game at https://sabr.org/gamesproj/game/september-2-2006-kevin-kouzmanoff-blasts-first-big-league-pitch-for-grand-slam/. There are other players who hit a grand slam in their first at-bat, but not on the very first pitch.

2   Ian Browne, "Nava's Mom Always Supportive of Unpredictable Career," MLB.com, May 10, 2013. https://www.mlb.com/redsox/news/daniels-navas-mom-supportive-of-red-sox-ofs-career/c-47067034.

3   Danny Wild, "Nava's Journey to Majors Hard to Believe," milb.com, October 28, 2010. https://www.milb.com/news/gcs-15795320.

4   Mike Andrews, "Meet Daniel Nava, the Best Red Sox Minor Leaguer You've Never Heard Of," espn.com, April 8, 2010. https://www.espn.com/blog/boston/red-sox/post/_/id/2090/meet-daniel-nava-the-best-red-sox-minor-leaguer-you%E2%80%99ve-never-heard-of. Asked later if 70 pounds was really correct, Nava said, "Technically, I was lighter than that – 68

pounds – but I rounded it up." Conversation with Daniel Nava, February 20, 2024.

5 Author interview with Daniel Nava on January 9, 2024. Hereafter, "Nava interview."

6 Marc Normandin, "Meet Daniel Nava, Unlikely Major Leaguer," SBNation.com, June 1, 2012. https://www.sbnation.com/2012/6/1/3056853/daniel-nava-unlikely-major-leaguer-red-sox.

7 Nava interview.

8 Nava interview.

9 Andrews.

10 Andrews.

11 He pitched once for Lancaster, the only time did so professionally. He faced seven batters, walked three and gave up two base hits, one of them a home run. He was charged with three earned runs.

12 Nava interview.

13 Nick Cafardo, "Lowell Showcases His Value," *Boston Globe*, June 12, 2010: C5.

14 Nate Taylor, "Nava Enjoys a Debut Loaded with Excitement," *Boston Globe*, June 13, 2010: C1, C6.

15 Taylor. Nava had watched some video of Joe Blanton before the game. Conversation with Daniel Nava, February 20, 2024.

16 Hermida was still with the team when Nava hit his homer, and later on June 12, or the next day, mentioned to Nava that he had hit a grand slam in his own first at-bat. In July the Red Sox visited Oakland for a three-game series from July 19-21 and Kevin Kouzmanoff was with the Athletics at the time. It struck Nava at the time that on that field were three of the four players – Hermida, Kouzmanoff, and himself – who had hit grand slams in their debut at-bats. Bill Duggleby, who hit his grand slam back in 1898, was remembered but not present. Conversation with Daniel Nava on February 20, 2024.

17 Nick Cafardo, "Red Sox Win, but Lose Matsuzaka," *Boston Globe*, June 13, 2010: C1, C6.

18 McDonald had played for other teams before coming to Boston, but homered in his first Red Sox at-bat.

19 "Daniel Nava: Cinderella, After the Ball," *Boston Globe*, March 22, 2011: A10.

20 Peter Abraham, "Stability Helped Set Sox Straight," *Boston Globe*, October 1, 2013: C4.

21 He was hit by pitches 15 times, second only to Shane Victorino's 18.

22 Peter Abraham, "Napoli to Start Game 3, and Gomes May, Too," *Boston Globe*, October 15, 2013: C5. Nava had typically batted against right-handers during the season, and Farrell said "it's been very difficult" to sit Nava, giving Gomes the nod more often on what he called as something of a "hunch." Peter Abraham, "Gomes Start Was Feel-Good Story," *Boston Globe*, October 20, 2013: C7.

23 At the end of his playing career, one sees he batted .281 against right-handers and .211 against southpaws. https://www.baseball-reference.com/players/split.fcgi?id=navada01&year=Career&t=b.

24 "They had a couple of prospects who were left-handed hitters. I was told, basically, you're going to be going there as the fourth outfielder and if it there's a tough, tough lefty to protect these guys against, we might give them a blow and you can go in there and balance us out a little more on the roster since you can also bat right-handed." Nava interview.

25 See Julian Benbow, "Nava Is Making Most of Chances," *Boston Globe*, April 12, 2015: C7.

26 Nava interview.

27 Nava interview.

28 Peter Abraham, "Nava's Goal Is to Get Back, as Coach or Manager," *Boston Globe*, January 7, 2024: C6.

PAUL GILLESPIE

BY MIKE COONEY

Paul Gillespie was a high school second-team catcher at 17, a minor-league all-star outfielder at 19, and a major-league catcher at 21. In a career that spanned 89 games from 1942 to 1945, he became the first big-leaguer to hit a home run in both his first and last regular season at-bat. Only one other man has done it since: John Miller (in 1966 and 1969).

Paul Allen Gillespie was born September 18, 1920 in Cartersville, Georgia.[1] He was the second of three children born to Virgil E. Gillespie, a painter and a carpenter, and Rebecca Allen Gillespie.[2]

At the age of 14, Gillespie started playing baseball with the Inman Park Cardinals, an American Legion team. At 15, he played for the YMCA Crackers, another American Legion team.[3] When he reached high school age, Gillespie played football for the Northwest Tigers sandlot football team.[4]

Gillespie enrolled at Tech High School in Atlanta, Georgia. In high school, he "wasn't good enough to make first string . . . and sat out his Tech High career on the bench."[5]

Despite playing a backup role, Gillespie got a hand from his friend and fellow Carterville resident Rudy York, who was playing for the Detroit Tigers. York arranged for Tigers manager Mickey Cochrane to check out Gillespie.[6] Shortly after Cochrane's observation, Tigers' scout Eddie Goosetree signed Gillespie to a contract.[7]

Less than two months after leaving Tech High, the 17-year-old was playing professional baseball for the Brownsville Charros of the Class D Texas Valley League. *The Brownsville Herald* reported, "Paul Gillespie is the new catcher. He hails from somewhere in Georgia, we're not sure where, but he is a big boy and looks like he might go places."[8] Indeed, Gillespie had good size at 6-feet-3 inches and 195 pounds when fully grown.

Gillespie signed as a catcher, but after playing his first game for Brownsville behind the plate, he shifted to third base for the next several weeks.[9] By mid-July, however, he had returned to catching duties. On July 25, he drove in three runs with a triple in the seventh inning but had to leave the game when he split a finger reaching for a foul tip.[10] Yet just two days later, Gillespie was back in action and drove home the winning run with a single in the fifth inning.[11]

After 183 at-bats and a .213 batting average for Brownsville in 1938, Gillespie moved to the Lake Charles (Louisiana) Skippers of the Evangeline League (also Class D) for the 1939 season. He started the season as the Skippers' catcher, but soon found himself in the outfield. By late July, he'd been selected the North Team utility outfielder for the Evangeline League all-star game.[12]

Following the all-star game, Gillespie found himself in the lineup at catcher, left field, first base, and third base.[13] He even

Paul Gillespie, Chicago Cubs – Courtesy of Chicago Cubs Archives

appeared as a pitcher when he moved from third to get the final out of a 11-1 Skippers loss.[14]

After finishing the season with a .312 batting average, Gillespie was looking forward to advancing in the Detroit Tigers organization. He was ticketed for Beaumont in the Texas League.[15] Instead, he became one of 92 players declared a free agent by Baseball Commissioner Kenesaw Mountain Landis in a "drastic decision aimed at eliminating 'misuse of working agreements as a camouflage for covering up players' by the Detroit Tigers and 15 farm teams.'"[16]

The Montreal Royals, the Brooklyn Dodgers' top farm team, quickly signed Gillespie.[17] After the start of spring training, Royals manager Clyde Sukeforth was impressed with Gillespie's hitting against International League pitching and his work behind the plate. Still, Gillespie was optioned to the Class A Elmira Pioneers of the Eastern League in late March.[18]

Pioneers business manager Charlie Miller described Gillespie as "a possible first-string receiver."[19] When the Pioneers broke training camp to begin the Eastern League season, Miller called Gillespie "another Bill Dickey."[20] Elmira manager Bill Killefer was also impressed with Gillespie's "hustle behind the plate and his handling of the willow."[21]

With the start of the 1940 season, Joe Just was announced as the starting catcher for the Pioneers. Having a shortage of outfielders, Killefer commented that in 89 games in the outfield the previous season, Gillespie had "covered the territory well and made only six errors." Killefer went on to say Gillespie might move to the outfield.[22]

After the first four games of the season, Gillespie was 5-for-6 at the plate and had won a starting position in left field. He continued his role as backup catcher.[23] By May 20, Gillespie was leading the Eastern League in hitting with a .457 average.[24] Three days later, playing catcher, Gillespie injured his thumb and had to leave the game.[25]

By mid-June, Brooklyn Dodgers president Larry MacPhail conceded the Dodgers would not make the 1940 World Series. However, he was confident the Dodgers would win the 1941 pennant with a revised lineup. One of the names mentioned was Paul Gillespie – MacPhail said he was highest on him, "We signed him for $7,000. I'd value him at $150,000 right now." He added that Bill Killefer touted Gillespie as "the greatest he's ever seen – including himself. The boy handles himself like a Dickey, throws a 'soft' ball to second, and leads the Eastern League in batting . . . at the moment!"[26]

In mid-July, Elmira manager Killefer commented, "Gillespie . . . may need more experience but he's on his way."[27] But by mid-August, Gillespie's batting average had fallen from over .400 during the first six weeks of the season to .258. The downward spiral led him to be demoted to the Class C Grand Rapids Dodger Colts of the Michigan State League.[28]

After sending Gillespie to Grand Rapids, Charlie Miller "conceded that 'we guessed wrong twice this year. Paul Gillespie, the catcher who looked so good in the spring camp was a disappointment behind the plate and at the plate.'"[29]

Despite finishing out the 1940 season with Grand Rapids, Gillespie found himself getting "lots of work" during spring training with Brooklyn in 1941.[30] After playing in the major-league camp, the Dodgers planned to assign Gillespie to the Montreal Royals, even though Royals manager Clyde Sukeforth felt that he would probably never make the major-league grade.[31]

When spring training started for the Royals, Gillespie stayed in the Brooklyn camp, getting plenty of work and participating in exhibition games daily.[32] Then, at the start of the season, Gillespie was traded from Montreal to the Class A1 Knoxville Smokies.[33]

Smokies manager Freddie Lindstrom said he was "tickled pink" that he was able to trade for Gillespie, who had played in the same league previously against a new teammate, Woody Johnson. According to Johnson, Gillespie was a left-handed hitter who "always drove the ball a long way against our club. . . I can recommend him to the limit for the way he played against us.'"[34]

Lindstrom quickly lost his excitement for Gillespie. After seven at-bats for Knoxville, Gillespie was sent to Gadsden in the Southeastern League (Class B) in a 'farming' arrangement on 24-hour recall.[35] After 41 at-bats with Gadsden, Gillespie was demoted further to the Class D Salina Millers, a Cleveland Indians farm club in the Western Association.

After batting close to .200 in his brief stints with Knoxville and Gadsden, Gillespie regained his hitting prowess with Salina (.323 in 189 at-bats). Even so, Knoxville, which still owned Gillespie's contract, decided to outright him to the Oklahoma City Indians in the Class A1 Texas League.[36] Despite hitting just .196 in 59 games, Gillespie quickly became a "one-man catching staff."[37]

Either toward the end of the 1941 season or shortly thereafter, Gillespie registered for the draft, listing the Oklahoma City Baseball Club as his employer.[38] With World War II raging, Gillespie returned to the Indians for the 1942 season. As the opening game approached, John Cronley of the Daily Oklahoman evaluated the club's roster. He wrote, "Catching – Paul Gillespie, period." Cronley added a note of concern that "the army call is just around the spring corner for Gillespie."[39]

Gillespie, whom teammates had named "perpetual motion Paul," showed another side of his personality on a rainy day in April.[40] As described by John Cronley, some of the rainy day antics around the hotel were classics. Gillespie and outfielder Hershel Martin teamed in the top act. With Martin at the piano, Gillespie "rigged up a strip tease pantomime that brought down the house . . . 'A little fan-fare,' Paul calls, there is a tinkle of the ivories, and Gillespie glides forth, about as much of an Astaire as a cow on ice."[41]

Despite opening the season as Oklahoma's starting catcher, Gillespie was soon catching behind Danny Doyle.[42] However, he had regained his starting position by late July.[43] The game of July 26 was a highlight as Gillespie "applied a hilarious finish with a clean theft of home as the flabbergasted Buff infield stood around arguing about a popfly."[44]

Yet the franchise did not experience much hilarity during the season as it fought through financial problems. By August 1, the Indians, "desperately needing cash to meet another pay roll, . . . disposed of catcher Paul Gillespie . . . to Tulsa."[45]

At the time Gillespie was sold to the Tulsa Oilers (also in the Texas League), he had the Tribe's second-best batting average at .266. After a brisk start at the plate, he had lost time due to an injury. However, he was still considered the team's top big league prospect.[46]

The Oilers – then the top farm affiliate of the Chicago Cubs – felt Gillespie would help "unless waived in by the Cubs."[47] It didn't take the Cubs long to reach for him. On August 11, less than two weeks after he'd been acquired from Oklahoma City, Gillespie was sold to Chicago "for delivery when and if the Oilers fade from the Texas League playoff picture."[48]

Exactly one month after the Cubs purchased his contract from Tulsa, Gillespie made his major-league debut. On September 11, 1942, he settled in behind the plate in a game against the New York Giants. He also settled in at the plate with a home run off Harry Feldman in his first major-league at-bat. He later singled in a second run.[49]

Following an offday, the Cubs travelled to Boston to take on the Braves in a doubleheader. Gillespie was the starting catcher in the first game. In the eighth inning, he hit his second major-league home run, this time against Braves pitcher Tom Earley.[50]

After homers and two RBIs in each of his first two games, Gillespie had positioned himself as potentially the Cubs' catcher of the future. However, that was put on hold because he was scheduled to report to the Army on November 1.[51]

But instead of the Army, Gillespie, who was one of 13 Cubs in the military, reported for Coast Guard training in New Orleans.[52] Once his training was complete, he found himself catching for the Coast Guard team during the 1943 season.[53] By season's end, Gillespie had teamed with pitcher Al Jurisich, who made his major-league debut with the St. Louis Cardinals in 1944, to win the USO championship.[54]

During his Coast Guard enlistment, Gillespie served in New Orleans, Ringold, Mississippi, Baltimore, Maryland, and on board the *USS William M. Black*.[55]

At the start of the 1944 season the Cubs had six catchers, including Gillespie, in the military.[56] Gillespie, though, was able to report to the Cubs on September 2 after receiving a medical discharge from the Coast Guard because of a knee injury. Still, after reporting to the Cubs, he had to wait to play until September 13 when his transfer from the national defense list became effective.[57]

Cubs manager Charlie Grimm said, "From what I've seen of Gillespie, I think he has a chance to be the best catcher on our staff. He has a good arm, looks as if he packs some power at the plate and he's a big guy, just like old Gobby [sic] Hartnett."[58]

Once Gillespie became eligible, Grimm immediately inserted him into the lineup against the Cincinnati Reds.[59] He finished the season having played nine games and hitting one home run, against New York Giants pitcher Bill Voiselle on September 21.[60] Perhaps as an attempt at revisionist history, Gillespie would later claim that he homered in his first at-bat after returning from the Coast Guard.[61]

With the approach of the 1945 season, Mickey Livingston, the Cubs' starting catcher in 1943, was given a medical discharge from the army.[62] With Livingston's return, Gillespie became one of four catchers competing to be Livingston's backup.[63]

Gillespie helped his position early in the 1945 spring training when he belted a pair of homers off Walt "Boom Boom" Beck.[64] As the season progressed, Gillespie asserted himself as not only a backup catcher but one of starting caliber.

During the season, officials from several teams questioned whether wearing an honorable discharge service patch known as the "ruptured duck" should be allowed. At the time, the patch was being worn by four Cubs (Gillespie, Hiram Bithorn, Peanuts Lowrey, and Mickey Livingston) and Red Ruffing of the Yankees. In response, on July 17, American League president Will Harridge wrote to all teams: "I will leave it to your judgment as to whether or not this is desirable." It appears that no other major league players wore the "ruptured duck" patch on their uniforms.[65]

A highlight of the regular season came in an August 15 game against the Brooklyn Dodgers. when Gillespie hit a grand slam in the first inning and a two-run homer in the fourth.[66] A week later, he was credited with a steal of third in a game against the New York Giants.[67]

Gillespie's last regular-season at-bat in the majors – in which he homered – was a fourth-inning shot off Pittsburgh's Rip Sewell on September 29. He came out of the game after that at-bat. He appeared again in the field the next day, finishing the game in right field, but did not make a plate appearance.

It is not known if the August steal aggravated his old knee injury, but the Cubs were concerned about his bad knee as they prepared for the 1945 World Series. Even with their concern, the Cubs anticipated having Gillespie catch when Detroit used a right-handed pitcher.[68]

Although Gillespie had hit .288 against Livingston's .254, Livingston remained the starting catcher for the Cubs. However, as planned, Gillespie was inserted into the lineup for the second game of the series when right-handed pitcher Virgil Trucks was named the Tigers' starter.

In the ninth inning, Gillespie swung at a Trucks pitch and "half fell after hitting a ball down to first base," aggravating his old left knee injury. Cubs manager Charlie Grimm said that Gillespie, with his twisted knee, would probably be lost for the remainder of the series."[69] Even so, Gillespie entered two more games as a pinch-hitter. He finished the series going hitless in six at-bats, but was one of 30 Cubs to receive a full Series share of $3,931.22.[70]

Three weeks after the Cubs lost the World Series to the Tigers, Gillespie underwent an operation in the Illinois Masonic hospital. Dr. Walter Fischer performed the operation on what was described as "an injured external cartilage."[71] While recuperating from that procedure, Gillespie stayed active. The *Daily Oklahoman* reported: "Red Smith, who doubles as coach of the baseball Cubs and football Giants under Steve Owen, says he gets a play a day (football) from Paul Gillespie."[72]

Once out of the hospital, Gillespie took a break from baseball. On January 5, 1946, he married ex-Marine sergeant Pat Ozant.[73] The couple went on to have four daughters.[74]

After returning from his honeymoon, Gillespie signed his 1946 playing contract with a boost in salary.[75] When spring training started, he was described as "moving around as if forgetting all about the (knee) operation."[76] His recovery was important. Even though he had led Cub catchers in hitting in 1945, he was in an eight-man competition that included former starting backstop Clyde McCullough, who was returning from the Navy.[77]

Gillespie's effort to make the 1946 Cubs roster took a hit on March 18 when he "was banged on the little finger of his bare hand, the wallop sending him away for repairs."[78] Three weeks later, on April 10, he was optioned to the Class AA Nashville Volunteers of the Southern Association.[79]

In a May 17 game against the New Orleans Pelicans, Gillespie was hit on the right side of the head by a pitch and knocked unconscious.[80] Two days later, he still had a knot on his forehead so large that he could not wear a mask.[81]

By mid-June, Gillespie had returned to be one of the Southern Association's top hitters.[82] In mid-July, he was one of three catchers selected to the all-star team. In a note of irony, Gillespie, who was the Volunteers' primary catcher, received eight votes while Teddy Pawelek, the Vols' reserve backstop, got 11 votes – making the backup the starter and the starter the backup.[83]

In an August 17 game against the Atlanta Crackers, Gillespie was bowled over when Charley Glock tried to score. The following day, Gillespie collided with Cracker catcher Mike Ulicny, injuring Ulicny's knee so badly that he was lost for the season.[84]

A week later, Gillespie was on the sidelines with a split finger.[85] While rehabbing that injury, he contracted the flu. The *Tennessean* reported that he returned to uniform on August 30, still in a weakened condition.[86] However, when the year-end Southern Association all-star team was named, Gillespie was one of three catchers selected.[87]

With a successful season behind him, Gillespie was requested to report to the Cubs for the 1947 spring training.[88] But before camp started, Gillespie was sold outright to the Oakland Oaks of the Pacific Coast League on a "30-day look."[89] This meant that manager Casey Stengel had until May 1 to decide to keep him or to send him back to the Cubs.[90]

Gillespie returned the first Oaks contract he was offered, unsigned. Oakland then sent him a revised pact.[91] Gillespie finally reported to training camp on February 25.[92] Two days later he signed.[93]

In the midst of the Oaks spring training, Gillespie was hospitalized with a severe cold. At the time, Stengel felt that the catcher's hitting was impressive but that his throwing had yet to come under scrutiny.[94] Two days later, Gillespie was released from the hospital 15 pounds lighter than when he went in.[95]

When the Oaks broke camp to begin the 1947 season, Gillespie was named the starting catcher.[96] Yet, his tenure didn't last long. Just two weeks into the season he was turned over to the Los Angeles Angels.[97] He joined the Angels on a similar 30-day look. In reporting the move, the *Oakland Tribune* commented, "The big fellow is a good man with the willow but he can't throw."[98] Gillespie was hitting .300 when the Oaks released him.[99]

By May 20, Gillespie had increased his Pacific Coast League average to .321.[100] But at the end of the season, it had dipped to .257.[101]

Gillespie was scheduled to return to the Angels for the 1948 season, returning his signed contract on February 17.[102] Early in spring training, Angels manager Bill Kelly indicated that he was not happy with his catching candidates. In describing Gillespie, Kelly said he "can hit, but he's not Hartnett behind the plate."[103]

By May 23, Gillespie was relegated to being the Angels' bullpen catcher.[104] His 1948 season got worse on September 15 when he underwent an appendectomy at Bell Mission Hospital.[105]

On October 5, after a season where Gillespie played in only 21 games and hit .107, he was released by the Angels.[106]

The start of the 1949 season found Gillespie with the Class-A Macon Peaches, where he played in 12 games, hitting .350. After he reinjured his knee, he found himself without a team until being recruited by Tom Hicks, a former teammate and manager of the Tyler Trojans of the Class-C East Texas League.[107]

It appears that Gillespie's tenure with Tyler was short-lived. Even though the 1949 Tyler Trojans records do not show that Gillespie was ever a part of the team's official roster, he actually played his first game for the Trojans on June 16.[108] One week later, while Gillespie was shown as one of two catchers on the Trojans roster, he was being held out because of an injured arm.[109]

By early August, Gillespie was playing for Bolton Post 156 in the Atlanta Amateur Baseball Federation Tournament.[110] After the tournament, Gillespie continued to play amateur ball with Bolton in the Chattahoochee League. After a September 4 game, the *Atlanta Constitution* reported, "Paul Gillespie, former Chicago Cubs catcher, smacked two homers to pace Bolton 156 to a 14-13 triumph."[111]

With a disappointing 1949 season behind him, Gillespie decided to attempt a comeback in 1950 with the Beaumont Roughnecks of the Texas League (by then Class AA). Competing against three other established catchers, he failed to make the roster despite a determined fight.[112]

After his baseball career came to an end, Paul Gillespie lived in Atlanta, Jacksonville, Florida, and Anniston, Alabama. He worked as a sales representative for the Adler Typewriter Company. Not quite 50 years old, he died in Anniston on August 11, 1970 after a short illness.[113]

Paul Gillespie is buried at the Westview Cemetery in Atlanta, Georgia.[114]

ACKNOWLEDGMENTS

This biography was reviewed by Rory Costello and Chris Bouton and fact-checked by Kevin Larkin.

SOURCES

In addition to the sources cited in the Notes, the author also consulted Baseball-Reference.com.

NOTES

1   U.S., Baseball Questionnaires, 1945-2005. From the American Baseball Bureau and found on ancestry.com.

2   United States Census, 1930 and 1940.

3   U.S., Baseball Questionnaires, 1945-2005.

4   "Banquet to honor Northwest Tigers," *Atlanta Constitution*, December 19, 1946.

5 "Ex-Tech High boy catches for Cubs," *Atlanta Constitution*, October 4, 1945.

6 Gary Joseph Cieradkowski, *The League of Outsider Baseball: An Illustrated History of Baseball's Forgotten Heroes* (New York: Touchstone Books, 2015), 59.

7 "Ex-Tech High boy catches for Cubs," *Atlanta Constitution*, October 4, 1945.

8 "Ramblin through the sports news," *Brownsville Herald* (Brownsville, Texas), June 22, 1938.

9 Based on a review of box scores from the *Brownsville Herald*.

10 "Gillespie drives in Brownsville runs," *Valley Morning Star* (Harlingen, Texas), July 26, 1938.

11 "Brownsville Charros divide twin bill with Cardinals," *Valley Morning Star*, July 28, 1938.

12 "Indians place four stars on Northern Nine," *Clarion-News* (Opelousas, Louisiana), July 27, 1939.

13 Based on a review of box scores from *Town Talk* (Alexandria, Louisiana).

14 "Evangeline loop boxscores," *Town Talk*, September 4, 1938.

15 Charlie Roberts, "Ex-Smithie catcher hits homer in major debut," *Atlanta Constitution*, September 20, 1942.

16 "Tigers suffer blow in action of Landis feeing 92 players," *Detroit Free Press*, January 15, 1940.

17 "3 free agents to Dodger farm," *Daily News* (New York, New York), February 3, 1940.

18 "Pioneers get new catcher; start drills on Monday," *Star-Gazette* (Elmira, New York), March 23, 1940.

19 "Pioneers get new catcher; start drills on Monday."

20 "Pioneers to face Roanoke team Wednesday," *Star-Gazette*, April 13, 1940.

21 "Killefer May use Gillespie in Pioneer outfield," *Star-Gazette*, May 2, 1940.

22 Killefer May use Gillespie in Pioneer outfield."

23 "Gillespie, Templeton start against Albany; Hofferth's hit wins," *Star-Gazette*, May 7, 1940.

24 "Eastern Big Six," *Star-Gazette*, May 20, 1940.

25 "Pioneers bow to Laurels, play Springfield tonight," *Star-Gazette*, May 24, 1940.

26 Hy Turkin, "Hits," *Daily News*, June 16, 1940.

27 Tommy Holmes, "Tour gives Dodgers line on farmhands," *Brooklyn Daily News* (Brooklyn, New York), July 14, 1940.

28 "Locals swap Gillespie for Sosh," *Star-Gazette*, August 16, 1940.

29 Harry O'Donnell, "'We guessed wrong on two,' Miller says," *Star-Gazette*, August 22, 1940.

30 Judson Bailey, "Baseball Banter," *Selma Times-Journal* (Selma, Alabama), February 17, 1941.

31 Marc. T. Mcheil, "Casual Close-ups," *Gazette* (Montreal, Quebec, Canada), February 21, 1941.

32 "Royals await Bramham's decision after hearing -Sukeforth in Macon," *Gazette*, March 30, 1941.

33 "Smokies obtain pitcher and new catcher," *Knoxville News-Sentinel* (Knoxville, Tennessee), April 13, 1941.

34 "Smoky Skipper tickled over players," *Knoxville News-Sentinel*, April 13, 1941.

35 "Sugar Cain released by Knoxville Manager," *Huntsville Times* (Huntsville, Alabama), May 9, 1941; Bob Wilson, "Sugar Cain is given release after defeat," *Knoxville News-Sentinel*, May 9, 1941.

36 "Changes are plentiful in Southern loop," *Montgomery Advertiser* (Montgomery, Alabama), July 27, 1941.

37 John Cronley, "Tribe squeezes in win before curtain drops (No Encores)," *Daily Oklahoman* (Oklahoma City, Oklahoma), September 8, 1941.

38 Paul A. Gillespie, "Georgia World War II Draft Registration Cards, 1940-1945."

39 John Cronley, "Giants are hitting clean-up." *Daily Oklahoman*, April 5, 1942.

40 "Perpetual Motion Paul," *Daily Oklahoman*, April 19, 1942.

41 John Cronley, "Indians mire deep in the mud of Texas," *Daily Oklahoman*, April 9, 1942.

42 John Cronley, "The city makes a sizeable assist to keep Indians here," *Daily Oklahoman*, June 26, 1942.

43 "Club can't draw, some shows will," *Daily Oklahoman*, July 24, 1942.

44 John Cronley, "Indians jolt Buffs twice," *Daily Oklahoman*, July 27, 1942.

45 "Gillespie, Butcher peddled to Tulsa," *Daily Oklahoman*, August 2, 1942.

46 "Gillespie, Butcher peddled to Tulsa."

47 John Cronley, "Once over Lightly," *Daily Oklahoman*, August 5, 1942.

48 "Gillespie is sold to Cubs," *Daily Oklahoman*, August 12, 1942.

49 Hy Turkin, "Giants win in ninth, 4-3," *Daily News*, September 12, 1942.

50 "Cubs, Braves split twin bill," *Danville Morning News* (Danville, Pennsylvania), September 14, 1942.

51 Hy Turkin, "Giants win in ninth, 4-3," *Daily News*, September 12, 1942.

52 Arch Ward, "In the Wake of the News," *Chicago Tribune*, December 9, 1942.

53 Arch Ward, "In the Wake of the News," *Chicago Tribune*, December 9, 1942; "Beauregard opens baseball season," *Town Talk* (Alexandria, Louisiana), May 18, 1943.

54 Cieradkowski, *The League of Outsider Baseball*, 60.

55 "Paul Gillespie weds Louisiana belle," *Atlanta Constitution*, January 28, 1946.

56 Fritz Howell, "Baseball-1944," *Pantagraph* (Bloomington, Illinois), April 19, 1944.

57 "Former Indian catcher joins Cubs' roster," *Daily Oklahoman*, September 14, 1944.

58 "Former Indian catcher joins Cubs' roster."

59 "Secory belts homer; Cincy, Cubs divide," *Decatur Herald* (Decatur, Illinois), September 14, 1944.

60 Irving Vaughan, "Cubs win over Giants twice, 11-8 and 6-4," *Chicago Tribune*, September,22, 1944.

61 Paul Gillespie, "My big thrill," *Daily Chronicle* (De Kalb, Illinois), June 29, 1946.

62 "Livingston to join Cubs next season," *Daily Chronicle*, November 9, 1944.

63 Edward Burns, "Talent hunters setting traps for Cub chiefs," *Chicago Tribune*, December 8, 1944.

64 "Reds 5, Bruins 4," *Daily Oklahoman*, April 7, 1945.

65 http://exhibits.baseballhalloffame.org/baseball_enlists/at73.htm

66 "Cubs' 4 homer attack routs Dodgers, 20-6," *Chicago Tribune*, August 16, 1945.

67 "Hack comes through," *Chicago Tribune*, August 22, 1945.

68 "Cubs shakeup puts Nicholson on sidelines," *Chicago Tribune*, August 28, 1945.

69 "Tigers even series with Cubs," *Daily Oklahoman*, October 5, 1945.

70 "30 Cubs get $3,930.22 as series share," *Chicago Tribune*, November 2, 1945.

71 Irving Vaughan, "Cubs add four teams to farm system," *Chicago Tribune*, October 30, 1945.

72 Hal Middlesworth, "On the level," *Daily Oklahoman*, November 13, 1945.

73 "Paul Gillespie weds ex-marine sergeant," *Chicago Tribune*, January 15, 1946.

74 "Obituaries," *Anniston Star* (Anniston, Alabama), August 12, 1970.

75 "Paul Gillespie signs Cub pact," *Atlanta Constitution*, January 24, 1946.

76 Irving Vaughan, "Grimm works Cubs 4 hours, but easy like." *Chicago Tribune*, February 21, 1946.

77 Vaughan, "Grimm works Cubs 4 hours, but easy like."

78 Irving Vaughan, "Lowrey smacks double; Gillespie injured," *Chicago Tribune*, March 19, 1946.

79 "Paul Gillespie joins Vols," *Atlanta Constitution*, April 11, 1946.

80 Raymond Johnson, "Nashville overcomes five-run lead to win," *Tennessean* (Nashville, Tennessee), May 18, 1946.

81 Raymond Johnson, "One man's opinion," *Tennessean*, May 20, 1946.

82 Arch Ward, "In the Wake of the News," *Chicago Tribune*, June 22, 1946.

83 Raymond Johnson, "One man's opinion," *Tennessean*, July 19, 1946.

84 "Ulisney takes beating in blocking plate," *Tennessean*, August 19, 1946.

85 "Alderson, Hausmann shelled by Pelicans," *Tennessean*, August 28, 1946.

86 "Ailing list mounts," *Tennessean*, September 1, 1946.

87 "8 Crackers on Southern all-star nine," *Atlanta Constitution*, February 9, 1947.

88 Raymond Johnson, "Vols recall 18 farm hands for next season," *Tennessean*, September 8, 1946.

89 "Gillespie sold to Oakland," *Chicago Tribune*, February 6, 1947.

90 "Ex-Cub catcher signed by Oaks," *Oakland Tribune* (Oakland, California), February 5, 1947.

91 "Max Marshall only Oakland holdout," *Oakland Tribune*, February 21, 1947.

92 "Gillespie in camp," *Oakland Tribune*, February 26, 1945.

93 "Scarsella comes to terms with Oakland ball club," *Oakland Tribune*, February 28, 1947.

94 Alan Ward, "Acorns in double bill," *Oakland Tribune*, March 11, 1947.

95 "Oak hurlers worry Stengel," *Oakland Tribune*, March 13, 1947.

96 Walter Judge, "Oaks pick starters," *San Francisco Examiner*, March 27, 1947.

97 "Oaks, Senators clash tonight," *Oakland Tribune*, April 15, 1947.

98 "Oaks, Senators clash tonight."

99 "White of S.F. leads hitters," *Oakland Tribune*, April 15, 1947.

100 "Jo Jo White top PCL hitter," *Oakland Tribune*, May 20, 1947.

101 "Pacific Coast League batting marks for '47," *Los Angeles Times*, November 30, 1947.

102 "Angels, Stars sign players," *Los Angeles Times*, February 18, 1948.

103 Frank Finch, "Angel Hurlers biggest worry, says Kelly," *Los Angeles Times*, April 4, 1948.

104 Al Wolf, "Raiders beat Angels twice," *Los Angeles Times*, May 24, 1948.

105 "Angels Gillespie loses appendix," *Los Angeles Times*, September 16, 1948.

106 "Angels release two players," *Los Angeles Times*, October 6, 1948.

107 "Trojans give away orchids to lure customers to park," *Longview News-Journal* (Longview, Texas), June 21, 1949.

108 "Ten-Minute Break," *Tyler Morning Telegraph* (Tyler, Texas), June 18, 1949.

109 "Dean on sports," *Tyler Courier Times* (Tyler, Texas), June 26, 1949.

110 "Mountain View to use team of Deans, Mabrys in amateur baseball meet," *Atlanta Constitution*, August 7, 1949.

111 "Chandler vets cop pennant in Suburban," *Atlanta Constitution*, September 5, 1949.

112 "Hopes high in Beaumont on opening day," *Miami Daily News-Record* (Miami, Oklahoma), April 11, 1950.

113 "Obituaries," *Anniston Star* (Anniston, Alabama), August 12, 1970.

114 www.findagrave.com/memorial/46621852.

CARLOS LEE

BY JOEY ELLEDGE

With 358 major-league round-trippers, Carlos Lee is the all-time leader in home runs among players born in Panama.[1] He was a career .285 hitter with a .339 on-base percentage and never struck out more than 100 times in a season. Lee had five consecutive 30-homer seasons and 11 consecutive 20-homer seasons. He also stole double-digit bases in seven seasons and played in 140 or more games in all but one season.

In his 14-year major-league career, mainly spent as an outfielder and third baseman with the Chicago White Sox and Houston Astros, Lee collected 2,273 hits His 17 grand slams tie him with Ted Williams and Jimmie Foxx for seventh place on the career grand-slam list, more than Babe Ruth and Hank Aaron among others. As of 2024 he was the *only* player to hit three grand slams in extra innings, two of which were walk-off smashes.

Lee was born on June 20, 1976, in Aguadulce, Panama, a small town about 85 miles from Panama City. He was the second of three children born to Carlos and Olga Lee. His family were cattle farmers, but his father was a manager in a communications company and his mother taught at the local school. Carlos Senior played amateur baseball in Aguadulce.

Young Carlos was playing third base on the provincial all-star team when he was scouted and signed for the White Sox in 1994 by Miguel Ibarra.[2] The 18-year-old struggled at his first stop in the White Sox minor-league system, the GCL White Sox, going 7-for-56 (.125).

After 67 games with the 1995 Bristol White Sox (rookie-level Appalachian League), in which he batted .346 and hit 7 home runs, Lee was promoted to the Hickory Crawdads of the Class-A South Atlantic League. Playing in 63 games, he batted .248 with 4 home runs. Back in Hickory in 1996, Lee, now 20 years old, was the regular third baseman, playing in 119 games, and led the team with 70 RBIs. He hit .313, with 8 home runs. Lee had the lowest strikeout rate on the team at 9.73 percent.

Lee was moved up to High A in 1997 at age 21, to Winston Salem of the Carolina League. On a team that featured 11 future major leaguers, Lee showcased his future all-star caliber slugging ability. He hit for a .317 batting average with 17 homers and 82 RBIs in 139 games. *Baseball America* ranked Lee the number 43 major-league prospect. He continued his climb up the baseball ladder in 1998 and rose to *Baseball America's* number 28 prospect after batting .302 with 21 home runs and 106 RBIs in 138 games for the Birmingham Barons of the Double-A Southern League.

Lee started the 1999 season with the Charlotte Knights of the Triple-A International League, one step away from the major leagues. His tenure with the Knights was brief: After 25

Carlos Lee, Chicago White Sox – Courtesy of MLB.com

games, in which he batted .351 with 4 home runs and 20 RBIs, the 23-year-old Lee was called up to the White Sox in early May and soon made history in his first at-bat.

On May 7, 1999, Lee got a chance to live out his childhood dream of playing professional baseball at the highest level. Lee replaced outfielder Jeff Abbott, who was optioned to Charlotte after hitting .158 with 2 home runs and 6 RBIs to start the season.[3] This was considered a puzzling move by the White Sox; Lee had very little experience playing left field, as throughout his minor-league journey he was mostly a third baseman. Asked why the club decided to send Abbott down to Charlotte and bring up Lee, White Sox general manager Ron Schueler said simply, "(His) bat's hot, and right now we need offense."[4]

Lee himself was perplexed. He told a sportswriter, "I didn't expect to get called up when I was playing left field for a week and a half. When they called me up I was like 'Where am I going to play?'"

His lack of experience playing left field aside, Lee's bat stole the show in his debut.[5]

The White Sox were a charter member of the American League. Never had a White Sox player hit a home run in his first at-bat. When Lee came to bat in the second inning against the Oakland Athletics' Tom Candiotti, Lee took a Candiotti knuckleball deep for career homer number one in a game the White Sox won 7-1.

Outfield inexperience aside, in his rookie season, the 6-foot-2, 270-pound Lee established himself as the team's left fielder, playing in 127 games and batting .293 with 16 home runs and 84 RBIs. In 2018, Hall of Famer Frank Thomas, rookie Lee's teammate, explained why he had been very impressed with the young slugger: "I see a young me in Carlos Lee. The way he goes through pitches and how he hits the ball to right field. I watch him hit and think: those are the things I used to do [at that age]. I think he's the second coming."[6]

In 2000 Lee, firmly ensconced in left field, batted .301 in 152 games with 24 home runs and 92 RBIs. On July 9 he hit two home runs against the crosstown rival Chicago Cubs in a 9-6 defeat at Wrigley Field. Lee had four games with four hits during the season – June 6, July 7, July 27, and September 4. On June 23, Lee hit a game-tying home run in the ninth inning off the best closer in baseball, future Hall of Famer Mariano Rivera. The 95-67 White Sox had the best record in the American League but were swept 3 games to none in the opening round of the playoffs by the Seattle Mariners, despite having home-field advantage. Lee had 12 plate appearances in the series but could muster only one hit, a double, though he drove in a run with a sacrifice fly. This was a disappointing performance for Lee, despite his regular-season success, and it wound up being Lee's only major-league postseason appearance.

In 2001 Lee's offensive performance fell off: He batted .269 with 24 home runs and 84 RBIs. During the season, Lee had seven games in which he had three hits, and in four of these games, Lee hit a home run. On June 8 Lee hit a 10th-inning walk-off grand slam against the Cubs at Comiskey Park. The next day he had four hits – all singles – in a 10-inning loss to the Cubs. After his four-hit game, Lee was batting .320, but his output fell steadily the rest of the season. The White Sox (83-79) finished third in the AL Central and missed the playoffs.

Lee's batting average dropped slightly in 2002, to .264. He hit 26 home runs and drove in 80 runs. He had three two-home-run games, on June 16 against the Cubs, June 26 against the Minnesota Twins, and July 14 vs. the Detroit Tigers. In the Tigers game, Lee collected four hits and scored three runs in a 6-4 win. In the June 16 game against the Chicago Cubs at Wrigley Field, one of Lee's home runs was a grand slam in the top of the third inning against Cubs starting pitcher Kerry Wood. The White Sox went 81-81 and fell short of the postseason.

Lee's true breakout season was 2003. The White Sox (86-76) finished in second place in the AL Central Division. Lee had his best offensive production year to date. Lee finished second on the team in home runs (31; Frank Thomas had 42) and led the team in runs scored (100), RBIs (113), and stolen bases (18). At age 27, Lee established himself as a perennial slugger with

consistent power. So much so that his stats in 2004 mimicked those of 2003 (.305, 31, 99). In 2004 Lee batted .305 with 31 home runs and 99 RBIs. Lee led the team in hits (180) and runs scored (103). The 2004 White Sox once again finished the season second in the AL Central Division.

Despite back-to-back career years for Lee, the White Sox determined that Lee's tenure with the ball club would end after the 2004 season. On December 13 they traded Lee to the Milwaukee Brewers in a deal that sent Scott Podsednik, Luis Vizcaíno, and Travis Hinton to the White Sox. Lee's tenure with the Brewers further solidified his reputation as a reliable power hitter. In 2005 he batted .265 with 32 home runs and a career-high 114 RBIs. Lee also earned his first All-Star appearance and his first Silver Slugger award.

Lee continued to hit well for the Brewers in 2006, but on July 28, at the trade deadline, he was sent to the Texas Rangers with Nelson Cruz for Francisco Cordero, Kevin Mench, and Laynce Nix. At the time of the trade, Lee was batting .286 with 28 home runs and 81 RBIs in 102 games. With the Rangers as a left fielder and designated hitter, he batted .322 with 9 home runs and 35 RBIs. Between both the Brewers and the Rangers, Lee hit a career-high 37 home runs while driving in 116 runs in 161 games. Lee earned another All-Star appearance with the Brewers before he was traded, once again reflecting his reputation as one of the best sluggers in baseball. After the 2006 season, Lee was a free agent and had the opportunity to pick where he played next, and he had an ideal landing spot.

On November 24, 2006, Lee signed with the Houston for $11.5 million, the richest contract in the franchise's history to that point. Before signing, Lee had made it known to several top Texas cattlemen that his preference was to land in Houston via free agency because of a ranch and a bull he owned in nearby Wharton County.[7] (Lee owned Slugger Ranch in Texas, where he raised prize-winning Brahman cattle, and nine ranches in his native Panama. In 2006 Lee's entry was the Brahman Grand Champion at the Houston Livestock Show and Rodeo.[8]) In 2008 Lee donated $25,000 and over 300 bales of hay to support Texas ranchers whose properties were ravaged by Hurricane Ike.[9]

In 2007, his first year with the Astros, Lee played all 162 games and batted .303 with 190 hits, 43 doubles, and 32 home runs. On April 13, in the face of 20-mph winds, he hit three home runs at Philadelphia's Citizens Bank Park in a 9-6 win over the Phillies. Admiring Lee's feat, Astros manager Phil Garner said, "Carlos Lee must have hit 1,200 feet worth of homers on a night when I didn't think anyone would hit any homers."[10] Lee finished 2007 with another All-Star Game appearance and his second Silver Slugger Award.

Lee spent six seasons with the Astros (2007-12). His home-run production declined over that span – 32 homers in 2007, then 28, then 26, then 24, and 18.

In 2008 Lee was on pace to have his best statistical year, but injuries limited him to 115 games. Injuries had never plagued Lee's career as he played 150 or more games in 10 seasons and twice played all 162 games. Despite playing 47 fewer games in

2008 than in 2007, he batted .314, hit 28 home runs and drove in 100 runs. Lee again played all 160 games in 2009, once again establishing himself as a durable player who served as a power bat for his team. He batted .300, led the team with 26 home runs and 102 RBIs, and finished second on the team with 183 hits.

In 2010 the 34-year-old Lee's production fell drastically. He played in 157 games and batted only .246 with 24 home runs and 89 RBIs. In 2011, Lee raised his batting average to .275 and had 94 RBIs but only 18 home runs on a team with the worst record in baseball (56-106). Still, at age 35 he played in 155 games and led the team in homers, doubles (38), RBIs (94), and runs (66).

As the 2012 trading deadline approached, the Astros were shopping the 36-year-old Lee around to other teams, and a deal with the Los Angeles Dodgers was heavily rumored.[11] However, on July 2 discussions between the Astros and Dodgers had ended because of Lee's opposition to being traded to the Dodgers.[12] Two days later, on July 4, the Astros traded him Miami to the Marlins for Matt Dominguez and Rob Rasmussen. At the time of the trade, Lee was batting .287 for the Astros with 74 hits in 66 games but had only 5 home runs and 29 RBIs. After the trade, he played 81 games for the Marlins, hitting .243 with 4 home runs and 48 RBIs.

In an interview with MLB.com in 2010, Lee had stated his desire to retire after the 2012 season.

Lee said, "I don't know if I'm going to play after this contract is up. I'm ready to go home. We spend so much time away from our family. I can't spend any other time with my kids. I get home at 10 o'clock, 11 o'clock and they're sleeping, and they get up at 6:30 in the morning to go to school and I see them 10, 15 minutes. I want to be able to spend time with my kids when they're still young and healthy. I want to enjoy them."[13]

Released by the Marlins after the 2012 season and unsigned in the offseason, Lee announced his retirement as a player on June 21, 2013.[14]

Before Lee signed his contract with the Astros, his father said the slugger wanted to be remembered as Panama's best hitter.[15] Lee's biggest competitor for this title is Rod Carew, the Hall of Famer also from Panama. While Carew had over 3,000 hits, Lee was the better power hitter. Carew hit only 92 major-league home runs.

In an all-time Panama baseball team roster selected by *USA Today*, Carew was chosen as the best first baseman.[16] Lee was selected as the best designated hitter from Panama – an honor that seems very appropriate for the power hitter from Panama.

SOURCES

In addition to the sources cited in the Notes, the author consulted Baseball-Reference.com and Retrosheet.org.

https://www.baseball-reference.com/register/player.fcgi?id=lee---004car

https://www.retrosheet.org/boxesetc/L/Plee-c001.htm

NOTES

1   Andrew Mearns, "The Hall of Fame Case: Carlos Lee," Cut4, January 9, 2008. https://www.mlb.com/cut4/the-hall-of-fame-case-for-carlos-lee-c264297312.

2   Chris Kamka, "When They Were Prospects: Carlos Lee," NBC Sports Chicago, July 30, 2018. https://www.nbcsportschicago.com/mlb/chicago-white-sox/when-they-were-prospects-carlos-lee/381146/.

3   Jimmy Greenfield, "Carlos Lee Replaces Slump-Mired Abbott," *Chicago Tribune*, May 8, 1999. https://www.pro-quest.com/chicagotribune/docview/418819288/fulltext/B5953D5CDC32451BPQ/1?accountid=69&sourcetype=Newspapers.

4   Greenfield.

5   Greenfield.

6   Kamka.

7   Jose De Jesus Ortiz, "Astros' $100 Million Slugger Is a Breed Apart," *Houston Chronicle*, February 11, 2007. https://www.chron.com/sports/astros/article/astros-100-million-slugger-is-a-breed-apart-1834678.php.

8   Ortiz.

9   Ortiz.

10 Andrew Mearns, "The Hall of Fame Case: Carlos Lee."

11 Brett Logiurato, "Carlos Lee Trade Talks between Dodgers, Astros Officially off the Table," *Sports Illustrated*, July 2, 2012. https://www.si.com/si-wire/2012/07/02/carlos-lee-trade-dodgers-astros-rumors-los-angeles.

12 Logiurato.

13 Drew Silva, "Astros' Lee Says He May Retire after 2012 Season," NBC Sports, May 6, 2010. https://www.nbcsports.com/mlb/news/astros-lee-says-he-may-retire-after-2012-season.

14 "Former OF Carlos Lee Retires," ESPN.com, June 21, 2013. https://www.espn.com/mlb/story/_/id/9411658/carlos-lee-retires-baseball.

15 Ortiz, "Astros' $100 Million Slugger Is a Breed Apart."

16 "All-Latino Baseball Team: The Best All-Time Lineup of Players Born in Panama," *USA Today*, September 24, 2021. https://www.usatoday.com/story/sports/mlb/2021/09/24/best-panamanian-baseball-players-top-mlb-stars-panama/8362835002/.

CLYDE VOLLMER

BY NELSON "CHIP" GREENE

On May 31, 1942, the Cincinnati Reds prepared to host the Pittsburgh Pirates in a Memorial Day doubleheader. The previous two days had been disastrous for the Reds; a rash of injuries had decimated their outfield ranks. Ival Goodman was already nursing an injured ankle as the series began. On Friday, Hank Sauer, too, suffered an ankle injury that left him unavailable for the next afternoon's game. During Saturday's game three more outfielders went down: center fielder Mike McCormick broke his leg while sliding into second base, replacement center fielder Harry Craft suffered a concussion after an outfield collision with right fielder Gee Walker and was carried from the field on a stretcher, and Walker could not bat when his turn came up. Things had gotten so bad on the injury front that at one point the Reds took the field with catcher Dick West playing left field and pitcher Bucky Walters playing center.

With few outfield options available to manager Bill McKechnie, Cincinnati GM Warren Giles contacted the Syracuse Chiefs, his club's Double-A (top-level) minor-league affiliate, "begging for the best help available."[1] He asked manager Jewel Ens to "give us somebody who can play the field respectably."[2] That night, 20-year-old Clyde Vollmer boarded a 1:00 A.M. train for Cincinnati to join his hometown team in the major leagues.

Clyde Frederick Vollmer was a big youth. At 6 feet 1 inch tall and a solid 190 pounds, his teammates called him Big 'Un. Born in Bridgetown, a Cincinnati suburb, on September 24, 1921, Vollmer had first starred at age 14 in the Bridgetown Baseball League, where in 1935 he led his team to the Hamilton County Grade School championship. Later, he played American Legion ball as a member of Cincinnati's Bentley Post. By the time he left Western Hills High School in 1938 (a school that would also produce, among others, Don Zimmer, Russ Nixon, Eddie Brinkman, and an infielder named Pete Rose), Vollmer had been well scouted by the Reds. The following year, 1939, Frank Lane, Cincinnati's farm director, signed the 17-year-old to a Cincinnati contract for $75 a month.

Almost immediately Vollmer showed he was a legitimate major-league prospect. He began his professional career in 1939, in the Class-D Bi-State League, playing in the outfield for the Bassett (Virginia) Furniture Makers. In 77 games, he produced a .310 batting average, smashed six home runs, and slugged an impressive .461. Returning to Bassett in 1940, the big slugger was even better, as he played in 119 games and posted averages of .366 batting and .607 slugging, with 21 home runs and 45 doubles.

He also proved to be a fine defensive player. Indeed, it wasn't his hitting that recommended Vollmer for promotion to

Clyde Vollmer, Cincinnati Reds – SABR-Rucker Archive

Crosley Field; rather, it was for his fielding. While compiling a fine .970 fielding average at Bassett in 1940, Vollmer committed only seven errors and totaled 21 outfield assists. So impressed were the league's sportswriters that Vollmer was the unanimous choice as right fielder on the Bi-State League All-Star team.

In 1941, Vollmer was promoted to the Columbia (South Carolina) Reds, in the Class-B South Atlantic League. While the big right-handed slugger had proved to be a consistent .300 hitter against Class-D pitching, he struggled in the faster Class-B ball. In 112 games, Vollmer batted just .248, although he again displayed good power, leading the league with 17 home runs while also stroking 22 doubles and 4 triples. During the September playoffs, Vollmer hit four home runs, two in one game, as Columbia defeated Macon, four games to two.

By the opening day of the 1942 season, Vollmer had once again earned a promotion: He was now the starting center fielder for the Syracuse Chiefs of the Double-A (later Triple-A) International League. Playing for manager Ens, Vollmer started slowly. After 32 games, he was batting just .214, with only one home run and a dismal slugging average of .325. Vollmer remained steady in the field. Just three years removed from Western Hills High, the young man from Cincinnati was wearing the uniform of his hometown team.

When Vollmer finally arrived at the Cincinnati Terminal that Sunday afternoon, the first game of the doubleheader was already under way. Hurriedly, he called home and told his father, Albert, a railroad worker, to get to the stadium, as Vollmer might see action in the second game. (In addition to Clyde, the third child and second son, Albert and his wife, Mabel, also produced Bernard, Myrtle, Melba, and Jewel.) Manager McKechnie started the rookie in left field in the second game, and Vollmer took his place in the Crosley Field outfield.

It took his father 2½ innings into that second game to get to the stadium. By chance, however, the Reds rookie left fielder had yet to come up for his first at-bat. Just as the public address announcer said, "The Cincinnati batter is Clyde Vollmer, left field," Clyde's father was settling into his seat. Several weeks later, manager McKechnie recalled for the press what happened next:

"He got to bat for the first time in the third inning," related McKechnie. "Well, before he steps up he moves over to me and says, 'Mr. McKechnie, I don't know what the take sign is.' And I say to him, 'Young man, never mind the take sign. Just swing at the first pitch.' Well, Max Butcher is the Pittsburgh pitcher, and Vollmer followed instructions perfectly … swung at the first pitch and knocked it on a line off the top of the laundry roof in left field."[3]

Vollmer became one of only 24 major leaguers (through 2008) to hit a home run on the first pitch thrown to him in the major leagues.

It was an auspicious debut. Yet it was the lone highlight of a brief first stay in the major leagues. Over his next 33 at-bats, Vollmer struggled mightily, managing just two more hits. A week after his historic home run, McKechnie sent the young outfielder to the bench, telling the press, "He is a big boy with power and class in the field. Some day he will make me a fine outfielder. But I doubt that he is ready yet."[4] In fact, he wasn't.

On June 21, after just three hits in 34 at-bats (.088), Vollmer was optioned to Birmingham. He wasted no time getting his hitting back on track. Perhaps more relaxed away from the glare of his hometown, Vollmer made an immediate impact. In his first game he belted a triple and two singles and made three spectacular catches in the outfield; by July, it was reported that "no less a baseball brain than Pie Traynor advises … Clyde Vollmer is the best-looking prospect in the Southern Association."[5] In August, when Birmingham split a doubleheader with the Atlanta Crackers, Vollmer's two-run homer in the first game was "only the fifth home run ever hit into the left-field stand at Atlanta Park."[6] And by September, Vollmer had played in 83 games for the Barons, batted .309, and compiled a .462 slugging average. On September 6, when the Reds expanded their roster, Vollmer was recalled to Cincinnati. Yet he played in only two games, produced a single in six at-bats, and finished the season with the Reds with a .093 batting average and one historic home run in 12 games. It was more than three years before the Big 'Un had the chance to hit another.

When the Reds opened their 1943 spring training in Bloomington, Indiana, Vollmer was thousands of miles away and wearing a much different uniform: He had joined the Army on October 31, 1942. Vollmer remained in the Army for three years, until he was discharged in the fall of 1945.

By the following spring, Vollmer was ready to resume his career. As training got under way in Tampa, Florida, in February 1946, he was one of 52 players in the Reds' camp. With their outfield situation unsettled, management was hopeful that Vollmer could win a starting position, and General Manager Giles was pleased with the slugger's performance in spring training, so much so that he made a rather startling comparison.

"Not only do I believe Vollmer will be our regular left fielder," Giles opined to the press in March, "but what's more, I feel he may develop into another Joe DiMaggio. He has all the potentialities. He's built along the same lines as DiMaggio. He uses the same stance at the plate as does the Yankee Clipper. He has the speed and throwing arm of a great outfielder. … You'll hear a lot of Vollmer."[7]

Whether or not Giles truly believed his own assessment or was simply trying to instill confidence in his young hometown player is unclear. Though he made the team, Vollmer's stay was very brief: He saw action in only one game, striking out as a pinch-hitter on April 24, before the Reds determined he was still not ready and optioned him again to the minors. This time, though, they loaned him to another team, the Rochester Red Wings, the St. Louis Cardinals Triple-A International League affiliate. Vollmer played in 103 games and batted .275, while blasting nine home runs among 146 total bases (his slugging average was .432), before being recalled to the Reds on August 12. Over the remainder of the National League season, however, Vollmer played just eight games for Cincinnati, collected four hits in 21 at-bats, and wound up the season with a .182 average and one RBI. After two failed stints with the Reds, it appeared Vollmer's chances with his hometown team were dwindling.

The 1947 campaign appeared last best chance. Playing for a new manager, Johnny Neun, who was determined to rebuild the Reds with youth, Vollmer finally spent the entire season on the Cincinnati roster. Vollmer once again failed to live up to his promise. After starting in center field on Opening Day and batting fourth, Vollmer was soon benched, and rarely played during the remainder of the season. In the end, he appeared in only 78 games, totaled just 155 at-bats, and finished the season with a paltry 34 hits and a .219 batting average. Moreover, his power all but disappeared, as Vollmer recorded an anemic slugging average of .303, hitting just one home run and driving in 13 runs. While he opened the 1948 season again on the Reds' roster, he appeared in only seven more games, singled once in nine at-bats, and was finally released by the Reds to Syracuse on May 15, 1948. Almost six years to the day from when he had homered in his hometown on his first major-league pitch, Vollmer's Cincinnati career had come to an end.

"That was my lowest point in baseball," he later said. "The Reds were through with me. They sold me outright to Syracuse, and I figured I'd never get back into the big leagues."[8]

This time in Syracuse, Vollmer turned his career around. Perhaps he had his new wife to thank for inspiration. After the 1947 season, Vollmer had married Margaret Oberberg, and it proved to be a wonderful, 59-year union that produced one daughter, Claudia. More likely, however, Vollmer's modest success after his Cincinnati release had more to do with getting out from under the pressure of playing before family and friends. Warren Giles said in 1951, when asked why he had let Vollmer go: "He couldn't make good for us. Don't forget, he was a Cincinnati boy, and to me it looked like the old story of the hometown boy trying too hard to make good and suffering because of it."[9]

For whatever reason, though, in Syracuse, Vollmer finally gave an explosive performance and posted the kind of numbers Giles had always predicted. In 122 games, the 27-year-old hit 32 home runs and drove in 104 runs, had 255 total bases for a slugging average of .580, and finished with 127 hits and a .289 batting average. Vollmer proved he could be a productive player and it didn't take long before he was in the major leagues once again. On September 26, while the Chiefs were in Montreal, Vollmer learned that he had been traded to the Washington Senators (for outfielder Carden Gillenwater – as well as, according to some reports, Sammy Meeks and $25,000 cash), so he packed his bags and headed to the American League.

Switching leagues proved to be just the change Vollmer needed. About his trade to Washington, the slugger later related, "I was glad to get away from the National [League]. All I remembered over there was failures with the Reds."[10] He arrived in Washington in time to play one game that season, starting in center field on October 2 and collecting two singles in five at-bats, and then headed home to prepare for 1949.

The '49 season was a study in contrasts. On the one hand, Vollmer gained the distinction of hitting at least one home run in every stadium in the league; on the other, he never made much of an impression on Senators management. Vollmer said in 1950, a year after he had been traded away from the Senators, that Washington manager Joe Kuhel "didn't even know my name. That's a fact. I had been with the Nats all season and it was late in August when Kuhel started to introduce me to someone. He got the first name all right, but spluttered around with my second until he finally came out with 'Milan – Clyde Milan.' Milan, of course, was a coach with us."[11]

It was symbolic of Vollmer's 1949 season in Washington. Platooned for most of the first month, he was then used mainly as the starting center fielder, but ultimately failed to impress as a consistent run producer. Playing in 129 games, Vollmer batted .253 with 14 home runs and 59 runs batted in, producing a slugging percentage of just .391. By the time the 1950 season opened, Vollmer was deemed expendable, and on May 7, after playing in just six games for the Senators, he was traded to the Boston Red Sox for outfielder Tom O'Brien and infielder Merrill Combs.

Vollmer was pleased with the trade. "Getting a chance to hit in Fenway Park was wonderful," he said a year later. Washington's Griffith Stadium "is really big. I knew a lot of the balls I was hitting there would reach that Boston fence."[12] For the next

Vollmer played parts of five seasons with Washington from 1948-54. – SABR-Rucker Archive

season and a half they did, and the Big 'Un hit home runs far more frequently than before.

If Vollmer was expected to play every couple of days and add occasional power to the Boston lineup, circumstances soon dictated a larger role for the 28-year-old. First, Vollmer realized a singular achievement. On June 8 at Fenway Park, the Red Sox annihilated the St. Louis Browns, 29-4, and the outfielder, batting leadoff, became the only player in history to come to the plate eight times in eight innings (he finished 1-for-7, walking once and hitting a double). Then, on July 11, in the All-Star Game in Chicago, Ted Williams fractured his elbow. When the Sox resumed their season after the All-Star break, manager Steve O'Neill played Vollmer in Williams' spot, starting him in left and batting him third. "He's a good outfielder, pretty good hitter and fast," O'Neill said. "He gets away from the plate faster than [Vern] Stephens or [Walt] Dropo and he's less likely to be doubled up. I'd thought of moving and Dropo up in the order, but this may work out better."[13]

In his first game starting in place of Williams, on July 13 at Fenway Park, Vollmer hit a home run and two doubles in an 8-7 victory over the White Sox. In the 32 games in which he filled in, he batted a respectable .281, with three home runs and 22 RBIs. Returning to a part-time role after Williams returned, Vollmer then provided even grander heroics when, as a pinch-hitter, he blasted his first-ever grand slam, at Fenway Park against Cleveland on August 27. The blast propelled the Red Sox to an 11-9 victory. In all, Vollmer appeared in 57 games after the trade from Washington, batted a major-league career-best .284, and hit seven home runs, drove in 37 runs and posted a slugging mark of .467. Acquired to add depth to the Boston outfield, Vollmer helped keep the Red Sox in contention in 1950 with his clutch hitting.

And then came 1951 and one of those inexplicable streaks that power hitters sometimes experience. When it was over he deemed his performance "the greatest satisfaction I've ever got out of baseball."[14]

Before the Fourth of July, Vollmer got his season off to a good start, but not one that suggested fireworks. As Boston's fourth outfielder, Vollmer played in 33 games, batted 73 times, posted a .260 average, and hit four home runs. On July 4, at Philadelphia's Shibe Park, in the first game of a doubleheader, he hit a solo home run, and over the next 23 days he had one of the most impressive streaks in baseball history.

Consider this performance: July 6 — a two-run triple in a 6-2 win over New York; July 7 – a grand slam in the first inning of a 10-4 win over New York; July 8 — a two-run homer that gave Boston a 4-3 lead in an eventual 6-3 win over New York; July 12 — a two-run homer in the first game of a doubleheader against Chicago, won by Boston, 3-2; in the second game drove in the winning run with a sacrifice fly in a 6-5 win; July 13 — a homer in the fifth inning and an RBI single in the 19th in a 5-4 loss to Chicago; July 14 – a two-run single in the ninth that defeated Chicago, 3-2; July 18 — a solo home run for the first Boston run in a 4-3 win over Cleveland; July 19 — two home runs in a 5-4 loss to Cleveland; July 21 – a home run, double, and single, with four RBIs, in a 6-3 win over Detroit; July 26 – three home runs driving in six runs in a 13-10 win over Chicago; July 28 — singled in the 15th inning to tie the score, 3-3, against Cleveland, and hit a grand slam in the 16th to give Boston an 8-4 victory.

It was an amazing run. In 24 games from July 4 through July 28, Vollmer collected 30 hits in 98 at-bats (.306); totaled 13 home runs and 38 RBIs; and smashed 74 total bases for a .755 slugging average. His 13 home runs contributed to 12 Boston victories, and his three-home-run game on July 26 made Vollmer only the fourth hitter in history to hit that many in one game at Fenway Park.

He had been an unlikely hero. Indeed, asked during the streak to explain his performance, Vollmer told the press, "A hero today, a forgotten man tomorrow. … I can't honestly explain what has been happening. I'm swinging the same bat in the same groove. Nothing is different. I just hit a hot streak."[15]

Vollmer was reticent when interviewed. "I don't know what they want me to say," he explained. "Nobody ever tried to make a hero out of me before. Newspaper guys never bothered me much until now. I don't mean that they bothered me. I mean they never paid me any attention, or asked me any question.

I'll say one thing, however," he concluded. "It's more fun when you're hitting home runs."[16]

It also put money in Vollmer's pocket. At the start of the season, he was the lowest-paid player on the Boston roster, at a salary of $7,500. At midseason, however, it was reported that Red Sox owner Tom Yawkey had rewarded Vollmer for his performance by raising his salary to $12,500.

Through it all, the sudden notoriety seemed to have little effect on Vollmer's disposition; he remained a quiet and reserved player. That came as no surprise to Ruth Hatch. A 50-ish widow, Mrs. Hatch ran a rooming house on Bay State Road, close to Fenway Park, where Vollmer roomed with half a dozen other Red Sox players. (Clyde's wife and daughter were back home in Ohio.) The men were the "town's heroes," and Mrs. Hatch shielded the players from local "bobby-soxers." She was sure that Vollmer would stay grounded. "Clyde won't get any swelled head like some of the others did," she said.[17] And Clyde never did.

The 1951 season was the pinnacle of Vollmer's career. After posting a .251 average in 1951, scoring a career-high 66 runs, and compiling 22 home runs, 85 RBIs, and a .456 slugging average in 115 games, Vollmer returned to Boston in 1952 and, again in a reserve role, posted solid numbers: a .264 batting average in 90 games, with 11 home runs, 50 RBIs, and a .476 slugging average. That was his final full season with Boston. In 1953, after making one appearance for the Red Sox (he walked as a pinch-hitter), on April 22 he was sold back to the Senators in a cash transaction somewhere around the waiver price of $10,000. The deal brought Vollmer back to Washington to provide help with the Senators' depleted outfield. He played in 118 games and batted .260 with 11 home runs and 74 batted in, and then played one final season in Washington, appearing in only 62 games (.256, two home runs). On September 17, 1954, the 32-year-old Vollmer asked for and was granted his unconditional release. In 10 major-league seasons, he had compiled a .256 batting average with 69 home runs, 40 of which came while he played in a Red Sox uniform.

Still, Vollmer wasn't done. Over the next two seasons, he bounced around with three minor-league clubs, playing in Charleston (American Association) and Buffalo (International League) in 1955, and Buffalo and Little Rock/Montgomery (Southern Association; the franchise moved during the season) in 1956. And then, at the age of 35, he left the game for good.

Vollmer lived a full life after baseball. For more than 20 years, he owned the Lark Lounge in Florence, Kentucky, across the Ohio River from Cincinnati, and was a member of the American Legion, the Fraternal Order of Eagles/Cheviot Aerie, and the Delhi Senior Citizens. He died on October 2, 2006, in Florence. He was survived by his wife, Maggie; daughter, Claudia; and a brother.

SOURCES

Alton Evening Telegraph (Ohio), *Baseball Digest, Blytheville Courier News* (Arkansas),

Boston Post, Connellsville Daily Courier (Ohio), *Charleston Daily Mail* (West Virginia),

Charleston Gazette (West Virginia), *Coshocton Tribune* (Ohio), *Dunkirk Evening Observer* (New York), *Lima News* (Ohio), *Mansfield News Journal* (Ohio), *Marion Star* (Ohio), *Middlesboro Daily News* (Kentucky), *Piqua Daily Call* (Ohio), *Portsmouth Times* (Ohio),

The Sporting News, Syracuse Post-Standard, Syracuse Herald Journal, Van Wert Times-Bulletin (Ohio), *Washington Post, Van Wert Times* (Ohio), and *Zanesville Times Recorder* (Ohio)

NOTES

1   Russ Needham, "A Dream Comes True Values Change Quickly," *Columbus Dispatch*, June 4, 1942: 4-B.

2   Sy Burick, "Vollmer, the Enbalmer," *Baseball Digest*, September 1951: 79.

3   The Old Scout, "Reds Continue Seeking Picket," *Springfield* (Massachusetts) *Union*, June 13, 1942: 12.

4   The Old Scout.

5   Sid Feder, "Weinstock is Aspiring for Kessler Team," *Wilkes-Barre Leader*, July 18, 1942: 11.

6   United Press, "Travelers Keeping Up Pace Against Vols in Drive for S.A. Flag," *Knoxville New-Sentinel*, August 26, 1942: 9.

7   "Reds Meet Detroit Tigers in Exhibition Game Today," *Zanesville (Ohio) Signal*, March 15, 1946: 13.

8   Bob Ajemian, "Vollmer Fires Bosox Victory Rockets," *The Sporting News*, July 25, 1951: 3.

9   Shirley Povich, "All Vollmer Can Say: 'It's Fun to Hit Homers'," *Washington Post*, July 29, 1951: C1.

10   Ajemian.

11   Gerry Moore, "Vollmer's Grand Slam on Al Benton's Curve First He Has Ever Hit," unidentified newspaper clipping, August 1950, in Vollmer's player file at the National Baseball Hall of Fame.

12   Ajemian.

13   Ajemian.

14   Ajemian.

15   Jim Wood, "Big Clyde hits popularity streak," *Statesville (North Carolina) Daily Record*, July 27, 1951: 14.

16   Wirt Gammon, "Just Between Us: Quotable Quotes," *Chattanooga Daily Times*, July 31, 1951: 11.

17   "Vollmer 'Reveals' Recipe – 'Meeting the Ball' Better," *The Sporting News*, August 8, 1951: 12.

EARL AVERILL

BY JOSEPH WANCHO

Four cutouts of larger-than-life baseballs adorned the royal blue outfield wall at Cleveland Stadium. Each baseball sported a player's name and the corresponding jersey number that had been retired by the Indians. Even the most casual of Cleveland fans would be familiar with Bob Feller's number 19 and Lou Boudreau's number 5. They may have also been familiar with Mel Harder, whose uniform number 18 was the most recent to be retired in 1990.

The last baseball on the wall displayed the number 3, which belonged to Cleveland outfielder Earl Averill. He was likely the least recognizable of the quartet. His years (1929-1939) in Cleveland were not punctuated with a pennant. The team finished no higher than third place and no lower than fifth in the American League standings during Averill's tenure. Cleveland had competitive teams with good players; however, during the decade of the 1930s, when Averill was with the Indians, they could not put it all together for one season. New York, Philadelphia, Detroit, and Washington all won pennants during those years, while Cleveland was left looking forward to next season.

Despite the club's lackluster performance, Averill's offensive impact could not be overlooked. When he was traded to Detroit in 1939, he was the Indians' team leader in seven offensive categories. In 2024 Averill remained the franchise leader in runs (1,154), RBIs (1,084), triples (121), total bases (3,200), and extra-base hits (724). Averill is also in the top five in five other offensive categories.[1]

Averill finally reached the World Series with the Detroit Tigers in 1940. Although he was a backup outfielder at this point of his career, Averill proved how valuable he could be, batting .308 as a pinch-hitter.

In 1975 the Veterans Committee elected Averill to the National Baseball Hall of Fame. Finally, 34 years after he played his last professional season, he took his rightful place with the game's greatest players.

Howard Earl Averill was born on May 21, 1902, in Snohomish, Washington. He was the youngest of three children (brother Forrest and sister Valera) born to Jotham and Anna (Maddox) Averill. Jotham Averill died in 1904 and Anna had to take on work in a shingle factory to support her family.

Averill dropped out of high school his freshman year. He worked in lumber mills and on road crews. He was not a big man (5-feet-9½, 160 pounds), but the hard labor resulted in brawn and muscle in his upper body. Averill played baseball on the Snohomish town team, battling neighboring cities after work and on the weekends. Although the players did not receive a salary, fans often took up a collection for the player who

Earl Averill, Cleveland Indians – SABR-Rucker Archive

distinguished himself the most in the game. Averill was often the recipient of this largesse, one time receiving a pot of $80.

On May 15, 1922, Averill married Gladys Loette Hyatt in Mount Vernon, Washington.[2] Earl and Loette were married 61 years and had four sons: Howard, Bernard, Earl, and Lester.[3]

In 1924 citizens of Snohomish raised money to send Averill to Seattle to try out for the Seattle Indians of the Pacific Coast League. However, manager Red Killefer was not as impressed with his abilities and sent Averill home.

The Averill family grew to four when Bernard was born in 1925. Averill played two days a week for Bellingham (Washington), earning $15 a game. He also worked for the county painting bridges and picked up other jobs to support his growing family. After a few weeks in Bellingham, he moved on to Anaconda (Montana), where the baseball team paid $250 a month.[4] Averill batted .430 at Anaconda, drawing interest from the San Francisco Seals of the PCL.

Averill won a spot on the Seals' roster during spring training in 1926. Before long he was slashing line drives all over Recreation Park in San Francisco as well as the other venues in the league. In his three years with Seals, Averill averaged 250 hits and 50 doubles, 26 home runs, and a .342 batting average.[5]

What was the secret to Averill's hitting success? Why, it was sauerkraut juice. When Averill mentioned to Seals manager Nick Williams that he might give up the bitter elixir in favor of milk, Williams balked. "If you do, I'll run you clean out of the joint," threatened Williams. "If there are base hits in sauerkraut juice, as I suspect, you are going to drink lots of it and what is more, I think I'll drink some myself and hit in a pinch."[6]

In 1928 Cleveland general manager Billy Evans had a pocket full of cash as he headed to the West Coast to sign players. The first player on his list was Seals outfielder Roy Johnson. But Detroit beat Evans to the punch and signed Johnson. Next was another outfielder, Smead Jolley. Seals pitchers Duster Mails and Dutch Ruether interceded, sending Evans in a different direction. "Forget Jolley. Forget Johnson, too. Buy that Averill," they told Evans.[7]

Evans took their advice, plunking down $45,000 to acquire Averill. "The Snohomish slugger came fast last season," wrote the *San Francisco Examiner*. "He was always a good hitter, but last season he polished up his play in the outfield; learned how to play for batters and once he learned the lesson, did not forget it."[8]

When Indians owner Alva Bradley first saw Averill, he said to Evans, "You paid all that money for a midget."[9] Bradley and the rest of the Indians would soon learn that Averill packed plenty of power in his compact body.

In 1929 Roger Peckinpaugh was in his second season as the Cleveland skipper. The year before, the team finished the season with a 62-92 record. Averill and fellow rookie outfielder Dick Porter garnered many of the headlines during the '29 spring training. However, Irving Vaughan, beat writer for the *Cleveland Plain Dealer*, doused any hope that Cleveland fans might have for their team, writing, "There may be some improvement if a rookie comes through, but while these happenings are always looked for, they occur only about as often as Halley's comet whistles through the heavens."[10]

Maybe he wasn't a comet, but Averill quickly became a star. Cleveland opened the 1929 season on April 16 against Detroit at League Park. Averill, playing center field and batting third in the lineup, came to bat in the bottom of the first inning. Detroit starter Earl Whitehill threw the rookie a fastball on a 0-and-2 count. The left-handed-hitting Averill sent a towering drive over the 45-foot right-field fence. The blast warmed the chilled crowd as Averill became the second American League player to homer in his first big-league at-bat.[11]

Later in the game, in the top of the sixth, the Tigers had a baserunner on first when Averill lunged forward and caught a sinking line drive off the bat of Detroit's Marty McManus. Both plays contributed to the Cleveland 5-4 win. "Whitehill apparently thought he could slip a fast one by me," said Averill. "I was all set, took a healthy swing and as the ball hit the bat, I knew it was going somewhere."[12]

Decimating minor-league pitching on the West Coast was one thing, but hitting against major-league talent was another. Averill batted .332 his rookie season and set a team record for

home runs in a season at 18. As a team, the Indians finished in third place.

Averill also demonstrated a keen batting eye. While some home-run hitters tend to be free swingers and would rack up the whiffs, Averill did not. In the first 11 seasons of his career, he totaled more walks than strikeouts. He was the perfect hitter who combined hitting for power and average.

Despite his size, Averill wielded one of the heaviest bats in the league. His bat was 36 inches long and weighed 42 ounces. Averill would also swing a 44-ounce bat from time to time.[13]

While many batters stand toward the back of the batter's box to better pick up a pitch, Averill had a different philosophy. "I virtually straddled the plate," he said. "The farther you stand in front, the smaller the break on the ball when you meet it. I kept two things in mind at the plate. One was that I was up there to swing; the other was to keep my eye on my target. That was the pitcher's cap. I always aimed for that, tried to go to the middle. But, if the ball was outside, I'd hit to left."[14]

One of Averill's signature games occurred on September 17, 1930, at League Park. In a doubleheader against Washington, he smashed three home runs in the opener and drove in eight runs to set a team record in Cleveland's 13-7 victory. In the second game, Averill came to the plate in the first inning with two runners aboard and smacked a drive to deep center field. He raced around the bases for an inside-the-park home run, his fourth home run and 11th RBI for the day.

Averill was not the only formidable batsman in the Cleveland lineup. In 1930 the Indians hit .304 as a team. Besides Averill, who hit .339, their lineup consisted of Porter (.350), Johnny Hodapp (.354), Eddie Morgan (.349), Charlie Jamieson (.301), and Joe Sewell (.289). But opposing teams batted .305 against the Indians pitching staff. The result was an 81-73 record, earning the club a fourth-place finish, 21 games behind first-place Philadelphia.

Peckinpaugh was replaced as manager by Walter Johnson on June 9, 1933. Peckinpaugh was a players' manager and Averill was sorry to see him go. "He knew more baseball than the rest of them put together," Averill said, comparing Peckinpaugh to his other managers.[15] Johnson had recent success as a field manager, guiding the Senators to 92 and 93 wins in 1931 and 1932. However, he had been replaced by Joe Cronin, who led the Senators to the AL pennant in 1933.

The 1933 season was a historic one for major-league baseball. The year marked the first-ever All-Star Game, pitting the best players of the NL against the AL. Billed as "The Game of the Century," the game was played on July 6, 1933, at Chicago's Comiskey Park. Cleveland pitchers Oral Hildebrand and Wes Ferrell joined Averill as members of the American League squad. Averill was the only one of the trio to see action, pinch-hitting for Washington pitcher Alvin Crowder in the bottom of the sixth inning. Averill singled sharply to center field to drive Cronin in from second base, giving the AL a 4-2 lead that ended up being the final score.

Hal Trosky moved into the Cleveland lineup as the starting first baseman in 1934. Averill and the young Iowa slugger each played in all 154 games. They combined for 66 home runs and 255 RBIs. Trosky became another solid player in the lineup, one who could hit for power and average.

After the season, Averill joined a traveling all-star team that went to Japan. Babe Ruth, Jimmie Foxx, Lefty Gomez, Lou Gehrig, Lefty O'Doul, and manager Connie Mack were among the party who made the trip.

Averill was awarded a Japanese sword for being the first American player to hit a home run against the All-Nippon Stars. He treasured the gift for years.[16] "The Earl of Snohomish has been doing some long-distance clouting on his own hook in the land of cherry blossoms," wrote Ed Bang of the *Cleveland News*. "Truth be, he has experienced no trouble in holding to the pace of the other sluggers. It so happens that Averill is the smallest member of the 'Big Four' home run manufacturers and that being the case, he should inspire the Japanese players far more than those Goliaths – Ruth, Gehrig and Foxx.[17]

"The Japanese are small in size, and their main drawback is our national pastime, which they appear to have adopted as their own, has been their inability to pack enough force to drive the ball for the well-known bacon-getting route. However, since they have not seen Averill, who, while small, still is well-muscled and has perfect timing at the plate, they have evidently concluded they, too, can develop the well-known punch at bat."[18]

On June 28, 1935, the Indians had a day off and were enjoying a team picnic. "Earl threw a firecracker that didn't go off," said Mel Harder. "When he picked it up, it exploded. Joe Vosmik and I put him in a car and took him to St. Luke's Hospital. It looked bad. There was a lot of blood."[19] This incident resulted Averill getting his nickname, Rock.[20]

Averill missed three weeks as his right hand healed from the burns and scars caused by the firecracker. Vosmik replaced Averill for the All-Star Game, which in 1935 was played at Cleveland Stadium.

There had been weeks of speculation, especially in the Cleveland media, about the security of Walter Johnson's job as manager. He dismissed popular players Willie Kamm and Glenn Myatt from the team because he felt that they were no longer useful. The Indians (37-26-1) were 2½ games behind New York (40-24) on June 30. They went 2-13-1 from July 1 to July 18. Obviously, Averill's injury did not help the situation. "I'm 100 percent for Walter and I think the whole team is for him," said Averill, "The boys have found Walter is on the level and has plenty of guts."[21]

Despite Averill's stance, Johnson was fired on August 5 and replaced by Steve O'Neill, a former Indians catcher and a coach on Johnson's staff.

In 1935 Averill did not bat over .300 for the first time in his career. He rebounded the next season in a big way, posting a .451 batting average in the month of July. His season average was .374 and climbed to over .380 in August. Averill was leading the AL in hitting going into September, but Chicago's Luke Appling batted .477 in September to surpass Averill, .388 to .378, for the season. Averill led the league in hits with 232.

While Averill was hitting line drives around AL ballparks, a teenager from Van Meter, Iowa, joined the Indians. Bob Feller was 17 years old when he started his first game for Cleveland, against the St. Louis Browns on August 23, 1936. The right-handed fireballer threw a complete-game six-hitter against the Browns. He struck out 15 in the 4-1 win. Feller became, and still is, the face of the Cleveland franchise.

Another game Averill is known for, perhaps infamously, is the All-Star Game on July 7, 1937, at Washington's Griffith Stadium. The American League had taken a 2-0 lead on Lou Gehrig's two-run home run off Dizzy Dean. Averill stepped to the plate and sent a liner back to the mound. "Diz threw that big curve," said Averill. "The last thing I remember is seeing it break toward the outside of the plate. I was already into my swing. I connected and saw the ball hit him in the toe and bounced right into the second baseman's glove.

"That was the third out. Not many people remember that. We passed as Diz was on his way to the dugout. He said, 'Hey, you didn't have to hit me with it.' I laughed. Heck, I wasn't trying to pull the ball at him, I was just trying to hit the thing."[22]

Dean's left toe was broken, his plant foot when he pitched. He was not the same pitcher for the rest of his career.

Off the field, a highlight of 1937 was when Averill appeared on the cover of Wheaties cereal boxes. There was a tradition by General Mills to choose an athlete, either national or regional, to be in the advertisement on a box of the popular cereal. In Averill's case, he often started his day with a bowl of Wheaties.[23]

Cleveland manager O'Neill failed to move the needle in a positive direction and was fired after the 1937 season. He was replaced by Oscar Vitt. They were like night and day: O'Neill was a friendly, outgoing sort while Vitt was a taciturn, disciplinary type of manager. Club owner Bradley also gave Vitt the power to make trades, undermining general manager Cy Slapnicka and causing tension between the two. Vitt also didn't make many friends when he stated that he "had only two major leaguers, Feller and Harder."[24]

Averill began the 1938 season on a hot streak. After his average climbed to .397 on May 5, he began to have back pain in Philadelphia. He played through the pain. However, his average started to drop. A groin injury in early September kept him on the bench. Averill hit .330 in 1938, which for most players would have been a very successful season. Cleveland dealt Averill to the Detroit Tigers on June 14, 1939, for left-handed pitcher Harry Eisenstat and cash. Averill was inserted as the Tigers' starting left fielder. He batted a career-low with the Tigers, hitting .262 with 10 home runs and 58 RBIs. Detroit finished in fifth place with an 81-73 record, 26½ games behind the red-hot Yankees with a record of 106-45, who went on to sweep the Cincinnati Reds in the World Series.

The 1940 AL pennant race came down to Detroit and Cleveland. The Tigers held a two-game lead over the Indians heading into the season's final three games at Cleveland Stadium. The Tigers won the first game, clinching the pennant.

Cincinnati defeated Detroit in the World Series in seven games. Averill went 0-for-3 in three pinch-hitting appearances. He made the final out of the Series, a 2-1 Reds win.

Averill was released by Detroit and signed with the Boston Braves for the 1941 season. With just two singles in 17 at-bats, he was released after eight games. Averill then returned to the Pacific Coast League, joining the Seattle Rainiers. Also on the Rainiers was Earl Torgeson, also of Snohomish. After the season, Averill retired from professional baseball. In his 13-year career, he hit 238 home runs, 401 doubles, and 128 triples. Averill batted .318 (2,019-for-6,353) and drove in 1,164 runs.

In retirement, Averill worked in a greenhouse he owned with his brother, Forest. For 20 years, he also owned and operated the Averill Motel in Snohomish. Averill spent time keeping tabs on his son, Earl Douglas Averill, too. Sometimes mistakenly referred to as Earl Jr., the younger Earl carved out a modest baseball career for himself. Primarily a catcher, with some time in the outfield, Earl Douglas played seven seasons with Cleveland (1956, 1958), the Chicago Cubs (1959-1960), the Chicago White Sox (1960), the Los Angeles Angels (1961-1962), and the Philadelphia Phillies (1963). He had a lifetime batting average of .242 with 44 home runs and 159 RBIs.

On February 3, 1975, the elder Earl Averill was elected to the Hall of Fame unanimously by the Veterans Committee. Also elected were Billy Herman, Bucky Harris, Judy Johnson, and Ralph Kiner. Averill was outspoken about how long it took for his election to the National Baseball Hall of Fame. He was also candid about players who he believed merited inclusion but had not been elected, urging that the voting rules be changed.[25]

"It's been a long time coming, but better late than never," said Averill. "It is wonderful to make it while you are still alive. I'm going on 73. In fact, I told my sons that if I didn't make it while I was still alive, that they turn it down if I made it afterward."[26]

"My ambition is reached. I really longed for this. And, you know, a lot of good ballplayers never make it. I understand that it was a unanimous vote. That kind of makes up for the long wait."[27]

Not everyone agreed with the election of Averill. Jack Lang of the New York Daily News wrote, "The moment he's inducted, Averill pops off that it took baseball too long. Funny thing, but all the while he was waiting to get in, he expressed no resentment. If we are going to have these old geezers popping off after they've received the tributes, maybe they don't deserve them to begin with."[28]

On June 8, 1975, the Cleveland Indians retired Averill's uniform number 3, joining Feller (19) and Boudreau (5).

In 1983 the All-Star Game was held at Comiskey Park to commemorate its 50th anniversary. The living All-Stars who played in the first game in 1933 were invited to Chicago to take part in the festivities.

About six weeks later, on August 16, Averill died from respiratory problems brought on by pneumonia. He was survived by his wife, Gladys Loette; four sons; numerous grandchildren; and six great-grandchildren. "He had a real good time in Chicago, but when he got back he was really down," said his son Earl. "Of the 33 All-Stars in 1933, only 13 were left. Now with Dad's death, there are only 12."[29]

Center fielder Doc Cramer, a contemporary of Averill's, said "Earl Averill was a great hitter and a fine outfielder all around. … Whatever you write about Earl won't be enough."[30]

NOTES

1   *Cleveland Guardians 2024 Media Guide*, 272.

2   Ancestry.com marriage records, Howard Earl Averill, accessed June 8, 2024.

3   A.C. De Cola, "Earl Is Pal to His Sons," *Cleveland Press*, July 2, 1936: 21.

4   Vince O'Keefe, "'Hard Rock' Earl Averill dies," *Seattle Times*, August 17, 1983: E1.

5   It must be noted that the Pacific Coast League played 190-game schedules.

6   Abe Kemp, "Earl Averill's Bat Impresses Pirate Leader," *San Francisco Examiner*, March 23, 1928: 1.

7   Gordon Cobbledick, "Hometown Fans' Cash Started Averill on Career to Fame," *Cleveland Plain Dealer*, July 26, 1936: 4.

8   Abe Kemp, "Young Star Outfielder Will Go Up to Big Top," *San Francisco Examiner*, November 20, 1928: P-3.

9   Bob Dolgan, "A Man of Talent, Consistency, Class," *Cleveland Plain Dealer*, August 7, 1996: D-6.

10 Irving Vaughan, "Vaughan Sees Tribe Improved This Year," *Cleveland Plain Dealer*, March 19, 1929: 26.

11 Luke Stuart of the St. Louis Browns hit an inside-the-park home run at Washington's Griffith Stadium on August 8, 1921.

12 Earl Averill, "The Biggest Thrill of My Career," *Cleveland News*, undated, 1930. Player's Hall of Fame clippings file.

13 Hy Zimmerman, "Gab Session With the Earl of Snohomish," *The Sporting News*, December 25, 1965: 5.

14 "Gab Session With the Earl of Snohomish."

15 Doug Simpson, "The Earl of Snohomish," *Baseball Research Journal*, 1982. https://sabr.org/journal/article/the-earl-of-snohomish/. Accessed June 15, 2024.

16 Penny Sopris-Kegerreis, "Cast a Vote for the 'Rock' of Snohomish," *Monroe* (Washington) *Monitor and Valley News*, January 27, 1999: 8.

17 Ed Bang, "Scribbled by Scribes," *The Sporting News*, December 6, 1934: 4.

18 "Scribbled by Scribes."

19 "A Man of Talent, Consistency, Class," *Cleveland Plain Dealer*, August 7, 1996: D-1.

20 Bob Broeg, "Averill Shy, Except at the Plate," *The Sporting News*, March 8, 1975: 8.

21 Henry W. Thomas, *Walter Johnson: Baseball's Big Train* (Washington DC: Phenom Press, 1995), 326.

22 Don Duncan, "Earl Averill Recalls Infamous '37 Game," *Seattle Times*, July 15, 1979: J3.

23 "Cast a Vote for the 'Rock' of Snohomish."

24   William H. Johnson, *Hal Trosky: A Baseball Biography* (Jefferson, North Carolina: McFarland, 2017), 80.

25   Transcript of Earl Averill Hall of Fame Induction Speech, Cooperstown, New York, August 18, 1975, in player's Hall of Fame clippings file.

26   Hy Zimmerman, "The Earl of Snohomish Feels Like a King," *Seattle Times*, February 3, 1975: B1.

27   "The Earl of Snohomish Feels Like a King."

28   Jack Lang, "Reds Respectful of Mets Pitching," player's Hall of Fame clippings file.

29   "His Son Recalls Earl Averill," player's Hall of Fame clippings file.

30   Simpson, "The Earl of Snohomish."

JAY GAINER

BY JOE ADONA

In their inaugural season of 1993, few will dispute that the biggest bat in the Colorado Rockies lineup belonged to Andres "Big Cat" Galarraga. Aided by the rarefied air in Denver, Galarraga won the NL batting title that year with a .370 average, had an OPS of 1.005, and drove in 98 runs in 120 games.

On May 14 Galarraga was dealing with a torn hamstring that landed him on the disabled list. His roster spot was filled by Jay Gainer, a 26-year-old left-hand-hitting first baseman.

At the time of his call-up from Triple-A Colorado Springs, Gainer had been hitting .331 with 5 home runs and a Pacific Coast League-leading 39 RBIs.

Gainer arrived in Cincinnati three hours before game time and when he got to Riverfront Stadium, he discovered that Rockies manager Don Baylor had enough confidence not only to plug him in as the starting first baseman, but to also bat him in Galarraga's usual cleanup spot.[1]

In major-league baseball history, only 2.6 percent of all players made their debut as their team's cleanup hitter.[2]

"No hesitation at all," Baylor told the *Colorado Springs Gazette Telegraph* of batting Gainer cleanup. "He's only going to remember his first major league at-bat anyway so what difference does it make where he bats?"[3]

Born Johnathan Keith Gainer on October 8, 1966, in Panama City, Florida, Gainer began his baseball journey as a self-described "clumsy 11-year-old kid" who was given the opportunity to receive guidance from two of his early coaches and mentors, Jim Stafford (Little League) and Dave Goodwin (American Legion).[4]

Gainer's natural abilities were cultivated as his career progressed through Rutherford High School in Panama City and the University of South Alabama, where he drew the attention of scouts and was selected by the San Diego Padres in the 24th round of the 1990 amateur draft. The signing scout was Hosken Powell. Gainer was listed as 6 feet tall and 190 pounds, batting and throwing left-handed.

Gainer started his professional career that year with the short-season Spokane Indians (Northwest League) where he played first base and led the league in batting (.356) average and hit 10 home runs in 76 games. He moved up to the high-A High Desert Mavericks (California League) for 127 games in 1991 (.263/32/120), leading his team in both homers and RBIs for manager Bruce Bochy. He was promoted to Double-A Wichita (Texas League) in 1992 and hit .261 in 105 games with 23 home runs and 67 RBIs.

Unfortunately for Gainer, the Padres already had future Hall of Famer Fred McGriff entrenched at first base.

Jay Gainer, Colorado Rockies – Courtesy of Colorado Rockies

In late March of 1993, in the midst of the expansion Colorado Rockies' first spring training, they swapped left-handed pitcher Denis Boucher to the Padres for Gainer. Little did Gainer know that another roadblock loomed: Galarraga.[5]

"At first, I thought I'd done something wrong," Gainer recalled of the day he was told he'd been traded. "It turned out it wasn't a bad deal. I was actually OK with the idea of being the left-handed bat off the bench behind McGriff. But I guess my success with the Padres pushed me into a spot where I'd gotten exposed a little bit."[6]

Gainer continued to put up impressive numbers rising through the ranks to Triple-A Colorado Springs, where he was regarded as one of the Rockies' top prospects.

There's a reason why coaches at the minor-league level are constantly telling their players to be ready at the drop of a hat – or in this case, the pull of a hamstring. With Galarraga tearing up the NL, Gainer figured his season would be spent in the Pacific Coast League. Then on May 13, Galarraga began the first of two stints on the disabled list.

Colorado Springs manager Brad Mills gave Gainer the news that he was going to join the Rockies in Cincinnati.

"The ride from the airport to the ballpark in Cincinnati was like 30 miles," Gainer remembered. "So I had a lot of time to reflect. People ask me if I was nervous. No, I just took things in stride and did what I always did. I walked into the clubhouse and put my bags in my locker. The lineup card was right in front of my face. I saw that I was hitting cleanup. I said OK, here we go. I was going to come out swinging."[7]

Pitching for the Reds that evening was Tim Pugh, a 6-foot-6 right-hander. Pugh retired the Rockies in order in the first inning, meaning Gainer would lead off the top of the second.

The first pitch to Gainer was what he remembered as a "sinker that didn't sink."[8] Gainer connected and sent the offering 375 feet over the outstretched glove of right fielder Reggie Sanders and into the seats.

"I told the guys at Triple A that I was going to swing at the first pitch and try to hit one out," Gainer said. "But I was joking. No one does that. Afterward, I was thinking, my God, what did I do? It was like I did something I shouldn't have done."[9]

"I was off and running, man," Gainer said. "By the time I looked back up and saw the umpire giving the home run sign, I was already rounding second base."[10]

Gainer became the 67th player to hit a home run in his first major-league at-bat, a list that through the 2023 season had grown to 135.[11]

Gainer was the first Rockies player to accomplish the feat and through 2023 was still the only one to do so.

Even rarer, Gainer's homer came on the first pitch to him, making him at the time the 15th player to do so and one of 31 through 2023.[12] (Cincinnati, however, won the game, 13-5.)

Gainer appeared in 11 games in May, batting .172 with no further homers or runs batted in, and then was sent back to Colorado Springs. He was recalled in early September and got into another 12 games.

Gainer finished the season having played in 23 major-league games. He went 7-for-41 (.171). Three of his hits were home runs (as it happened, all in team losses). He drove in six runs, all via homer. On September 20 at Mile High Stadium in Denver, he pinch-hit and slugged a fourth-inning grand slam off the San Diego Padres' Doug Brocail. He hit his third home run off Rod Beck of San Francisco on September 28 at Candlestick Park. Gainer played in his final major-league game on October 2 as a pinch-hitter for Lance Painter.

Gainer returned to Colorado Springs for the next two seasons and never played in a big-league

game again. After Galarraga moved on, first base was taken over by future Hall of Famer Todd Helton.

The players strike that shut down the major-league season in mid-1994 threatened the coming 1995 season. Baseball prepared for a shortened 144-game campaign with all 30 teams bringing in replacement players.

Had the strike not ended, we could have seen a very different starting nine in Coors Field's debut season. Gainer planned to cross the picket line.[13]

The "Replacement Rockies" were actually the first team to play professional baseball at the newly opened Coors Field. On March 31 and April 1 of 1995, the Rockies welcomed the New York Yankees for a two-game exhibition series in which both teams fielded rosters of replacement players who had chosen to cross the picket line.[14]

Players from all levels of the minors and former big-leaguers crossed the picket line and played in what was the first game held at Coors Field, in front of a near-capacity crowd of 47,563.[15]

The strike ended when Judge (and future Supreme Court Justice) Sonia Sotomayor of the US District Court in Manhattan issued a preliminary injunction against the owners on March 31. On April 2, the day before the season was scheduled to start with the replacement players, the strike came to an official end at 232 days, sending all of the replacement players back to their previous gigs. For Gainer, this was Triple-A Colorado Springs.

Gainer remained a part of the Rockies organization through the 1996 season, with his best campaign coming in 1995 when he blasted 23 homers and logged 86 RBIs along with a .291 average. After he left the Rockies organization in 1995, Gainer's baseball journey grew geographically. He ended up playing 11 seasons as a professional, with stops in Taiwan, the Mexican League, and in Italy with the Grosseto Baseball Club.

"Taiwan … it was like another planet," Gainer told an interviewer. "A lot of the (American) guys couldn't handle the social stuff and the change in baseball. It was a very different game. Still a bat and a ball and three outs and three strikes, but they played the game very differently. We were treated like the hired help."[16]

Not one to have his baseball experience limited again, Gainer moved on to Mexico for three seasons. In 2000, playing for the Olmecas de Tabasco, he led his team with 31 home runs and 81 RBIs.

After that, Gainer finished his playing days in Italy and eventually with Allentown, New Jersey, of the independent Northern League East in 1991.

"It was about Double-A level ball," he said, referring to his stint in Italy. "I was only making barely enough money to cover my expenses there and back home, but I couldn't pass up a chance to see Europe. I had a lot of fun."[17]

Overall, Gainer hit .275 with 121 home runs and 484 RBIs in 11 minor-league seasons spanning 1990-2001. After retiring, he was the hitting coach and manager of Yakima (Washington), an Arizona Diamondbacks' farm team in the Northwest League, and other minor-league teams including the Visalia Oaks of the California League.

In retirement, Gainer designed a training program for players called Baseball Advantage.

As of 2024, he was the coach of the A.C. Davis High School baseball team in Yakima, continuing a career in baseball that's now surpassed 40 years.

SOURCES

In addition to the sources cited in the Notes, the author consulted Baseball-Reference.com.

Attempts to get input or feedback from Jay Gainer for this biography were unsuccessful.

NOTES

1   Steve Acoo, "Jay Gainer Homered in His First Major League At-Bat, on the First Pitch He Saw; Saw 23 Total ML games," greatest21days.com, October 9, 2022. http://www.greatest21days.com/2022/10/jay-gainer-homered-in-his-first-major.html.

2   J.G. Preston, "They Batted Cleanup in Their First Major League Game," The J.G. Preston Experience, March 23, 2013. https://prestonjg.wordpress.com/2013/03/23/they-batted-cleanup-in-their-first-major-league-game/.

3   Acoo.

4   "Jay Gainer." https://www.babattingcages.com/jay-gainer.html.

5   Mark Knudson, "Jay Gainer Made Every Swing Count," *Fort Collins* (Colorado) *Coloradoan*, June 1, 2018. https://www.coloradoan.com/story/sports/professional/denver/2018/06/01/jay-gainer-professional-baseball-mlb-colorado-rockies-san-diego-padres/657979002/.

6   Knudson.

7   Knudson.

8   Knudson.

9   Tim Kurkjian, "And What a Year It Was," *Sports Illustrated*, October 4, 1993. https://vault.si.com/vault/1993/10/04/baseball.

10   Knudson.

11   Of all the major-leaguers who homered in their first at bat, two are in the National Baseball Hall of Fame (Earl Averill and Hoyt Wilhelm) and one is in the NFL Hall of Fame (Ace Parker). Parker homered for the Philadelphia Athletics, pinch-hitting in the top of the ninth inning at Fenway Park in Boston, a two-run homer off Wes Ferrell that bought the A's to within 10 runs of the Red Sox, who won 15-5. He was a running back for the NFL Brooklyn Dodgers and a longtime football coach at Duke University.

12   See the list provided by Major League Baseball at https://www.mlb.com/news/home-run-in-first-at-bat-c265623820.

13   Evan Lang, "The Replacement Rockies That Could Have Been," PurpleRow, SB Nation, January 13, 2022. https://www.purplerow.com/2022/1/13/22878513/colorado-rockies-news-thursday-rockpile-the-replacement-rockies-that-could-have-been.

14   Lang.

15   Patrick Lyons, "Rockies Review: March 31, 1995 – Coors Field Unofficially Opens." https://thednvr.com/rockies-review-march-31-1995-coors-field-unofficially-opens/.

16   Kevin Henry, "Colorado Rockies: May 14 Holds an Interesting Piece of trivia for the Team," Roxpile.com, May 14, 2017. https://roxpile.com/2017/05/14/colorado-rockies-may-14-marks-interesting-piece-trivia-rockies/.

17   Henry.

GATES BROWN

BY DAVE GAGNON

Gates Brown, Detroit Tigers – Courtesy of Trading Card Database

sk any serious Tigers fan over a certain age and they'll tell you that the sound of Tiger Stadium was always a little bit louder than normal when Gates Brown was announced as a pinch-hitter. And why not? After 13 seasons in Detroit, not only did the "Gator" retire as the American League's all-time pinch-hitting king, but so many of his hits were of the clutch variety, either tying the game or putting the team ahead. One would think that in order to have enjoyed that kind of success off the bench, Brown would've had to be ready to hit at all times. You would think he studied pitchers like a hawk for nine innings – trying to gain any advantage he could for when he took the plate. But surprisingly, that wasn't always the case for Gates Brown.

Once in 1968, Mayo Smith decided to put in his pinch-hitting specialist far earlier in the game than normal. Brown, who usually didn't come off the bench until a tight spot near the end of the game, was caught off-guard. "I was sitting at the end of the dugout, eating a couple of hot dogs," he recalled. "It was only the fifth inning (and) I never expected Mayo to call on me to pinch-hit that early." Since he didn't want Smith – who often harped on Brown to lose a few pounds – to see him eating during the game, Brown quickly shoved the hot dogs down his shirt before heading to the plate. "That's the only time I ever wished I'd strike out," he said. But being the clutch hitter he was, he didn't get his wish. Instead, he cracked a double and ended up having to slide head-first into second. While Tigers fans roared and cheered, Brown realized he had made quite a mess of himself. "I had mustard and squashed meat all over me," he laughed, recalling that all his teammates were bent over laughing.[1]

So despite his success as one of the greatest major-league hitters off the bench, Gates Brown wasn't a pinch-hitting robot after all. He was simply one of the guys. He played poker with teammates. He snored. He played catch with relievers during games. He was a press favorite. But most importantly, he always supported his teammates – so much so that his first big-league manager, Charlie Dressen, often referred to him as "Governor Brown." But that was Gates Brown in a nutshell – a team player who always said and did the right things to help his team win.

William James "Gates" Brown was born in Crestline, Ohio, on May 2, 1939 (the same day that Lou Gehrig's consecutive games streak came to an end). His father, John William Brown, a Georgia native, was a laborer working for the US government's Depression-fighting WPA. Crestline was a town along the Cleveland, Columbus and Cincinnati Railroad, and by the time of the 1950 census he was listed as "laborer, railroad." He and Phyllis Brown, a native Ohioan, had six children.

Gates grew to be 5-feet-11 and 220 pounds. He batted left-handed, but threw right-handed and played in 1,051 major-league games, all for the Detroit Tigers.

He was nicknamed Gates by his mother when he was a toddler. He claimed he didn't know why. "I had it long before I went to school. … Maybe it had something to do with the way I walk – kind of bowlegged, I really don't know."[2]

Crestline, like much of northern Ohio in the 1940s and '50s, wasn't the greatest area to grow up in. It was flat, desolate, and poor. Most youngsters from the area got in trouble with the law at some point. A sociologist would say it wasn't their fault they turned to a life of crime, but was a result of where they grew up.

Brown didn't make it out of Crestline with a clean record. Even though he was a standout football star at Crestline High School, he got into more than his fair share of trouble growing up. When he turned 18, he was arrested for breaking and entering and was sent to the nearby Mansfield State Reformatory. (The prison was used in the film *The Shawshank Redemption*.)

Even though Brown had played some baseball in high school, it was in Mansfield that his talents as a ballplayer were developed. At 5-feet-11 and 200-plus pounds of pure muscle, he was encouraged by a prison guard who coached the institution's baseball team to try out at catcher. In awe of his raw ability with the bat – and encouraged that baseball might lead Brown out of a life of crime – the coach, Chuck Yarman, wrote to several major-league teams, including the Tigers.[3]

In the fall of 1959, Detroit sent scouts to the prison to see Brown. Impressed, one of them called onetime Tiger Pat Mullin, later the team's top scout. Mullin made the trek from Detroit to see for himself. After Brown belted a daunting home run in Mullin's presence, the Tigers decided to help him get paroled a year early. He was signed to a $7,000 bonus pact almost immediately upon his release.

Brown has said that other clubs, including the Cleveland Indians and Chicago White Sox, were interested in springing him. But he stuck with Detroit because "they didn't have any Negroes at that time and I figured they'd have to have some soon."[4] In fact, Ozzie Virgil, a Puerto Rican, had joined the Tigers in 1958 – becoming the Motor City's first Black ballplayer. But Brown was right in that the Tigers obviously lacked the integration of most other big-league clubs in the late 1950s.

Before Brown's first professional season, 1960, Mullin advised him to give up catching and switch to the outfield. More concerned about staying out of trouble than he was about a position change, he was fine with the new position.

Brown – on legal probation from Mansfield during his first season – joined the Tigers' organization in Duluth that year. He shined almost immediately – especially for someone only a few months out of prison. In 121 games, he hit .293 with 10 homers. He also led the Northern League with 13 triples and was second in stolen bases (30) and runs scored (104). But his real character test wouldn't come until later.

The following year he headed south to Durham of the Carolina League. It was here that Brown found out firsthand that being Black and an ex-con was fuel for the fire for Southern crowds. "It was tough just being a Negro down there," he said. "I had to contend with people calling me 'n-----'' and other stuff."[5]

Being an ex-con didn't help as Southern newspapers printed stories about his criminal history, leading to more quips and threats from the crowds. "They called me all the names, 'Con,' 'Jailbird,' the whole thing. They were pretty vicious," Brown recalled. But he had to learn to ignore the jeers and to use the negativity as motivation to improve. "Some of the guys wanted to go up into the stands after those people, but I told them to just let it lay. It made me do better. It made me try harder. I decided that they could beat me physically, but no way were they going to beat me mentally. And do you know something, I hit the ball hard that season and led the league in hitting," topping the circuit in 1961 with a .324 mark. His outstanding play began to win over the same Durham fans who had heckled him earlier in the season. "By the end of the year, they were all on my side," Brown said, laughing.[6]

After showing continued success at the minor-league level – including another .300 campaign for Denver in 1962 – it was

clear that Brown was on the fast track to join the big club. And with the Tigers' lack of early-season success in 1963, Brown was called up from Triple-A Syracuse on June 17 – one day before Dressen was named the team's new manager. It would be Dressen who would call on Brown to take his first major-league hacks.

Brown officially debuted for the Tigers against the Boston Red Sox on June 19 at Fenway Park. With Boston up 4-1 in the fifth inning, Brown entered the game as – what else – a pinch-hitter for pitcher Don Mossi.

With Dressen getting his first look at the young outfielder, the situation was much like when Pat Mullin saw Brown play at Mansfield for the first time. As it happened, Mullin was at Fenway Park that day – having been made Dressen's first-base coach. Again, as he had during his Mansfield tryout, Brown did not disappoint his onlookers. He hit a 400-foot home run well into the Boston sky, becoming only the third Tiger in history to homer in his first at-bat.

Brown remained with the club for the rest of the season, primarily as a pinch-hitter. Detroit rebounded with him on the team and had a winning record for the rest of the year. Overall, Brown hit .268 with two home runs in his rookie season. He stuck with the Tigers in 1964, primarily as the starting left fielder. Playing alongside Al Kaline in right field and a troika (Bill Bruton, George Thomas, and Don Demeter) in center, Brown hit .272 with 15 home runs and was second on the team with 11 stolen bases.

Despite his solid 1964 season, however, Brown lost his starting job in the outfield in 1965 to the young power hitter Willie Horton. And even though he was disappointed in returning to his role as a pinch-hitter and reserve outfielder, Brown would never let his personal frustration get in the way of the team. He slugged 10 home runs that season in barely half the at-bats he had in 1964. And despite his stocky 225-pound frame, he also stole six bases and was regarded unofficially as the fastest Tiger on the team. Brown didn't know it then, but he was on his way to becoming the most successful pinch-hitter in American League history.

Despite Brown's clutch contributions, his reserve status – and a budding mix of young outfielders – made it difficult for him to get raises from his bosses in Detroit. In fact, prior to the 1965 season, Brown had to pass up winter ball for the first time. With a wife and child plus a second on the way, Brown took a second job as a furniture salesman in the offseason.

Brown pressed on, however, and returned in 1966 and had similar success in the same role – batting .325 as a pinch-hitter. Overall he hit .266 with 7 home runs in 169 at-bats. Although he remained quietly disappointed with his role, it was clear that Brown was the Tigers' best offensive option off the bench.

Tragedy befell Brown and the Tigers that season, however. Charlie Dressen died on August 10. Dressen had been suffering from heart and kidney problems for most of the season.

Brown struggled with injuries in 1967 before finally being shelved with a dislocated wrist. Even when he played, he never could find his swing under new manager Mayo Smith. As a pinch-hitter, he hit only .160 (4-for-25). However, that Tigers team nearly made the World Series before they were beat out by the "Impossible Dream" Red Sox on the final day of the season. Mayo Smith and the rest of the Tigers vowed to return to the 1968 season with a vengeance. But the greatest turn-around of all would come from Brown.

Discouraged by his poor season in 1967, Brown came to spring training on a mission in 1968. He was no longer upset about a lack of playing time, he just wanted to contribute. The Tigers, however, weary of Brown's poor and injury-filled campaign in 1967, decided to bring back Eddie Mathews as the team's primary left-handed pinch-hitter. General manager Jim Campbell and Smith even said that they thought about trading Brown, but couldn't come close to pulling a trade because Brown had packed on a few pounds while waiting for his wrist to heal, a turnoff for prospective trading partners.

Brown got his chance to prove them wrong, however, on the second day of the season; when Smith, having already used Mathews earlier in the game, called on Brown to pinch-hit in the ninth inning in a tie game. Brown grabbed a bat and hit a game-winning home run off John Wyatt of the Boston Red Sox. It was how the 1968 Tigers won their first game of the season.

Brown did everything he could to tarnish the image of what would be known as the Year of the Pitcher. He hammered six hits in his first 10 pinch-hit at-bats on his way to an AL-record 18 pinch hits that season. Tigers fans soon became accustomed to watching him come off the bench and deliver over and over in key situations. But none was more key than during a Sunday doubleheader on August 11 against the defending American League champion Red Sox.

In the lidlifter that day, the Tigers were in an extra-inning struggle with the Red Sox until Mayo Smith finally found a time for Brown to get in the game in the bottom of the 14th inning. Tiger Stadium erupted when he was announced. But their cheers were nothing compared to when Brown smacked the game-winning home run a minute later.

Then in the second game, Brown strode to the plate in a tie game in the bottom of the ninth. With Mickey Stanley creeping off third, he singled to right to drive in the winning run, Giving him an unheard-of two game-ending hits in the same day. Even 16-year vet Kaline admitted he had never heard the Tiger Stadium crowd cheer the way they did for Brown that day.

In fact, Brown hit so unbelievably well in 1968 that Smith even started him in 16 games. Not bad for a guy who was trade bait when the season began. In the end, Brown hit an astounding .370 in 1968 – more than over 100 points higher than his career average, 135 better than the team average, and 140 better than the American League's collective average. He was the only full-season Tiger to hit above .300 that season. He also averaged an extra-base hit every 6.9 at-bats – a remarkable stat when you consider that the mighty Álex Rodríguez averaged one every 7.2 at-bats in his MVP season of 2007.

Brown was not only clutch with the bat in 1968, he was also clutch as a teammate. One night during the season, he inter-rupted a melee between Denny McLain and Jim Northrup and made them understand the importance of what the team was trying to accomplish as a whole. During a road trip in the middle of the 1968 season, Brown was playing poker with a bunch of other players, including Northrup and McLain. Halfway through a hand, Northrup caught McLain cheating. Enraged, he flew across the bed and grabbed McLain by the throat. John Hiller, who was seated next to Brown, recalls Northrup screaming, "I'm gonna kill you, you bastard! I'm gonna kill you!" Red-faced and exasperated, Northrup continued to wring McLain's neck in anger. But he was eventually pulled off from behind by Brown. A shocked Hiller remembered Brown looking Northrup dead in the eye and saying, "You're not gonna touch him until after we win the pennant. Then he's all yours."[7]

Brown also remained popular with the Detroit writers that season. When asked about his remarkable success in the clutch, he developed a common response to give to reporters: "I'm square as an ice cube, and I'm twice as cool." Detroit media couldn't get enough of Gates.

Neither could Tigers fans. When the World Series rolled around and the Tigers lost Game One to St. Louis's Bob Gibson – who also struck out 17 – Mayo Smith was bombarded by letters to put Brown into the starting lineup. One Tigers fan even wrote Smith asking him to start Brown at shortstop and bat leadoff during the series. "That guy must be nuts," reacted Brown when told of the letter.[8]

Brown had only one appearance during the World Series: a pinch-hit fly out to left off Gibson in Game One. But for anyone who remembers how untouchable Gibson was that October day, it's a miracle any man could come off the bench and even touch the ball.

Throughout the rest of his career, Brown enjoyed continued success as a pinch-hitter – including a .346 pinch-hitting campaign in 1971 – but nothing quite like the 1968 season, although he did enjoy more time in the baseball spotlight by becoming Detroit's first designated hitter in 1973, a position tailor-made for the game's Gates Browns.

Moreover, Brown became so beloved that some sportswriters who were adamantly against the DH when it was first implemented eventually said it didn't bother them as much as they thought it would. One of the reasons: It was great for Tigers fans to see Brown at the plate every day.

The whole country got a chance to see Brown in July 1974 when Joe Garagiola, host of NBC's pregame show *Baseball World of Joe Garagiola*, did an unusual two-part story on Brown. Garagiola rarely devoted his weekly show to anyone for two separate shows, but did so for Brown. The shows featured Brown and Garagiola back in Brown's old stamping grounds at the Ohio State Reformatory in Mansfield. The program consisted of an interview in Brown's former prison cell, as well as several rap sessions with current inmates.

Brown said he agreed to the interview inside the prison itself because "if I can help a few people who are mixed up by doing this [interview], it will be well worth it." But he also mentioned that even if you did make the mistake of breaking the law, incarceration didn't mean the end. "Just because a man has been in jail doesn't mean it has to be the end of his whole life," Gates told the inmates.[9]

After suffering through a 102-loss Tigers season in 1975, Brown decided to hang up his spikes at age 36. However, he loved the game too much to give it up completely. So he became a scout for the club less than three weeks after the season ended. Almost immediately Brown went from sitting in a major-league dugout to scouting teams in Florida, assisting in the free-agent draft; instructing the Tigers' rookie-league team, and visiting various colleges nationwide to find new talent.

Brown continued his work as a scout until 1978, when he returned to the Tigers to become the new hitting coach under manager Ralph Houk. The Tigers' team batting average rose from eighth in the American League in 1977 to second overall in Brown's first season. That year the Tigers also enjoyed their first winning season in five years.

When Sparky Anderson arrived in Detroit in 1979, he kept Brown on. He helped bring along the hitting talents of Kirk Gibson, Alan Trammell, and Lou Whitaker. Brown remained with the Tigers through their World Series championship in 1984. He wanted to continue coaching the Tigers beyond 1984 but couldn't agree with the team on a contract extension. He quit on November 14, 1984 – almost 25 years after he signed his first professional contract fresh out of Mansfield.

Things weren't always rosy for Brown in his years since the 1984 championship. In 1991 he was part of a business group that purchased Ben G Industries, a plastics molding company that was relocated from the Detroit suburb of Mount Clemens to Detroit after its purchase. The company was doomed almost from the start. First it was alleged that the previous owners had stolen $458,000 from Ben G before it was sold to Brown's group. Then the Internal Revenue Service got involved and found that as the company's president, Brown had failed to oversee the payment of taxes during his first two years of ownership. A civil suit against Brown by the IRS sought more than $61,000.[10] However, he never faced criminal charges.

Brown also had to settle another IRS allegation a few months before the Ben G trial began. This time it was at the personal level. Brown and his wife, Norma, were accused of shorting income on their personal taxes and ordered to pay more than $36,000 in back taxes and penalties dating from 1992 to 1997.

Brown was not forgotten by the baseball world, however. He was inducted into the Michigan Sports Hall of Fame in 2002. Beside Brown during his acceptance speech were his former hitting pupil, Lance Parrish, and former big-league pitcher Jim Kaat.[11] Many of the voters said that Brown's amazing story was a huge reason why they chose him.

Brown always liked to revisit and reflect upon that magical season of '68. He had reached the pinnacle of his profession. He was a World Series champion. His climb from a prison cell to shaking hands with the likes of Bob Hope and Ed Sullivan was a great comeback story. But if you asked Brown, his contribution to the 1968 season was for his parents.

"I can never make up for all the grief I gave them in my life. I can never make up for all the humiliation they suffered, all the torture, when I spent time in (Mansfield)," Brown said. "But I promised them, when I got out of there I would never go back. If I didn't make it in life, it would not be because I didn't try. You know, you can do bad things in a big city and nobody ever knows about them. But do something wrong in a small town [Crestline's population was 6,000] and everybody knows. That's why I was so happy we won it all. I could finally give them something else to talk about."[12]

In 2009 Crestline honored Brown by naming its high school baseball diamond Gates Brown Field. He said, "You dream about something like this, but you don't ever think it's going to happen. I didn't want no fanfare when I was with the Tigers, but this is quite an honor."[13]

In his 13 years as a player with Detroit, Brown was a part of nine winning ballclubs. He was part of seven more as a coach. Most Tigers fans will tell you that, despite his reserve role, Brown was a huge part of the successful era in Motown. His ability to come through in the clutch has not been matched in the AL. His .370 average in '68 was the eighth-best season ever for a pinch-hitter. He had 107 pinch hits in his career, the most ever in the American League. He also still holds the AL records for pinch-hit at-bats (414) and home runs (16). Talking about his records in pinch-hitting, he once told a reporter, "Well, one thing, I didn't do a lot of playing or I wouldn't have been pinch-hitting."[14]

But it wasn't just with his bat, but with his attitude, that Brown became so successful on the diamond. He was everyone's favorite teammate. He was a huge crowd favorite. He was an underdog who went from prisoner to champion.

Brown suffered from diabetes and a bad heart, dying at age 74 on September 27, 2013, at a nursing home in Detroit.[15] He and Norma had four children: Pamela, Rebekah, Lindsey, and William.

"It's just a shame," former manager Jim Leyland said in an MLive story. "We knew his health wasn't good. To this day, a lot of people think maybe Gates Brown is maybe the best pinch-hitter of all time. Hopefully Gates is in a better place."[16]

SOURCES

Brown's quotes about being hounded by Southern fans while in the minors: Rich Koster article, *St. Louis Globe Democrat*, October 19, 1968.

Joe Garagiola interview information and quotes: Detroit Tigers press release, July 1, 1974.

Poker story with McLain and Northrup and quotes: *Detroit Tigers Encyclopedia*, 99.

Reference to Mayo Smith receiving letters to start Gates at shortstop during the World Series: Rich Koster article, *St. Louis Globe Democrat*, October 19, 1968.

*This biography originally appeared in a SABR publication: Mark Pattison and David Raglin, eds., *Sock It to 'Em, Tigers* (Hanover, Massachusetts: Maple Street Press, 2008). It has been brought up to date with additional research and writing by Bill Nowlin and David Raglin.

NOTES

1   Detroit Tigers press release, August 18, 1978. See Gates Brown player file at the National Baseball Hall of Fame. See also Dave Kindred, "Baseball's Comic Relief," *The Sporting News*, April 25. 1994.

2   Associated Press, "'On Track' Gates Shows Youngsters Straight Path," *Bakersfield Californian*, July 7, 1942: 42.

3   Brown later said, "He was in love with baseball and knew a few scouts, and he paved the way for them to come in and see me. … Other than that, I don't know where I'd be today." George Sipple, "Ex-Tiger Brown to Be Inducted, Twice." *Detroit Free Press*, November 1, 2009, found in Brown's Hall of Fame player file.

4   Rich Koster, "Gates Brown – Hero in Detroit," *The Sporting News*, October 19, 1968: 8.

5   Associated Press, "Gates Brown Not Forgetting Past," *High Point* (North Carolina) *Enterprise*, July 7, 1974: 42.

6   Joe Falls, "Gates Brown's Life an Example for LeFlore," *The Sporting News*, March 22, 1975: 18.

7   *Detroit Tigers Encyclopedia*, 99.

8   Rich Koster, "Gates Brown – Hero in Detroit."

9   Jim Hawkins, "Gates Picking Up Rust as Tiger Spot Swinger," *The Sporting News*, July 27, 1974: 23.

10   David Shepardson, "Trial Begins for Former Tiger," *Detroit News*, undated article in Brown's Hall of Fame player file.

11   Mike Brudenell, "Parrish, Six Others Enter Hall of Fame," *Detroit Free Press*, April 18, 2002.

12   Joe Falls column, *The Sporting News*, March 22, 1969: 2.

13   Jon Spencer, "Crestline Goes to Bat for Brown," *Mansfield* (Ohio) *News-Journal*, March 17, 2009: 9.

14   William Yardley, "Gates Brown, Tigers' Clutch Pinch-Hitter, Is Dead at 74," *New York Times*, September 28, 2013.

15   Terry Foster, "Tigers Family Mourns Pinch-Hitting Legend Gates Brown," *Detroit News*, September 27, 2013.

16   Brendan Savage, "The Complicated Story of Gates Brown, the MOST CLUTCH HITTER on the 1968 Tigers," MLive, August 2, 2018. https://www.mlive.com/tigers/2018/08/not_all_memories_were_good_one.html. Accessed August 6, 2024.

CHARLTON JIMERSON

BY JUSTIN KRUEGER

Charlton Jimerson was named the Most Outstanding Player of the 2001 College World Series for the champion Miami Hurricanes. He also had nine major-league at-bats. At 6-feet-3-inches tall with a playing weight of 210 pounds, Jimerson was a combination of speed and power.

Charlton Maxwell Jimerson was born on September 22, 1979, in San Leandro, California, to Eugene and Charlene Jimerson. He had two older brothers, Derell and Eugene Jr., an older sister, Lanette, and a younger brother, Terrance. In a memoir he noted of his childhood: "I had no idea that I was born into a generational curse of anger, addiction, and misfortune."[1]

When Charlton was a child, his mother moved the family to Hayward, a city about 20 miles south of Oakland. Life was not easy. Issues of poverty, his mother's drug use, and getting into trouble dotted his youth. Jimerson wrote of his mother's unemployment: "She was content with government funding being our only reliable source of income."[2] Poverty exacerbated the lack of a stable home situation and led to Jimerson living in foster homes, homeless shelters, with a friend's family, and later with his older siblings.

By high school, Charlton had moved in with his sister, Lanette, and gained a much-needed stabilizing force in his life. He played baseball, football, and basketball at Mount Eden High School in Hayward, California. A conflict with the head baseball coach led him to walk away from the team in his junior year. He returned to the diamond for his senior year under a new coach and hit .424 with 4 home runs. His efforts drew the attention of local Houston Astros scout Gene Wellman.[3]

The Astros drafted Jimerson in the 25th round of the 1997 amateur draft as a high-school senior but he did not sign. Instead, at the behest of his sister, he decided to go to college. As told in his memoir, Jimerson made his choice of school after seeing a commercial for the University of Miami. He planned to walk-on to the baseball team.

The Hurricanes were one of the most dominant programs in Division 1 baseball at the time. It wasn't an easy task for a player hoping to make the team as a walk-on, but Jimerson did in his freshman year. Many of his teammates were highly recruited and much more polished in their baseball skills and acumen. Teammates included future major leaguers Aubrey Huff, Jason Michaels, Pat Burrell, and Bobby Hill.

Jimerson's raw athletic ability allowed him to make the squad as a backup outfielder. He made the occasional start, but largely came in as a pinch-runner or played in the late innings of games. He was still developing his baseball knowledge. Case in point: he did not play for the Hurricanes during the College

Charlton Jimerson, Houston Astros – Courtesy of Houston Astros

World Series in either 1998 or during their 1999 championship runs. He sat on the bench. Frustrated.

Jimerson's senior season in 2001 began again with him as a backup outfielder. In April an injury to his roommate, outfielder Marcus Nettles, moved him into the starting lineup. In his first game in his new role, Jimerson batted leadoff against Florida State. He led the game off with a home run. Now with the opportunity to start, he made the most of it and remained a starter for the last month of the season.

On June 5, 2001, shortly after a Super Regionals victory over Clemson and with a return trip to the College World Series secured, Jimerson was drafted for the second time by the Astros, in the fifth round of the Amateur Draft. Three teammates were drafted above him: Mike Rodriguez (second round), Chris Sheffield (fourth round), and Brian Walker (fourth round), and seven were drafted below him.

The team still had the College World Series to play. For Jimerson, it was a memorable week in Omaha. He hit leadoff home runs in the first two games. Both were victories – the first game 21-13 over Tennessee, and the second game 4-3 over the University of Southern California. A second victory over

Tennessee moved Miami into the championship game, and the Hurricanes defeated Stanford 12-1 for their second championship in three years. For his efforts on the field, which included a home-run-robbing catch against USC and seven stolen bases in the series, Jimerson made the All-Tournament team and was named the tournament's Outstanding Player.

Soon after, he signed a major-league contract and began his professional career with the Pittsfield Astros in the Low-A New York-Pennsylvania League. He had a particularly embarrassing introduction to the differences between college and professional baseball during his first road game. Showing up to the bus fully dressed in his playing uniform, he noted:

> "Everyone, including Mike [Rodriguez, who was also his teammate at the University of Miami] was crying laughing when I walked on the bus. All my teammates were properly dressed in collared shirts and jeans. I was the only idiot on the bus in my Pittsfield Astros uniform."[4]

In 51 games with Pittsfield, Jimerson hit 9 home runs, drove in 31 runs, and stole 15 bases. He also exhibited a proclivity for striking out – 79 times in 197 at-bats – and a low batting average (.234). Both would become perpetual parts of Jimerson's game.

Jimerson spent the 2002 season with Lexington of the South Atlantic League, where he was named a South Division all-star. He stole 34 bases in 43 attempts and put up solid offensive numbers with 14 home runs and 57 RBIs. His strikeouts climbed to 168 in 439 at-bats.

In 2003 Jimerson advanced to High A with Salem of the Carolina League. He continued to show speed and decent power with 27 stolen bases in 31 attempts along with 12 home runs and 55 RBIs. Again, his strikeouts were glaring in their frequency: 109 in 336 at-bats. Still, at .265, he delivered the highest batting average of his young professional career. Most important, however, was a conversation he had with hitting coach Pete Rancont about showing up early and putting in extra work in the batting cage to get better. In *Against All Odds*, Jimerson wrote: "Pete Rancont saved my career on that summer day in Myrtle Beach. He was the only one who cared enough to talk to me honestly, without reserve."[5]

In 2004 Jimerson advanced to Round Rock of the Double-A Texas League. He stole 39 bases in 45 attempts and hit 18 home runs, his career high in a season so far. After the season he played with Scottsdale of the Arizona Fall League, where Tony Gwynn Jr. was a teammate. That association led to Jimerson's getting hitting advice from Gwynn's father, Hall of Famer Tony Gwynn. The instruction and insight he received helped him to better understand the strengths in his swing. Tony Sr. invited Jimerson to San Diego to work on his batting approach in the offseason. Jimerson reflected:

> "There were things that major-league hitters do that I wasn't doing. The inner third of the plate, if there was anything that

wasn't thrown in the zone, I wouldn't hit. Maybe I'd hit for a week or so, but overall, it was obviously exposed at the Double-A level."[6]

Jimerson played the 2005 season with Corpus Christi, the Astros' new affiliate in the Texas League. Despite the offseason work on his swing and batting approach, strikeouts continued to plague his offensive game: 145 in 425 at-bats. However, his speed and defense in the outfield were continued strengths. A late-season promotion to the Round Rock Express, now the Astros' Triple-A affiliate, saw him go 7- for-23 and nab three steals on three attempts.

With the 2005 minor-league season over, Jimerson headed back home to South Florida for the offseason. But an injury to Willy Taveras on September 13 meant the Astros needed a player. Jimerson made his major-league debut the next day as a ninth-inning defensive replacement in center field. Jimerson did not get another game appearance with the Astros that season but stayed with the team until the end of the regular season. He was not on the playoff roster; instead, he again played in the Arizona Fall League, with Surprise, and in 20 games, he hit five home runs and stole eight bases.

A full season in 2006 with Round Rock, now in the Pacific Coast League, yielded a career-high 183 strikeouts in 470 at-bats. Jimserson also hit a career-high 27 doubles and stole 28 bases in 36 attempts. On May 28 against Albuquerque, Jimerson had the first three-home-run game of his professional career,[7] and he once again earned a September call-up to the Astros.

Jimerson's first major-league at-bat came as a pinch-hitter for Roger Clemens in Philadelphia on September 4, 2006. When he came to bat in the top of the sixth inning, the Phillies' rookie pitcher Cole Hamels was tossing a perfect game.

Jimerson hit Hamels' fourth pitch over the 409-foot sign in center field at Citizens Bank Park, tying the game, 1-1, and ending Hamels' perfect game. The Astros went on to lose the game, 3-2 in 10 innings.

Jimerson appeared in 16 more games that season, usually as a defensive replacement. In his five other at-bats, he hit a single, stole two bases, and scored a run.

Just before the Opening Day in 2007, Jimerson asked the Astros for his release. He had recently been out-righted back to Double-A Corpus Christi. Astros general manager Tim Purpura commented: "His request at that point was to find a trade for him and, if not, would we be willing to release him? We tried the last couple of days to trade him and couldn't come up with anything, so we released him."[8]

After his release, Jimerson called the 29 other major-league teams looking for another shot. One team called him back – the Seattle Mariners. Mariners director of player development Greg Hunter said, "We just needed a player at Double A."[9] With major-league experience, Jimerson fit the bill and he signed with the Mariners.

Sent to West Tennessee (Jackson) of the Double-A Southern League, Jimerson had the strongest offensive production of his professional career: 23 home runs, 73 RBIs, 30 stolen bases, and a .276 batting average in 82 games. On May 29, 2007, a year and a day after his first three-home-run game, Jimerson launched three homers, including a ninth-inning walk-off shot against the Tennessee Smokies (Knoxville), for the second three-home-run game of his career.[10] He was named the Jaxx Player of the Year and earned a call-up to Triple-A Tacoma. Then, for the third season in a row, Jimerson got a September call-up to the major leagues. He saw action in 11 games with the Mariners, went 2-for-2, and scored five runs. The second and last home run of his major-league career was another pinch-hit shot, a solo home run in the ninth inning off Tampa Bay pitcher Brian Stokes. In the offseason, he played in the Venezuelan Winter League with the Cardenales de Lara.

With a strong showing in spring training, Jimerson made the 2008 Opening Day roster for the Mariners as a backup outfielder. His first action of the season was as a pinch-runner for catcher Kenji Johjima in the second game of the season. He appeared in one more game before being designated for assignment. Released by the Mariners, he re-signed with the team on April 16 on a minor-league contract and was sent to Tacoma. He never made it back to the majors and was released on July 11. He played briefly for Sioux City in the independent American Association of Professional Baseball.

Jimerson spent the 209 full season with Newark of the independent Atlantic League. In 103 games he showed power, speed, and increased plate discipline, but at 29 years old, he was nearing the end of his professional career. He hit 21 home runs, drove in 62 runs, stole 38 bases in 43 attempts, batted .335, and slugged .567. He also played a handful of games in the Mexican Pacific Winter League with the Tomateros de Culiacan.

Hoping to extend his career, Jimerson signed a free-agent contract with the Minnesota Twins in February 2010, but was released before Opening Day.

Wanting to play professional ball a bit longer, Jimerson signed with Bridgeport in the independent Atlantic League. In 48 games he batted .346, slugged 10 home runs, had 43 RBIs, and was a perfect 12-for-12 in stolen bases.

His efforts in Bridgeport, against weaker competition, allowed Jimerson one final professional contract. On July 15, 2010, the Los Angeles Angels of Anaheim purchased his contract from Bridgeport. Manager Willie Upshaw commented: "Charlton has worked tremendously hard to get back to this level. He was an exemplary teammate both on and off the field and we wish him the best of luck."[11]

In 43 games with Double-A Arkansas, Jimerson knocked in 25 runs and stole 9 bases. It was his last professional season. He was released after the season.

In 10 professional seasons Jimerson slugged 172 home runs, drove in 554 runs, stole 301 bases, and hit 221 doubles and 32 triples. Always a free swinger with not enough plate discipline, he struck out 1,339 times. His major-league stats were a .444 batting average (4-for-9), two solo home runs, eight runs scored, and 4-for-4 in stolen bases.

In 2015 Jimerson published *Against All Odds: A Success Story*. Divided into nine chapters (innings), the book explores his life and culminates with his home run off Hamels in his first major-league at-bat.

After his playing career, Jimerson earned a bachelor's degree in computer science and has worked as an IT consultant and program manager in the public and private sectors.

He lives in the Houston area with his wife, Candace, and their four children.

SOURCES

The author gathered research material from Charlton Jimerson's player file at the National Baseball Hall of Fame, baseball-reference.com, baseballalmanac.com, and mlb.com FILM ROOM.

NOTES

1 Charlton Jimerson, *Against All Odds: A Success Story* (North Charleston, South Carolina: CreateSpace, 2015), 1.

2 Jimerson, 6.

3 Jimerson, 33.

4 Jimerson, 75.

5 Jimerson, 89.

6 Jose de Jesus Ortiz, "Astros' Charlton Jimerson Deals With Hole Truth," *Houston Chronicle*, March 10, 2005. https://www.chron.com/sports/astros/article/astros-charlton-jimerson-deals-with-hole-truth-1953135.php.

7 Eric Justic, "Express' Jimerson Hits Three Homers," MiLB.com, May 29, 2006. https://www.milb.com/news/gcs-85001.

8 Brian McTaggart, "Astros Notes: Jimerson Released," *Houston Chronicle*, March 29, 2007. https://www.chron.com/sports/astros/article/ASTROS-NOTES-Jimerson-released-1597824.php.

9 George Bell, "His Latest Challenge," *Spokane Spokesman-Review*, March 23, 2008. https://www.spokesman.com/stories/2008/mar/23/his-latest-challenge/.

10 Ryan McConnell, "Walk-Off Blast Caps Hat Trick," MiLB.com, May 30, 2007. https://www.milb.com/news/gcs-250279.

11 "Angels Organization Signs Bluefish OF Jimerson," *Connecticut Post* (Bridgeport, Connecticut), July 20, 2010. https://www.ctpost.com/baseball/article/angels-organization-signs-bluefish-of-jimerson-583234.php.

JON NUNNALLY

BY GISELLE STANCIC

On April 29, 1995, rookie right fielder Jon Nunnally became the first Kansas City Royals player to hit a home run in his first big-league at-bat. Five years later, on June 28, 2000, Nunnally did it again, when he homered on his first plate appearance as a player for the Orix BlueWave in Osaka, Japan. He became the first and, as of 2024, the only player to hold the distinction in both US major-league baseball and Nippon Professional Baseball.

Jonathan Keith Nunnally was born on November 9, 1971, in Danville, Virginia, and he grew up in nearby Pelham, North Carolina.[1] Jon's father, Solomon Tyrone Nunnally, was a laborer, and his mother, Mary Alice (Galloway) Nunnally, cared for their 12 children – five daughters and seven sons. Jon is the youngest son.[2]

Nunnally attended high school at Hargrave Military Academy in Chatham, Virginia, where he played on the Tigers baseball and football teams.[3] He was drafted out of high school as a catcher by the Baltimore Orioles in the 39th round of the June 1990 amateur draft. But he declined the offer and decided to go to Miami Dade College, where he was moved to the outfield.[4]

Adjusting to the new position was a challenge for Nunnally, but he worked hard to make the transition. "My first year in college, I made six errors out there. The next year, I didn't make any," he said.[5]

In 1992 the left-handed-hitting Nunnally batted .410 and was named Junior College Conference Player of the Year.[6] In June he was drafted in the third round by the Cleveland Indians.

Nunnally played three seasons in the Indians farm system, with three different Class-A teams. In his third season, 1994, with the Kinston Indians of the Carolina League, he hit 22 home runs and had an .826 OPS. The 22-year-old's numbers attracted attention and after the season Nunnally was chosen by the Kansas City Royals in the Rule 5 Draft.[7] Nunnally's journey to the big leagues was delayed by the players strike that began on August 12, 1994, and ended 232 days later, on April 2, 1995, one day before the season would have started with replacement players.[8]

Nunnally made the leap over Double A and Triple A to take part in three weeks of spring training. "I came straight out of A-ball so there was a lot of development things going on there," he said. "But the one thing I knew I could do was hit a fastball so I really wasn't that worried. I had a pretty good zone. The main thing was just getting to know pitchers and knowing what they were going to do."[9]

He boarded the plane to Kansas City with the team after spring training, still not knowing if he had made the roster. When they arrived in KC, the bus to the hotel made a stop at

Jon Nunnally, Kansas City Royals – Courtesy of Kansas City Royals

Kauffman Stadium. "The other young guys ended up going to the dugout. But I started looking around. I was like, wow, this is amazing. Like hey, I'm here. You see this place and this would be awesome."[10]

During the next day's practice, Royals manager Bob Boone walked out to right field to give Nunnally the good news that he was officially on the team.

The Royals' 1995 season started at home on April 26 against the Baltimore Orioles, the team that drafted Nunnally out of high school. He came in to pinch-run in the bottom of the eighth and scored his first major-league run in the 5-1 Royals' win.

Nunnally made his next appearance in a day game against the New York Yankees on April 29. He arrived early at the ballpark (around 7:00 A.M.) and had to ask the security guard to let him into the clubhouse.

"It's dark in the clubhouse, the only thing I saw was a Budweiser sign. It was lit up. I put my uniform on and I was sitting at my locker in the dark, looking at that sign. Then all of a sudden, Bob Boone comes in, and I think I scared him because I'm sitting in my locker. ... He goes into his office and he comes back out and he goes, 'Hey, you playing today and you leading off.' And I said, 'OK, I'm ready.'"[11]

Rain delayed the game for 81 minutes, moving the start time to 2:56 P.M. for the 14,431 in attendance.[12] Under still-drizzling skies, New York picked up a run in the top of the first inning. Then Nunnally was up for the Royals as the leadoff hitter. But his walk to the plate was interrupted. "I forgot my batting helmet," he said after the game. "I got out of the dugout and somebody yelled, 'Hey where's your helmet?' I had to go back and get it."[13]

When Nunnally stepped up into the box to face Yankees right-hander Mélido Pérez, he remembered the advice Royals starter Mark Gubicza had given him, that Pérez would pitch him fastballs away. Nunnally stayed patient and, sure enough, Pérez threw three fastballs off the plate, running the count to 3-and-0.[14]

On the next pitch, Boone gave Nunnally the take sign. Pérez threw a fastball down the middle of the plate. On the 3-and-1 count, Pérez threw another fastball right down the middle. Nunnally crushed the ball to deep center field. He became the first Royal to hit a home run in his first big-league at-bat.

"It's an awesome feeling to be able to do it," Nunnally reflected in 2021. "You have all those fans there, but I didn't hear a thing. I guess I was so focused and locked in to where I was that I couldn't hear nobody. I heard nothing until I touched home plate."[15]

Nunnally's attention-grabbing debut was the only bright spot for the Royals on a day that ended with a 10-3 Yankees win. But his performance earned him a spot in the next day's lineup, and he stayed with the big-league club for the rest of the season. "That was a great group of guys that that I was with. They were young and it was easy for us to grow together in the game."[16]

The veterans on the team also mentored the younger players like Nunnally. "Gary Gaetti helped me out a lot. I love Gary. Also Greg Gagne, and Wally Joyner and me became really close."[17]

Nunnally batted .244 in the 1995 season, hitting 14 homers, including two walk-offs, and had 42 RBIs. He played in 119 games, 92 of them in right field. He was known to have a strong arm, a credit from his days behind the plate, and he made a point of staying sharp on the field.

"I work hard on my defense during batting practice and things like that, trying to get jumps and reads. That's where you get all your work," he told an interviewer in 1999. "Trying to get some balls off the bat, trying to see the true jump, and how the ball actually comes off the bat. In batting practice, the ball actually comes off a lot harder than it does in the game."[18]

In 1996 Nunnally was on the Royals' Opening Day roster. However, he was sent down to Triple-A Omaha a couple of times during the season. "I wasn't discouraged because I always knew what I could do," he said. "I had experience up there in the big leagues. I had to come down to learn the league. Once you came to Triple A, you had a lot of older veteran dudes who were major-league guys themselves who were going through the same things."[19]

While in Omaha, Nunnally batted .281 with 25 homers and 77 RBIs. He was recalled by the Royals in mid-August and hit four home runs playing out the rest of the season. Nunnally started 1997 in Omaha, but he was called up on June 22. His stint with the club was a short one this time. On July 15 Nunnally was traded, along with Chris Stynes, to the Cincinnati Reds for Héctor Carrasco and Scott Service.

The move to Cincinnati resulted in more playing time for Nunnally, mostly in center field. He also got the opportunity to work with Ken Griffey Sr., one of the three hitting coaches he credited with helping him the most to shape his approach at the plate. His other two mentors were Mitchell Page and Gene Tenace, from his days in the Royals and Boston Red Sox organizations respectively.

"Those three guys put together helped shape and mold my mind into what I wanted to do as a hitting coach," Nunnally said. "I got a mechanical side. I got an approach side. I got direction. Those three guys helped me out tremendously."[20] Nunnally ended the 1997 season with Cincinnati batting .318 with 13 home runs and 35 RBIs.

Nunnally started the 1998 season with Cincinnati but was sent down in June to Triple-A Indianapolis. He came back to the Reds in September. Then in March 1999, the Reds traded Nunnally to the Red Sox for minor-league player Pat Flury. Nunnally played for the Triple-A Pawtucket Red Sox and had 23 home runs before he was a late-season call-up to Boston.

Despite all the twists and turns of his career, Nunnally stayed focused on the goal. "I just keep going out there battling and

Jon Nunnally – Courtesy of Kansas City Royals

battling and hopefully one day I'll rise to the top. Hopefully one day someone will give me the opportunity to have 500 at-bats. If I don't do anything, I'll deserve what I got. If I do something with them, which I know I will, I'll be happy."[21]

In the offseason, Nunnally was traded again, this time to the New York Mets for Jermaine Allensworth. Nunnally played his last major-league game with the Mets on May 31, 2000. His big-league stats included 42 home runs and 125 RBIs, with a batting average of .246.

Nunnally's next move would be much farther away. His contract was purchased from the Mets by the Orix Blue Wave[22] of Japan's Nippon Professional Baseball. On June 28, 2000, he hit a home run in his first at-bat with Orix, becoming the only player (as of 2024) to hold the distinction in two different major leagues.[23]

"I was hitting second in that game, Ichiro was hitting third. ... So [the pitcher] throws a curveball. I let him release it. He threw it and it hung and I was like oh, that's it right there. Boom."[24]

Nunnally returned to the States after a season with Orix. He played on the Royals' Omaha Triple-A club in 2001, and in the Fall League he hit his third first at-bat homer. He returned to Omaha for 2002, then moved between Triple-A teams until 2005, playing in the Cardinals, Brewers, and Pirates organizations. In April 2005 while with Indianapolis, he tested positive for steroids and served a 15-game suspension.[25] He retired from playing after Mexican winter league ball in 2006.

Nunnally stayed in the game, however, taking a different role. While playing in the minors, he had enjoyed mentoring younger players and helping to develop new talent. So in 2006, he began coaching in the Indians farm system.

"I'm always talking to the player. I want to know what the player wants," he said. "What is he trying to do? I like to understand their mind first, and then going on to whatever we're seeing and plan an approach. I like to make sure those guys can be external thinkers not internal thinkers. Then you go and do your work, and it becomes a little more simple. ... I always enjoyed helping other guys do what they do. That made it fun for me."[26]

In 2010 Nunnally became the Cleveland Indians' hitting coach, a role he held through June 28, 2011. He then coached in the minors for the Toronto Blue Jays (2012-2014) and the Red Sox (2015-2016). Nunnally joined the Los Angeles Angels staff as their outfield and baserunning coordinator for 2017-2018. He then returned to the minors in 2019 as a hitting coach in the Pirates organization, where he stayed until October 2023. Nunnally as of 2024 was a baseball consultant.

Through all of Jon Nunnally's years of playing, on different teams, in different levels of baseball, and internationally, he's kept an even-keeled perspective on the game, with one goal in mind. "I just wanted to go play and win. I just loved the game."[27]

Baseball continued to be a part of Nunnally's family, too. Jon and his wife, Tammy, were married in 1994 in Danville, Virginia. (They are now divorced.)[28] The couple have three children, Kristen, Josie, and Jonathan Jr.[29] Jon Jr., an outfielder and right-handed pitcher, was drafted out of high school by the Toronto Blue Jays in the 38th round of the 2013 free-agent draft, but decided to play college baseball at Arizona Christian University.[30] Jon Jr. then went on to pitch independent-league baseball for four years. As of 2024, he was the executive director of the Legacy Church in Chandler, Arizona.[31]

ACKNOWLEDGMENT

Special thank-you to Jon Nunnally. Telephone interview with author on June 22, 2024.

SOURCES

In addition to the sources cited in the Notes, the author consulted Baseball-Reference.com, Baseball Almanac, and Retrosheet.org for background information on players, teams, and seasons.

NOTES

1   Jon Nunnally was born in a Danville, Virginia, hospital, but he was brought home to the family home in Pelham, North Carolina, which he considers his hometown. Phone interview with Jon Nunnally, June 22, 2024.

2   "Solomon Tyrone Nunnally, Sr., Obituary," Fisher & Watkins Funeral Home, Inc., April 3, 2017. https://www.fisherandwatkinsfuneralhome.com/obituaries/print?o_id=4184837, accessed May 10, 2024.

3   Ian Hamilton, "Jon Nunnally Jr. Hitting His Stride with the Regina Red Sox," *Regina* (Saskatchewan) *Leader-Post*, July 11, 2016. https://leaderpost.com/sports/baseball/jon-nunnally-jr-hitting-his-stride-with-the-regina-red-sox, accessed May 10, 2024.

4   Tyler Kepner, "Nunnally's Hitting Has Mets Noticing," *New York Times*, March 9, 2000: D2.

5   Rick Brown, "Quiet Leader Emerging on PawSox," *Attleboro* (Massachusetts) *Sun Chronicle*, July 1, 1999. https://www.thesunchronicle.com/sports/brown-quiet-leader-emerging-on-pawsox/article_6069cda3-be6c-5910-bfd1-b3f2cd894263.html, accessed May 10, 2024.

6   "Quiet Leader Emerging on PawSox."

7   "The Rule 5 Draft allows clubs without a full 40-man roster to select certain non-40-man roster players from other clubs. There's a fee paid to the club providing the player, and the pick is assigned directly to the drafting club's 26-man roster." For more information see "Rule 5 Draft," https://www.mlb.com/glossary/transactions/rule-5-draft.

8   Mark Maske, "After the Strike, Baseball's Disgusted Fans Decide to Strike Back," *Washington Post*, April 29, 1995. https://www.washingtonpost.com/archive/politics/1995/04/30/after-the-strike-baseballs-disgusted-fans-decide-to-strike-back/07c1f121-3de0-4887-8609-45c8c35d876e/, accessed May 10, 2024.

9   Tony Boone, "Nunnally Returns to Omaha with Indy," mlb.com, May 29, 2021. https://www.milb.com/news/former-omaha-player-returns, accessed May 9, 2024.

10   Phone interview with Jon Nunnally, June 22, 2024.

11   Phone interview with Jon Nunnally, June 22, 2024.

12   "Perez Ends Five-Game Losing Streak against Royals," *Santa Cruz* (California) *Sentinel*, April 30, 1995:14. Fans were slow to come back to the ballpark after the strike.

13   Doug Tucker, "KC's Nunnally Clubs Homer in First At-Bat," *Salina* (Kansas) *Journal,* April 30, 1995: 39.

14   Tony Boone, "Nunnally Returns to Omaha with Indy," mlb.com, May 29, 2021. https://www.milb.com/news/former-omaha-player-returns, accessed May 9, 2024.

15   "Nunnally Returns to Omaha with Indy."

16   Phone interview with Jon Nunnally, June 22, 2024.

17   Phone interview with Jon Nunnally, June 22, 2024.

18   Rick Brown, "Quiet Leader Emerging on PawSox."

19   Tony Boone, "Nunnally Returns to Omaha with Indy."

20   Glenn Jordan, "Jon Nunnally Helping to Make Sea Dogs' Offense a Hit," *Portland* (Maine) *Press Herald*, August 1, 2016. https://www.pressherald.com/2016/08/01/jon-nunnally-leads-sea-dogs-hit-parade/, accessed May 10, 2024.

21   Tyler Kepner, "Nunnally's Hitting Has Mets Noticing."

22   "Orix Buffaloes," JapanBall.com. https://japanball.com/baseball/npb-teams/orix-buffaloes/, accessed May 11, 2004. The team became the Orix Buffaloes in 2005 after a merger with the Kintetsu Buffaloes.

23   Nippon Leagues history, first at-bat home runs research conducted by Yoshihiro Koda, SABR Tokyo Chapter.

24   Phone interview with Jon Nunnally, June 22, 2024.

25   "Three Pirates Minor Leaguers Suspended for Failing Drug Tests," ESPN.com, April 6, 2005. https://www.espn.com/mlb/story?id=2031240&src=desktop&rand=ref~%7B%22ref%22%3A%22, accessed May 10, 2024.

26   Tony Boone, "Nunnally Returns to Omaha with Indy."

27   "Nunnally Returns to Omaha with Indy."

28   Phone interview with Jon Nunnally, June 22, 2024.

29   Jon Mozes, "Callix Crabbe Named Curve Manager for 2023 Season at Peoples Natural Gas Field," milb.com, December 21, 2022. https://www.milb.com/news/callix-crabbe-named-curve-manager-for-2023-season-at-peoples-natural-gas-field, accessed May 10, 2024.

30   Ian Hamilton, "Jon Nunnally Jr. Hitting His Stride with the Regina Red Sox."

31   "Our team," Legacy Church, https://www.legacyaz.church/leadership-staff, accessed June 29, 2024.

DON ROSE

BY MICHAEL TRZINSKI

Just before Christmas 1971, Don Rose was included in what many baseball experts consider one of the worst or best trades of all time. Rose went on to play in only 19 big-league games over the next three years for three different teams. But in one of those games, he did something that very few pitchers have ever done in major-league history. He hit a home run in his first major-league at-bat, on the first pitch, and collected his first (and only) big-league victory in the same contest.

Donald Gary Rose was born on March 19, 1947, to R. Porter Rose and Josephine (Delmonego) Rose in Covina, California, a Los Angeles suburb. His father was an apprentice pharmacist at a drugstore, and his mother was a homemaker.[1] Older brother Michael was born one year before.

Donald attended Covina High School and earned All-Conference honors in baseball his junior and senior years. His high-school coach was Floyd Roenicke, father of future major leaguers Gary Roenicke and Ron Roenicke, and grandfather to Josh Roenicke, who also played in the majors.

In addition to his four years of high-school baseball, the 6-foot-3, 190-pound Rose played football all four years as a linebacker and played basketball one year.

In the summer after Rose's senior year, his Covina Post 207 baseball squad outlasted the field of 74 teams and captured the annual Anaheim American Legion tournament championship.[2]

Rose entered Stanford University in the fall of 1965. The next spring he played on Stanford's freshman team and led them to a 27-1-2 mark. Rose earned first-team honors in the Bay Area Freshman Baseball League, compiling a 9-0 record with an ERA of 0.40 in league play.[3] Overall, he was 11-1 with a 0.69 ERA.[4]

Going into Rose's sophomore season, coach Dutch Fehring had high hopes for his young right-hander, and for the whole staff. Said Fehring of Rose, "Don can be one of the best pitchers we ever have had. He has all the pitches."[5]

Stanford finished third in the College World Series in Omaha in 1967, losing 4-3 to eventual champion Arizona State in 14 innings in the semifinal round.[6] Rose ended the season 5-2 with an ERA of 2.87.

Rose had a bad start to his junior season: He was ineligible after missing some final exams, and sat out the first 20 games of the campaign.[7] He still managed to pitch well for the season, finishing with an ERA of 0.41, best in the Pacific Eight conference. He won twice against one loss in conference play, and earned postseason honorable mention.[8]

As a junior, the Stanford pitcher was selected in the 11th round of the 1968 amateur draft by the New York Mets. He signed with the Mets, thus ending his college career. He was

Don Rose, California Angels – Courtesy of Trading Card Database

assigned to Memphis in the Double-A Texas League. Rose was roughed up in his first start, lasting only one inning while giving up two hits, five runs (one earned), and a pair of walks. Rose got his only win for Memphis on July 6, pitching a complete game and allowing four hits and two earned runs. He struck out 11 and walked six. Rose's season ended a few weeks later, when on July 30 he was put on the disabled list with tendinitis in his elbow.[9]

In December, Rose married Kathleen Kinney at the Methodist Community Church in Los Altos, California. His uncle, Rev. Charles Rose, performed the ceremony, along with Rev. Charles Cox.[10]

Rose began the 1969 season again with Memphis, but after struggling to an 0-4 record and 4.70 ERA, he was sent to Visalia in the Class-A California League. "[Memphis manager Pete Pavlick] didn't let me pitch regularly, (so) I asked to be sent down," he said.[11]

Rose performed well for Visalia, winning 13 games (tied for fourth in the league). He completed 12 of his 20 starts, ranking third in the circuit. Both numbers were remarkable since he missed the first month of the season while still in Memphis. After the season, Rose pitched for the Mets team in the Florida Instructional League, winning four of five decisions and posting a 2.45 ERA in 44 innings.

The right-hander returned to Memphis for the third straight year in 1970. He was named to the Texas League Eastern Division all-star team and was 7-11 with a 3.09 ERA, third-best in the league. Memphis won the Eastern Division championship but fell to Western Division champion Albuquerque in the Texas League playoffs. Rose and his wife, Kathleen, welcomed daughter Lisa to the family on May 29.[12]

Rose was promoted to Triple-A Tidewater for the 1971 season. With a record of 11-10, 3.33, he was among the International League's top five leaders in shutouts (3) and strikeouts (156), and was in the top 10 in victories and ERA. The highlight of his season was a 14-strikeout performance against Winnipeg in August, tying a club record.[13] In a September call-up, he pitched two scoreless innings in one game.

In the offseason, Rose's name popped up in a couple of big-name trade rumors. First came an offer of San Diego's first baseman Nate Colbert for Rose and two others, but the trade didn't happen.[14] Another rumor had Braves first sacker Orlando Cepeda coming to New York for Rose and a starter, but that also fell through.[15]

On the last day of the trading period, the California Angels traded Jim Fregosi to the New York Mets for Francisco Estrada, Leroy Stanton, Nolan Ryan, and Rose.[16] Fregosi played in 146 games for the Mets before he was sold to the Texas Rangers in July 1973. Estrada never played in the big leagues after the trade. Stanton gave the Angels five solid years, and everyone knows what Nolan Ryan did. California general manager Harry Dalton said, "Rose and Estrada are young prospects, and both have a chance to make our club."[17]

Rose was playing winter ball in Barquisimeto, Venezuela, when he got a phone call in his hotel room at 3 A.M. from Joe McDonald, director of minor-league operations for the Mets. McDonald told him about the trade to the Angels and told Rose not to tell anyone. "Who am I going to tell? It's 3:00 in the morning and everybody here speaks Spanish," recalled Rose.[18]

In 1972 Rose went to spring training in Palm Springs hoping to win a spot on the big-league roster, but after making only one appearance (two innings, no runs) he was reassigned to the Angels minor-league camp.[19] Rose was moved to Triple-A Salt Lake City. "I kind of knew ahead of time I wasn't going to make the (Angels) out of spring training," he said.[20]

Major-league players went on strike at the start of the season and were out for 13 days. Rose pitched decently at Salt Lake City in his first six starts, winning four against no losses. His reward was to get called up to the majors on May 18 when Andy Messersmith, Clyde Wright, Paul Doyle, Lloyd Allen, and Nolan Ryan were injured.[21] California manager Del Rice said, "It's hard telling what (Rose) will be doing here with our injury situation."[22] But it was expected that Rose would be pitching in relief.

That prediction came true, as the lanky right-hander made three appearances out of the bullpen in his first three days as an Angel and fared well. He pitched four perfect innings, striking out two. Then on May 24, he became part of baseball history.

The beginning of the season had been a struggle for the Angels, and on the morning of the 24th they had a record of 11-21, 10 games behind the AL West-leading Chicago White Sox. The Angels had won back-to-back games only twice in the first six weeks of the '72 season.

On that Wednesday evening in late May, a small crowd of 3,042 fans saw an exciting game at Oakland-Alameda County Stadium, featuring the scuffling Angels against the eventual 1972 World Series champion Oakland A's. The weather was fair in the Bay Area, with a game-time temperature in the high 60s.

The game was scoreless when Rose came to the plate in the top of the third with the bases empty and one out. Oakland pitcher Diego Segui sent his first pitch to Rose, who slugged the ball over the left-field fence for a home run.

"Players always say the game has to slow down, but to my mind, that ball stopped, and I was able to adjust and take a good whack at it. It probably went 400 feet," Rose remembered years later.[23]

After the Angels scored two more runs in the inning, Rose walked to the mound with his head held high in the bottom of the third, leading 3-0.

California added a run in the top of the fifth, giving the Angels a 4-0 lead. In his first four innings, Rose had allowed three hits and one walk while striking out six. But in the bottom of the fifth, the A's tied the game on two-run home runs by Joe Rudi and Mike Epstein. The Angels came back and scored twice in the top of the sixth off Vida Blue, and took back the lead, 6-4.

Dave Duncan hit a leadoff homer for the A's in the bottom of the sixth, making the score 6-5. Rose then settled down and retired the side. His day was done. He pitched six innings, allowed seven hits and five earned runs, walked two, and struck out seven. Steve Barber pitched the final three innings to earn the save for the Angels. Rose took the win for what would turn out to be his only victory in the majors. Blue, making his season debut, ended up with the loss.

"I dreamed last night that I would hit a homer and pitch a shutout in my first start in the big leagues," Rose said with a laugh after the game. "I didn't get my shutout but I'm happy nevertheless."[24]

Rose became the third pitcher to hit a home run in his first official big-league at-bat and earn his first win in the game. The others were Bill Duggleby (1898) and Hoyt Wilhelm (1952). John Montefusco joined that exclusive club in 1974.[25] But when you consider that Rose hit his homer on the first pitch he saw, the company is even more rare. He became the 10th player, and third pitcher, to smash his first offering for a home run.[26] "I bet (Montefusco) five dollars that he couldn't tie my record," laughed Rose years later.[27] Montefusco hit a home run, but not on the first pitch, so Rose won the bet.

Five days later Rose got another start and pitched well against the Chicago White Sox at home, lasting seven innings and giving up five hits, three earned runs, and three walks while striking out six. Although he gave up two home runs, the Angels led 4-2 when Rose exited in the eighth after giving up a home run and a single. Reliever Lloyd Allen coughed up a three-run homer to Bill Melton and the White Sox grabbed a 5-4 lead, which they held.

Over the next two months, Rose made two more starts – both losses – and nine relief appearances. He was sent down to Salt Lake City to make room for catcher Jack Hiatt.[28] Rose had a record of 1-4 with an ERA of 4.22. His main problem was giving up home runs – nine in 42⅔ innings. Rose finished his Triple-A season with an 8-2 record with an ERA of 3.19 in 14 starts.

Rose then played winter ball in Puerto Rico, where he developed an ulcer and lost 35 pounds. For a 6-foot-3 guy who weighs 190 pounds, that's a pretty big loss. "I had no strength, I had nothing," recalled Rose. "I couldn't even run my sprints but eventually I pulled out of it."[29]

The next spring, new Angels manager Bobby Winkles praised Rose and Dick Lange for their control and it seemed both had a chance to make the big-league team out of training camp.[30] But when cutdown day came, both were sent back to Triple A.

Rose struggled in the early going of the 1973 campaign, posting a record of 1-7 and ERA of 5.47. At the end of June, he was traded along with Bruce Christensen to San Francisco for pitcher Ed Figueroa. Rose spent the whole year at Triple-A Phoenix and went 6-5 with an ERA of 3.16 in 111 innings.

The 1974 season was shaping up to be the same story, but then a key Giants pitcher was injured in a freak accident. Ron Bryant, – the only pitcher in the NL to win 20 games in 1973, received 25 stitches in his right side in a swimming-pool accident in mid-March, giving Rose a chance to join the big-league team. He began the season with San Francisco but didn't get into a game until April 20, in the Giants' 15th game of the season.

He ended up pitching in only two games for San Francisco, mostly because Bryant returned on April 26. In Rose's first game, on the 20th, he pitched one inning in relief and allowed one hit in a 4-2 loss to Los Angeles. Three days later, he was rocked in an 8-4 loss to Montreal. Rose faced four batters, yielding three hits and a walk. "I was disappointed that I didn't get much work while I was with the big club," said Rose. "They told me I'd have all the work I could handle, but it was 15 days into the season before I got into a game."[31]

The game on April 23 was Rose's last in the major leagues.

Rose said, "Charlie Fox (Giants manager) called me in and told me, 'We've seen enough' and they sent me down. I just lost all interest and I felt (playing in the majors) just wasn't going to happen for me."[32]

Rose was shipped back to Phoenix on May 11 and pitched decently, going 9-6 with an ERA of 3.81, third best in the league.

He had some arm issues during the season and missed a couple of starts but performed well otherwise. One good piece of news: Rose and his wife welcomed their second child, a son, Brian, on June 18.[33]

Rose began spring training with the Giants in 1975, but was sent down to Phoenix, where he pitched all season. He made 21 starts among his 34 appearances and struggled, posting a record of 7-16 and a ERA of 6.30.

During the offseason, Rose retired from baseball and worked at a few odd jobs before re-enrolling at Stanford. He worked at National Semiconductor (on the 3-to-midnight shift) while finishing up his political-science degree.

After graduation, Rose took a customer-service job at the company, working in Santa Clara, California. Rose continued in the computer business in various roles, including as a senior operations manager for Hitachi, meeting with factory management to plan the output and enhance the supply chain. In addition, he was responsible for importing, warehousing, and distribution. Rose also met with large customers, such as GM, to discuss their material needs. He retired in 2005.

As of 2024, Don and Kathleen resided in the San Diego area, They celebrated their 55th anniversary in December 2023. They have three grandsons.

NOTES

1   US Census Bureau, 1950 US Census.

2   Mike Kelly, "Covina Captures Legion Tournament Crown," *Anaheim Bulletin*, August 30, 1965: B2.

3   "Indian Nine Tops Frosh Star Squad," *Oakland Tribune*, May 27, 1966: 58.

4   Reed Nessel, "Make Room for Fabulous Frosh Athletes," *Palo Alto (California) Times*, June 2, 1966: 30.

5   Dick O'Connor, "Cards Blessed with Best-Ever Mound Staff," *Palo Alto Times*, February 22, 1967: 37.

6   Dick O'Connor, "'We'll Be Back': Stanford Coach," *Palo Alto Times*, June 19, 1967: 29.

7   Dick O'Connor, "Shank Pitches 2-Hit Shutout," *Palo Alto Times*, February 24, 1968: 17.

8   "Shank Named All-Pacific 8," *Redwood City (California) Tribune*, June 5, 1968: 18.

9   Bill E. Burk, "Blues' Fans Find the Action," *Memphis Press-Scimitar*, July 30, 1968: 18.

10   Kathleen Kinney-Donald Rose wedding announcement, *Palo Alto Times*, December 25, 1968: 18.

11   Bill E. Burk, "Blues Begin Chase for Texas League Flag," *Memphis Press-Scimitar*, April 17, 1970: 18.

12   Bill E. Burk, "Gags Not Surprised at Trade to Cubs," *Memphis Press-Scimitar*, May 30, 1970: 9.

13   "Tides, 5-1," *Richmond (Virginia) Times-Dispatch*, August 21, 1971: B-4.

14   Dick Young, "Hot Stove Confidential," *New York Daily News*, December 2, 1971: 131.

15 "King-to-Angels Still Only Rumor," *Richmond Times-Dispatch*, December 7, 1971: 6-B.

16 Joe Trimble, "Big Deal! Mets Trade 4 for Fregosi," *New York Daily News*, December 11, 1971: 28.

17 "Jim Fregosi Traded to N.Y. Mets," *Anaheim Bulletin*, December 10, 1971: A1.

18 Don Rose, telephone interview with author, January 11, 2024.

19 "Ryan Wild on Mound; A's Whip Angels, 6-0," *Los Angeles Times*, March 22, 1972: 3, 2.

20 Don Rose, telephone interview with author, January 11, 2024.

21 "Angels Upset Oakland, Mound Injuries Persist," *Barstow* (California) *Desert Dispatch*, May 19, 1972: 4.

22 Steve Jones, "Angels Win, but Dalton's Hurlers Need Blue Cross," *Anaheim Bulletin*, May 19, 1972: C-5.

23 Don Rose, telephone interview with author, January 11, 2024.

24 "Vida Pitches but Can't Hold Out," *Anaheim Bulletin*, May 25, 1972: C1.

25 https://www.baseball-almanac.com/feats/feats5.shtml.

26 https://www.baseball-almanac.com/feats/feats6.shtml.

27 Don Rose, email correspondence with author, January 12, 2024.

28 Don Merry, "May 4-Hitter Halts Texans," *Long Beach* (California) *Independent Press-Telegram*, July 30, 1972: S-4.

29 Don Rose, telephone interview with author, January 11, 2024.

30 "Angel Duo Bidding to fill Spots," *Escondido* (California) *Daily Times-Advocate*, March 5, 1973: A-11.

31 Bob Eger, "Rose Ready, Hurls Tonight," *Arizona Republic* (Phoenix), May 20, 1974: C1.

32 Don Rose, telephone interview with author, January 11, 2024.

33 Bob Eger, "Giants Lose to 'New' Hudson, 6-3," *Arizona Republic*, June 20, 1974: E1.

GAREY INGRAM

BY BOB WEBSTER

"Chicken Strikes Again" was a newspaper headline after Garey Ingram had a particularly good game with the Pawtucket Red Sox. His manager, Gary Jones, called him "Chicken." The nickname came from a college teammate who first called him "Blue Chicken" about 10 years earlier. He wondered where that name came from since the team colors were black, gray, and white. Ingram didn't like "Blue Chicken," but was okay with "Chicken." Since then, everyone on campus started calling him "Chicken." He started writing it on his bat and batting gloves and it stuck.[1]

Garey Lamar Ingram was born in Columbus, Georgia, on July 25, 1970. As a child, he liked football first, basketball second, and baseball third. One reason he picked baseball over the other sports to pursue was that his uncle was a baseball player, and Garey watched him play while he was growing up. His uncle was a pitcher, but a finger injury kept him from being drafted. However, Garey did not have many baseball friends as a kid because most the other kids he knew got footballs and basketballs as gifts, and not many received baseball equipment.[2]

Garey was a member of the National Little League All-Stars of South Columbus, District 8. In 1981 the team won the Georgia state Little League championship and advanced to the South Regional Tournament in St. Petersburg, Florida. There, the youngsters from Columbus were eliminated in the opening round by Clemmons (North Carolina) Southwest Forsythe.[3]

At Columbus High School, Ingram was a teammate of future Hall of Famer Frank Thomas for two years. When Ingram was a freshman, Thomas was a junior.[4] Thomas didn't know it, but Ingram tried to imitate him and his swing, because Ingram knew Thomas was going to be good.

The Los Angeles Dodgers selected Ingram in the 43rd round of the June 1988 draft but he did not sign, choosing to play for Middle Georgia State University in Macon, Georgia. In 1989 Ingram led the team to the Junior College World Series District 17 Tournament by going 5-for-12 with five runs scored, two RBIs, and a double, while taking home the tournament MVP Award. With the win, Middle Georgia State advanced to the Junior College World Series to meet San Jacinto College.[5]

In the championship game, Ingram broke up a no-hitter in the sixth inning against San Jacinto's Robert Henkel. San Jacinto still won the game, 5-0.

The Dodgers drafted Ingram again in 1989, in the 44th round. He didn't sign until June 3, 1990. Playing for the Great Falls Dodgers of the Rookie-level Pioneer League in 1990, he hit .343 with an on-base percentage of .415 in 56 games and was named a league all-star.[6] Great Falls visited Salt Lake for the first two games of the best-of-five Pioneer League championship and

Garey Ingram, Los Angeles Dodgers – SABR-Rucker Archive

swept the two games on the road. Ingram hit a two-run homer in the bottom of the eighth inning of the championship-clinching game three at Legion Park in Great Falls to give the Dodgers its third straight league title.[7]

The 20-year-old started the 1991 season as an outfielder at Bakersfield of the High-A California League and played 118 games there, hitting .297 in 445 at-bats.

The Dodgers made a few September call-ups from the Albuquerque Dukes of the Triple-A Pacific Coast League on September 1, and the San Antonio Missions of the Double-A Texas League sent four players to Albuquerque to replenish their roster. That left eight nonpitchers to fill a San Antonio nine-man batting order. Ingram was brought up from Bakersfield, but due to bad weather, his flight was delayed. Pitcher Mike Wilkins had to start the game in left field until Ingram arrived in the second inning. Then the game was called after five innings because of rain. It was the last game of the season, so Ingram's Double-A 1991 stint lasted a total of four innings.[8]

Ingram returned to San Antonio to begin the 1992 season. But in just the fourth game, he broke a finger when he was hit by a pitch on the right hand. He was out until June.[9] He finished the season batting .288 with an on-base percentage of .406 in 65 games. He played 61 games on defense in the outfield.

After losing Eric Young Sr. and Roberto Mejía in the 1992 expansion draft, the Dodgers moved Ingram from center field to second base to begin 1993 with San Antonio.[10] "I haven't played second base in a regular season since I was a sophomore in high school," said Ingram. "It was a little bit rough at first, but I feel like I'm making strides and picking up things a day at a time."[11]

Learning to play second base defensively takes some time, but the on-field change didn't hurt Ingram's offensive game. Then injuries started to take their toll. Ingram was placed on the seven-day disabled list on April 26 with a twisted right knee.[12] Back in the lineup on May 12, and hitting .359, Ingram was involved in a collision at second base with Shreveport's Barry Miller. Ingram missed almost a month with a broken bone in his left leg.[13] He finished the 1993 season hitting .269 in 84 games.

Ingram started the 1994 season at San Antonio but was called up to the Dodgers in mid-May. But Ingram didn't believe it, at first.

On May 14, the Missions were playing the Tulsa Drillers in San Antonio. In the eighth inning, San Antonio manager Tom Beyers told Ingram to shower and pack his bags for Los Angeles. His teammates gathered around to give Ingram high-fives, but he wasn't buying it. With so many pranks played on baseball players, Ingram thought this was just one more. He stayed in the dugout until his turn to bat came up, but he was replaced by a pinch-hitter. Only then did he realize there was no joke.[14] The call-up happened because Dave Hansen of the Dodgers had been placed on the 15-day disabled list and Ingram had experience in center field as well as second base.[15]

Earlier in the season, Dodgers President Peter O'Malley and executive vice president Fred Claire were at a Missions game scouting Korean pitcher Chan Ho Park when they noticed Ingram, who was playing well in the series. They were impressed with Ingram's progress in learning to play second base as well as his confidence, so he was the choice when Hansen went down. "Yeah, it was a big surprise," said Ingram.[16]

On May 15, the day after joining the Dodgers, Ingram entered their game against the San Diego Padres in the ninth inning as a defensive replacement. On the fifth pitch, the Padres' Tony Gwynn hit a grounder to Ingram who threw to first to retire Gwynn. After the game, Gwynn presented Ingram with an autographed ball.[17]

In his next game action, on Thursday, May 19, Ingram was called on to pinch-hit for Orel Hershiser in the eighth inning against the Colorado Rockies at Mile High Stadium in Denver, in front of 51,515 fans. On a 2-and-2 pitch from Rockies reliever Mike Munoz, Ingram hit a long drive into the seats in left-center with the wind blowing in from center. With that mighty swing, Ingram became the second Los Angeles Dodger to homer in his first major-league at-bat. (José Offerman was the first.)

"When I hit it, I just took off running, I was so excited," said Ingram. "Brett Butler was there waiting for me and he was smiling, it made me feel good." Butler was on deck when Ingram hit the home run. Butler later said, "I told him someday you will be bouncing your grandchildren on your knee, and you will be telling them about your first major league at-bat.'"[18]

On May 25 second baseman Delino DeShields lacerated the middle finger on his left hand. Later in the same game, backup Jeff Treadway sprained his right wrist and Ingram became the Dodgers' starting second baseman.[19] "It's not that I'm trying to show them I should be starting regularly," said Ingram, "I'm just here to help us win any way I can. I'm filling in until they are ready, and we don't have to worry about that right now. Whatever role they want me to play, that's what I'll do."[20]

On June 3 the Dodgers visited Atlanta to begin a three-game series with the Braves. At least 25 of Ingram's family and friends were in attendance. They held up a sign that read, "Garey Ingram, Yo' Mama Is Right Here." The sign was so big that three or four people were needed to hold it.[21] Ingram responded by going 2-for-3 with a walk and scored twice, raising his batting average to .379.

DeShields and Treadway were activated from the disabled list on June 19, and Ingram was sent back to San Antonio. Ingram, who was expected to provide speed off the bench with the Dodgers, had started 21 games at second base, hitting .282 with three home runs and eight runs batted in. "I'm kind of surprised myself," said the 23-year-old Ingram. "I was kind of nervous at first. I learned more playing in games up here and I think it will help me when I go back to San Antonio."[22] Ingram played in 99 games for the Missions in 1994, hitting .258 with eight home runs and 28 RBIs.

Ingram started 1995 on the Dodgers roster and played third base as well as some second and four games in the outfield. He hit .200 in 66 plate appearances. On May 31 the Dodgers claimed infielder Chad Fonville off waivers from the Montreal Expos and optioned Ingram to Triple-A Albuquerque. In another move, the Dodgers designated Eddie Pye for assignment. Pye had been playing second base at Albuquerque and Dodgers executive vice president Fred Claire said, "By optioning Ingram to Albuquerque, it will give him the opportunity to play on an everyday basis so he can gain experience."[23] Playing in 20 of the Dodgers' 32 games to that point in the season, Ingram registered 10 hits in 40 at-bats, with 3 RBIs. In his 63 games with Albuquerque, he hit .246.

On August 11, the Dodgers placed outfielders Todd Hollandsworth and Chris Gwynn on the disabled list and brought up outfielder Roger Cedeño and Ingram from Albuquerque.[24] Ingram remained with the Dodgers for the remainder of the season.

After Ingram was assigned to Albuquerque to begin the 1996 season, a strained right shoulder landed him on the disabled list in April. After shoulder surgery, he missed the rest of the season.[25]

On November 20, 1996, the Dodgers claimed Nelson Liriano off waivers and designated Ingram for assignment.[26]

However, he was back in the Dodgers organization for the 1997 season with San Antonio. On August 26 Ingram, batting

.299 with 28 doubles, 12 homers, and 52 RBIs in 92 games, and playing second base and left field, was called up to the Dodgers to replace Roger Cedeño, who was out with a broken toe. Charlie Blaney, Dodgers vice president for minor-league operations said, "The big-league club is in a pennant race and they needed someone who can do the kinds of things Garey can do."[27] In 10 plate appearances in 12 games for the Dodgers, Ingram was 4-for-9 with a walk.

Albuquerque was Ingram's team for 1998. Now 27 years old, in 108 games, he batted .302, with 8 homers, 58 RBIs, and 20 stolen bases.

On December 16, 1998, Ingram signed a minor-league deal with the Boston Red Sox and was assigned to the Pawtucket Red Sox for the 1999 season. He batted .247 with 9 home runs and 39 RBIs in 85 games. He was back with Pawtucket in 2000, and in 103 games, the 29-year-old hit .238 with 10 home runs and 36 RBIs.

In May 2001 Ingram signed with the Elmira Pioneers of the Northern League. In 79 games, he hit .294 with 13 home runs.

Ingram started the 2002 season with the Las Vegas 51s of the Pacific Coast League, where he hit .318 in 25 games before breaking his wrist. In July he announced that he would be leaving the 51s to coach for the Rookie League Gulf Coast Dodgers in Vero Beach.[28]

Thus, his playing days behind him, Ingram began his coaching career. Ingram also married and had four children, but the marriage ended in divorce.

In addition to the Gulf Coast Dodgers, Ingram was a hitting coach in the Dodgers organization from 2002 to 2008, with the Class-A South Georgia Waves, Columbus Catfish, and Great Lakes Loons. Ingram coached future major leaguers Russell Martin, Matt Kemp, Eric Stults, Blake DeWitt, Eduardo Pérez, Iván De Jesús Jr., Kenley Jansen, and Clayton Kershaw.

In 2009 Ingram was the hitting coach for the Connecticut Defenders, the San Francisco Giants' affiliate in the Double-A Eastern League. Ingram worked for the Atlanta Braves from 2010 to 2016, as the hitting coach for the Mississippi Braves of the Double-A Southern League and the Gwinnett Braves of the Triple-A International League.

Some of the future major leaguers Ingram taught along the way were Phil Gosselin, Evan Gattis. Andrelton Simmons, Cory Rasmus, Tommy La Stella, Mallex Smith, Dansby Swanson, and Ozzie Albies.

Ingram was the third-base coach for the Charlotte Knights of the Triple-A International League in 2017 and 2018. The Knights were a Chicago White Sox affiliate.

Ingram was part teacher and part mentor in Charlotte. He said, "In Triple A, it's a lot different than when you're at the lower levels because you have older guys who've been around the game a longer time."[29] He added, "Some of them are former major leaguers and they know how to prepare themselves on an everyday level to get back to the major leagues. When you're dealing with the younger levels, you're dealing with a lot smaller details that you have to pay attention to, especially developing those kids to get to this level."[30]

After his coaching career ended, Ingram became a talent acquisition consultant at Atrium Health Wake Forest Baptist. An avid fisherman, he hosts the YouTube channel Cove Ultimate Fishing.

SOURCES

The author used Retrosheet.org and Baseball-Reference.com for stats and game information, as well as the baseballcube.com for coaching information.

Garey Ingram requested that his family information remain private.

NOTES

1   The story of the moniker was recounted by Ingram in a 2017 interview with two radio hosts. See Jeff Schaefer and Tommy Viola, "Schaefer Baseball Report," September 30, 2017. https://soundcloud.com/user-896163922/garey-ingram-on-schaefer-baseball-report.

2   Schaefer and Viola.

3   "Georgia Little League Champions," Columbus (Georgia) Ledger, August 16, 1981: 27. See also https://www.unpage.org/south/sr-1981.htm.

4   Schaefer and Viola.

5   Chuck Thompson, "Warriors Silence DeKalb," Macon Telegraph, May 14, 1989: 12; "Warriors Wary as Play Begins," Macon Telegraph, May 19, 1989: 41, 45.

6   Scott Mansch, "Dodgers Begin Title Trek on Road," Great Falls (Montana) Tribune, September 1, 1990: 13, 17.

7   George Geise, "Dodgers Win Third Pennant," Great Falls Tribune, September 4, 1990: 1.

8   Tim Griffin, "Missions Go Out in style, Top Diablos," San Antonio Express News, September 3, 1991: 26; Jerry Briggs, "Missions Wind Up with Win," San Antonio Light, September 3, 1991: 7.

9   "Missions Report," San Antonio Light, April 14, 1992: 37.

10 Tim Griffin, "Youthful Missions Open Play Friday," San Antonio Express News, April 4, 1993: 51.

11 Tim Griffin, "Missions Open Year at Midland," San Antonio Express News, April 9, 1993: 25.

12 "Missions Notes," San Antonio Express News, April 27, 1993: 20.

13 "Elster lifts Missions to Victory over Captains," San Antonio Express News, May 13, 1993: 19; "Missions Notes," San Antonio Express News, June 10, 1993: 38.

14 Guerry Clegg, "It's No Joke, Ingram Learns," Columbus (Georgia) Ledger-Enquirer, May 17, 1994: 17.

15 Clegg.

16 Clegg.

17 Clegg.

18 Maryann Hudson, "Nervous Rookie Homers First Time Up," Los Angeles Times, May 20, 1994, https://www.latimes.com/archives/la-xpm-1994-05-20-sp-59930-story.html.

19 Associated Press, "LA Rookie Is Looking Good," *Birmingham News*, June 15, 1994: 32.

20 "LA Rookie Is Looking Good."

21 Charles Odum, "Ingram Made Dream Come True," *Columbus Ledger-Enquirer*, June 5, 1994: C12.

22 "Dodgers Activate DeShields," *Delaware State News* (Dover, Delaware), June 20, 1994: 14.

23 Brian Bujdos, "Infielder Pye to Be Replaced at Second Base," *Albuquerque Tribune*, June 1, 1995: 16; "Baseball Focus," *Springfield* (Massachusetts) *Republican*, June 1, 1995: 27.

24 Brian Bujdos, "Look, LA, Daal Didn't Walk the Guy, But…," *Albuquerque Tribune*, August 11, 1995: 34.

25 "Hot Hitting Piazza Slides to a Halt with Bad Knee," *Albuquerque Tribune*, May 29, 1996: 16.

26 "Dodgers Sign Infielder," *Hemet* (California) *News*, November 21, 1996: 12.

27 David King, "S.A. Loses Ingram to L.A.," *San Antonio Express News*, August 27, 1997: 27.

28 Mark Anderson, "51s' Chen in Hitting Groove," *Las Vegas Review-Journal*, July 2, 2002: 29.

29 Herbert L. White, "Garey Ingram Brings Experience and Mentoring to Knights Bench," *Charlotte* (North Carolina) *Post*, April 13, 2017, https://www.thecharlottepost.com/news/2017/04/13/sports/garey-ingram-brings-experience-and-mentoring-to-knights-bench/.

30 White.

JEREMY HERMIDA

BY JACOB POMRENKE

When Jeremy Hermida stepped up to the plate for his first at-bat in the major leagues on August 31, 2005, he wasn't thinking about accomplishing something no one in baseball had done for more than a century. With the bases loaded and the game out of reach for the Florida Marlins, the 21-year-old rookie was sent up to pinch-hit for the pitcher in the seventh inning. He just wanted to swing the bat and get a hit.

But he did much more than that. On the third pitch he saw from Alberto Reyes of the St. Louis Cardinals, Hermida smashed a line drive over the right-field wall – a grand slam in his first at-bat.

"You always dream of coming in and maybe not getting a home run in your first at-bat, but just getting a hit," Hermida said afterward. "To do something like that, it's something I couldn't even describe. … It didn't really hit me until I crossed home plate."[1]

Hermida became the second known major-league player – the first since Bill Duggleby of the Philadelphia Phillies in 1898 – to hit a grand slam in his first at-bat. (Two others have done it since, as of 2024.)[2] His parents, Larry and Tammy, were back home in Georgia watching the nationally televised game on ESPN.

"We'd seen too many of his hits. We absolutely knew the ball was gone," Tammy Hermida said. "I think I ran out of the room. And my husband fell to the floor, screaming, 'That's my boy! That's my boy!'"[3]

Hermida's stirring start raised expectations, but the former first-round draft pick struggled to live up to them. He had several productive seasons with the Marlins and provided a few more memorable moments, but a series of injuries limited him to part-time status after the age of 25. He spent time with the Boston Red Sox, Oakland A's, Cincinnati Reds, San Diego Padres, and Nippon-Ham Fighters in Japan before calling it a career after the 2015 season.

Jeremy Ryan Hermida was born on January 30, 1984, in Atlanta. His parents were both Florida natives and his father, Larry, worked in the home-building industry. Jeremy was a natural right-hander, but at around 4 years old, he began swinging left-handed with his father's guidance off a tee in the backyard of the family home in suburban Marietta.

"There was no time limit. Early in the morning, late at night, he was ready [to hit]," said Larry, a self-described "Tampa park rat" who would occasionally bring his son along on work trips with their baseball equipment stored in the car. "There's not a park or batting cage we didn't pull over at as he was growing up."[4]

Jeremy Hermida, Florida Marlins – Courtesy of MLB.com

Jeremy admired Seattle Mariners star Ken Griffey Jr. because "he did so much so young," but often wore the number 7 because his father's idol was Mickey Mantle.[5] At the age of 14, Jeremy joined East Cobb Baseball, a prestigious club program that produced future major leaguers Michael Barrett, Corey Patterson, and Adam Everett, among others. He began swinging with a wood bat to build stronger habits and received hitting instruction from former Atlanta Braves outfielder Terry Harper and East Cobb coach Danny Pralgo.[6]

Wheeler High School coach David McDonald was in his 27th year when Hermida arrived as a freshman in 1999. By mid-season, McDonald had inserted the young lefty outfielder into the starting lineup. "I guess I was doing my best coaching job not to coach him," McDonald said. "I could see as a ninth-grader he had his mind set to do things after high school."[7]

Hermida was teammates with star shortstop Josh Burrus, who was taken in the first round by the hometown Braves in the 2001 amateur draft. Hermida signed a letter of intent with

Clemson University that fall, but midway through his senior season, his own draft stock suddenly went up after a power-hitting display during batting practice.

On April 9, 2002, more than 50 scouts showed up to watch Wheeler play against Parkview High School, featuring multi-sport star and fellow Clemson signee Jeff Francoeur. Hermida and Francoeur both put on a dazzling show in the batting cage. As Mike Berardino of *Baseball America* wrote in 2003:

> Some scouts called Hermida the best high school hitter since Eric Chavez. Others saw a young Andy Van Slyke or Paul O'Neill. Hermida himself identified more with Shawn Green. Whichever comparison you prefer, there's no denying his polished hitting approach and advanced maturity. He has a smooth, quick stroke, top-notch plate discipline, a strong work ethic and first-rate makeup.[8]

Hermida finished his senior season with a .485 batting average and 7 home runs, and he was named to the All-Cobb County team by the *Atlanta Journal-Constitution*. Even Francoeur, who went on to spend 12 seasons in the big leagues, raved about Hermida's abilities: "He has such a sweet swing. It's one of the prettiest lefty swings you'll ever see."[9]

The 2002 draft class of Georgia high-school seniors was one of the strongest in the state's history. Hermida and Francoeur were at the top of the rankings, but the list also included catcher Brian McCann from Duluth, pitcher-third baseman Micah Owings from Gainesville, and pitcher Jonathan Broxton from Burke County. The eight future major leaguers from that senior class would go on to combine for more than 60 Wins Above Replacement in their careers.[10]

It was Hermida, not the highly touted Francoeur, who was ultimately selected first. The Florida Marlins snagged him with the number 11 overall pick and signed him for a bonus of just over $2 million. Francoeur went to the hometown Braves with the number 23 selection. Both players turned down their scholarship offers from Clemson in order to turn pro. "It's very fairy tale-ish," Hermida said.[11]

The *Atlanta Journal-Constitution* published a first-person essay with Hermida's byline in which he described the draft day experience at his house: "With my family and friends huddled around me, I anxiously leaned toward the computer screen and listened to the draft picks live. … It went fast … and then at pick 11, I heard my name. It was without a doubt the best moment of my life. … It's an honor to be where I am."[12]

Hermida joined the Marlins' instructional-league team in Florida to make his professional debut, and then was soon called up to Low-A Jamestown (New York), where he hit .319 over the final two weeks of the season. He spent most of 2003 in Class A with the Greensboro Bats, hitting 6 home runs and stealing 28 bases in 133 games.

Before the 2004 season, Hermida was ranked among the top 30 prospects in the game by *Baseball America*. He moved up to the top 20 after a strong season with High-A Jupiter in the Florida State League.

He had a breakout year in 2005, hitting 18 home runs and posting a .457 on-base average for the Double-A Carolina Mudcats. He was named MVP of the Southern League All-Star Game and participated on the US team (along with old friend Jeff Francoeur) in MLB's Futures Game at Comerica Park in Detroit.

In August Hermida injured his left wrist and suffered a bone bruise that kept him out of the Mudcats' lineup for more than a week. The Marlins flew him to Florida, where he was examined by a specialist and he began hitting off a tee and working out with the big-league team. Team officials did not tell Hermida when or if he would return to the minor leagues.[13]

About three hours before the Marlins' game on Wednesday, August 31, Hermida was told he would be in uniform. "It happened so quickly that no one from his family was on hand for his historic debut at Dolphins Stadium," the *Miami Herald* reported.[14]

In the seventh inning, manager Jack McKeon sent Hermida up as a pinch-hitter for pitcher Brian Moehler with the Marlins trailing 10-0. He stepped to the plate against 35-year-old right-hander Alberto Reyes with the bases loaded. Hermida swung at a strike, took a ball low, and then smashed a Reyes changeup over the right-field wall, a blast estimated at 373 feet.

"I pretty much already made up my mind I was going to swing at the first pitch up there, just to get the jitters out," Hermida said. "After that I was like, 'All right, sit back and trust yourself.' And he just happened to leave one over the middle a little bit."[15]

Hermida quickly circled the bases with his head down and ran back into the dugout. He missed the crowd of 20,656 – plus 687 dogs for Dog Day in the Park – clamoring for a curtain call. "Honestly, I didn't even see it. I was just running," he said afterward. The Marlins' bullpen traded two signed baseballs in a deal with the fan who caught the home run.[16]

After their loss in Hermida's historic debut, the Marlins fell out of first place in the NL wild-card race and they stumbled to an 83-79 finish. Hermida was mostly used as a pinch-hitter down the stretch, but he hit home runs in three of the team's final four games. His memorable start earned him a ranking as *Baseball America's* number 4 prospect entering his first full rookie season.

In spring training, Hermida said he tried "not to pay too much attention about what is written or said about me. When you're standing in the batter's box, it sure doesn't matter what kind of a prospect you were rated. The pitcher is going to try to make it tougher on you, not easier."[17]

The Marlins were full of unproven prospects in 2006, having traded away veterans Carlos Delgado, Josh Beckett, Mike Lowell, Juan Pierre, and Luis Castillo in a fire sale during the offseason. Miguel Cabrera (age 23) and pitcher Dontrelle Willis (24) were the only returning starters as the Marlins fielded the youngest team in the majors.

Hermida was touted as a potential Rookie of the Year candidate, but a hip flexor strain in mid-April put him on the injured list and caused him to miss more than 30 games. He got hot in June, hitting .345 with 11 doubles, but he couldn't sustain that performance in the second half. An ankle injury down the stretch limited him to just seven plate appearances as a pinch-hitter in September.

After a slow start in 2007, Hermida finally broke out in a way the Marlins front office had always thought he was capable of. He hit .340 with 10 home runs over the second half and played a key role in the final weekend as the last-place Marlins spoiled the New York Mets' bid for a National League East Division title.

Hermida, who was still the Marlins' youngest starting position player at the age of 24, took a step back in 2008 but he did enjoy some of his finest individual days in a big-league uniform that year. He recorded his first two-home-run game on April 11 as the Marlins set a club record with six homers in a win over the Houston Astros at Minute Maid Park. He also hit two home runs on July 26 against the Chicago Cubs at Wrigley Field. The inexperienced Marlins were a surprise contender for a postseason berth before falling out of the wild-card race in September. Hermida batted .249 with 17 homers and played in a career-high 142 games.

His third and final game with two home runs came on April 18, 2009, when his three-run blast tied a game at Nationals Park with two outs in the ninth inning against Washington closer Joel Hanrahan. In the 11th inning, he put Florida in the lead for good with a three-run homer off Wil Ledezma. Hermida's five RBIs that afternoon were a career best.

But that was his only major highlight in his final season as a Marlin. He hit .259 with 13 home runs but missed almost all of September with a rib injury. After the season, Florida traded its once-prized prospect to the Boston Red Sox for two pitchers, José Álvarez and Hunter Jones. The Red Sox intended to use Hermida as a backup for starting outfielders J.D. Drew, Jacoby Ellsbury, and Mike Cameron.

"You have to come out here with a purpose every day," Hermida said about accepting a reserve role for the first time. "Take pride, look at yourself in the mirror and make sure you're doing it on a daily basis. That's all you can ask of yourself."[18]

On May 18, 2010, Hermida endeared himself to Red Sox fans by hitting a go-ahead two-run double off future Hall of Fame closer Mariano Rivera at Yankee Stadium. But a few weeks later, he was placed on the injured list with fractured ribs following a collision with third baseman Adrian Beltré. That meant he was not in uniform when Boston's Daniel Nava hit a grand slam in his first at-bat on June 12, drawing comparisons to Hermida's magical debut.[19] After playing in just 52 games, Hermida was released by the Red Sox at the end of August and signed with the Oakland Athletics. He hit one home run in the season's final 25 games.

Hermida signed as a free agent with the Cincinnati Reds in 2011 and spent most of the year at Triple-A Louisville, where he had a strong season (.319/.400/.524, 17 home runs in 105

games). But at age 27, his days as an up-and-coming prospect were now past him.

The San Diego Padres claimed Hermida on waivers and he appeared in 33 games with the big-league club over two seasons. But in early 2012, he sustained a sports hernia injury that required surgery and a lengthy rehab stint at Triple-A Tucson. He never made it back to the majors.[20]

Hermida signed minor-league deals in 2013 with the Cleveland Indians and in 2014 with the Milwaukee Brewers. In 2015, he inked a deal with the Nippon-Ham Fighters in Japan's Pacific League, where he hit .211 with one home run in 50 games.

Hermida may not have lived up to the promise of his spectacular major-league debut, but he invested his money wisely. He now helps other athletes do the same as a business development officer for BIP Wealth, a wealth management firm founded by two former Georgia Tech baseball players.[21]

As of 2024, Hermida lived in suburban Atlanta raising his three children with wife Lindsey (Sherman), a New Jersey native and former Philadelphia Eagles cheerleader whom he married in 2011. He spends his time golfing, traveling, and coaching his son's baseball team. He also occasionally works as a television analyst for Georgia Tech baseball games.

SOURCES

In addition to the sources cited in the Notes, the author consulted Baseball-Reference.com, Retrosheet.org, and Newspapers.com.

NOTES

1   Tim Reynolds (Associated Press), "Rookie Makes Grand Debut," *The Columbian* (Vancouver, Washington), September 1, 2005: B5.

2   In addition to Duggleby and Hermida, the other major-league players to hit a grand slam in their first at-bat entering the 2024 season were Kevin Kouzmanoff (2006) and Daniel Nava (2010).

3   Tim Reynolds (Associated Press), "Hermida's Historic Homer Has Family 'Still Shaking,'" *Stuart* (Florida) *News*, September 2, 2005: C5.

4   Juan C. Rodriguez, "Kid's Got Pop," *South Florida Sun-Sentinel* (Fort Lauderdale), February 24, 2006: 18.

5   Jeff D'Alessio, "Gimme 5," *Atlanta Journal-Constitution*, February 1, 2007: B2.

6   Mike Berardino, "Top Ten Prospects: Florida Marlins," *Baseball America*, November 19, 2003. Accessed online August 29, 2024, via Archive.org.

7   Rodriguez, "Kid's Got Pop."

8   Berardino, "Top Ten Prospects: Florida Marlins."

9   Guy Curtright, "Splashy Rookie Thrills Marlins," *Atlanta Journal-Constitution*, March 3, 2006: F1.

10 Three other Georgia high-school seniors from the 2002 draft also made the major leagues: Barret Browning, Matt Capps, and Brandon Moss. The record for any single draft (as of the 2024 season) is 10 Georgia seniors taken in 2010, led by Delino DeShields

Jr. All information from the Baseball-Reference.com Draft Index, accessed August 29, 2024.

11 Carlos Frías, "Bonus Should Outlast Career," *Atlanta Journal-Constitution*, June 4, 2002: C2.

12 Jeremy Hermida, "As a Clemson Tiger or Florida Marlin, at 18 I Can't Lose," *Atlanta Journal-Constitution*, June 13, 2002: JG13.

13 Juan C. Rodriguez, "Prospect Needs Wrist Examined," *South Florida Sun-Sentinel*, August 31, 2005: 3C.

14 Clark Spencer, "History, Heartache," *Miami Herald*, September 1, 2005: D1.

15 Reynolds, "Rookie Makes Grand Debut."

16 Reynolds, "Rookie Makes Grand Debut." Joe Capozzi, "Miss, and a Swing," *Palm Beach* (Florida) *Post*, September 1, 2005: 5C.

17 Curtright, "Splashy Rookie Thrills Marlins."

18 Kevin Thomas, "Sox Hope Hermida Comes to the Fore as a Backup," *Portland* (Maine) *Press Herald*, March 28, 2010, accessed online August 29, 2024, at https://www.pressherald.com/2010/03/28/sox-hope-hermida-comes-to-the-fore-as-a-backup_2010-03-28/.

19 Nate Taylor and Nick Cafardo, "It Doesn't Get Grander Than Nava's Debut," *Hartford Courant*, June 13, 2010: E6.

20 Alex Williams, "Hermida's Rehab Gives Outfielders a Break," *Arizona Daily Star* (Tucson), June 30, 2012: B5.

21 "Jeremy Hermida," BIP Wealth, accessed August 27, 2024, at https://bipwealth.com/team/jeremy-hermida.

BASEBALL LIFER CHUCK TANNER SHOWS HE'S HERE TO STAY WITH A HOME RUN ON THE FIRST PITCH

April 12, 1955: Milwaukee Braves 4, Cincinnati Redlegs 2, at County Stadium, Milwaukee

BY TARA KRIEGER

Chuck Tanner is a household name in much of Western Pennsylvania, after a 19-year major-league managerial career that included nine seasons with the Pirates and a championship in 1979.

He was a much more remarkable manager than he was a player. In eight major-league seasons with four teams between 1955 and 1962, Tanner batted .261 with a career OPS+ of 92 and WAR of -0.2. He was a pinch-hitter in almost as many games (200) as he played in the field (202).

However, despite hitting just 21 career home runs, Tanner shared in a notable accomplishment achieved by less than 0.7 percent of all major leaguers – homering in his first at-bat, on April 12, 1955.

But perhaps Tanner's first-at-bat glory buries the lede, as his pinch-hit home run for the Milwaukee Braves in the eighth inning tied the game they eventually won against Cincinnati, 4-2.

April 12 was Opening Day at County Stadium in Milwaukee for the home team (Cincinnati had traditionally opened at home at Crosley Field the day before, this year against the Cubs.) The Milwaukee Braves were hosting their largest opening day crowd, 43,640, since moving to the Midwest.[1]

The Braves had high expectations of both winning the pennant and setting attendance records that season, just their third in Brewtown.[2] They finished third in 1954 with essentially the same squad, though now with another year of experience.

Milwaukee's lineup included third baseman Eddie Mathews, runner-up for the 1953 National League Most Valuable Player Award; sophomore sensation Henry Aaron, fourth in Rookie of the Year voting; Shot Heard 'Round the World hero Bobby Thomson, recovering from a broken ankle but still formidable; two-time All-Star catcher Del Crandall;[3] speedster Bill Bruton, on his way to his third straight NL stolen-base title; and rising young talents Johnny Logan and Joe Adcock.

Future Hall of Famer Warren Spahn, coming off his fifth 20-win season in six years, was on the mound for his fourth

Chuck Tanner, Milwaukee Braves – Courtesy of Trading Card Database

straight home opener. Tanner would eventually pinch-hit for Spahn.

Although remarking a year earlier that he "wasn't ready" for the majors,[4] the 26-year-old Tanner[5] tore it up in Atlanta in 1954, batting .323 with 20 homers and 101 RBIs as the Crackers won the Southern Association championship.[6]

Lou Chapman of the *Milwaukee Sentinel* described Tanner as "a husky kid with a crew cut and a pleasing smile" and "like the boy next door," who learned how to hit from Pirates Hall of Famer Paul Waner, the Braves' special hitting instructor.[7] After toiling nine seasons in the minors as a lefty spray hitter, Tanner took some pointers from Waner on power and started pulling the ball to right.

"I'm the kind of guy who likes to be told when I'm doing a good job and Paul gave me that necessary confidence at the plate," Tanner said.[8] Waner thought Tanner could be another Dusty Rhodes, who had risen to prominence with the New York Giants in the World Series of the prior fall. Rhodes also would be better remembered for his pinch-hitting abilities.

Like Tanner, Spahn batted as a lefty. He was a career .194 hitter, not bad for a pitcher, but certainly not the person you'd want at the plate when the team is down to its final five outs. He'd pitched well in the game, shutting out Cincinnati on five hits through the first seven innings before giving up a two-run homer to Ted Kluszewski in the top of the eighth.[9] Kluszewski's blast traveled 390 feet; he'd also gone yard the day before.[10]

The Redlegs' pitcher that day was 34-year-old Gerry Staley, a two-time NL All-Star on the decline as a starter. The right-handed sinkerballer spent his first seven seasons with the Cardinals but was traded to Cincinnati in the offseason after a 7-13 1954 campaign.[11] He'd allowed an RBI double to Thomson in the bottom of the first that scored Bruton, but otherwise limited the Braves to four hits at the end of seven innings. With one out in the eighth, he'd retired 10 of the last 11 batters he faced – the lone baserunner reaching on an error and forced out on a double play.

Crandall grounded out to start the eighth when Braves manager Charlie Grimm called on Tanner. The rookie stepped up to the plate and drove the first pitch he saw 325 feet to right field.

Before Tanner, six men had homered on their first major-league pitch, and four others had gone long in their first at-bat as a pinch-hitter. But only one before him – Eddie Morgan of the Cardinals, on April 14, 1936 – delivered a pinch-hit home run on the first pitch thrown to him in the big leagues.[12]

"I wasn't thinking about anything in particular when I came to bat against Staley, except to try to hit the ball and get on base," Tanner said. "Staley pitched, I swung and started for first base. I don't know if I touched the bag in rounding it, or any of the others – I was floating on air – but I saw the bleacher fans scrambling for the ball and I turned for second and the rest of the trip to home plate was just a dream."[13]

Tanner also said afterward that he "didn't even know where the hit landed."[14]

Staley fell apart quickly after Tanner's home run. His next pitch, to Bruton, resulted in a single. Then Aaron tripled to the center-field fence to drive in Bruton for the go-ahead run – and chase Staley off the mound.

"I saw Billy running and I just kind of tried to drag it to right field," Aaron said. "If I had taken a full swing I'da knocked it out of the ball park."[15]

The Redlegs bullpen didn't fare much better. Lefty reliever Jackie Collum walked Mathews and then was done. His replacement, righty Jerry Lane, allowed Aaron to score an insurance run on Thomson's sacrifice fly to center fielder Gus Bell.

Milwaukee's Dave Jolly then recorded a perfect ninth for the save.

Spahn, who allowed two runs on seven hits and one walk, with five strikeouts, had now won all three of his Braves' home openers in Milwaukee.[16] The 1955 season would not be one of Spahn's best – he finished 17-14 with a 3.26 ERA – but he won at least 20 games the next six years after that.

Staley, tagged with all four runs on seven hits, took the loss. He would be waived by the Redlegs, after going 5-8 with a 4.81 ERA, before the season was out.[17]

Hitting highlights for Milwaukee included Thomson's 2-for-3 day, even though he was still nursing a sore shoulder out of spring training. Bruton also had two hits for the Braves. For Cincinnati, Kluszewski and Johnny Temple also had two-hit days.

As for Tanner, he still seemed in disbelief even after hitting the showers.

"And to think I was ready to give it up all last spring," he said. "It happened after the Braves sold me to the Atlanta club after using up all my options."

"It's hard to realize I've finally made it, not only the majors but getting a homer on my first try – and the first pitch too. I was more nervous after it happened."[18]

Those nerves could have come from Tanner's concern about his place on the Braves' major-league roster when the team made further cuts on May 12.[19] But Grimm said Tanner had little to worry about. "There's a good chance Chuck will stay come cut-off time," Grimm said. "We've liked him all spring. He's got a fine, level swing and should be a good hitter."[20]

Tanner then placed a long-distance call to his wife, Barbara, in their hometown of New Castle, Pennsylvania, where she was caring for their two sons, Mark, 4 years old, and Gary, almost 2.

"Looks like I've finally made it, honey," he said, "and after nine years, too."[21]

Tanner had a middling rookie season, batting .247 with 6 home runs and 27 RBIs in 97 games, playing left and right field on defense. He played for Milwaukee all season and the season after that, although his hitting numbers started to diminish. He then moved around the Cubs, Indians, Red Sox, and Angels organizations before finding his calling as a manager in 1963. Tanner worked in baseball in some capacity for the rest of his life.

Perhaps his first-at-bat home run did signify the moment that he'd "finally" made it.

SOURCES

In addition to the sources cited in the text, the author consulted Baseball-Reference.com and Retrosheet.org.

https://www.baseball-reference.com/boxes/MLN/MLN195504120.shtml

https://www.retrosheet.org/boxesetc/1955/B04120MLN1955.htm

NOTES

1   This was the first year the Milwaukee Braves had opened at home. In 1953 and 1954, they played the Redlegs in Cincinnati first, and then their second game at County Stadium.

2   Red Thisted, "In Milwaukee, It's a Matter of Only Counting Up Fans, Later Raising the Pennant," *The Sporting News*, April 20, 1955: 9. The Braves hit neither of those goals – although their attendance, at more than 2 million fans, was still league-best. In the standings, they finished a distant second place (85-69) to the champion Brooklyn Dodgers, 13½ games out. It would be another two years – 1957 – before they would set that new attendance record and win the World Series.

3   Crandall also made the NL All-Star team in 1955 and five more years after that (1956, 1958, 1959, 1960, 1962).

4   Red Thisted, "First Swing in Majors Puts Tanner in Records," *The Sporting News*, April 20, 1955: 9.

5   Although Tanner was born on July 4, 1928, the Braves' media guide listed his birthdate as July 4, 1929; the team apparently lied about a lot of their players' birthdates when they were first signed. David Briggs, "Tanner, Managed '79 Champion Bucs, Dies," MLB.com, https://web.archive.org/web/20110214071121/http://mlb.mlb.com/news/article.jsp?ymd=20110211&content_id=16621286&vkey=news_mlb&c_id=mlb.

6   Tanner was invited to the Braves camp in 1953, but he tore a muscle in spring training and didn't make the team.

7   Lou Chapman, "Tanner Tabbed by P. Waner as 'Possible Dusty,'" *The Sporting News*, March 16, 1955: 15.

8   Chapman.

9   Lou Smith of the *Cincinnati Enquirer* put it colorfully: "Prior to the eighth, the Reds couldn't have hit a circus fat lady with a hand full of buckshot at five pages in the jam. They 'blew' scoring opportunities in each of the first two frames and again in the fourth and fifth stanzas." Lou Smith, "Rookie's Punch Homer Sinks Reds, 4-2," *Cincinnati Enquirer*, April 13, 1955: 40.

10 Newspaper accounts conflict on whether the ball traveled to right field or left.

11 Staley had a resurgence as a closer with the pennant winning "Go-Go" Chicago White Sox in 1959. He made both AL All-Star teams in 1960, at 39 years old.

12 Morgan, who lasted just eight games with St. Louis and then another 31 with the Brooklyn Dodgers in 1937, never hit another. As of 2024, eight players have pinch-hit a home run on the first pitch thrown to them, the most recent being Willson Contreras for the Cubs on June 19, 2016.

13 Thisted, "First Swing in Majors Puts Tanner in Records."

14 Associated Press, "New Castle Rookie Hits First Pitch for Homer," *Pittsburgh Post-Gazette*, April 13, 1955: 18.

15 United Press, "Chuck Tanner Finds 'Home' in Milwaukee," *Pampa* (Texas) *Daily News*, April 13, 1955: 8. Aaron was running so fast that he lost his hat. When asked why, the second-year slugger compared himself, perhaps presciently, to another young star: "That Willie Mays ain't got no monopoly," he said. "I run better with my hat off."

16 The streak would be broken in 1956, when Lew Burdette got the Opening Day start.

17 Fortuitously, the New York Yankees would claim Staley off waivers in September. Although he would pitch just two innings for them that year (allowing three runs), he was on the bench as the team chased down the 1955 American League pennant.

18 Associated Press, "Rookie's Homer Sparks Braves to Opening Win," *Janesville* (Wisconsin) *Daily Gazette*, April 13, 1955: 18.

19 Until 1968, major-league rosters included an expanded "tryout period" to start the season. But teams had to trim down to 25 active players after the first month.

20 "Rookie's Homer Sparks Braves to Opening Win." Grimm was more emphatic with the United Press: "You're damn right Tanner made the team with that homer. If we did anything else with a guy like that people would start wondering if we knew what we were trying to do. He's found a home." "Chuck Tanner Finds 'Home' in Milwaukee."

21 Jack Varick, "Chuck Tanner's Pinch-Hit Homer Sparks Braves to 4-2 Win," *LaCrosse* (Wisconsin) *Tribune*, April 13, 1955: 23.

GARY GAETTI

BY BRYAN LAKE

Gary Gaetti did it all over 20 seasons (1981-2000) for five major league teams. He spent the first decade of his career with the Minnesota Twins, where he was a two-time All-Star and four-time Gold Glove winner at third base. In 1987, when the Twins won the first championship in franchise history, he was the MVP of the League Championship Series and handled the final out of the World Series. By the time he retired after stints with the Angels, Royals, Cardinals, Cubs and Red Sox, he had amassed 2,280 hits and 360 home runs, and only two players in history had played more games at the hot corner.[1] With his durability and hard-nosed style, Gaetti displayed a blue collar grit that he learned growing up in a small Midwestern town.

Gary Joseph Gaetti was born on August 19, 1958, in Centralia, Illinois, a place he would later describe as "14,000 and dying."[2] He recalled, "When I was growing up, two things were big in that area: baseball and beer."[3] Gary and his older sister, Cheryl, were raised by their mother, Jackie (Shahan), and father, Bill. Jackie was a secretary and office manager. Bill was a blue collar railroad man, always up early to start a hard day's work. When the elder Gaetti got home in the afternoon, his son would be waiting for him, ready to play ball. Gary Gaetti recalled that his dad "devoted time every day to hitting me grounders and playing catch. I think he loved baseball."[4]

Busch Stadium in St. Louis was about an hour's drive west of Centralia. Each year the Gaetti family made a handful of trips to see the Cardinals play, which gave young Gary opportunities to gather a trove of treasured memories and mementos, including an autograph from Lou Brock ("He was real nice") and a bat from Dick Schofield ("It was so huge, man, it was a club").[5]

Gaetti had talent to match his passion for baseball. As a 13-year-old, he blasted a home run halfway up a towering tree 250 feet away. It was so impressive that the opposing players all shook Gaetti's hand.[6] At Centralia High School, he earned all-state honors in baseball and football.[7] On the gridiron he was a free safety and quarterback. Bill Gaetti recalled Gary's football coach telling him, "I've never seen a kid with so much competitiveness and aggressiveness and charisma. We don't have anything, but with him in there, those kids feel like they can't be beat."[8]

Gaetti's family did not let the star athlete get too full of himself. "The biggest thing," Gaetti recalled, "is how my family raised me. I didn't grow up with an overinflated opinion of myself."[9] Still, his dad could see his son's talent. Bill Gaetti thought that Gary was as good as the minor league players he'd seen.[10] For Gary, the key moment came in high school when he was at a Cardinals-Reds game and realized that he could

Gary Gaetti, Minnesota Twins – SABR-Rucker Archive

throw as well as Pete Rose. "I'm not saying I thought I could be as good as him," Gaetti said, "but knowing I could do one important thing as good as him made me think. That was a turning point for me."[11]

As talented as he was, Gaetti was not heavily recruited out of high school, so he attempted to get a railroad job, figuring his dad, who had decades of tenure, could pull some strings. But Bill Gaetti had other ideas. "He used his pull to not get me a job," Gary recalled. "At the time, he had more ambition for me than I had for myself."[12] Nudged away from his father's path, Gaetti went on to play baseball at Lincoln Land Community College. He made a big enough impression that the Cardinals drafted him in the 4th round of the January 1978 draft, but the Redbirds only offered him a $500 signing bonus, which he declined.[13] The young prospect also turned down the White Sox after they picked him in the third round of the 1978 summer draft.

A year later, after transferring to Northwest Missouri State University and starring as a shortstop, Gaetti was picked in the first round (11th overall) by the Minnesota Twins. "Growing up, I'd never even heard of the Minnesota Twins," Gaetti recalled. "I didn't even know who they were."[14] Looking back on it, however, Gaetti realized that it was "the biggest break of my life."[15] Assigned to the Twins' Rookie-level club in Elizabethton, Tennessee, Gaetti slugged 14 homers in 66 games against Appalachian League pitchers in 1979. The following year he led the Midwest League with 22 home runs for Class-A Wisconsin Rapids, and in 1981 he moved up to the Southern League and blasted 30 bombs for Class-AA Orlando. His performance earned him a September call-up to the big leagues. In his first at bat in the majors, Gaetti belted a home run off Charlie Hough.

He never went back to the minors.

The 1982 season was Gaetti's first full year in the majors. On Opening Day he displayed his two trademarks—power (two home runs) and aggressiveness (thrown out trying to stretch a triple into another home run). He went on to have a 25-homer, 25-double, 84-RBI campaign that earned him a 5th place finish on the AL Rookie of the Year ballot.[16] Gaetti's manager, Billy Gardner, thought he had star potential. "Heck," Gardner said, "he's capable of hitting 30 home runs and driving in 100 runs."[17]

Gaetti eventually fulfilled his promise, but not before taking some big league lumps. His stats stayed fairly steady in 1983 but his power vanished in 1984 when he hit just five homers. Late that year, with Minnesota's playoff hopes on life support, his devastating throwing error hastened the Twins' collapse as they blew a 10-0 lead in a crushing loss to Cleveland. Afterward, he was brutal in his self-assessment: "It's hard to throw with both hands around your neck."[18] Though he struggled in 1984, he never took a day off, playing all 162 games. According to Gaetti, the daily question was: Would Pete Rose play today? "If the answer was yes, then it was a no-brainer, you just went out and played."[19] Being in the lineup every day fit the G-Man's blue collar roots. "I don't always feel like playing," he said. "The legs certainly don't. But come 7 o'clock, I'm ready to go." Thinking of his dad, perhaps, he added, "I guess it's kind of like the guy who gets up at 6:30 every morning and drives off to work. I don't know any other way."[20]

Gaetti's power stroke started to return in 1985, and in 1986 he blossomed into a star, hitting .287 with 34 home runs, 34 doubles, and 108 RBIs. Among American Leaguers he was third in homers, fifth in slugging percentage and RBIs, sixth in total bases, and eighth in OPS. In addition, he won his first Gold Glove for his outstanding defense at third base. The key to Gaetti's newfound success was getting out of his own head. During his struggles, the young third baseman "started listening to other people telling me I should do this and do that, trying to change me. And I would listen. When you're young, you do that."[21] The flood of advice made him overthink at the plate. "You reach a point where you're thinking about where your shoulders are and if you're striding too far and where your head is and before you know it, you forget the object of the game is to hit the ball."[22]

The other object of the game is to win, and going into the 1987 season, Gaetti's Twins had not done much of it, averaging 90 losses per year from 1982 through 1986. In 1987, however, the Twins took the AL West crown. Their charismatic third baseman helped lead the way, hitting 31 home runs, driving in 109 runs, and finishing 10th on the AL MVP ballot. He also earned his second consecutive Gold Glove. Gaetti's defense at the hot corner led teammate Don Baylor to offer the most complimentary comparison a third baseman could get, saying Gaetti reminded him of Brooks Robinson.[23]

Gaetti's teammates and opponents already knew how good he was, but his coming out party was the 1987 ALCS, when the Twins defeated the heavily-favored Tigers in five games. Gaetti, who was named Series MVP, stepped on the national stage in Game One and belted home runs in his first two at bats. In Game Two, he doubled and scored the Twins' first run as they rallied from behind to beat Detroit. In the pivotal Game Four, he signaled catcher Tim Laudner for a pickoff play in the sixth inning with one out, Tiger runners on second and third, and the Twins clinging to a one-run lead. The throw and tag nabbed Darrell Evans, a momentum-swinging play that led to a Twins win. Minnesota took the AL title the next day with Gaetti singling and scoring his team's first run.

The Twins went on to win the World Series in seven games against the St. Louis Cardinals, with Gaetti snatching a grounder and firing to first for the final out. In the clubhouse, reflecting on what he and his teammates had just accomplished, he said, "When I'm 65 years old, I'm going to take my grandchild to his first baseball game," he said. "We'll take our seats, and I'll say to him, 'Baseball is the national pastime, the greatest game in the world. And the greatest thing you can do in baseball is win a World Series.' Then I'll pause and say, 'I once played for a World Series winner.'"[24]

A bona fide star entering the 1988 season, Gaetti had a year that was notable both on and off the field. On the diamond, he had another standout season with his bat and glove, earning his first All-Star selection and third Gold Glove. But his on-field production was overshadowed by his sudden born-again Christian experience in the middle of the season. The seeds of his transformation were planted after the Twins' World Series victory. "It was nice, it was satisfying—but only in a baseball sense, in a human sense of accomplishment," he said, "because it doesn't mean anything the minute you win. It's fleeting and you realize it."[25]

In the middle of the 1988 season, while recovering from arthroscopic knee surgery, Gaetti examined his life, had some discussions with Christian teammates, and decided to radically change his ways. The hard-living Gaetti was known for chugging beers, smoking like a chimney, cursing like a sailor, and celebrating victories with shots of whiskey. But almost instantly, he abandoned those habits and dedicated himself to Jesus Christ. Gaetti's conversion caused some tension in the clubhouse as his teammates tried to adjust to the new Gary, who also separated from his wife, Debby, who he had been with throughout his professional baseball career. On the field, though, he continued to produce, earning his fourth Gold Glove and second All-Star selection in 1989. Early in the season, *Sports Illustrated* asked the 12 American League managers who they thought was the best third baseman in the league. Ten of them picked Gaetti, and one more split his vote between Gaetti and Wade Boggs.[26]

By 1990, however, the G-Man's production was noticeably slipping as he turned 31 years old. That season he hit only 16 homers and batted just .229, and his four-year Gold Glove streak ended. He did take part in a unique bit of baseball history, though, starting two triple plays in a game against Boston on July 17, the only time in major league history that a team has turned two triple plays in one game.[27] Now a free agent, he faced a skeptical market. A Yankees official recalled that some scouts thought Gaetti was washed up.[28] The California Angels, however, had enough confidence in him to sign the two-time All-Star to a four-year, $11.4 million contract.

The Angels regretted their decision almost instantly. Gaetti's batting average and power numbers were subpar in 1991 and worse in 1992. His world-class defensive abilities vanished, too, frustrating the club and its fans. A game story from 1992 reports that Gaetti's "hitting and fielding failures sent boos cascading from the seats in Anaheim Stadium."[29] In another game, after he "failed to make two critical plays," he "was booed by the home crowd and received a standing ovation for every ball he handled cleanly thereafter."[30]

After the 1992 season, Gaetti asked the Angels for a trade, but they could not grant his wish because, as an Angels official bluntly put it: "Right now we haven't been tempted by anybody, because there has been no interest."[31] He started the 1993 season buried on the Angels bench, and did not help himself when he was given opportunities to play, hitting just .180 with zero homers in 50 at bats. He performed so poorly that the Angels decided to eat the remaining year and a half on his contract and released him in early June.

Gaetti soon latched on with the Kansas City Royals. "We took a shot," said Royals manager Hal McRae. "It's hard to say what the guy will do."[32] What he did was drastically surpass expectations. A year later, McRae said, "He's been our most valuable player so far, among the position players."[33] During 1993 and 1994, Gaetti played 172 games for the Royals and hit 26 homers. He was just getting started.

After the 1994 season, Gaetti was divorced and married his second wife, Donna. Perhaps energized by his new love, the G-Man found the fountain of youth in 1995. While turning 37 years old, he thumped a career-high 35 round-trippers, knocked in 96 runs, garnered the Silver Slugger as the AL's top-hitting third baseman, and finished 10th in the MVP voting. Along the way he exacted revenge against the team that had released him by blasting a walk-off homer against the Angels in May. He did it again against the Brewers in June, part of a scorching streak of eight homers in ten games. Gaetti did not let himself get carried away with his exploits, though, saying, "I know how humbling baseball can be."[34]

At his age, Gaetti knew the next game, much less the next season, were not promised to him. "My physical condition is going to determine how long I last," he said in the middle of the 1995 campaign. "Right now, Advil is the key. I could do a legitimate commercial for Advil."[35]

He could afford plenty of Advil with the one-year, $2 million deal he reached with the St. Louis Cardinals before the 1996 season. It was a dream come true to join the team he had rooted for as a boy. He said, "I can't tell you how many times I stood in the front yard, the back yard, everybody's yard," pretending to be various Cardinals stars.[36] Gaetti started slowly due to injuries, but he finished strong and racked up 23 home runs and 80 RBIs. Continuing a career-long theme, the veteran slugger had a knack for dramatic home runs in 1996:

- Homered in his first at bat in his first Cardinals home game.
- Smashed a walk-off dinger on August 7 to restore the Cardinals' division lead.
- Belted a game-tying, momentum-changing homer on September 24 to help St. Louis clinch the division crown.
- Blasted a three-run bomb in the first inning of Game One of the NLDS against San Diego.
- Tagged Greg Maddux for a crushing grand slam in Game Two of the NLCS against Atlanta.

Maddux also gave up Gaetti's 2,000th career hit the following year, a shot off the pitcher's right ankle. "I couldn't have gotten a nice, clean hit," Gaetti said. "I had to dig it out and work for it. I guess it's fitting."[37] The gritty veteran also scored his 1,000th run in 1997. He knew 1,000 was a big number, but he thought it could have been higher: "I've probably been thrown out a thousand times at the plate, too."[38] He believed he could have had more career homers and a better batting average, too, "But I didn't learn how to hit a breaking ball for 10 years because nobody could throw a fastball by me and not a lot of people would try."[39]

Gaetti appreciated being in St. Louis, constantly reminded of childhood memories. He could stand on the field and "smell the same smell that I used to love as a kid coming over to watch the Cardinals. The hot dogs and the beer and the popcorn, and it just wafts in the air. I used to just love that as I kid because, you know, going to the ballpark is a special time. Times like that, I think I really am blessed to be in the position I'm in."[40]

Gaetti gave St. Louis two and a half seasons of solid production. But on July 31, 1998, the Redbirds acquired Fernando Tatis in a trade, and they no longer needed Gaetti's services. Eventually they released the veteran, freeing him to sign with the Cubs on his 40th birthday. He may have been over the hill, but he was as relentless and driven as ever. For the second time in his career, he responded to being released by turning back the clock. Gaetti appeared in 37 games for the Cubs down the stretch of the 1998 season. And he did not just play—he raked. The rejuvenated G-Man posted a .320 batting average, a .594 slugging percentage, and a .991 OPS. He also produced a cluster of clutch hits as the Cubs battled for a playoff spot. On September 17 he smashed a pinch hit homer in the 10th inning to beat the Padres. On September 26 he doubled and scored to tie a critical game against the Astros, then doubled again to drive home the deciding runs. Finally, in a Game 163 winner-goes-to-the-playoffs duel with the Giants, Gaetti hit a two-run home run to break up a scoreless tie in a game eventually won by the Cubs, 5-3.

Gaetti was back with the Cubs again in 1999, but the magic vanished from his bat and he struggled mightily at the plate. Retirement started to cross his mind. "It's a huge decision," he said. "What I'd really like is at least one more hot streak. Just to enjoy it again."[41]

It was not to be. After he hit just .204 in 113 games in 1999, nobody wanted to sign the 41-year-old with 19 seasons of major league mileage on his wheels. Finally, after every other major league club passed on him, Gaetti accepted an invitation to Boston's spring training camp. Entering his 20th big league season, his passion for baseball was as strong as ever. He said, "I'm sure I'm going to hear people say, 'Why don't you quit?' My answer to them is, 'Why don't you quit watching?' The game is in my blood as much as it is in yours."[42]

Surprisingly, Gaetti did well enough in spring training to make Boston's season-opening roster, but he could not hit regular season pitching. After an 0-10 start at the plate, he had a discussion with his wife and decided to retire. "I'm tired," he said. "I definitely didn't want to end up bitter at my lack of success, getting beaten physically and taking it home."[43] He went home to Louisiana, where, in 2002 he was hired as the hitting coach for the Houston Astros' Class-AAA team, the New Orleans Zephyrs. In the middle of the 2004 season, the Astros promoted him to the same role in Houston. Back in the majors as a coach, he fit in well. "[Gaetti] is just an upbeat guy," said Houston's Lance Berkman. "Everybody respects him for the kind of ballplayer he was."[44]

Gaetti was the hitting coach for the 2005 NL champion Astros, but he was fired at midseason in 2006. The following year, he landed in North Carolina as the hitting coach for the Class-AAA Durham Bulls. Gaetti then went on to manage the independent Atlantic League's Sugar Land Skeeters from 2012 to 2017. He guided the club to a league championship and was the skipper when Roger Clemens and Rafael Palmeiro made cameo appearances for the team.

Gaetti married his current wife, Joni, in 2014, and his family includes three children from previous marriages—daughter Gigi and sons Joe and Jacob. Joe turned out to be a talented ballplayer himself. He never got above Class-AAA, but in an interesting coincidence he married the daughter of Dan Gladden, Gaetti's teammate on the 1987 world champion Twins.

When Gaetti was inducted into the Twins Hall of Fame, his former teammate, Kent Hrbek, summed up his longtime buddy and got to the core of who he was. "Gary wanted to win more than anybody," Hrbek said. "Gary wasn't out there to make friends or headlines. He was just out there to win."[45]

ACKNOWLEDGMENTS

This biography was reviewed by Malcolm Allen and Norman Macht and fact-checked by Mark Sternman.

SOURCES

In addition to the sources cited in the Notes, the author also consulted www.baseball-reference.com

NOTES

1　When Gaetti retired, only Brooks Robinson and Graig Nettles had played more games at third base. Later, Adrian Beltre moved into second place behind Robinson.

2　Dennis Brackin, "Memories return for old Cardinals fan named Gaetti," *Minneapolis Star Tribune*, October 20, 1987: 3D.

3　Mike Eisenbath, "Centralia's Gaetti Discovering New Baseball Life With Royals," *St. Louis Post-Dispatch*, May 27 1994: 1G.

4　Mike Eisenbath, "Heavy-Duty Gaetti Was Built For The Game, And He Returns, Game As Ever," *St. Louis Post-Dispatch*, January 21, 1996: 3F.

5　Brackin, "Memories return for old Cardinals fan named Gaetti."

6　Norman Draper, "Gaetti's old town divided," *Minneapolis Star Tribune*, October 20, 1987: 3D.

7　Eisenbath, "Heavy-Duty Gaetti Was Built For The Game."

8　Dennis Brackin, "Playing for keeps," *Minneapolis Star Tribune*, August 16, 1987: 1C.

9　Eisenbath, "Centralia's Gaetti Discovering New Baseball Life With Royals."

10　Eisenbath, "Heavy Duty Gaetti Was Built For The Game."

11　Eisenbath," Heavy Duty Gaetti Was Built For The Game."

12　Craig Barnes, "Thanks To Dad, Gaetti Isn't Working On Railroad," *Fort Lauderdale Sun Sentinel*, March 13, 1988: 4C.

13　Robbie Andreu, "Just Call 'Em The Get-Well Cards," *Fort Lauderdale Sun Sentinel*, October 17, 1987: 4C.

14　Dan Barreiro, "Gaetti is having great time," *Minneapolis Star Tribune*, October 16, 1987: 1D.

15　Ted Silary, "The Tale Of 2 Cities: Youthful Twins Blaze Hottest Trail In West," *Philadelphia Daily News,* August 27, 1984: 82.

16　Cal Ripken Jr. won, and Gaetti's teammate Kent Hrbek finished second.

17　"Gaetti, Twins See A Bright Future – But Will They Enjoy It Together?" *Philadelphia Inquirer*, March 13, 1983: E12.

18　"Twins: 50 Years, 50 Moments," *Minneapolis Star Tribune*, June 28, 2010: C2.

19　R.B. Fallstrom, "At 39, Gaetti carves out a home with the Cardinals," *Milwaukee Journal Sentinel*, May 17, 1985: 5.

20　Dennis Brackin, "Unspoiled Gaetti still is dishing it out daily," *Minneapolis Star Tribune*, June 17, 1988: 1C.

21 Dan Barreiro, "Learning game proves a hit for Gaetti," *Minneapolis Star Tribune*, March 15, 1987: 1C.

22 Barreiro, "Learning game proves a hit for Gaetti."

23 Brackin, "Memories return for old Cardinals fan named Gaetti."

24 Steve Wulf, "Sweet Music," *Sports Illustrated*, November 2, 1987.

25 Hank Hersch, "The Gospel And Gaetti," *Sports Illustrated*, August 21, 1989.

26 Peter Gammons, "Baseball," *Sports Illustrated*, May 1, 1989.

27 Gaetti was involved in seven triple plays during his career.

28 Mike Penner, "With Gaetti's Release, Angels Cut Dead Weight," *Los Angeles Times*, June 4, 1993: 4.

29 Dennis Brackin, "With the past fading away, Gaetti battles the present," *Minneapolis Star Tribune*, June 23, 1992: 1C.

30 "Gaetti's fielding lapses at new position draw boos from all but the Blue Jays," *Baltimore Evening Sun*, July 22, 1992: 1B.

31 Bob Nightengale, "Angels Gaetti Is Free to Seek Own Trade," *Los Angeles Times*, February 27, 1993: 8.

32 Dennis Brackin, "He's no Angel – and glad of it," *Minneapolis Star Tribune*, June 22, 1993: 1C.

33 Dennis Brackin, "Gaetti of old returns with Royals," *Minneapolis Star Tribune*, June 26, 1994: 12C.

34 "'Washed Up' Gaetti Suddenly Carrying Royals Offensively," *St. Louis Post-Dispatch*, June 6, 1995: 4C.

35 Dennis Brackin, "Second chance has been a blessing to Royals' Gaetti," *Minneapolis Star Tribune*, June 25, 1995: 10C.

36 Rick Hummel, "Gaetti Finally A Cardinal," *St. Louis Post-Dispatch*, December 19, 1995: 1C.

37 Rick Hummel, "Gaetti Hits Plateau, And As Usual, Takes Everything In Stride," *St. Louis Post-Dispatch*, May 18, 1997: F3.

38 Ruck Hummel, "Gaetti Hits Another Milestone," *St. Louis Post-Dispatch*, May 30, 1997: D5.

39 Fallstrom, "At 39, Gaetti carves out a home with the Cardinals."

40 Jim Souhan, "Gaetti feeling right at home in St. Louis," *Minneapolis Star Tribune*, June 30, 1997: 5C.

41 Stephen Cannella, "Inside Baseball," *Sports Illustrated*, July 12, 1999.

42 Gordon Edes, "Not The First Choice At Third Gaetti Gives It Another Shot," *Boston Globe*, February 24, 2000: C6.

43 Godeon Edes, "It's A Painful Goodbye For Gaetti," *Boston Globe*, April 15, 2000: G3.

44 Derrick Goold, "Gaetti brings experience, positive attitude to Astros," *St. Louis Post-Dispatch*, October 15, 2004: F6.

45 Dennis Brackin, "Anniversary Summer: Twins' First World Championship – The 1987 Season," *Minneapolis Star Tribune*, August 17, 2007: C6.

BENNY AYALA

BY RORY COSTELLO

Benigno Ayala lives up to his given name, which means "kind" or "friendly." Following a productive career as a role player, he has bestowed greater gifts on the baseball world, through his work with the Baseball Assistance Team (BAT). Quite a few of his fellow Puerto Rican pros have fallen on hard times since they left the game. "There are really sad stories," said Ayala in 2009. "And most of them are unknown, because ballplayers are proud. They don't like to ask."[1] Ayala played five full seasons in the majors and parts of five others from 1974 to 1985. He qualified for a good pension and does not have to worry about life's necessities – now he is a voice for those in need.

In his playing days, the outfielder wasn't known for his defense, but he was a pretty fair batting threat in platoon. In its glory years, the Baltimore organization understood the importance of "deep depth," as manager Earl Weaver called it in 1979. Pitcher Steve Stone detailed the concept in *Tales from the Orioles Dugout*.

"They were a team that pretty much understood that the spare parts of a baseball team determine whether you win or lose. It's going and getting . . . [a] Benny Ayala. And then it's up to the manager after you get Benny Ayala to realize that . . . when they put soft-tossing lefthanders in the game, Benny was good for two hits. Earl put him in a situation where he could be successful. So Hank Peters went and got him, and Earl used him correctly."[2]

Ayala came to the plate 951 times in his big-league career, and 86 percent of those appearances were against lefties. It's no surprise that 35 of his 38 regular-season homers came off southpaws – as did his crowning blow as a pro, his two-run shot off John Candelaria in Game Three of the 1979 World Series.

Benigno Ayala Félix was born on February 7, 1951, in Yauco, a town in southwestern Puerto Rico. He was the first of two sons born to Benigno Ayala and Lillian Félix (there was also a half-brother). The island has sent over 300 men to the majors over the years, yet only three others have hailed from Yauco. The first was pitcher Tomás "Planchardón" Quiñones, a longtime local star who pitched briefly in the Negro Leagues in the 1940s. After Ayala came Mario Ramírez (1980-85) and Mike Pérez (1990-1997).

Ayala himself did not start playing baseball until the age of 11, but in retrospect, he saw some benefits from it. In 2010, he said, "If you start late, you don't get bored. And when you grow, you have to go through a process of adjustment. I asked guys like Tom Seaver and Rusty Staub about it."

On January 28, 1971, the New York Mets signed Ayala as a free agent (the amateur draft did not include Puerto Rico

Benny Ayala, New York Mets – Courtesy of Trading Card Database

until 1990). The scout was Nino Escalera, who covered Latin America for the Mets. "I was in my first year at Río Piedras Junior College. Whitey Herzog came to Puerto Rico. He was with the Mets at the time. Many years later, Nino told me and Angel Cantres that Whitey said, 'Go as high as $125,000.' He didn't give us the money – he gave us $7,000!"

Escalera, who died in 2021 aged 91, was 80 when Ayala was originally interviewed. Ayala observed, "You know what else he told me? 'Benny, out of all the guys I signed, you're the only one who has helped me.'"

Ayala's first pro team in the US was Pompano Beach in the Florida State League. He hit .279 with 8 homers and 34 RBIs in 63 games, which won him promotion to Visalia in the California League (high A). In the winter of 1971-72, he played in the Puerto Rican Winter League for the first time. "Nino Escalera was a coach for the San Juan Senadores, Roberto Clemente's team. Angel Cantres went to San Juan after he signed with the Mets, but I didn't. I said, I'll see what I can do in the US, then I'll see who's interested. I'll go to a club where I can develop. Arecibo was in the cellar. Cantres had more competition with San Juan."

Returning to Visalia in 1972, Ayala hit 19 homers, second on the club behind Ike Hampton's 21. He also had 66 runs batted in, one fewer than Greg Harts (who, like Hampton, appeared very briefly with the Mets). Visalia is an agricultural town with a large Hispanic population, but there were plenty of times when Ayala didn't feel welcome. "We lived in a bad neighborhood called 'Sin City' but it was the only thing we could afford. People threw rocks at us. I remember waiting in a barbershop, and when my turn came, they said, 'We don't cut that kind of hair.' The team owners were good people, though. I remember they owned a chain of hot-dog stands."

Ayala continued to climb the ladder steadily. In 1973 he was with Memphis (Double A). Serving frequently as a designated hitter, he led the team in home runs (17) and was second in RBIs (68). That winter he led the Puerto Rican league in homers for the first time, as his 14 tied with Jerry Morales. He also tied Jay Johnstone for the league lead in RBIs with 46 and hit .340. To emphasize how strong that circuit was then, the four men who finished ahead of him in the batting race were George Hendrick, Chris Chambliss, Mickey Rivers, and José Cruz, Sr. Yet Ayala won the MVP award.

Ayala did well in spring training 1974, hitting homers off veterans like Woodie Fryman and Bob Gibson. He wasn't quite ready, though, and Cleon Jones did not take well to an experiment in center field. Near the end of camp the Mets sent Ayala down to their top affiliate, Tidewater. Here too he was the club leader in homers (11) and RBIs (40). The big club called him up in August after Jones got hurt; to make room, pitcher Jack Aker went on the disabled list. Ayala still has the bat he borrowed from Joe Nolan, his teammate with the Tides and later the Orioles.

With that bat, on August 27, Ayala made a memorable big-league debut at Shea Stadium. Batting sixth in the lineup, he stepped in against Houston's Tom Griffin (a righty!) with one out and nobody on in the second inning. He pulled a high fastball – as he kept repeating on Ralph Kiner's postgame show, *Kiner's Korner* – down the line in left field. The ball stayed inside the foul pole, and Ayala became the first National Leaguer to homer in his first big-league at-bat since Cuno Barragan in 1961. Of course, that made him the first Met to do so too (not to mention, the first Puerto Rican).

A contributor to the Ultimate Mets fan website provided some extra detail. "We were sitting in the left field mezzanine at Shea among this group of 10 or 12 of Benny Ayala's cousins and extended family who were thrilled to see him in his first major-league game. When he homered in his first at-bat they went BERSERK, hugging and kissing everyone around, including me and my father of course. It was a great memory that I was able to recount with my dad that always drew a smile."

The rookie did not live with family, however, and although fellow Puerto Rican Félix Millán was present, he remembers that his most helpful teammates were John Milner and Jones. Manager Yogi Berra also did not stack up well against Weaver

in Ayala's estimation. "He was always laughing, he didn't pay too much attention to the game."

Ayala did not see any big-league action in 1975. The Mets acquired Dave Kingman in February, which severely impaired his chances of making the big club. In fact, he played just 65 games for Tidewater, missing a big chunk of the early season after Rochester's Bob Galasso broke his hand with a pitch.

In the winter of 1975-76, Ayala led the Puerto Rican league in homers once again with 14 in 60 games. He finished in a four-way tie for second in RBIs with 39. Coming off this very strong effort, he made the Mets roster in spring training 1976. The team's new manager was Joe Frazier, his skipper at Visalia, Memphis, and Tidewater. Ayala was not in the lineup on Opening Day but started the next two games. He would get just two more starts over the remainder of April and May, however, and he got only three hits in 26 at-bats (including a pinch-hit homer off Jack Billingham, his last off a righty in the majors). New York then called up Jack Heidemann and sent Ayala back to Tidewater, where he hit just .225 with 12 homers and 48 RBIs.

On March 30, 1977, New York traded Ayala to the St. Louis Cardinals in exchange for second baseman Doug Clarey, whose big-league career comprised nine games scattered across the '76 season. Ayala spent the bulk of 1977 with New Orleans in the American Association, where he had a good year (.298/18/73). The Cardinals called him up in September, but he got into just one game, singling in three at-bats.

The Cardinals had a new Triple-A affiliate in 1978, Springfield, but Ayala spent only part of the season there – he went to Columbus in the Pittsburgh organization on loan. As the *Pittsburgh Post-Gazette* wrote that August, "Columbus was so short of talent that it borrowed players from other minor-league clubs. Players like Hector Torres, an infielder, and Benny Ayala, an outfielder who has a problem. He can't catch a fly ball."[3] Ayala hit .340 for the Clippers in 59 games, though, lifting his overall mark for the year to .299. He totaled 11 homers and 56 RBIs.

On January 16, 1979, Ayala got the best break of his career. The Cardinals traded him to Baltimore for Mike Dimmel, another player whose big-league career was quite limited (39 games from 1977 to 1979). Ayala had considered going to play in Japan with the Taiyo Whales, but Doc Edwards, his manager in Puerto Rico, was also the manager at Baltimore's Triple-A team, Rochester.[4] Edwards persuaded Ayala to stay, farm director Clyde Kluttz liked what he saw too, and the Orioles called him up at the end of April after Doug DeCinces got hurt.

Earl Weaver used Ayala sparingly in '79, but he benefited from the AL's designated-hitter rule. In 86 at-bats across 42 games, he hit 6 homers, drove in 13, and hit .256. He had his only two-homer game in the majors on June 10 at Memorial Stadium. Both were solo shots off his former Mets teammate, Texas Rangers lefty Jon Matlack.

Weaver did not use Ayala in the American League Championship Series, but he got six at-bats in four games during the World Series. He singled off John Candelaria in his first at-bat in Game Three before reaching the Nuyorican for his homer. That blow brought the Orioles within a run at 3-2, and they proceeded to knock out Candelaria in the fourth inning. During that rally, righty Enrique Romo came out of the bullpen, and so Al Bumbry hit for Ayala.

The Associated Press write-up said, "Ayala also didn't know he was starting until he saw the lineup posted in the clubhouse. Ayala admitted that he never knows when Weaver is going to use him. 'He doesn't play me against certain lefthanders,' Ayala said. 'It's mostly if I can hit a certain lefthander.'" Many observers thought the lineup was unconventional, but Earl said, "It was one that helped us get here in the first place. . . . Benny has done that for us a number of times."[5]

Ayala enjoyed his best season in the majors in 1980 (.265/10/33 in a career-high 76 games). Always thinking positively, he said, "I don't mind my role here. I always have a chance to swing the bat with the Orioles and the way Earl uses me is decent." Frank Robinson, then a Baltimore coach, said, "Benny uses his time wisely, watching and studying the pitchers. He's not afraid to ask somebody about a certain pitcher either."[6]

Ayala's most dramatic hit that year may have come on September 5 at Memorial Stadium. This could have been the game described in a 1996 article in the *Los Angeles Times* about Earl Weaver's golden hunches. "One day, Weaver walked up to [pitching coach Ray] Miller and said, 'Ray, Benny Ayala. Don't forget that, Benny Ayala.' That night, Ayala hit an eighth-inning pinch homer. 'It just made sense to me in those days . . . to know if I had a hitter sitting on the bench in a situation that was hitting that pitcher good,' Weaver said. 'So I made up my lineups accordingly.'"[7] The three-run blow off Oakland lefty Bob Lacey brought the Orioles within a run at 6-5, and they won it 8-7 with another three runs in the bottom of the ninth.

In the strike season of 1981, Ayala served mostly as a platoon DH with Terry Crowley. During 1982 he was part of a three-man contingent in left field with John Lowenstein and Gary Roenicke. In his book *Weaver on Strategy*, Earl said, "By matching your bench-players' strengths to your starters' weaknesses, you can create a 'player' of All-Star caliber." He likened the trio's total output to having a Reggie Jackson in the lineup.[8]

That July Ayala told Steve Wulf of *Sports Illustrated*, "I try to think ahead of time. Say, we are playing Chicago in two weeks. I think how the lefthander pitched me the last time. Sitting on the bench I have a lot of time to think. I try not to be surprised." Another line in the same article showed his Zen-like calm. On May 19 he hit a three-run homer after a rain delay of an hour and 21 minutes. "When asked if he thought he was in a tough spot, having to face a two-strike count after sitting for so long, Ayala replied, 'Not really. I just felt like I was pinch-hitting for myself.'"[9]

Wulf's piece was strewn with juicy quotes on Ayala. Earl Weaver said, "He's so good he knocks himself out of games. I'll start him against a lefthander, and he'll hit a three-run homer off him. Then they'll bring in a righty, and Benny's back on the bench." According to Lowenstein, Ayala was "the most profound player on the Orioles. 'He will sit there, arms folded, for eight innings. If he's going to hit, I'll ask him what he's looking for. He'll say, 'Something white. Coming through.'"[10] Indeed, Ayala (like many Caribbean players) didn't walk or strike out much – he got his hacks.

"I always try to take three swings," Ayala said that summer. "I don't think the hitter should give the pitcher a strike by taking." With the arrival of Dan Ford, Ken Singleton had moved from right field to full-time DH, leaving Ayala with spot duty. Yet as always, he stayed positive. "Sure I would like to play more. But the important thing is to stay ready and then do your job when you're called on."[11]

In 2010 Ayala said, "I suffered a lot in the big leagues. It was hard for me to accept my role, but I accepted it quietly. If I don't play every day, I have it in my mind that I have to work harder. Rod Carew asked me one time, 'Benny, why are you over there by yourself? Don't you want to talk?' I told him I don't have time. I worked. I studied, so when I get that opportunity against Ron Guidry, I can say, 'I'm ahead of you.'" Ayala did far better than most against "Louisiana Lightning" – 9-for-28. Changeup artist Geoff Zahn was just his meat (11-for-30 with two homers), but the lefty whom Ayala owned was Mike Caldwell (11-for-21 with three HRs).

Ayala remained in his reserve role with the O's in 1983, but his effectiveness diminished, as he hit just .221. "I was a little disappointed with Joe Altobelli [who succeeded Weaver], he didn't give me a chance. Then when he knows he needs me for the postseason, he put me up against John Montefusco, a righty with that overhand curve."

Ayala hit a sacrifice fly in his only at-bat in the ALCS against the White Sox, capping the three-run 10th-inning rally that won Game Four and the series for Baltimore. He also made his lone at-bat in the 1983 World Series count. In the seventh inning of Game Three, pinch-hitting for Jim Palmer, he lined a single to left off Steve Carlton, past a diving Mike Schmidt. Rick Dempsey scored the tying run. Ayala then scored the go-ahead run, which would stand up as the margin of victory.

When asked about having a World Series ring, Ayala said, "Juan González turned down $150 million from Detroit because he thought there wasn't a chance for a ring. He should be in the Guinness Book of Records for that!

"You're on top. You're a champion. Even now, I'm signing autographs, and people request that I put '1983 World Series Champ' after my name. I'm lucky that I played with legends – six Hall of Famers."

In 1984 Ayala joked about his infrequent playing time. After getting just four at-bats in the month of June, he said, "I'm an eclipse player. You don't see me very often."[12] He hit just .212 for the year, and the Orioles announced in late September that they would not offer him a contract for 1985. Bumbry and Singleton were also part of the housecleaning.

Spring training also came and went without any offers. Even Ayala thought it might be the end of the line. "So what's left?" he said. "Mexico. And I don't look at myself as a Mexican

League player.[13] Looking back, he thought he should have paid his own way to camp, as he remembers players like Rob Picciolo and Kurt Bevacqua did.

On April 19, 1985, though, the Cleveland Indians signed the veteran to a minor-league deal. Although he went just 7-for-46 with the Maine Guides (Portland), the Indians called him up in May. Just days after he made it back, he missed a fly ball against the Boston Red Sox – but then drove in the game-winning run. Manager Pat Corrales said, "Benny looked a little ugly in left field, but he was Robert Redford at the plate."

Ayala spent the rest of the season with Cleveland, hitting .250 (19-for-76) in 46 games. "When I learned to hit to right field, I was 34 years old. I was a low-ball hitter. I liked to uppercut, even in street fights!" His last big-league homer came off Jimmy Key at Toronto's Exhibition Stadium on September 4. The Indians made him a free agent in November 1985, and Ayala's big-league career ended.

In December 2009, Ayala responded to blogger Bo Rosny's request for stories about his baseball cards. One anecdote captured a key part of his approach to the game. "In one of them the picture was taken in Chicago that I like a lot; Brooks Robinson [then an Orioles announcer] told me that I was looking good. That was a perfect day to take the picture. He said, 'Looking good, Benny, in case you have a bad game today.'

"After that I always shave before the game, good haircut, shine shoes, complete clean uniform, brand-new hat. In case I have a bad game, always looking good."[14]

In the winter of 1985-86, Ayala returned to the Puerto Rican Winter League after several seasons away. He regretted the hiatus. "After I established myself with the Orioles, I didn't go back. Relatives told me I was a little bored with the game. It was foolish. I should have played. I could have gone over 100 homers, I'd be one of the few there." He finished with 68 homers in his PRWL career.

In 1989 Ayala came back to play with the West Palm Beach Tropics of the Senior Professional Baseball Association. One of his teammates was Tim Stoddard., whose career had overlapped with Ayala's in Baltimore from 1979 through 1983. Ayala recalled, "I went there, I'm a low-mileage player. How can a player like me be injured? I hit very good, but one day I chased a fly ball and didn't get it. [Manager] Dick Williams said, 'We aren't going to stick with you.'"

After his playing days finally ended, Ayala got an interview with Doug Melvin about a job in the Orioles chain but went back home to Puerto Rico. For a couple of years he was batting coach with Arecibo, "but there was not much money, $1,200 a month, and I was nearly killing myself driving." After that, "I managed a couple of amateur teams, but they were not easy to handle."

Ayala was married in 1971 to Esperanza "Eppie" Martínez. "I was always visiting her when I was in college. I was in love. I didn't like school much!" The Ayalas had four children: sons Benigno III, Luis Mario, and Melvin, plus daughter Jesica.

In subsequent years, Ayala's main endeavor became his professional network. His goal: to help retired Puerto Rican players in such areas as pensions, health insurance, celebrity baseball clinics, training clinics for children, and more. In November 2007 Ayala (in tandem with the Calero & Sullivan Baseball Management firm) held a groundbreaking meeting with 118 former pros from the island and the Major League Baseball Players' Alumni Association. As a result, the Baseball Assistance Team was able to offer financial and medical support to various men who needed it. Ayala also got involved with setting up memorabilia signings to bring the players some additional money. His network came to include around 250 pros.

Ayala's role as BAT's liaison to the Puerto Rican community brings him and his fellow *boricuas* much joy. He helped his old teammate Angel Cantres after Angel lost a leg following a work-related accident in 2001. After former minor-league pitcher Jacinto Camacho received a new artificial leg to replace his homemade prosthesis, he walked off the plane home to greet his family and completely forgot about his wheelchair. "Times like these are when I know that the work I do with BAT really makes my life worthwhile," Ayala said.[15]

In the summer of 2009 Ayala also reached out to former big-league outfielder Ricky Otero. Otero, who had fallen into alcohol and drug addiction, was living homeless in Cancún, Mexico. Though Otero subsequently denied the report, Ayala was able to get him into a rehab program in New York.[16] As of 2024, Otero was doing well in Vega Baja, Puerto Rico.

Ayala, who turned 73 in 2024, remains actively involved in his professional network and on social media. He dresses with the same attention that he did to looking sharp in uniform. He is a cheerful and chatty man, but his baseball memories feature a serious undercurrent. He said, "Earl Weaver respected you as a major-leaguer. Some people had to be on the field first, but still I feel, 'Here they treat everyone the same.' I was very proud to wear that big-league uniform, with that Orioles name up front."

This biography was originally published in 2010. It was subsequently updated for Puerto Rico and Baseball (SABR, 2017) and again in 2024.

ACKNOWLEDGMENTS

Grateful acknowledgment to Benny Ayala for his memories (telephone interview, May 2, 2010). All quotations that are not otherwise attributed come from this interview.

Continued thanks to SABR member Jorge Colón Delgado (Puerto Rican statistics).

SOURCES

In addition to the sources cited in the Notes, the author also consulted retrosheet.org, ultimatemets.com, and caleroandsullivan.com, as well as Crescioni Benítez, José A., *El Béisbol Profesional Boricua* (San Juan, Puerto Rico: Aurora Comunicación Integral, Inc., 1997).

NOTES

1 Carlos Rosa Rosa, "Benigno con el prójimo," *El Nuevo Día* (Guaynabo, Puerto Rico), October 16, 2009.

2 Louis Berney, *Tales from the Orioles Dugout* (Champaign, Illinois: Sports Publishing LLC, 2004), 147.

3 Charley Feeney, "Columbus Turmoil Might Spell Peterson's Demise," *Pittsburgh Post-Gazette*, August 8, 1978: 13.

4 Steve Wulf, "It's the Right Idea for Left," *Sports Illustrated*, July 12, 1982.

5 Associated Press, "Baltimore Offense Is Ignited," October 12, 1979.

6 Ken Nigro, "Hitting Or Sitting, Ayala Happy," *The Sporting News*, August 2, 1980: 37.

7 Jason LaCanfora, "Beyond tantrums, was hidden Weaver," *Los Angeles Times*, August 4, 1996.

8 Earl Weaver and Terry Pluto. *Weaver on Strategy* (New York: Collier Books, 1984), 26.

9 Wulf, "It's the Right Idea for Left."

10 Wulf, "It's the Right Idea for Left."

11 Ken Nigro, "Benny Always Fit as Bird in Pinch," *The Sporting News*, August 9, 1982: 27.

12 Robert W. Creamer, "They Said It," *Sports Illustrated*, August 27, 1984.

13 Associated Press, "Indians won't be sending Ayala to Mexico," May 19, 1985.

14 http://borosny.blogspot.com/2009/12/one-more-card-story-from-benny-ayala.html

15 Baseball Assistance Team, Winter 2008 newsletter (mlb.mlb.com/mlb/downloads/y2009/bat/bat_winter_2008_newsletter.pdf)

16 "Ricky Otero: de Grandes Ligas a indigente en Cancún," *El Universal* (Mexico City, Mexico), September 4, 2009. "Madeja de Contradicciones," *Primera Hora* (Guaynabo, Puerto Rico), March 22, 2010.

MARCUS THAMES

BY RICHARD CUICCHI

Marcus Thames made an unforgettable debut with the New York Yankees on June 10, 2002, when he hit a home run off future Hall of Famer Randy Johnson in his first major-league at-bat. Hitting home runs became the trademark for the right-handed slugger, not because of the total number he amassed over his 10-year major-league career, but because of the frequency and timeliness with which he hit them. Thames never played a season as a full-time starter. He accepted his role as a part-time outfielder and designated hitter, whose value stemmed from his penchant for hitting home runs at opportune times.

Marcus Markley Thames (pronounced "TIMMS") was born on March 6, 1977, in Louisville, Mississippi, a small town in the central part of the state, approximately 100 miles northeast of Jackson. He was only 5 years old when his mother, Veterine Thames, became paralyzed as a result of an automobile accident. Ms. Thames was a passenger in an auto driven by G.W. Hughes, the father of four of her five children. Her spine was permanently damaged, leaving her unable to move her legs and torso. She was also unable to hold items.[1]

Marcus was the youngest of his siblings: sisters Tabitha and Carnetta, and brothers E.W. and Stacy. Hughes, who was not injured in the crash, was not significantly involved in the care of the children.[2]

With Ms. Thames unable to care for herself or her family, the children were moved into the homes of relatives in Louisville. When Stacy and Tabitha reached the age of responsibility for household duties, the children moved back home with their mother. The family's income consisted solely of welfare and food stamps.[3]

Thames's career was inspired by his mother's perseverance in dealing with her disability. In an interview with the *New York Times* in 2006, he said, "When you have somebody who can't get themselves a glass of water, you look at this baseball stuff and it's easy in comparison. You can't take life for granted. It just made me a stronger person."[4]

His former Louisville High School baseball coach Charlie Smith remarked about Thames, "He wanted to play, he wanted to be good, and he's talented. But I think the driving force of his mom is 90 percent of it for him."[5]

Thames emerged from his difficult upbringing to become involved in sports. As a 16-year-old, he played on the Louisville team that won the Mississippi Junior Dizzy Dean championship and finished fifth in the World Series in Jasper, Alabama.[6]

He went on to play baseball and football for Louisville High School. He joined the Mississippi National Guard after his junior year to earn extra money for the family. He came back

Marcus Thames, New York Yankees – Courtesy of Trading Card Database

from his nine-week basic training duty 20 pounds bigger and stronger. He learned mental toughness from the disciplined environment.[7]

Thames came into his own during his senior year. As a wide receiver on his football team that advanced to the state playoffs in 1994, he led the team with 11 receiving touchdowns.[8] He also earned a second-team all-state selection in 1995 as a senior infielder and pitcher.[9]

Thames received a baseball scholarship from East Central Community College, 50 miles from his hometown. He spent the 1996 season under head coach Jamie Clark, to whom Thames later attributed the development of his work ethic. He played well enough to attract the attention of the New York Yankees, who selected him in the 30th round of the 1996 amateur draft.

Thames did not sign after the draft, instead choosing to return to East Central for the 1997 season. The school had one of its best seasons in recent history, led by Thames's .420 batting average, 13 home runs, and 70 RBIs. The team finished in second place among junior colleges in Mississippi and fourth in Region 23 of the national junior-college postseason. Thames was named to all-state and all-region teams.[10] He didn't wait for the coming June draft, instead signing with the Yankees and scouts Joe Robison and Leon Wurth on May 16, 1997.[11]

Thames had a promising minor-league debut season in the rookie Gulf Coast League in 1997, earning league all-star team honors.[12] Yet a Tampa sportswriter characterized him as an "untamed talent with untapped potential." Lee Mazzilli, his manager at Tampa in 1998, saw him as coachable and willing to learn. Mazzilli said, "He's learning the strike zone. The situations of hitting. Knowing what his limitations are. Knowing how to hit in game situations. Not just going up there free swinging."[13] Thames ended the season with a respectable .285 batting average, 11 home runs, and 59 RBIs in 122 games.

Thames struggled for the next two seasons with Double-A Norwich. He would later say it was his inability to hit sliders that caused his performance to drop off. At one point he considered giving up the game.[14]

In 2001, his fifth minor-league season and his third with Norwich, Thames had a breakout year. He slashed .321/.410/.598, with 31 home runs (a Norwich franchise record) and 97 RBIs. With Juan Rivera (in a split-season between Norwich and Triple-A Columbus), Thames was named the co-winner of the Player of the Year Award for the Yankees' minor-league organization.[15] Norwich manager Stump Merrill remarked about Thames's impact, "I'm surprised Marcus didn't get the MVP of the league, but he's certainly been our MVP.[16]

Coming off the best season of his career, Thames impressed Yankee manager Joe Torre in spring training the next year, despite not having Triple-A experience. With Rondell White injured during spring camp, Thames became one of Torre's considerations for backfilling the veteran outfielder at the start of the season. Thames was enthusiastic about his opportunity to get visibility in the big-league camp as an up-and-coming outfield prospect, and his work ethic stood out to the Yankees' staff. He attributed his dedicated approach to his junior-college coach, Jamie Clark, whom Thames commemorated by writing his name on the inside of the bill of his cap.[17]

However, White healed by the end of camp and Thames was sent to Triple-A Columbus for more seasoning. He was in a slump, batting only .218, when he went on the injured list for two weeks.[18] But when Yankees outfielder Rivera, who had moved up to the majors in 2001, crashed into a golf cart while shagging flies during batting practice, Thames got his first call-up to the big leagues.[19]

He made his major-league debut with the Yankees on June 10 against the Arizona Diamondbacks at Yankee Stadium. Manager Joe Torre started Thames in right field, batting ninth in the lineup. In his first at-bat in the third inning, against hard-throwing lefty Randy Johnson, he hit Johnson's first pitch for a two-run home run off the screen in left-center above the Diamondbacks' bullpen. Shane Spencer hit a grand slam in the eighth inning to power the Yankees' 7-5 win.

Thames was only the second Yankee to hit a home run in his first plate appearance. John Miller first accomplished the feat in 1966. After the game, sitting in front of his locker, an elated Thames said, "I'm going to sit here in my uniform awhile and then go call everyone I know. I'm going to watch 'SportsCenter' and 'Baseball Tonight' all night."[20] According to *Baseball Digest*, Thames was the 17th player in the majors to hit a home run on the first pitch of his first at-bat.[21]

Thames saw action in six more Yankees contests before being sent back to Columbus to make room for hot-hitting Karim García, who was called up from Columbus.[22] Thames finished the season with the Clippers, batting only .207, with 13 home runs, 21 doubles, and 45 RBIs in 107 games.

After starting the season with Columbus in 2003, Thames was traded by the Yankees for Texas Rangers veteran Rubén Sierra on June 6. Following an initial assignment with Triple-A Oklahoma City, he joined the Rangers after the All-Star break. He was one of several prospects the last-place Rangers wanted to evaluate.[23]

In his first game with the Rangers, on July 17, Thames hit a two-run home run in the fifth inning off Tampa Bay pitcher Joe Kennedy. But that was his best showing during the balance of the season. A shoulder injury in September set him back.[24] He failed to hit another home run and batted a meager .205 in 30 games.

The Rangers released Thames to free agency after the season. Detroit signed him on December 7.

He was back in the minors with Triple-A Toledo to start the 2004 season. In one of the best games of his career, he hit three homers and a double for the Mud Hens on April 25 against Louisville.[25] He maintained a hot bat, and at the time of his call-up to Detroit on June 22, he was leading the International League with 24 homers while compiling 59 RBIs and batting .329. But his bat cooled off in his first days in the Tigers lineup. He had trouble making contact, unable to hit the ball out of the infield.[26] He collected only one hit in his first 20 at-bats.

Tigers manager Alan Trammell stuck with Thames, though, and he eventually rebounded to hit 10 home runs and get 33 RBIs in 165 at-bats for the season. It was the beginning of a trend he would continue for the balance of his career – a low rate of at-bats per home run. Thames's 10 home runs made him the 11th Tiger to reach double figures that season, a new major-league record.[27]

Coming out of spring training in 2005, Trammell kept outfielder Bobby Higginson over Thames, because Higginson had more major-league outfield experience. Thames, upset with being sent to Toledo to start the season, went 5-for-5 with a two-out homer in the ninth to tie the game in Toledo's home opener.[28] He was immediately recalled when outfielder Magglio Ordoñez had to miss several games with a viral infection. Thames responded with a grand slam in his first game back, on April 9.

He stayed with the big-league club while Ordoñez had an extended stay on the injured list. When Thames was in the lineup with some regularity, he hit for power. With 13 starts in 19 appearances in May, he averaged a homer for every 10.2

at-bats. But he also had a sagging batting average and on-base percentage.

Thames was sent back to Toledo by mid-June until he was re-called in September. He finished the season with 7 home runs, 16 RBIs, and a .196/.263/.411 slash line in 38 games with the Tigers. By contrast, in 73 games with Toledo, he slashed .340/.427/.679, with 22 home runs (one per 12 at-bats) and 56 RBIs.

For the first time in his five-year major-league career, Thames made the Opening Day roster in 2006. As he stood on the field for player introductions before the game, he said it was a dream he'd "never forget."[29] With Jim Leyland replacing Trammell as manager, Thames spent the entire season with the Tigers as they captured their first American League pennant since 1984.

Now 29 years old, Thames contributed to the team's success with a breakout season. He was in the starting lineup in 100 of his 110 games played, splitting time between the outfield and designated hitter. He relished the periods when he could play consecutive games regularly. Thames remarked, "I'm getting the chance to play ball, getting a chance to play in the major leagues. I never really had an opportunity like I'm getting now to go out there every day." He added, "I'm making the most out of it and trying to go out every day and keep working hard."[30]

Thames ended the season with a career-best 26 home runs (one per 13.3 at-bats) and 60 RBIs, while batting .256. He batted .333 in 15 at-bats in the Tigers' ALDS win over the Yankees. The first person he called after the series was his mother, wanting to share his and the team's successes with her. She had been his inspiration during his struggle to get to the majors and remain there. He said, "She's given me so much that I'm happy I'm able to give her a little something like this. And she kept reminding me about the power of believing in yourself when others aren't. Just keep fighting and keep battling."[31]

Thames saw limited action in the Tigers' defeat of the Oakland A's for the 2006 AL pennant and the loss to the St. Louis Cardinals in the World Series.

Thames spent another full season with the Tigers in 2007, except for a minor rehab appearance with Toledo. During spring training, Leyland asked him to play first base, to provide an option for a backup at the position and avoid the need for a separate backup first baseman.[32] Plus, after the Tigers' acquisition of Gary Sheffield in a trade with the Yankees during the offseason, Thames would see fewer opportunities to fill the designated-hitter role.

Thames ended up playing in a utility role: 33 games at first base, 46 games in the outfield, and 15 as a DH and pinch-hitter. He remained proficient in hitting home runs. Three games at the beginning of July, referred to as the "Thames Trilogy" by the *Detroit Free Press*, demonstrated the kind of impact he had. Thames hit a home run in the eighth inning to defeat Minnesota, 1–0, on July 1. He hit a grand slam in a series opening win against Boston on July 6, and he hit a 440-foot home run on July 8 to help sweep the Red Sox.[33]

The Tigers battled Cleveland for first place in the division during the majority of the season, holding a slim lead as late as August 16. But Cleveland broke away during September, leaving the Tigers in second place, eight games behind. Thames delivered 18 home runs (one per 15 at-bats) and 54 RBIs for the season. In an end-of-season assessment of Thames's future with the Tigers, Leyland asserted that he didn't project him as an everyday outfielder. Leyland explained, "I think he's a nice platoon (outfield) player, part-time DH, part-time first baseman. I think he's a very, very valuable player for this team."[34]

During the offseason Detroit acquired two All-Stars, first baseman Miguel Cabrera and shortstop Édgar Rentería, to complement an already talented team that included catcher Iván Rodríguez, second baseman Plácido Polanco, third baseman Carlos Guillén, outfielders Ordoñez and Curtis Granderson, and DH Sheffield. In 2008 Thames continued in his part-time role, splitting time with Matt Joyce in left field while also serving as an occasional DH and pinch-hitter.

Thames's confidence as a hitter was bolstered by his previous season's improvements in batting average with runners in scoring position (.315) and batting average against left-handed pitching (.310). During spring training, the New York Mets expressed interest in him as a needed right-handed power hitter. But Leyland's solid relationship with Thames squashed any consideration the Tigers' front office might be willing to entertain. Leyland insisted, "He can play on my team anytime."[35]

Thames made the headlines with a grand slam in a win over Seattle on May 21. It was the fifth slam of his career, which was also his 66th career home run. Tigers hitting coach Lloyd McClendon called attention to Thames's penchant for success with the bases loaded. "Marcus understands that when the bases are loaded, the pressure is on the pitcher. He's so darn strong that when he hits strikes, good things usually happen." McClendon was referring to the fact that coming into the game Thames had a career average of .556 and 31 RBIs when batting with the bases loaded.[36]

On June 17 against the San Francisco Giants, Thames hit a home run for the fifth consecutive game. He tied a team record shared with several Tigers greats: Rudy York (1937), Hank Greenberg (1940), Vic Wertz (1950), and Willie Horton (1969).[37] Thames missed a chance to potentially break the record the next day. He was hitless when he was replaced in the outfield by Brent Clevlen for defensive purposes in the sixth inning. If he had stayed in the game, he would have had at least one more at-bat. But Thames wasn't bothered by the move. "As long as we keep winning ball games, I'm happy." He added, "It's not about me; it's about the team."[38]

Thames's attitude made him one of the most popular players on the team. Teammate Brandon Inge said, "He's not for personal stats; he's for the team. You don't find too many guys like that. He's one of my favorites of all time." Pitcher Kenny Rogers echoed Inge's sentiments: "He has a great attitude. When he sat on the bench a lot the last few years, he never complained. He just waited for his shot. Those types of guys are nice to be around."[39]

Thames posted one of the best months of his career in June 2008. He hit 10 home runs and had 16 RBIs in 72 at-bats, while slashing .306/.375/.764. He was a key factor in the Tigers' 19-8 record during the month. Leyland said about his slugger, "The one thing I like about Marcus, and for me, the most important thing is Marcus hits [home runs] when they mean something."[40]

Yet June was the only month in which the Tigers posted a winning record. Except for one day in May, the team never rose above third place in the standings, despite the talent in its ranks. September's 8-18 record placed them last in the American League Central Division. Thames finished the season with 25 home runs (one per 13 at-bats) and 56 RBIs.

Despite speculation about the number of home runs Thames could hit if he were a full-time player, Leyland preferred to use him off the bench in 2009. When Detroit released Sheffield before the start of the 2009 season, Leyland saw a path to give Thames more at-bats as a designated hitter. Leyland said, "He's got the best home-run ratio – or one of them – in the last three years. That's a way to get him some at-bats. We were really going to have our hands tied (with Sheffield on the team) because I wasn't going to be able to find Marcus at-bats. Now I can."[41]

The Tigers bounced back in 2009. They led the Central Division for practically the entire season, with Minnesota never far behind. Detroit ended the season tied for first place with the Twins, but then lost a one-game tiebreaker.

Thames played in the outfield in only 20 games, while being predominantly used in DH and pinch-hitter roles in 73 games. A rib injury caused him to miss 43 games and included a 12-day injury rehabilitation assignment with Toledo.[42] He finished the season with 13 home runs and 36 RBIs, while batting .252. His home-run productivity declined (one per 20 at-bats), compared with previous seasons. At a time when the Tigers needed his powerful bat to maintain their distance with Minnesota in the standings, he failed to hit a home run in his last 29 games involving 71 at-bats (during August 14 to October 1).

After six years with the Tigers, Thames was let go and he entered the free-agency market. The Yankees, his first major-league team, signed him to a minor-league contract in February 2010. He went to spring training as a nonroster invitee to compete for a backup role in the outfield and a right-handed DH.

Thames didn't hit well during spring training but was put on the regular-season roster because the Yankees needed a right-handed-hitting outfielder. The Yankees' coaching staff looked back on his offensive productivity with the Tigers as a reason for awarding him a roster spot.[43]

Thames didn't disappoint. Through May he slashed .323/.443/.484 with 2 home runs and 10 RBIs in 21 starts. But in the middle of June, he went on the 15-day disabled list with a strained right hamstring. When he returned on July 4, he delivered a walk-off pinch-hit single in the 10th inning to increase the Yankees' lead over Boston by 1½ games.

From August 24 to August 30, Thames hit six home runs in five starts. The last one was his 10th home run in 151 at-bats for the season. As he maintained before, Thames said, "I've been

playing a little more and if you look at every year I've been playing, I've done something like this when I get more at-bats consistently."[44] He ended the season with 12 home runs, 33 RBIs, and a career-high .288 batting average in 212 at-bats.

The Yankees' season went down to the wire on the last day of the season, tied for the division lead with Tampa Bay. The Red Sox defeated the Yankees at Fenway Park, while Tampa Bay defeated the Kansas City Royals to claim the division championship. The Yankees went into the postseason as a wild-card entry. Thames hit a home run in Game Three of the ALDS. The Yankees swept the Minnesota Twins in three games.

Against the Texas Rangers in the ALCS, Thames was limited to only two hits in 16 at-bats, as the Rangers won their first pennant.

The Yankees made Thames a free agent in November, and he signed with the Los Angeles Dodgers on January 18, 2011. First-year Dodgers manager Don Mattingly planned to platoon Thames in left field against left-handed pitching, overlooking any defensive liabilities he might bring. Mattingly's interest was getting 20 to 25 home runs from the position, even though Thames admitted his shortcomings defensively.[45]

Neither Thames nor the other platoon players in left field delivered as Mattingly had hoped. He played sporadically in the field and didn't produce offensively as he had in the past. He spent a month on the disabled list with a quadriceps problem, which included a short rehab stint with Triple-A Albuquerque. Later he dealt with a strained calf muscle. With a .197 batting average, 2 home runs, and 7 RBIs in 70 plate appearances in mid-July, the Dodgers decided to go in a different direction. Thames was designated for assignment and released to make room for newly acquired outfielder Juan Rivera.[46] (Thames had replaced the injured Rivera when the two were with the Yankees organization in 2002.)

The Yankees reportedly re-signed Thames shortly after his release from the Dodgers,[47] but he did not appear in additional games in 2011. He returned to Mississippi after the 2011 season.

During his 10-year major-league career, Thames slashed .246/.309/.485, with 115 home runs and 301 RBIs. He finished with an AB/HR ratio of 15.6, which put him 15th among major leaguers with 80 or more career home runs from 2003 to 2010. He was ahead of noteworthy sluggers such as Sammy Sosa, Mark Teixeira, Gary Sheffield, Ken Griffey Jr., Vlad Guerrero Sr., and Chipper Jones during the same period.[48]

Back in his home state, Thames enrolled in classes at Mississippi State University and helped out with his mother. She died on September 23, 2012. During his time away from the game, Thames learned that he didn't want to sever his baseball ties. "When I lost my mother, that's when I knew I had to get back into the game of baseball before it was too late," Thames said. "I didn't want to stay out too long. I knew I eventually wanted to coach."[49]

Mark Newman, then the Yankees' vice president of baseball operations, contacted Thames before the 2013 season and offered him a coaching position with Yankees' Class-A affiliate at Tampa.

It was the opportunity Thames was looking for. He joined the team as hitting coach under manager Luis Sojo.[50] He advanced quickly as a coach through the Yankees' farm system, working with Double-A Trenton in 2014 and Triple-A Scranton in 2015.

In 2016 Thames joined the Yankees' major-league staff as assistant hitting coach with manager Joe Girardi. When Aaron Boone became manager in 2018, Thames was promoted to hitting coach. He stayed four more years with the Yankees.

Thames moved to the Miami Marlins in 2022, followed by a year with the Los Angeles Angels. As of 2024, Thames was a member of the Chicago White Sox staff as hitting coach.

Thames and his wife, Danna, have three daughters, Deja, Jade, and Ella Grace, and two sons, Marcus Jr. and Kole.[51]

NOTES

1   Jack Curry, "Marcus Thames's Mother Inspires and Amazes," *New York Times*, October 22, 2006. https://www.nytimes.com/2006/10/22/sports/baseball/22thames.html. Accessed February 28, 2024.

2   Curry.

3   Curry.

4   Curry.

5   Curry.

6   "Local Dizzy Dean Champs Place Fifth in World Series," *Winston County Journal* (Louisville, Mississippi), September 15, 1993: 11.

7   Curry.

8   MSHAA State Playoff Games, *Jackson* (Mississippi) *Clarion-Ledger*, November 25, 1994: 4C.

9   "Clarion-Ledger All-State Baseball," *Jackson Clarion-Ledger*, June 4, 1995: 6D.

10 "ECCC Has Successful 96-97 Season," *Winston County Journal*, July 9, 1997: 1-B.

11 *2002 New York Yankees Information & Record Guide*, 184.

12 *2002 New York Yankees Information & Record Guide*, 184.

13 Bill Chastain, "Thames an Untamed Talent with Untapped Potential," *Tampa Tribune-Times*, May 24, 1998: 5.

14 Stephanie Storm, "Thames Turns Corner," *Columbus* (Ohio) *Dispatch*, April 9, 2002: 6.

15 *2002 New York Yankees Information & Record Guide*, 183.

16 "Minor Leagues," *Yankee Magazine*, October 2001 (Vol. 22, No. 9): 70.

17 Anthony McCarron, "Thames Makes Marc on Yanks," *New York Daily News*, March 24, 2002: 56.

18 "Thames Goes From DL to Cleanup Spot," *Columbus Dispatch*," May 19, 2002: E7.

19 Roger Rubin, "Juan Lands on DL After Cart Mishap," *New York Daily News*, June 10, 2002: 61.

20 Roger Rubin, "D-Backs Back: Treats Champs to Grand Ol' Time, *New York Daily News*, June 11, 2002: 70.

21 *Baseball Digest*, October 2002 (Vol. 61, No. 10): 9.

22 Marty Noble, "El Duque to Start After All," *Newsday* (Long Island, New York), June 28, 2002: A84.

23 Carlos Mendez, "Thames, Drese Called Up From Minors," *Fort Worth Star-Telegram*, July 17, 2003: 5D.

24 T.R. Sullivan, "Few Questions Remain After Showalter's Season of Evaluation," *Fort Worth Star-Telegram*, September 29, 2003: 6D.

25 "Thames Leads Mud Hens," *Bryan* (Ohio) *Times,* April 26, 2004: 13.

26 Gene Guidi, "No New Spin for 2nd-Half Rotation," *Detroit Free Press*, July 12, 2004: 4D.

27 John Lowe, "Tram Seeks Late Fixes Next Season," *Detroit Free Press*, October 4, 2004: 3D.

28 John Lowe, "Ordonez May Miss Tribe Due to Virus," *Detroit Free Press*, April 8, 2005: 4G.

29 John Lowe and Jon Paul Morosi, "Opener Among 16 Games on TV 20," *Detroit Free Press*, April 8. 2006: 7C.

30 John Lowe, "Rogers, Family Ready for 200," *Detroit Free Press*, June 18, 2006: 13D.

31 Drew Sharp, "At Last, Redemption for All-American Rejects," *Detroit Free Press*, October 10, 2006: 4D.

32 John Lowe, "Thames Takes Big Bat to Infield," *Detroit Free Press*, February 24, 2007: B1.

33 "Best Moments," *Detroit Free Press*, July 12, 2007: 5C.

34 Jon Paul Morosi, "Jones Close to 300 Club," *Detroit Free Press*, September 16, 2007: 11D.

35 Jon Paul Morosi, "Mets Like Thames, but So Does Leyland," *Detroit Free Press*, March 7, 2008: 4C.

36 John Lowe, "Thames Grand With Bases Loaded," *Detroit Free Press*, May 22, 2008: 5C.

37 John Lowe, "Thames Homers in 5th Game in a Row," *Detroit Free Press*, June 18, 2008: 6C.

38 "Thames Homers in 5th Game in a Row," 7C.

39 John Lowe, "Teammates Call Thames an All-Star Person," *Detroit Free Press*, June 20, 2008: 1C.

40 "Tigers' Thames Finds Strength in Mother's Plight," *New York Times*, June 29, 2008. https://www.nytimes.com/2008/06/29/sports/baseball/29thames.html. Accessed February 28, 2024.

41 John Lowe and Jon Paul Morosi, "Thames Will Get Chance to Hit More Home Runs," *Detroit Free Press*, April 1, 2009: 14A.

42 Carlos Monarrez, "Tigers Welcome Thames's Big Bat," *Detroit Free Press*, June 8, 2009: 3B.

43 Mark Feinsand, "With Thames in a Fill-in Role, Just Smashing," *New York Daily News*, September 1, 2010: 57.

44 Peter Botte, Kristie Ackert, and Anthony McCarron, "Dallas Does Bronx," *New York Daily News*, August 31, 2010: 74.

45 Dylan Hernandez, "At Least the Price Is Right in Left," *Los Angeles Times*, February 26, 2011: C9.

46 Dylan Hernandez, "Dodgers Acquire Juan Rivera," *Los Angeles Times*, July 13, 2009: C4.

47 Greg Logan, "Thames Returning to Bronx?" *Newsday*, July 23, 2011: A43.

48 The data for the player AB/HR rankings was obtained using Baseball-Reference.com's Stathead Player Finder query function.

49 Thomas Golianapoulas, "Somebody to Lean On," *Yankees Magazine*, April 17, 2018. https://www.mlb.com/news/marcus-thames-goes-above-and-beyond-for-nyy-c272547142. Accessed February 28, 2024.

50 Golianapoulas.

51 *2020 New York Yankees Official Media Guide & Record Book*, 30.

TERRY STEINBACH

BY HERB SCHAPER AND STEW THORNLEY

Terry Steinbach grew up in an athletic family that focused on the fun of the games they played. Although he didn't give a lot of thought to college scholarships or professional aspirations during his formative years, Steinbach took his baseball talents to a 14-year career in the major leagues that included three World Series and three appearances in the All-Star Game.

Terry Lee Steinbach was born March 2, 1962 to Lloyd and Burnell "Nellie" Steinbach in New Ulm, a hotbed for amateur baseball in south-central Minnesota. Lloyd worked for the 3M Company in New Ulm and also with Marco out of Mankato, Minnesota, as a service technician for office copiers in addition to coaching youth sports. Nellie was a cook at the school. ("I think she did that to keep an eye on us," Terry said.)

Terry is the third son, behind Tim and Tom, and also has a younger sister, Tracy, another good athlete who played hockey and softball. Along with his siblings as well as other neighborhood kids and friends, Terry spent a lot of time in the Steinbach backyard, playing games with improvised rules. "We did a ton of stuff in our backyard," said Steinbach. "We had to be creative, make up our own games."

The family attended games of the Brewers and Kaiserhoff, the New Ulm town teams, at Johnson Field and picked up cracked bats. They broke some of them in two and used the short end for the backyard stickball games. A tennis ball hit into the garden or clothes on the line was an out; a drive off the side of the garage was a double while those coming down on the top of the garage or the roof of the Baptist Church gym, across the alley, were home runs. "We just played baseball for fun," said Steinbach, adding that competing with his older brothers meant he was "always playing up" and helped with his development as a player.

At New Ulm High School, Steinbach played football in ninth grade and ran on the cross-country team for three years, although his best sports were hockey and baseball. A typical spring and summer for Steinbach was baseball for the New Ulm Eagles high-school team, followed by more baseball with VFW and American Legion teams.

Steinbach started playing VFW ball at the age of 12. Four years later, in 1978, he played for the New Ulm American Legion team that won the state tournament (with Steinbach beating out Bloomington's Kent Hrbek for the Most Valuable Player [MVP] award) and the regional tournament in Rapid City, South Dakota, advancing to the American Legion World Series.[1]

In 1980, after graduating from high school, Steinbach played for the Kaiserhoff under manager Ken Brueske. The Kaiserhoff produced a 14-2 regular-season record and went on to win the

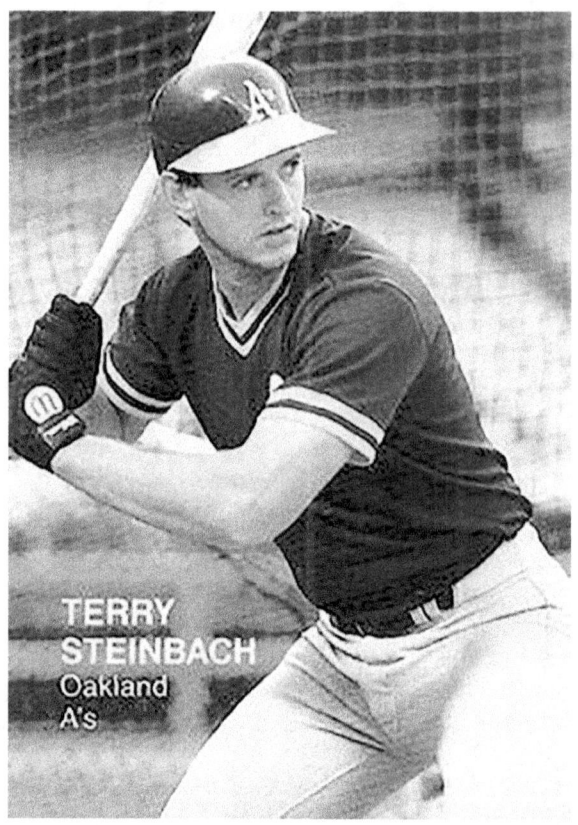

Terry Steinbach, Oakland A's – *Courtesy of Trading Card Database*

Class-B state amateur championship. Steinbach had two home runs in the championship game as the Kaiserhoff beat Dundas in 11 innings. With a batting average of .500 and 10 runs batted in (RBIs) in five games, Steinbach was named the tournament's Most Valuable Player.

The summer teams the Steinbachs played on included other fine players, including Jeff Schugel, a high-school teammate, and Doug Palmer, who had gone to Cathedral High School in New Ulm.

Steinbach didn't give much thought to college and professional scouts being at games, which kept him from pressing and possibly playing poorly. He said part of the reason was because of the attitudes of other New Ulm players he watched or played with. "In New Ulm, guys who were drafted or went to college didn't have egos. It kept baseball in perspective for me."

Steinbach considered attending a Division II college in Iowa, where he would be able to play hockey and baseball. However, after being drafted in the 13th round by the Cleveland Indians in 1980, he started to think more seriously about his future in baseball. Steinbach had numerous offers from larger colleges for a baseball scholarship and settled for the Minnesota Gophers, where his brother, Tom, had just wrapped up a standout season as a freshman.

Tom and Terry were joined by brother Tim on the Gophers in 1981. Tim, who had graduated from New Ulm High School in 1977, played two years of baseball and hockey at the University of Wisconsin, River Falls, before transferring to Minnesota. After sitting out a year because of the transfer, he joined the varsity, and the Gophers had three Steinbachs in the lineup.

Tim was a catcher while Terry played third base and Tom patrolled right field, often exhibiting his strong throwing arm. The Gophers finished first in the Big Ten West Division in 1981 (the first year the conference was split into divisions) but lost in the conference tournament. They went the other direction in 1982, finishing second in the West with an 8-8 conference record, but then won the Big Ten tournament and advanced to the National Collegiate Athletic Association playoffs. Steinbach had a .402 batting average in 1982 and drove in 65 runs, breaking the team record set by Tom Steinbach in 1981. (Both marks have since been surpassed by others.)

Steinbach had returned to the Kaiserhoff, along with many of his former teammates, in 1981, but in 1982 the group looked for the chance to play elsewhere. An avid outdoorsman, Steinbach hoped for an opportunity to play in the Alaska Summer League, but the invitation finally came after he had accepted an offer to play in the Cape Cod League on the East Coast. Even though it wasn't Alaska, Steinbach enjoyed his time on the Cape, "having fun and living the life of a rock star." Players were provided with jobs that allowed for their baseball schedule, working in the early morning and late afternoon before going to the ballpark.

On the Cape, Steinbach played first base for the Cotuit Kettleers. He led the league with a .431 batting average and received the Pat Sorenti Award as the league's Most Valuable Player. Steinbach said the Cape Cod was a valuable opportunity to play with more consistent competition. The Gophers played top-rate teams during the Texas spring trip and Big Ten schedule, but their season was mixed with a number of non-conference games with teams from smaller colleges in the area. On Cape Cod, Steinbach said almost all the players were Division I-caliber.

The Gophers finished first in the Big Ten West in 1983 but lost in the conference tournament. After the season, both Tom and Terry went into the pro ranks. Tom signed with the Seattle Mariners organization and Terry, who decided to forego his senior year at Minnesota, with Oakland. At the time, Tom and Terry were one-two in career runs batted in with the Gophers with 175 and 165, respectively. Tom also held the Gophers career mark for home runs with 45, a record that stood until Robb Quinlan broke it in the 1990s. Terry had a career .375 batting average, which at the time tied him for the team record with Greg Olson, who had wrapped up his college career in 1982 and, like Terry, would later play in the major leagues. In addition to the Steinbachs, the 1983 amateur draft by major-league teams included two other New Ulm players, Schugel and Palmer, who were drafted by the Minnesota Twins.[2]

Tom and Terry were both assigned to short-season Class-A teams in the Northwest League, Tom with Bellingham, Washington, and Terry with Medford, Oregon. They played against each other during the regular season and again in the league championship series, in which Medford defeated Bellingham. Terry hit .315 with six home runs and 38 RBIs in 62 games for Medford in 1983.

Tom did not do as well, and his stay in the professional ranks was briefer. Terry notes the "luck in pro ball," specifically that Oakland drafted players for only about 30-35 rounds in 1983 while Seattle, a team that had come into the majors only six years before, was still trying to stock its rosters and drafted through more than 50 rounds. This gave Terry the luxury of competing with a smaller mix of incoming players his first year while Tom got lost in the shuffle of all the players the Mariners had drafted. He was released by the Mariners after the 1983 season.

Terry progressed up the minor-league ladder. He came back to the region, playing for the Madison (Wisconsin) Muskies in the Class-A Midwest League in 1984. His manager there was Brad Fischer, who was also Steinbach's manager the next two years with Huntsville (Alabama) in the Class-AA Southern League.

Steinbach didn't begin catching until after his second year of pro ball. He had been hitting well, but the organization had a couple players in its system projected for the infield corners, Mark McGwire for third base and Rob Nelson at first base (Nelson did not last long with the A's and McGwire eventually took over first base). After the 1984 season, the A's sent Steinbach to the Arizona Instructional League to start catching.

Steinbach was a backup to Brian Dorsett at Huntsville in 1985, finding more time in the lineup as a designated hitter, but he became the starting catcher in 1986. He performed well, hitting .325 with 24 home runs and 132 RBIs, the latter figure breaking the league record of 122, set by Steve Balboni in 1980.[3] Steinbach was named the Southern League MVP. However, it was a long summer, squatting behind the plate in the heat of the southern U. S., made longer as Huntsville, which had won the Southern League title, advanced to the championship round again before losing to Columbus (Georgia).

His season earned him a promotion as a September call-up by the Oakland A's, and he joined the team in Cleveland. On Friday night, September 12, Steinbach entered the game as a defensive replacement for catcher Mickey Tettleton. He then led off the seventh inning, facing left-hander Greg Swindell. Steinbach made it a memorable debut, becoming one of a relatively few players to homer in his first at-bat in the majors.[4]

After the 1986 season, Steinbach had two days back in Minnesota before he and his wife, Mary, took off for winter ball with Licey in the Dominican Republic League. "I was fried," he said of spending two more months catching in hot weather before he finally returned home in late December. He did mention that the money in the winter league, more than he earned in the minors, was helpful to the couple, who had married two years earlier.

Steinbach started the 1987 season sharing the catching duties, but when Tettleton slumped at the plate, Steinbach took over the number-one spot.[5] He finished the year with a batting average of .284 with 16 home runs in 122 games (107 of them as a catcher). Besides exhibiting a solid bat, Steinbach did well behind the plate, particularly in throwing out runners trying to steal.

A freak injury early in the 1988 season put Steinbach on the disabled list when he was hit in the eye by a throw during batting and infield practice and suffered fractures around the orbital bone. He was still voted by the fans as the starting catcher for the American League in the All-Star Game, even though his batting average at the break was only .219.

While some questioned whether he deserved his spot on the All-Star team, Steinbach came through in the game itself. After two scoreless innings at Riverfront Stadium in Cincinnati, Steinbach led off the third with a home run to right off Dwight Gooden. In doing so, he became the first player ever to homer his first time up in the majors and his first time up in an All-Star Game. He came up the next inning with the bases loaded and hit a long fly to left, not quite far enough for a grand slam but deep enough to bring in from Dave Winfield from third. The sacrifice fly made the score 2-0, and the American League held on for a 2-1 win. By driving in both runs for his team, Steinbach was voted the All-Star Game MVP.[6]

Oakland won the American League West Division and then swept the Boston Red Sox in the league playoffs. He hit .364 in the World Series, although the A's lost in five games to the Los Angeles Dodgers (a series best remembered for the Dodgers' Kirk Gibson winning the first game with a two-out, two-run homer run in the last of the ninth off Dennis Eckersley).

The season concluded with Steinbach joining others from the summer All-Star team for a tour and series of games in Japan, an experience he enjoyed more than playing in the Dominican Republic League in 1986.[7]

Steinbach was again the starting catcher in the All-Star Game in 1989, and Oakland repeated as the American League champions, this time winning the World Series against the San Francisco Giants, although it was overshadowed by the earthquake that struck the Bay Area prior to the third game. Steinbach had caught the first two games of the series (hitting a home run in Game Two) with Dave Stewart and Mike Moore on the mound for the Athletics, who won both games. Bob Welch was the Game Three starter, and his regular catcher was Ron Hassey, so Steinbach relaxed in the dugout as he awaited the pre-game ceremonies at Candlestick Park in San Francisco.

"It got loud, we saw the overhang shake, and the dugout started shaking," is how Steinbach described what happened. "It was a weird feeling." The players jumped out of the dugout and initially did not realize the extent of the damage from the earthquake. The power in the stadium was out, but they thought it would be restored and the game still played. Soon they learned of how devastating the earthquake was. Steinbach found his wife and both were concerned about how their one-year-old

daughter, Jill, and her babysitter were doing at their home across the bay in Oakland.

The World Series did not resume for another 10 days. When it did, Oakland defeated the Giants on Friday night to take a three-game-to-none lead. The next night, the Athletics got off to an early lead, and Steinbach padded it with a two-run triple in the fifth inning. He capped the game's scoring with a bases-loaded walk in the eighth as Oakland won, 9-6, to capture the world championship.

Oakland made it three straight pennants in 1990, although the Athletics were swept in the World Series by Cincinnati. Steinbach had one more appearance in the postseason, hitting .292 with a home run and five RBIs in 1992, although the Athletics were defeated in the league playoffs, four games to two, by the Toronto Blue Jays.

Steinbach loved the Oakland organization and described it as "a great way to learn the game." He said Sandy Alderson and Walt Jocketty in the front office and manager Tony LaRussa "stressed the right attitude and effort." He also noted how the organization brought in veteran leadership with players such as Don Baylor, Dave Henderson, Reggie Jackson, and Dave Parker to go with the young talent they were developed. (Oakland had three straight Rookies of the Year from 1986 to 1988 in José Canseco, Mark McGwire, and Walt Weiss). Steinbach hung out with one of the veterans, Carney Lansford, who took him under his wing and taught him baseball and life lessons.

Steinbach's biggest year with Oakland came in 1996 when he hit 35 home runs and drove in 100. (His previous highs in those categories were 16 and 67, respectively.) Steinbach's 34 home runs as a catcher—one of his homers was as a pinch-hitter—set an American League record for the most home runs in a season by a catcher.

Steinbach was a free agent after the 1996 season and looked at the opportunity to go home. The Steinbachs, who had three children by this time (Jill and sons Lucas and Jake), maintained homes in Oakland and Minnesota as well as a place in Arizona for spring training. He said the constant shifting of was not a problem for Jill but that Lucas, about to start school, might have more trouble with it.

The scene in Oakland had been changing. Walter Haas no longer owned the team, and LaRussa and Jocketty were also gone. Steinbach decided to make a change himself, signing as with the Twins and enjoying the opportunity to come home and live full-time in Minnesota, even though it meant a cut in pay after his best season in the majors.[8]

Steinbach provided a young team in Minnesota with veteran leadership over the next three seasons and, in the final month of his career, had the chance to catch his second no-hitter. The first was in 1990 with Dave Stewart as the pitcher. In a Saturday morning game on September 11, 1999, Steinbach caught the no-hitter of the Twins' Eric Milton. He noted the difference in his roles in the games. Stewart was a veteran when he pitched his no-hitter and called his own game, using a wipe system if he wanted to change the catcher's signal. "I did a lot of following with him," Steinbach said of Stewart's no-hitter. "Milton, however, I'm the veteran. I was more nervous than he was in the seventh, eighth, and ninth innings. He's going to pretty much throw what I call, so I felt a tremendous amount more pressure not to blow it."

Steinbach retired after the 1999 season. He was one of several native Minnesotans who caught in the major leagues in the twentieth century. The list includes Wes Westrum, Tim Laudner, Brad Gulden (who was also born in New Ulm), Tim McIntosh, Greg Olson, and Don Wheeler.[9] Among that group, Steinbach has the best career batting average (.271) and slugging percentage (.420). His career includes more than 1,500 games and 5,000 official at-bats. In the field, he had exactly 8,400 putouts and assists and exactly 100 errors for a fielding percentage of .988.

In addition to 1,381 games behind the plate, Steinbach played 62 at first base, 22 at third, 15 in the outfield, and he was the designated hitter 69 times. He had more than 100 hits in 10 of his 13 full seasons. Steinbach finished his career with 162 home runs, approximately one every 33 official at-bats.

In 2000, Steinbach went back to playing with the Kaiserhoff in New Ulm,[10] although he had a couple of exciting offers. One was to catch the second half of the season with the St. Louis Cardinals, a chance to work again for Tony LaRussa, who was managing the Cardinals. The other was to play for the U. S. team in the Olympics in Melbourne, Australia.

He and his family went to their lake home to decide which opportunity to follow. However, Steinbach then tore his hamstring from the bone while waterskiing and wasn't able to do either.

When interviewed in 2008, Steinbach played in a 35-and-older league for the Hanska Bullheads that plays along the Hwy. 19 corridor to the west and south of the Twin Cities. He likes the shorter games (batters start with a 1-and-1 count) and that there are only two games a week. Brothers Tom (who had continued to play for many years with the Kaiserhoff) and Tim were also on the Hanska team. Steinbach says that getting "caught up in the hype of big-league ball" could cause a person to "lose sight of the love of the game that comes back with the town ball."

Steinbach had offers to play in the Roy Hobbs Tournament in Florida each November, but he never let anything to interfere with hunting in the fall. (Steinbach even skipped a team reception with President George Bush at the White House following Oakland's 1989 championship so he could go hunting.)

Steinbach has long been involved in the communities where he has played and lived. He now has an endowment, funded by money he receives for autograph requests, that is used for scholarships to students at the New Ulm high schools. "It keeps me on top of the fan mail," he says of the charitable program.

Steinbach also worked with catchers with the Twins during spring training and helped coach the Wayzata High School varsity baseball team. when his sons were on it. Later, he and Mary made frequent trips 150 miles to the north to watch Lucas and Jake play for the University of Minnesota, Duluth, Bulldogs.

The northern jaunts became less frequent when Steinbach accepted an offer from the Twins in 2013 to be a bench coach under manager Ron Gardenhire. He even served a couple games as acting manager in April 2014 when Gardenhire was absent to attend an out-of-state funeral.[11] Gardenhire was fired after the 2014 season. Steinbach indicated he'd like to be considered for the position. However, Paul Molitor got the job. As part of the reshuffling, Steinbach was among the coaches not rehired.

Jake Steinbach eventually played for the University of St. Thomas in St. Paul, making it easier for Terry and Mary to watch him play. They were present in April 2016 when Jake hit a grand slam, a thrilling moment but one tempered by a smashed windshield as Jake's drive came down on Terry's car.[12]

As of 2024, the Steinbachs continue to live in the western suburbs of Minneapolis. In August 2024 Steinbach was inducted into the Oakland Athletics Hall of Fame. Twenty-two years earlier, he had been inducted into the Cape Cod League Hall of Fame along with Darin Erstad, Chuck Knoblauch, and Robin Ventura.

SOURCES

Interview by Schaper and Thornley with Terry Steinbach, February 15, 2008. All quotations by Steinbach are from this interview unless otherwise noted.

Carl "Red" Wyczawski provided valuable information for this biography.

NOTES

1 Carl Wyczawski, "New Ulm Has Had Its Share of Professional Ballplayers," *Johnson Park: 50 Years of New Ulm Baseball Tradition*, Volume One, 1989, 20-25.

2 "Many Involved in 'Stats,'" *Johnson Park: 50 Years of New Ulm Baseball Tradition*, Volume One, 1989, 36.

3 "Don't Pinch Steinbach" by Kit Stier, *The Sporting News*, September 29, 1986: 21.

4 Al Doyle, "Terry Steinbach: The Game I'll Never Forget," *Baseball Digest*, July 2005: 76.

5 Kit Stier, "Steinbach Learns, Earns," *The Sporting News*, June 29, 1987: 15.

6 Dennis Dillon, "Unlikely Star, Improbable Script: Steinbach Leaves Boldest Signature on A. L.'s 2-1 All-Star Victory" *The Sporting News*, July 25, 1988: 16.

7 Jim "Red" Bastian "Steinbach Reflects on Great 1988 Season," *Johnson Park: 50 Years of New Ulm Baseball Tradition*, Volume One, 1989, 33-35.

8 E. M. Swift, "Cold Sweet Home," *Sports Illustrated*, January 27, 1997: 56.

9 Laudner was born in Iowa but grew up in the Twin Cities.

10 Jim Bastian, "Steinbach, Raabe Suit Up for 'K'," *New Ulm Journal*, June 3, 2000.

11 The funeral in Ohio was for the son of Michael Hirschbeck, son of umpire John Hirschbeck. The Twins scored 17 runs in twice beating Kansas City while Steinbach was managing.

12 https://bringmethenews.com/minnesota-sports/tommies-steinbach-breaks-dads-window-with-home-run-ball, accessed July 13, 2024.

ED SANICKI

BY MICHAEL TRZINSKI

As a teenager in the late 1930s, Ed Sanicki and his brother Emil would travel by train from New Jersey to Ebbets Field in Brooklyn. At the ticket office they would buy bleacher seat tickets, which was all they could afford. Occasionally Dodgers players would walk past the ticket office, and sometimes sign autographs. Babe Ruth, a Brooklyn coach in 1938, would hand out small cards he had autographed in advance. Ed Sanicki dreamed of becoming a Dodger.

In 1946 the Philadelphia Phillies offered Sanicki a contract with a $2,000 signing bonus. Sanicki asked Brooklyn general manager Branch Rickey if the Dodgers had any interest in signing him. Sanicki asked Rickey for $2,500, to which Rickey responded, "We can't do that, but we'll give you $2,500 if you go to Vero Beach and make the team." Sanicki said he couldn't afford to do that, being married and just out of the Navy. "He wished me luck, gave me a little cigarette lighter ... and I signed with the Phillies instead."[1]

" ... I would've given my right arm to play for the Dodgers," Sanicki said. "I just loved them so much."[2]

Edward Robert "Butch" Sanicki was born in Wallington, New Jersey, on July 7, 1923, to Michael Paul and Anna (Baciak) Sanicki. Michael was a delivery driver for a furniture company.[3] Edward was the youngest of four children. Joseph (1916), Helen (1917), and Emil (1919) came before him.[4]

In the mid-1930s Sanicki spent his spare time playing a baseball board game, dreaming of the day he might play in a real World Series.[5] His brother Emil was an amateur boxer and would pay Edward a nickel to help with his road training, by running together to a country store and back. Ed credited Emil with instilling in him good work habits and discipline.[6]

Ed grew up to be 5-feet-9 and 175 pounds. He perhaps developed his strong wrists and forearms from working on the heavy bag and speed bag with Emil as a teenager.[7]

Batting and throwing right-handed, Sanicki played baseball at Clifton (New Jersey) High School for four years, earning All-Passaic Valley honors his final three years, along with All-State accolades his junior and senior seasons.

Sanicki also was a standout on the football squad, playing three seasons and being named to the All-Passaic Valley team his final year. He played basketball his final two years and made all-conference teams both seasons.

He enrolled at Seton Hall University in the fall of 1941, choosing baseball over a football scholarship at Georgetown on the advice of a Brooklyn Dodgers scout. The Dodgers had lined up a baseball scholarship at Seton Hall, which no doubt helped make the choice easier.[8]

Ed Sanicki, Philadelphia Phillies – Courtesy of Jacob Pomrenke

Sanicki had a great freshman year, batting .372 (16-for-43) as Seton Hall won 10 straight games. The team went on to win 25 consecutive contests over two seasons.[9]

The summer after his freshman year, Sanicki played baseball with the Curtiss-Wright team in the semipro Passaic-Bergen Baseball League, participating in a summer league as he had done all through high school. A teammate on the Curtiss-Wright team was Larry Doby.[10] The two had played against each other in high school in both baseball and football, with Doby playing for Eastside High School in Paterson, New Jersey.

In the spring of 1943, Sanicki joined the US Navy and served as a signalman on a Liberty ship until the end of World War II in 1945. On July 18, 1945, he and Anna Krehel were married at Assumption of the Holy Virgin Mary Church in Clifton, New Jersey.[11]

In December 1945, Sanicki signed with the Phillies. New Jersey area scout Chuck Ward, who signed him, said, "Eddie has a fine disposition for a player and is gifted in all departments of the game."[12]

Sanicki was originally slated to start the 1946 campaign at Utica in the Class-A Eastern League. But there was a need for outfielders at Class B, and he was instead sent to the Wilmington Blue Rocks of the Interstate League.[13] In his first exhibition game with the Blue Rocks, Sanicki walked in the first inning and then connected with a two-run homer in the fourth inning off Vic Raschi.[14]

In Wilmington's opening game, Sanicki walked in his first plate appearance and then homered his next time up, one of the 16 hits pounded out by the Blue Rocks in a 17-1 thrashing of Lancaster.[15] In an exhibition game against reigning World Series champion Detroit Tigers in early June, Sanicki's ninth-inning double was the only extra-base hit in the contest. The Tigers won, 1-0, as Sanicki's double off Johnny Gorsica was one of four Wilmington hits in the game.[16]

A week later, with Sanicki having hit 11 home runs so far, Phillies President Bob Carpenter in a newspaper interview took notice of Sanicki, saying, "Maybe he won't make good, though I say he will."[17]

The Blue Rocks made it to the Interstate League championship series but lost in five games to the Harrisburg Senators. Sanicki led the league with 30 home runs and 144 RBIs. His home-run total tied the league record. Sanicki also finished in the top five in stolen bases and total bases, and in the top 10 in runs, hits, walks, and slugging percentage. He was the only player unanimously named to the Interstate League all-star team,[18] but earned only the runner-up spot in the most valuable player voting, losing out to Harrisburg catcher Ed Mutryn.[19]

Sanicki returned to Wilmington the following year. He kept up his prodigious home-run pace and in early August, he homered in six straight games.[20] After failing to homer on August 6, he hit round-trippers in each of his next two games to give him a mark of eight homers in nine games. Sanicki ended the 1947 season with 37 home runs, setting a new league record. He also paced the circuit in runs, slugging percentage, and total bases. His name was listed among the top five in walks and on-base percentage, while his 109 RBIs tied for sixth. This time he was named league MVP.[21] The Blue Rocks avenged the previous year's title loss by taking the championship in seven games over Allentown.

Sanicki enrolled for his junior year at Seton Hall that fall. He was invited to the Phillies' spring-training camp at Clearwater, Florida, in March, along with several others, including Curt Simmons, Stan Lopata, and Richie Ashburn.[22] But by the end of March, Sanicki was sent down to the Toronto Maple Leafs of the Triple-A International League.

During the 1947 campaign in Class B, the average age was 24 years old. Sanicki was 23. The next year, in Triple A, the average age for the league was 27, and Sanicki was three years younger. That might have had something to do with his struggles in 1948 in Toronto. After a month of play, Sanicki had a "batting mark … around the .200 figure."[23] Included in that were three home runs, far below the pace of his last two seasons.

Sanicki eventually got back into home-run form, knocking 16 balls out of the park from mid-May to mid-July, when he hit his 19th home run against Jersey City.[24] He struggled the last three weeks of the season, though, only managing two round-trippers and four RBIs. Even though all his numbers were down from the previous two years, he still finished 10th in International League Most Valuable Player voting.[25] Sanicki finished the season with a league-leading 107 RBIs. On defense, he set an International League record with 29 outfield assists.

The New Jersey product returned to Triple-A Toronto in 1949. He started out with a bang, hitting .364 (12-for-33), with 6 home runs.[26] His power numbers continued all season, but his batting average dropped off and he finished the season with a line of .268/.358/.482. His 33 homers ranked third, while his runs, hits, RBIs, and total bases were all in the top 10. Sanicki finished sixth in the MVP voting.[27]

After the International League season ended, Sanicki was called up to the Phillies on September 11.[28] He made his big-league debut on September 14 against the Pirates at Pittsburgh's Forbes Field, inserted into the lineup in right field in the bottom of the seventh.

Sanicki batted for the first time in the top of the ninth with the Phillies leading 9-4, with two on and nobody out, and drove a pitch from right-hander Rip Sewell into the Pirates' bullpen. "The count was 2-and-2 when I hit Sewell's slider, which didn't slide, into Hank Greenberg's Gardens. It was an inside pitch."[29]

Five days later, Sanicki hit another home run, this one off Cardinals pitcher Howie Pollet, and added a run-scoring fly for three more RBIs in a 4-3 win over St. Louis at Sportsman's Park. "Pollet served me a fastball when I connected for the circuit," said Sanicki, who was nicknamed "All or Nothing" by his Phillies' teammates.[30]

Just over a week later, Sanicki hit his third and final major-league homer, off the Giants' Sheldon Jones in a 2-0 win at Shibe Park. For the season, Sanicki batted a lowly .231 (3-for-13), but all three of his hits were home runs.

As 1950 rolled around, the Phillies staff expected much of Sanicki. "What probably isn't generally realized is that (Sanicki is) even better with the glove than he is with the bat," said Babe Alexander, the Phillies' public-relations director. "He can really go and get 'em in center field, probably as good as Richie Ashburn."[31]

Added Phillies manager Eddie Sawyer: "I really am exceptionally high on Ed Sanicki. Richie Ashburn is going to have to hustle with all he has to keep this kid from taking his job."[32]

Despite the high hopes, Sanicki's chance of breaking camp with the Phillies was scuttled by three crucial details: his less-than-stellar spring performance (8-for-35, .229 batting average); the hot hitting of Dick Sisler, who batted .380 with 5 home runs; and the resurgence of Ashburn, who won the center-field job with his sparkling batting mark of .417 (30-for-72).[33]

Sisler was battling with Eddie Waitkus for the first-base job, but after Waitkus earned the starting nod, Sawyer moved Sisler to the outfield. "You have one chance to play regularly," Sawyer told Sisler. "That's if you can give us another big stick in the outfield."[34] He did, and that was enough for the Phils to send Sanicki back to Toronto.

Meanwhile, Philadelphia manager Sawyer was calling Sanicki perhaps the best center fielder in all of baseball. "Sanicki, in other words, is now where Joe DiMaggio was when he came up," Sawyer said. "He's going to be truly great."[35]

Being sent down did not demoralize the young slugger. "As long as I'm playing ball," he said with a grin. "But maybe my chance will come again."[36] As far as his switch from center field to right, "I think it's great," he said. "I don't have as much territory to cover, so I think it will be easier than playing [center field]. But frankly, it doesn't matter to me which field I play."[37]

One thing did irritate Sanicki: the Phillies wanted him to change his batting style to that of a spray hitter. "How can you, in four years, not say a word and I had all these great years? All of a sudden, I'm up in the major leagues and now you tell me I gotta change my style?" grumbled Sanicki.[38]

"First thing, you know, you're all messed up. You try to get back to your old stance, the newspapers are riding you because you hit 33 home runs the year before and now you got about seven and the season's half-finished. So, I had a terrible year."[39]

The new right fielder was batting only .188 in late May and was even benched for a game or two in a couple of series. But Sanicki responded by raising his mark to .232 by the end of June. In a 10-game span at the end of the month, he batted .440 (11-for-25) and was being looked at as a call-up to aid the Phillies' pennant chances.[40]

In mid-July Sanicki was summoned to manager Jack Sanford's compartment on the train ride to Rochester. "Eddie, the Phillies are fighting for the pennant," said Sanford. "After we get through with this Rochester series, you'll be joining the Phillies as a defensive outfielder relieving [Dick] Sisler in late innings."[41] The next day, Sanicki attempted to make a running, diving catch and twisted his right knee. He was carried off the field by his teammates and later found out he had torn ligaments in his knee. The date was July 18, his fifth wedding anniversary.

Sanicki missed five weeks and returned as a pinch-hitter to Toronto on August 23. He joined the starting lineup a week later, just as his most disappointing season was coming to an end. His batting mark of .211 was his lowest ever, as was his .676 OPS. His 10 home runs and 42 RBIs were also career lows. "Last year, I was confident when I went to bat with men on base," said Sanicki after the season. "This year, I wasn't confident, and I couldn't drive them in."[42]

The Phillies, coined the Whiz Kids, appeared in the World Series that year for the first time since 1915 but were swept in four games by the New York Yankees.

Before the 1951 campaign, Sanicki was assigned to Philadelphia's new Triple-A team, the Baltimore Orioles. At the end of March, Sanicki was called up to the Phillies and started the regular season as an extra outfielder. He played sparingly, appearing as a pinch-runner five times, a pinch-hitter once, and a defensive replacement seven times. In 13 games, he batted .500 (2-for-4) and had one double and one RBI. His last major-league at-bat came on May 12, when he struck out against Giants pitcher Monty Kennedy.

After the series, on the train ride to St. Louis, Sanicki was given the news that he was going to be sent down. Not to Triple-A Baltimore, but to Single-A Schenectady in the Eastern League. "They brought me all the way into St. Louis to tell me the next day that I was leaving," said Sanicki later. "And I was going to 'A' ball, which is sort of a slap in the face, too."[43]

The highlight of Sanicki's 1951 season came on July 22, in the first game of a doubleheader at Albany. With his team trailing 11-2, Sanicki led off the top of the ninth with a home run against Hugh Mulcahy. The Blue Jays batted around and Sanicki came up with two runners on and smashed another homer over the left-field wall off reliever Bill Emmerich. The rally fell just short as Albany squeaked out an 11-10 victory. The game came three days after the birth of Sanicki's daughter Patricia. When asked how it felt to hit the home runs, Sanicki said, "Great." He added, "Don't forget, those homers were for my new daughter and her mom. I'm going to get a couple more for her, too."[44]

He hit five more round-trippers over the last few weeks of the season and despite missing two dozen games, he finished third in the league with 20 homers.

In December Cincinnati Reds affiliate Tulsa selected Sanicki in the annual minor-league draft.[45] Club President Grayle Howlett was high on Sanicki, making the former Phil his number-one draft choice in the draft.[46]

Sanicki began the 1952 season on a .344 (21-for-61) clip for the month of April. Things went downhill after that, however, and when he was sold to the league rival Houston Buffaloes in mid-June, he was batting .232 with 2 home runs and 20 RBIs in 56 games. He didn't fare much better in Houston, batting .241 in 286 at-bats over 90 games, with 7 homers and 28 RBIs. Those at-bats were the last of his Organized Baseball career. Sanicki hit 160 home runs during his seven-year stint in the minors, plus three in the major leagues.

In the summer of 1952, Sanicki sent his family back home to New Jersey because of the polio epidemic sweeping through Texas and other parts of the United States. That winter, Sanicki and his wife talked about the future, one in which a return to Texas was likely. Sanicki recalled his wife, Ann, saying, "Well, if you go down there again, our marriage is gonna be … kinda risky." She suggested he return to Seton Hall and earn his education degree, which Sanicki did, graduating in 1953.[47]

Sanicki taught special-education classes in his hometown of Clifton and was named Educator of the Year in his school system in 1974. He also coached the Clifton baseball team for five years in the 1960s. Sanicki retired from teaching in 1985.

In 1995 the city of Clifton dedicated the baseball field at Albion Memorial Park to Sanicki. At the ceremony, he received letters of congratulation from the Phillies, the National League, New Jersey Governor Christine Todd Whitman, and President Bill Clinton.[48]

Sanicki died three years later from prostate cancer, on July 6, 1998, just one day short of his 75th birthday. After services at St. Ambrose Roman Catholic Church in Old Bridge, New Jersey, he was buried in Holy Cross Burial Park, South Brunswick, New

Jersey. He was survived by his wife, Ann, two sons (Edward and Robert), two daughters (Patricia and Sandra), six grandchildren, and one great-grandchild.

SOURCES

In addition to the sources credited in the Notes, the author consulted Baseball-Reference.com and Retrosheet.org for background information on players, teams, and seasons.

NOTES

1   Dennis Snelling, *A Glimpse of Fame: Brilliant but Fleeting Major League Careers* (Jefferson, North Carolina: McFarland & Company, Inc., 1993), 23.

2   Snelling, 23.

3   US Census Bureau, 1920 US Census.

4   Ancestry.com.

5   Snelling, 21.

6   Snelling, 21.

7   Snelling, 21.

8   Snelling, 22.

9   Art McMahon, "The Sportsman's Corner," *Passaic* (New Jersey) *Herald-News,* May 27, 1942: 22.

10 Joe Gootter, "Sportograms," *Paterson* (New Jersey) *News,* June 17, 1942: 19.

11 Krehel-Sanicki wedding announcement, *Paterson News,* July 17, 1945: 13.

12 "Eddie Sanicki, Local Outfielder to Sign Contract With Phillies," *Paterson News,* December 26, 1945: 20.

13 Marty Levin, "Saltzgaver Selects Rock Team to Oppose Binghamton," *Wilmington* (Delaware) *Morning News,* April 26, 1946: 30.

14 Marty Levin, "Blue Rocks Register 6-3 Victory Over Binghamton," *Wilmington Morning News,* April 29, 1946: 14.

15 "Rocks Crush Roses, 17-1, in Opener Before 4,106," *York* (Pennsylvania) *Dispatch,* May 2, 1946: 1.

16 "Tigers Nip Wilmington, 1-0, on Mullin's Single," *Detroit Free Press,* June 7, 1946: 22.

17 "Phils' Farm Club Stars to Mean Pennant Team in Year or Two, Owner Says," *Wilmington News Journal,* June 18, 1946: 18.

18 "Wilmington Team Places Six Men In All-Star Crew," *Lancaster* (Pennsylvania) *Intelligencer Journal,* September 6, 1946: 29.

19 "Ed Mutryn Is Voted Honor," *Hagerstown* (Maryland) *Morning Herald,* September 11, 1946: 7.

20 "Sanicki Stopped," *Paterson Morning Call,* August 7, 1947: 24.

21 "Ed Sanicki Named," *York Dispatch,* August 19, 1947: 12.

22 "Sanicki to Be Given Chance at Phils' Spring Training Camp," *Passaic Herald-News,* December 4, 1947: 36.

23 Walter Taylor, "Wittig Hurls Five-Hit Game," *Baltimore Sun,* May 15, 1948: 12.

24 "Leafs Win Two; Sanicki Hits 19th," *Paterson Morning Call,* August 13, 1948: 23.

25 "Bloodworth Voted Most Valuable," *Passaic Herald-News,* September 3, 1948: 14.

26 "Toronto Star on Rampage," *Asbury Park* (New Jersey) *Press,* April 30, 1949: 13.

27 "Royals' Morgan Voted MVP in International; Sanicki Sixth," *Passaic Herald-News,* September 2, 1949: 13.

28 "Phils Call Up Hurler, Infielders From Farm," *Arizona Republic* (Phoenix), September 12, 1949: 9.

29 Joe Lovas, "The Sportsman's Corner," *Passaic Herald-News,* September 28, 1949: 27.

30 Lovas, 27.

31 Gayle Talbot (Associated Press), "Phillies Loaded for Flag Chase," *Spokane* (Washington) *Spokesman-Review,* January 8, 1950: 36.

32 "Flock, Cards and Braves Threat to Phils: Sawyer," *New York Daily News,* January 30, 1950: 42.

33 Statistics compiled from box scores in *Philadelphia Inquirer,* March-April 1950.

34 "Dick Sisler's Clouting Edging Out Ed Sanicki," *Passaic Herald-News,* March 29, 1950: 30.

35 "Sawyer Thinks Ed Sanicki Is Game's Best," *Rapid City* (South Dakota) *Journal,* April 26, 1950: 12.

36 Milt Dunnell, "Leafs Show Sign of Being Clutch Club," *Toronto Daily Star,* April 21, 1950: 18.

37 Neil MacCarl, "Ed Sanicki Likes Switch From Centre to Right, Sanford Explains It," *Toronto Daily Star,* April 22, 1950: 16.

38 Snelling, 27.

39 Snelling, 27.

40 "Phils May Call Up Sanicki Soon as Long-Ball Hitting Threat," *Paterson News,* June 24, 1950: 20.

41 Snelling, 27.

42 Milt Dunnell, "Lost Confidence, Sanicki Accepts Blame," *Toronto Daily Star,* September 12, 1950: 10.

43 Snelling, 30-31.

44 Marvin R. Pike, "Two Homers in One Inning, Ed Sanicki's Dynamic Greeting to Newborn Daughter," *Paterson Morning Call,* July 26, 1951: 27.

45 Jack Hand (Associated Press), "66 Players Drafted at Convention of Minor Leagues," *Paterson Morning News,* December 4, 1951: 26.

46 John H. Turner, "Hot Stove Baseball," *Tulsa Daily World,* February 3, 1952: Sports 3.

47 Snelling, 31.

48 Robin Gadsden, Edward Sanicki obituary, *Hackensack* (New Jersey) *Record,* July 9, 1998: L-6.

DON LEPPERT

BY JOHN FREDLAND

Don Leppert signed his first professional contract shortly after his 23rd birthday, scouted on Korean War-era military-service teams in a sport he had not intended to play as a pro. He reached the majors a few months before his 30th birthday, when the defending World Series champion Pittsburgh Pirates sought to strengthen their bench.

He was right on time for a 41-year career as a player, coach, manager, and coordinator. Leppert homered his first time up in the major leagues, hit three home runs in another game, made an American League All-Star team, and coached first base on a World Series winner, while earning esteem as a catcher, brawler, mentor, and outdoorsman.

Donald George Leppert[1] was born on October 19, 1931, at the Indianapolis home of his parents, William and May Leppert.[2] His father worked as a factory machinist and tool and die maker,[3] and his mother sold cosmetics for Avon.[4]

Leppert's love of the outdoors developed during childhood. "My father was a great outdoorsman," he noted in 1972. "I've gone along ever since I was old enough."[5] Later coverage of Leppert's baseball career frequently referenced his outdoor pursuits, including winter goose and deer hunting, ice fishing, and in-season fishing trips.[6]

Leppert graduated from Washington High School on Indianapolis's West Side in 1949.[7] He played baseball for the Continentals and also distinguished himself in football.[8] Leppert was described as Washington's "husky left half" and "chief offensive weapon" in a 1948 loss to West Lafayette High School. West Lafayette's "strong-armed" halfback, Bob Friend, was Leppert's batterymate in his major-league debut 13 years later.[9]

He enrolled at Wabash College, a private, all-male liberal arts college in Crawfordsville, Indiana.[10] The brawny, 6-foot-2 Leppert competed in football and track at Wabash.[11]

"I never had any intention of playing pro baseball," Leppert recalled. "I didn't even go out for baseball in college. I always considered football my best sport and in the spring I was [in javelin and discus] on the track team."[12]

Leppert was a pre-law student at Wabash, but when the Korean War began in June 1950,[13] he enlisted in the Air Force and was sent to Japan as a military policeman.[14]

He played football and threw discus for Air Force teams in Japan.[15] He also got back into baseball, catching for a Nagoya Air Base team that won the Far East Air Force title in 1953. The military newspaper *Stars & Stripes* praised Leppert for his play in the championship game, where he scored the game-winning run.[16]

Don Leppert, Pittsburgh Pirates – Courtesy of Trading Card Database

A spot on the military all-star team that played the New York Giants on their barnstorming tour to Japan after the 1953 season brought about Leppert's opportunity in professional baseball.[17]

"[Leo Durocher] was the [Giants] manager and he, or somebody must have remembered me," Leppert said in 1961. "I came home from the service and intended to go back and finish school, but a Giant scout called me."[18]

Leppert's service in Japan left him two months short of an honorable discharge.[19] He went to Carswell Air Force Base in Fort Worth, Texas, where he played for the base's baseball team, the Carswell Bombers, and drew more attention from professional scouts.[20]

His time as a Bomber included one of the hallmarks of his playing and coaching career: an active role in on-field fights. In a game against Texas Christian University in March 1954, the Horned Frogs' Les Mattison slammed into Leppert at home after they had argued during Mattison's time at bat. As the *Fort Worth Star Telegram* reported, "fists began swinging" between Leppert and Mattison, leading to a bench-clearing brawl.[21]

Six big-league teams pursued Leppert while he was on the Bombers.[22] He signed with the Milwaukee Braves on the day of his military discharge in February 1955.[23] Developing catchers was a Braves' priority; a 1962 *Milwaukee Journal* article listed Leppert among 11 then-active major-league backstops who had been with Milwaukee's organization.[24]

From the earliest days of Leppert's career, Braves leadership heralded his big-league potential. Bob Coleman, a Deadball Era catcher in the 1910s and a major-league manager in the 1940s, was Leppert's first minor-league manager, with the Evansville Braves of the Class-B Illinois-Indiana-Iowa League in 1955. Coleman called Leppert a "cinch to make the major leagues."[25] "I don't know how much he'll hit, but he has power," the manager observed.[26]

A year later in Triple A, Wichita Braves manager George Selkirk, who had played on five World Series champion teams with the New York Yankees, and coach Johnny Riddle, a former major-league catcher, echoed Coleman's forecast.

"Leppert is a long-hitter and has all the earmarks of becoming a major-leaguer," Selkirk said.[27]

But Milwaukee struggled to get Leppert consistent playing time, owing to his relative lack of experience for his age. In 1955 he served as Evansville's backup catcher for the season's first month and a half, before getting reassigned to the Corpus Christi (Texas) Clippers of the Class-B Big State League.[28]

At Triple A in 1956, Leppert played infrequently in the last two months of the season, stuck behind three catchers with broader professional backgrounds.[29] "He has only two years of professional baseball behind him and the wisdom needed for catching maturity doesn't come quick," the *Austin American* summarized in 1957.[30]

Still, Leppert made his abilities apparent. He homered in his second professional plate appearance with Evansville in May 1955 and hit .349 with 3 home runs in 43 at-bats with the team.[31]

His playing time increased at Corpus Christi, where the Clippers won the Little Dixie Series by sweeping the West Texas-New Mexico League champs, the Pampa Oilers, in four games.[32] Leppert hit a grand slam in Game Three of the Little Dixie Series and drove in the go-ahead run in Game Four.[33] He hit .239 with 10 home runs in 58 games with Corpus Christi.

Even while buried on Wichita's depth chart in 1956, Leppert showed potential. He hit a 400-foot home run in the second-ever game at Minnesota's Metropolitan Stadium.[34] On a visit to his hometown of Indianapolis, Leppert caught Joey Jay's two-hit shutout, tagged out Roger Maris at home, and drove in the game's only run with a sacrifice fly.[35]

During the 1956-57 offseason, Leppert played for the Mexico City Aztecas in the Winter Veracruz League,[36] but his season ended early when he was hit in the face by a foul ball, fracturing his cheekbone.[37] Nevertheless, it was the first of many winters he spent in Latin American leagues as a player, coach, and manager.[38]

Leppert went down a classification in 1957, to the Double-A Texas League's Austin Senators. He won the Senators' starting catching job in spring training.[39]

"I'm gambling on Leppert's hitting because hitting and the long ball are what we need," manager Sibby Sisti, a 13-season big-league player, said in April 1957.[40]

Leppert validated Sisti's judgment. He led the '57 Senators with 20 home runs, despite chronic injuries. His right hand was frequently battered by foul tips.[41] A knee injury resulted in an offseason knee operation in Indianapolis.

"The knee was in a mess but the doctor and those nurses had me up and walking down the hallway in four hours," Leppert recalled in March 1958.[42]

However swift his treatment was, Leppert did stay in the hospital long enough to meet 20-year-old Daphine Hope, a Kentucky native who worked there.[43] Their courtship moved quickly during the 1957-58 offseason, and Don and Daphine were married in Austin, Texas, on April 9.[44]

Leppert's toils as a catcher often led to a trainer's table or doctor's office or involved enduring physical pain on the field.[45] Most frequent were injuries to his hands. Newspapers reported Leppert being sidelined or impaired by hand, finger, or thumb injuries in nine of his 12 professional seasons.[46]

His hand troubles were most persistent in 1958, his second year in Austin.[47] "[T]he bad thumb on his left hand keeps getting bruised and he's an uncertainty at the plate because he can't swing the bat with authority as bruised as his hands are," the *Austin American* reported.[48] Leppert was batting .319 on May 11,[49] but injuries dragged his final average to .229.[50]

After the 1958 season, on November 10, Don and Daphine's first son, Steve, was born. They had four more children: Kimberly (born in 1960),[51] Mike (1961),[52] Joe (1964),[53] and Tim (1970).[54] Steve Leppert played in the Cincinnati Reds system for three seasons in the 1980s.

Around the time that Leppert became a father, he considered moving on from baseball.[55] A February 1959 article in the *Paducah* (Kentucky) *Sun-Democrat* indicated that a conversation with Braves farm director John Mullen had convinced him to stick with his career.[56]

But his time in Milwaukee's organization was almost up. Leppert went to spring training with the Braves' Triple-A club in 1959 before getting reassigned to Austin.[57] The Senators then sold him to the Dallas Rangers, an unaffiliated expansion club in the American Association.[58] He was no longer property of the Braves, but he was back in Triple A.

Leppert remained relatively healthy in 1959 and caught 119 games, his most of any professional season.[59] His .271 overall batting average was his highest yet.

The National and American Leagues' attempt to block a potential rival league, the Continental League, from the Dallas-Fort Worth area led to both cities jointly operating an American Association club in 1960.[60] The rebranded Dallas-Fort Worth Rangers were affiliated with the Kansas City Athletics, and they owned 17 of the '59 Rangers outright, including Leppert.[61]

On a team managed by former big-league catcher Jim Fanning – Leppert's manager in Venezuela during the 1959-60 offseason – Leppert was again the primary catcher. His 17 home runs topped the Rangers and his 63 RBIs were second on the team.

Less than a year from his 30th birthday and now with two children, Leppert weighed options outside of baseball.[62] But a December 1960 transaction turned out to be his breakthrough. The Triple-A International League's Columbus Jets, a Pittsburgh Pirates affiliate, acquired him in a minor-league deal with the Rangers.[63] Two months earlier, Pittsburgh had won its first World Series since 1925.

As with John Mullen before the 1959 season, mentoring from a baseball executive helped to persuade Leppert to continue in the game. This time, his mentor was Pirates general manager Joe L. Brown.

In a June 1961 interview, Leppert recounted Brown's advice from spring training: "With expansion as it is now and with maybe even more in the future, baseball offers more and more opportunities, not only for more players, but with more clubs they're going to need more managers, coaches, scouts, and front-office people."[64]

A game out of first place on May 24, the '61 Pirates lost 11 of their next 16 and sank to fourth.[65] The club's pinch-hitting and backup catching struggled.[66] In Columbus, Leppert was leading the league in batting average at .386.[67] League managers chose him unanimously for the league's all-star game, scheduled for late June.[68]

By then, however, Leppert no longer was at Triple A. Brown remade the Pirates' bench at the June 15 trading deadline, and Leppert's contract was purchased.[69]

On June 18 Leppert was catching and batting seventh in the opener of a Sunday doubleheader with the St. Louis Cardinals at Forbes Field, in a battery with veteran right-hander Friend, his high-school football foe from Indiana. Of the 112 players to debut in the majors in 1961, Leppert was fourth oldest.[70]

Leppert made his first trip to a big-league batter's box with one out in the second. Five pitches passed without a swing, and the count was full.[71] Lefty Curt Simmons, a 14-year veteran, threw a curveball, and Leppert drove it into Forbes Field's left-field light tower.[72] He was the 32nd player in NL or AL history to homer in his first major-league at-bat.[73]

Leppert remained in the majors for the rest of the 1961 season, recording a .267 average and three homers in 22 games. In 1962 he made a major-league Opening Day roster for the first time, backing up Smoky Burgess. Leppert played in 45 games in 1962, hitting .266 with three home runs. On April 24, his two-run, opposite-field homer against emerging San Francisco Giants star Juan Marichal put the Pirates ahead to stay in a 7-3 win.[74]

An enduring thread in Leppert's minor-league days was his involvement in baseball brawls, dating to 1955, when a local newspaper documented him as "leading the combatants" after a fight broke out in a Big State League game in 1955.[75] His reputation as an enforcer continued to grow in the majors.

After a 1961 Pirates-Philadelphia Phillies skirmish, teammate Harvey Haddix recounted, "That Leppert was all over the place. He came out and was trying to pry someone apart when he got hit. Then he just went swinging at every white uniform within range."[76]

The Pirates traded Leppert to the Senators for a minor-league pitcher and cash in December 1962,[77] reuniting him with Selkirk, who had become Washington's general manager.[78] In the 1963 season's third game, on April 11, the Senators faced Boston Red Sox righty Ike Delock at Washington's D.C. Stadium. Leppert, using a 31-ounce bat – three ounces lighter than his regular model because of a shipping mistake[79] – drove a Delock fastball into the second deck in left field for a solo home run in the fourth inning.

He added a three-run blast off lefty Chet Nichols in the sixth and a 410-foot solo homer against Nichols in the eighth. It was the first three-homer game for the Senators, in their third season as an expansion franchise. Leppert also caught starter Tom Cheney's one-hit, one-walk, 10-strikeout shutout that night.[80]

Through mid-May, Leppert started a majority of the Senators' games. He homered off Detroit Tigers lefty Hank Aguirre on May 1.[81] The next time the Senators faced the Tigers, on May 18, Leppert hit another home run against Aguirre, giving him five for the season. An inning later, Aguirre hit Leppert on the elbow with a pitch, and he missed the next 11 games.[82] Dragged down by injuries, Leppert batted only .207 after May 18, with just one more home run.

In the meantime, Leppert achieved an unexpected distinction. Yankees manager Ralph Houk was picking the reserves for the AL All-Star team. Houk had to select an All-Star from the Senators, who were headed for 106 losses and the worst record in the AL, and he wanted a third catcher. He chose Leppert for the July 9 game in Cleveland.[83]

With the AL trailing the NL by two runs in the ninth, Leppert was on deck to hit for New York's Tom Tresh, but Bobby Richardson grounded into a game-ending double play, and Leppert did not get to bat.[84]

Another injury sidetracked Leppert's 1964 from the start. Three days before Opening Day, he broke his right thumb catching batting practice.[85] He hit .156 in 50 games while rookie Mike Brumley took over Washington's starting job. Leppert's season highlight was a home run off Hall of Fame-bound Whitey Ford on July 10 at D.C. Stadium, denying Ford a shutout.[86]

Leppert spent 1965 in the Triple-A Pacific Coast League with the Hawaii Islanders. The Islanders played in Honolulu Stadium. Only two players had ever hit home runs over the left-field bleachers: one in a local league in the 1930s, and Joe DiMaggio twice for a military service team in 1944.[87] In April 1965, Leppert became the third player – and the first in a professional game – to clear the left-field bleachers, against Paul Lindblad of the Vancouver Mounties.[88]

Still, Leppert's time as a big-leaguer appeared to have passed. Newspapers rumored that he was considering playing in Japan.[89] He again contemplated leaving baseball entirely. "I was the night terminal manager for Greyhound in my hometown of Indianapolis, and the job seemed to have a good future," he said in 1980.[90]

His doorway to major-league coaching was the same for his big-league playing career: the Pittsburgh Pirates. Larry Shepard, Columbus's manager when Leppert played there in 1961, still piloted Pittsburgh's Triple-A club. He contacted Leppert and offered a leadership role as a player-coach. Leppert accepted the opportunity, and Columbus purchased him in November 1965.[91]

Leppert concluded his playing career with a .229 batting average in 66 games with the '66 Jets. More relevant for his base-ball future were his coaching duties in Columbus.[92] The Pirates and Braves contacted Leppert about managing in the minors in 1967,[93] and he accepted an offer for Pittsburgh's Gastonia (North Carolina) club in the Class-A Western Carolinas League. Gastonia came in at 61-59, second in the league but 17½ games behind the first-place Spartanburg Phillies.

On October 13, Shepard, who had served as the Philadelphia Phillies' pitching coach in 1967, was hired as Pittsburgh's man-ager.[94] Four days later, Leppert returned to the majors when Shepard added him to the coaching staff.[95]

The move was the beginning of a long tenure in Pittsburgh for Leppert. He remained on the coaching staff when Shepard was fired and replaced by Danny Murtaugh after the 1969 season.[96] When Murtaugh retired, Bill Virdon was hired after Pittsburgh won the 1971 World Series.[97] Then the Pirates fired Virdon and brought back Murtaugh during their unsuccessful bid to win the NL East Division in 1973.[98] Leppert stayed on the staff during all the managerial changes.

Leppert coached in the bullpen in 1968 and 1969, then he was moved to first base from 1970 through 1973. He returned to the bullpen from 1974 through 1976.[99] He made headlines in Game Four of the 1971 World Series because of his animated argument with the umpires, who had ruled Roberto Clemente's deep drive to right a foul ball instead of a home run.[100]

Leppert's reputation for developing young catchers began to grow with the Pirates. In 1969, 25-year-old Manny Sanguillén won Pittsburgh's starting job in his first full major-league season. Sanguillén, who praised Leppert's coaching, served as the Pirates' primary backstop through 1976.[101] Three young catchers whom Leppert coached with the Toronto Blue Jays – Alan Ashby, Rick Cerone, and Ernie Whitt – went on to catch more than 1,200 games in the majors apiece.[102] Leppert's approach included tracking pitchers' and catchers' release times, measured to hun-dredths of a second, in order to counter stolen-base attempts.[103]

Becoming a coach did not end Leppert's days of on-field fights. A 1973 *Pittsburgh Press* article discussing "tough" athletes highlighted Leppert, "the 6-[foot]-1, 215-pounder [who] has biceps that bulge when his arms are at his side even though he is 41-years-old."[104]

"I don't know of any fights that Leppert has started," Virdon added. "[B]ut he has ended quite a few."[105]

Leppert was heavily involved in a heated Pirates-Reds encounter in July 1974. He kicked Cincinnati's Darrel Chaney hard enough to tear the Reds infielder's uniform pants, then got wrestled to the ground and punched by Chaney. Later in the scuffle, Leppert's tight grip on César Gerónimo led manager Sparky Anderson to plead for him to release Gerónimo.[106]

Even after his 50th birthday, Leppert was active in fights, delivering what the *Houston Post* labeled a "haymaker" to Derrel Thomas in a June 1983 Astros-Dodgers bench-clearing brawl. He also accused the Giants' Dusty Baker of giving him a "cheap shot" in an August 1984 skirmish.[107]

While with the Pirates, Leppert managed winter ball teams in Venezuela.[108] Newspapers occasionally suggested him as a future Pirates manager.[109] Soon after the 1976 season ended and Murtaugh retired, however, the Pirates informed Leppert that he was "no longer under consideration [for manager and was] free to go ahead and try to get a job with someone else."[110]

He had a new job within days. The Blue Jays, preparing for their inaugural season as an AL expansion franchise, added him to manager Roy Hartsfield's staff as a bullpen coach and catching instructor.[111]

Leppert also temporarily took on another duty in Toronto – umpiring. On August 25, 1978, AL and NL umpires went on strike. The Blue Jays were hosting the Twins that afternoon, and Toronto's management found three local amateur umpires to officiate the game. One of the amateur umpires, however, did not make it to Exhibition Stadium in time for the first pitch.

When the game began, the umpiring crew included the two amateur umpires, alongside Leppert at second base and Twins coach Jerry Zimmerman at third. After the first inning, which passed without incident, the third amateur umpire arrived, and the game continued with a three-man crew. Leppert and Zimmerman went back to their coaching duties.[112]

Leppert was in Toronto for three seasons. The Blue Jays fired Hartsfield on the final day of the 1979 schedule, Toronto's third straight year with at least 102 losses.[113]

As in 1976, Leppert was on to his next job before the World Series ended. Virdon had managed the Astros since September 1975, and Houston had come in second to the Reds in the NL West in 1979. Leppert joined the Astros' coaching staff that October.[114]

Under Virdon, Leppert served as a third-base coach for the first time in his career.[115] Virdon managed in Houston until August 1982, when the Astros fired him and promoted Bob Lillis from their coaching staff. Leppert, again surviving a managerial firing, moved to first-base coach in 1984.

Leppert remained with the Astros until Houston reshuffled its coaches in June 1985. The Astros added a second pitching coach, which put them at the major-league limit of five coaches.[116] The organization reassigned Leppert to a minor-league position, but Leppert spoke critically to a local newspaper.

"The Astros want everyone to be a gentleman, to look nice on the airplanes, to have no beer on the (team) bus," Leppert told a *Houston Post* columnist. "Sometimes I think they believe that's more important than winning games. They want to make it a Sunday school church game."[117]

After the remarks, the Astros immediately terminated Leppert's employment.[118] For the first time in more than 30 years, he was away from professional baseball that summer.

Bob Lee, general manager of the Kenosha Twins, Minnesota's Class-A Midwest League affiliate, had pitched for Corpus Christi in 1955. Lee returned home to Wisconsin after professional baseball and founded a plumbing business.[119] He called on Leppert, his batterymate in his professional debut,[120] to manage Kenosha in 1986.

"I was looking forward to fishing a lot this summer," Leppert said. "Then Bob Lee called me and wanted me to manage his team in Kenosha. I told him no, but he kept telling me how great it would be and how good the fishing is around here and finally I agreed."[121]

In Leppert's first season in Kenosha, the Twins' 46-92 record was the worst in the 12-team league. He returned in 1987, and the Twins improved to 82-58, 11 games ahead of the second-place team in the Midwest League's North Division. The Springfield Cardinals' 94 wins topped the league during the regular season, but the Twins beat them, three games to one, to take the championship series.[122] Leppert was named Midwest League Manager of the Year.[123]

After the 1987 season, the Twins moved Leppert to their minor-league field coordinator position.[124] Catcher Damian Miller, who played in nearly 1,000 major-league games with five franchises, credited a 1991 conversation with Leppert with encouraging him to stick with professional baseball.[125]

Leppert became Minnesota's Florida operations coordinator in 1993.[126] He retired from the game after the 1996 season.[127]

In 2003 Leppert was inducted into the Indiana Baseball Hall of Fame.[128] He and Daphine lived in Florida during their retirement years.[129] Don Leppert died at age 91 on April 13, 2023, four days after their 65th wedding anniversary.

He left a record of 190 appearances in big-league box scores and several marks on the game's lore, a testament to his own perseverance and confirmation of the judgment of baseball lifers like Coleman, Selkirk, Riddle, and Sisti. Joe L. Brown's advice on baseball's future also was prescient, as Leppert played for one expansion club and coached for two others.

Leppert became a lifer himself, contributing his experiences, passion, and teaching skills to generations of ballplayers, from Manny Sanguillén to Damian Miller.

The game he did not initially seek to play professionally brought decades of joy.

"I used to get a thrill just watching Roberto Clemente play for the Pirates," Leppert recalled. "It was thrilling every time [Hall of Fame Pittsburgh second baseman] Bill Mazeroski turned a double play. It's thrilling to watch [Astros' strikeout king] J.R. Richard pitch when he is so awesome. Those things make my heart pump."[130]

ACKNOWLEDGMENTS

SABR members Gary Belleville and Kurt Blumenau provided insightful comments on an earlier draft version. The author thanks Don Leppert's daughter, Kimberly Leppert Rosenberg, for sharing her memories in a phone conversation in May 2024.

SOURCES

In addition to the sources cited in the Notes, the author relied on Baseball-Reference.com and Retrosheet.org.

NOTES

1   Leppert was no relation to Donald Eugene Leppert, an infielder with the 1955 Baltimore Orioles.

2   Certificate of Birth, Donald George Leppert, Indiana State Board of Health.

3   "William Leppert," *Indianapolis News*, October 21, 1960: 9.

4   "Mrs. Leppert Dies; Mother of Coach," *Indianapolis Star*, May 30, 1972: 14.

5   Bill Williams, "The Outdoorsman," *Bradenton* (Florida) *Herald*, March 2, 1972: 6-B.

6   Williams, "The Outdoorsman"; Jim Peterson, "Day Off? Senators' King, Leppert Tackle Tonka Pike," *Minneapolis Star Tribune*, August 29, 1964: 11; Jimmy Jordan, "Field and Forest," *Pittsburgh Post-Gazette*, December 10, 1971: 20.

7   "Leppert is the only senior and only [returning] letterman [for Washington], but he leans into a delivery with zest," reported the *Indianapolis News* on the Continentals' appearance in the 1949 city tournament. Angelo Angelopolous, "Scouts Scan Tourney for 'Bonus' Players," *Indianapolis News*, May 3, 1949: 24.

8   "Scouts Scan Tourney for 'Bonus' Players."

9   "Scarlets Take to Air to Down Washington, 14-6," *Lafayette* (Indiana) *Journal and Courier*, September 18, 1948: 7.

10 Andy Kent, "Lep's a Handy Guy to Have Around: Former Catcher Don Leppert of Naples Has Experienced Almost Everything on a Baseball Field – And He Has the Hands to Prove It," *Naples* (Florida) *Daily News*, March 16, 2003: 1C.

11 "Sycamores' Frosh Whip Wabash in Dual Track Meet," *Terre Haute* (Indiana) *Star*, April 28, 1950: 30; Paul Horning, "'Expansion' Is Key Word in Don Leppert's Career," *Columbus Dispatch*, May 30, 1961: 5B.

12 "'Expansion' Is Key Word in Don Leppert's Career."

13 Kent, "Lep's a Handy Guy to Have Around."

14 Horning, "'Expansion' Is Key Word in Don Leppert's Career"; Kent, "Lep's a Handy Guy to Have Around."

15 Cpl Tino Venzor, "Russell's Three Victories Spark AF Japan Track," *Pacific Stars & Stripes*, June 21, 1952: 13; "Itazuke Uses Field Goal to Defeat Brady; Keeps Undefeated Record," *Pacific Stars & Stripes*, November 3, 1952: 14.

16 PFC Lou Welt, "Nagoya Cops AF Baseball Title With 9 to 8 Win Over Johnson," *Pacific Stars & Stripes*, September 9, 1953: 13.

17 Horning, "'Expansion' Is Key Word in Don Leppert's Career."

18 "'Expansion' Is Key Word in Don Leppert's Career."

19 Kent, "Lep's a Handy Guy to Have Around."

20 "Lep's a Handy Guy to Have Around"; The New York Yankees, New York Giants, Cleveland Indians, Chicago Cubs, and St. Louis Cardinals were also interested in signing Leppert. United Press, "Indianapolis Recruit Is Snared by Braves," *Terre Haute* (Indiana) *Tribune*, February 9, 1955: 11.

21 Burnie Key, "Frogs Stave Off Carswell by 4-3," *Fort Worth Star Telegram*, March 17, 1954: 15.

22 United Press, "Indianapolis Recruit Is Snared by Braves."

23 "Indianapolis Recruit Is Snared by Braves."

24 Cleon Walfoort, "Catchers Are Prize Catch," *Milwaukee Journal*, June 10, 1962: Sports News, 3.

25 Daniel W. Scism, "Sew It Seams," *Evansville* (Indiana) *Courier*, May 5, 1955: 27.

26 Dick Anderson, "Coleman Hopes Don Leppert Will Be Another Crandall," *Evansville* (Indiana) *Press*, April 15, 1955: 18.

27 Bill Hodge, "Rookie Catcher Catches Eye of Wichita Braves Manager: Leppert Vies With Two Vets," *Wichita Eagle*, March 21, 1956: 7C.

28 "Sew It Seams," *Evansville* (Indiana) *Courier*, April 26, 1956: 31.

29 Wichita's other catchers in 1956 were Charlie White, Billy Queen, and Bob Roselli. Pete Lightner, "Braves Seek Season Split With Omaha," *Wichita Eagle*, September 5, 1956: 10A; Pete Lightner, "The Morning After," *Wichita Eagle*, October 14, 1956: 2B.

30 Lou Maysel, "Top O' Morn," *Austin American*, April 10, 1957: 20.

31 Daniel W. Scism, "Rehm Fires Six-Hitter as Evansville Defeats Raiders, 6-2: Leppert Keeps Braves' Homer Streak Moving," *Evansville* (Indiana) *Courier*, May 4, 1955: 26.

32 Stan Hochman, "Clippers Rip Pampa 8-2, to End Series: Take Little Dixie Title on 11th Straight Win," *Corpus Christi* (Texas) *Caller*, September 26, 1955: 1B.

33 Joe Scherrer, "Clippers Rout Pampa, 14-4, for 2-0 Lead," *Corpus Christi Caller*, September 22, 1955: 3B; Hochman, "Clippers Rip Pampa 8-2, to End Series."

34 Bill Hodge, "Braves Lose 9-8 in 10th: Stanky Finally Wins Point as Umpire Waves in Marker," *Wichita Eagle*, April 26, 1956: 6B.

35 Bill Hodge, "Jay, Leppert Lauded for Play by Selkirk," *Wichita Beacon*, July 23, 1956: 8A; Max Greenwald, "Tribe Streak Ends on 1-0 Job by Jay," *Indianapolis Star*, July 24, 1956: 23.

36 Pete Lightner, "The Morning After," *Wichita Eagle*, November 16, 1956: 3C.

37 Pete Lightner, "The Morning After," *Wichita Eagle*, January 22, 1957: 3C.

38 Merrell Whittlesey, "Leppert Packs Wicked Wallop," *Washington Evening Star*, February 21, 1963: D-4; "Pirates Name Oceak, Osborn New Coaches: Leppert, Virdon Back; Grammas Gets Job Elsewhere," *Pittsburgh Press*, October 12, 1969: 4, 5; Milt Dunnell, "This Jays Coach Keeps His Cool," *Toronto Star*, March 2, 1977: C1.

39 "Ted Laguna Bound for Atlanta Team," *Austin American*, April 9, 1958: 21.

40 Lou Maysel, "Top O' Morn," *Austin American*, April 10, 1957: 20.

41 Lou Maysel, "Top O' Morn," *Austin American*, July 21, 1957: C-8.

42 Charley Eskew, "Big Season Due Leppert," *Austin American*, March 22, 1958: 12.

43 Phone interview with Kimberly Leppert Rosenberg, May 28, 2024.

44 State of Texas Marriage License, No. 519, recorded April 10, 1958, accessed May 18, 2024, https://www.ancestry.com/discoveryui-content/view/40714957:9168.

45 James Elkins, "Braves' Don Leppert Lives at Elk City," *Paducah* (Kentucky) *Sun-Democrat*, February 23, 1959: 8; "Surgery Set for Leppert," *Pittsburgh Post-Gazette*, February 1, 1962: 27; Russ White, "Will Leppert Change His Spots?" *Washington Daily News*, July 9. 1963: 35; Lester J. Biederman, "Leppert Willing to Catch a Leftover Job," *Pittsburgh Press*, March 10, 1965: 57.

46 Leppert had hand, finger, or thumb injuries in 1957, 1958, 1959, 1960, 1961, 1962, 1964, 1965, and 1966. Maysel, "Top O' Morn," *Austin American*, July 21, 1957; Lou Maysel, "Late Austin Rally Dumps Padres, 4-2," *Austin American*, May 21, 1958: A16; Elkins, "Braves' Don Leppert Lives at Elk City"; "Rangers Bow to Weather," *Dallas Morning News*, June 24, 1959, 2,1; "Rangers' Jablonski Gets Recall from Kansas City," *Fort Worth Star-Telegram*, August 2, 1960: Lester J. Biederman, "First World Series Still Stands as Top Thrill in Musial's Career," *Pittsburgh Press*, September 18, 1961: 27; Lester J. Biederman, "Francis Draws Acclaim in Tough Loss to Dodgers: Durocher Awed by Pirate Hurler; Murtaugh Happy Despite Defeat," *Pittsburgh Press*, April 30, 1962: 31; Associated Press, "Senators' Leppert Fractures Thumb," *Minneapolis Star-Tribune*, April 11, 1964: 15; United Press International, "Don Leppert Injures Finger," *Honolulu Advertiser*, May 17, 1965: B-7; Eddie Fisher, "Roberts Likes Hen Pitching," *Columbus Dispatch*, July 7, 1966: 16A.

47 Elkins, "Braves' Don Leppert Lives at Elk City."

48 Lou Maysel, "Top O' Morn," *Austin American*, June 5, 1958: 19.

49 "Senatorial Record," *Austin Statesman*, May 13, 1958: 19.

50 Elkins, "Braves' Don Leppert Lives at Elk City."

51 Phone interview with Kimberly Leppert Rosenberg, May 28, 2024.

52 "Memorial Hospital Notes," *Edinburg* (Indiana) *Courier*, October 21, 1961: 1.

53 "Memorial Hospital Notes," *Franklin* (Indiana) *Evening Star*, July 20, 1964: 2.

54 "Daily Vital Statistics," *Indianapolis News*, November 12, 1970: 44.

55 Elkins, "Braves' Don Leppert Lives at Elk City."

56 Elkins, "Braves' Don Leppert Lives at Elk City."

57 Charley Eskew, "Sens Get Don Leppert for Outfield Work," *Austin American*, April 8, 1959: 23.

58 "Rangers Buy Don Leppert," *Dallas Morning News*, April 20, 1959: Section 2, 3.

59 Leppert missed a few games in June with hand and back injuries. "Rangers Bow to Weather," *Dallas Morning News*, June 24, 1959: Section 2, 1.

60 Bill Van Fleet, "Cities to Unite in Association Ball," *Fort Worth Star-Telegram*, January 17, 1960: Section 2, 1.

61 Van Fleet, "Cities to Unite in Association Ball."

62 Horning, "'Expansion' Is Key Word in Don Leppert's Career."

63 The trade sent Tom Burgess, Chick King, and Ken Toothman to Dallas for Leppert. Jack Hernon, "Roamin' Around," *Pittsburgh Post-Gazette*, March 14, 1961: 24.

64 Horning, "'Expansion' Is Key Word in Don Leppert's Career."

65 Lester J. Biederman, "Pirates Get Logan, Moryn and Leppert for Better Bench: Cimoli, Oldis Take Departure Hard After Whirl with Championship Team," *Pittsburgh Press*, June 16, 1961: 31.

66 Through June 15, Pirates pinch-hitters had only 7 hits in 45 at-bats, a .156 average. Backup catcher Hal Smith, a lifetime .279 hitter with a key home run in Game Seven of the 1960 World Series, was batting just .202. Third-string backstop Bob Oldis, regarded as an outstanding defender, had appeared in only four games.

67 Earl Flora, "Jets Blast off with Power Win," *Columbus Dispatch*, April 20, 1961: 19A; Eddie Fisher, "Shepard Tabs Francis as League's Best Righty," *Columbus Dispatch*, June 2, 1961: 25B; Eddie Fisher, "Jets Well Off, Avers Cooper," *Columbus Dispatch*, June 18, 1961: 37B.

68 Fisher, "Jets Well Off, Avers Cooper."

69 "Pirates Land Logan, Moryn in Shuffle: Cimoli Traded, Waivers Asked on Gene Baker," *Pittsburgh Post-Gazette*, June 16, 1961: 18. The Pirates sent third-string catcher Oldis to Columbus, traded outfielder Gino Cimoli to the Braves for shortstop Johnny Logan, purchased outfielder Walt Moryn from the Cardinals, and released infielder Gene Baker.

70 Leppert was 29 years, 242 days old on the day of his debut. The only older rookies that season were pitcher Chi-Chi Olivo of the Braves (35 years, 79 days), briefly Leppert's minor-league teammate in 1958 and 1959; catcher Mike Roarke of the Detroit Tigers (30 years, 162 days), whose time in the Braves' organization had overlapped Leppert's; and outfielder Bobby Prescott of the Athletics (30 years, 82 days).

71 United Press International, "Bucs to Look at Potential Mound Toiler," *Simpson's Leader Times* (Kittanning, Pennsylvania), June 19, 1961: 13.

72 United Press International, "Bucs to Look at Potential Mound Toiler"; Lester J. Biederman, "Hoak Injury Adds to Pirate Woes: Top Hitter Hurts Eye as Card Split Keeps Bucs on Treadmill," *Pittsburgh Press*, June 19, 1961: 23.

73 Ed Eagle, "Players with Home Run in First At-Bat," MLB.com, September 1, 2023, https://www.mlb.com/news/home-run-in-first-at-bat-c265623820.

74 Will Doerge, "Friend Seeks Fourth Straight Win: Al McBean Muzzles Giants, 7-3; Pirates Lead by 3 Games," *Pittsburgh Press*, April 25, 1962: 54.

75 Stan Hochman, "Vega Wins No. 25, Inspires Fist Fight," *Corpus Christi* (Texas) *Caller*, August 6, 1955: 4B.

76 Jack Hernon, "Roamin' Around," *Pittsburgh Post-Gazette*, August 10, 1961: 29.

77 Merrell Whittlesey, "Senators Purchase Leppert from Bucs," *Washington Evening Star*, December 16, 1962: C-1; "Catcher Leppert Dealt to Senators for Pitcher, Cash," *Pittsburgh Press*, December 15, 1962: 7.

78 Whittlesey, "Senators Purchase Leppert from Bucs."

79 Herb Ralby, "Cheney's Win 3d Over Red Sox," *Boston Globe*, April 12, 1963: 29.

80 Russ White, "Senators Get Charge From Hot Battery," *Washington Daily News*, April 12, 1963: 42.

81 Merrell Whittlesey, "Cheney's Great Getaway Best in Memory for Coach," *Washington Evening Star*, May 2, 1963: B-6.

82 Merrell Whittlesey, "Senators Top Tigers, 7-5, After Blowing Opener, 6-3," *Washington Evening Star*, May 19, 1963: D-1; White,

"Will Leppert Change His Spots?"; Merrell Whittlesey, "Senators Win, 8-4; Lock Raps Pair: Don's 5 RBI Lead Pasting of Tigers," *Washington Evening Star*, July 28, 1963: G-1.

83 Associated Press, "Bunning or Bouton to Start for All-Stars: Houk Fills Squad; Leppert Selected," *Washington Evening Star*, July 2, 1963: A-21.

84 Bill Christine, "All-Star Flashbacks, Medium Rare," *Pittsburgh Post-Gazette*, July 22, 1974: 13.

85 "Senators' Leppert Fractures Thumb."

86 Joe Trimble, "Tired Ford Last [*sic*] 6, Wins 4 to 1," *New York Daily News*, July 11, 1964: C22.

87 Carl Machado, "Leppert in Rare Circle," *Honolulu Star-Bulletin*, April 26, 1965: B-6.

88 Tom Hopkins, "Islanders' Winning Streak Stops at 4," *Honolulu Star-Bulletin*, April 26, 1965: B-6.

89 "George Case to Return as Islander Pilot," *Honolulu Star-Bulletin*, October 16, 1965: B-4.

90 Harry Shattuck, "Catch This Coach: Helping Astros' Receivers Is Key Part of Leppert's Job," *Houston Chronicle*, May 11, 1980: Section 3, 4.

91 "Catch This Coach."

92 Max Greenwald, "Leppert's Moment of Decision Near," *Indianapolis Star*, October 30, 1966: Section 4, 9.

93 "Leppert's Moment of Decision Near."

94 Lester J. Biederman, "Larry Shepard Named Pirate Manager in '68: '67 Phil Coach Signs for Year," *Pittsburgh Press*, October 13, 1967: 1.

95 "Bucs Name Leppert Boss of Bullpen," *Pittsburgh Press*, October 17, 1967: 43.

96 "Pirates Name Oceak, Osborn New Coaches: Leppert, Virdon Back; Grammas Gets Job Elsewhere," *Pittsburgh Press*, October 12, 1969: Section 4, 5.

97 "Virdon Keeps Buc Coaches," *Pittsburgh Post-Gazette*, November 24, 1971: 20.

98 "Ricketts Fired, Skinner Hired," *Pittsburgh Press*, October 5, 1973: 32.

99 Bob Smizik, "Pirates Grounded by Reds, 9-4: Umpires Plague Bucs Again in Fourth Straight Home Loss," *Pittsburgh Press*, July 14, 1974: D-1.

100 Al Abrams, "'Home Run' No Issue in Long Run," *Pittsburgh Post-Gazette*, October 15, 1971: 26; "Fair Or Foul? At Least It Was a Rhubarb," *Newsday* (Long Island, New York), October 15, 1971: 118.

101 Al Abrams, "Sidelights on Sports," *Pittsburgh Post-Gazette*, February 26, 1970: 28.

102 Associated Press Photo, "It's a Bird, It's a Plane, It's A," *Toronto Star*, February 28, 1978: B1.

103 Neil MacCarl, "Jays on Defensive Against Stolen Bases," *Toronto Star*, May 10, 1978: B-6; Shattuck, "Catch This Coach." As a first-year expansion club in 1977, the Blue Jays, with Leppert coaching their catchers, threw out 47 percent of runners who tried to steal, tying them for second in the AL.

104 Dan Donovan, "Who Is the Toughest of Them All?," *Pittsburgh Press*, May 27, 1973: D-2.

105 "Who Is the Toughest of Them All?"

106 Hal McCoy, "Reds Weren't Listening During Sermon," *Dayton Daily News*, July 15, 1974: 14.

107 Kenny Hand, "Fighting Words: Astros Resume Old Feud With L.A.," *Houston Post*, June 26, 1983: 1C.

108 Milt Dunnell, "This Jays Coach Keeps His Cool," *Toronto Star*, March 2, 1977: C1.

109 Bob Smizik, "Handicapping a Successor," *Pittsburgh Press*, August 23, 1976: 19.

110 "Peterson Seeks Manager," *Pittsburgh Press*, October 5, 1976: 41.

111 "Two More Coaches Sign With Blue Jays," *Toronto Star*, October 16, 1976: D4.

112 Neal MacCarl, "Absent Umps Steal Woods' Thunder," *Toronto Star*, August 26, 1978: B1.

113 Alison Gordon, "It's Official: Hartsfield Is Out," *Toronto Star*, October 1, 1979: B1.

114 Harry Shattuck, "Leppert Named Astros' Coach," *Houston Chronicle*, October 18, 1979: Section 2, 6.

115 Shattuck, "Catch This Coach."

116 Ivy McLemore, "Astros Hire Moss, Fire Leppert," *Houston Post*, May 29, 1985: 4D.

117 Kenny Hand, "Leppert Red Hot About Being Left Out in the Cold," *Houston Post*, June 3, 1985: 1C.

118 "Leppert's Comments Earn Pink Slip From Rosen," *Houston Post*, June 4, 1985: 1E.

119 Paul McKillip, "City Welcomes Minor League Baseball," *Kenosha* (Wisconsin) *News*, December 31, 1983: YEAR END, 8.

120 Louis Anderson, "Harlingen Takes 9-6 Win Over Clippers," *Corpus Christi* (Texas) *Caller*, June 23, 1955: 4B; "Braves Bonus Pitcher Joins Clipper Squad," *Corpus Christi Caller*, June 23, 1955: 4B.

121 John McIntrye, "Old-Timers Anxious to Get Out to Ballpark," *Kenosha* (Wisconsin) *News*, January 23, 1986: 23.

122 John McIntyre, "Twins Are Champs Once More," *Kenosha* (Wisconsin) *News*, September 9, 1987: 15.

123 Three Clinton Giants Receive All-Star Honors; Angels Ignored," *Quad-City* (Iowa) *Times*, August 30, 1987: 2C.

124 "Twins Shuffle Their Lineup in the Minor Leagues," *Minneapolis Star Tribune*, October 31, 1987: 7D.

125 Jeff Brown, "Quite a Ride: Once a Journeyman, Damian Miller Looks Back on His Road to the Major Leagues," *La Crosse* (Wisconsin) *Tribune*, December 24, 2000: B-3.

126 Sid Hartman, "Warg Is Convinced Oilers Plan to Move," *Minneapolis Star Tribune*, November 5, 1993: 2C.

127 "Twins' Minor League Positions Nearly Set," *Minneapolis Star Tribune*, October 26, 1996: C2.

128 Pat McKee, "State Basketball Hall Honors IHSAA's Roy," *Indianapolis Star*, January 21, 2003: D5.

129 Kent, "Lep's a Handy Guy to Have Around."

130 Shattuck, "Catch This Coach."

MARK WORRELL

BY TOM SCHOTT

Pitcher Mark Worrell, who was known for his funky sidewinder delivery, will forever be linked to two home runs – one he hit and the other he gave up. In his second major-league game, on June 5, 2008, Worrell blasted a three-run homer in his first career at-bat. Three years later, in his final game in the big leagues, on July 24, 2011, he gave up the first career round-tripper hit by future perennial All-Star Mike Trout.[1]

The right-hander, whose major-league career consisted of eight games, described his pitching mechanics as "unorthodox." In a *St. Louis Post-Dispatch* story on June 3, 2008, writer Derrick Goold said: "As Worrell begins his delivery, he bends over and then springs up to throw sidearm while stepping almost toward first base."[2]

Mark Robert Worrell Jr. was born on March 8, 1983, in Palm Beach Gardens, Florida, the son of Nancy Worrell. Later a sister, Jennifer, was born. He is not related to fellow major-league pitchers Todd Worrell (1985-97) and Tim Worrell (1993-2006).

Worrell attended the Benjamin School in Palm Beach Gardens as a high-school freshman, winning five games. He then moved to John I. Leonard High School in Lake Worth, Florida, earning three letters from 1999 to 2001.[3] He posted a 10-2 record as a sophomore and was named second team All-State. Worrell went 6-2 and 8-3 as a junior and senior respectively, being voted team captain and earning first-team All-State honors both seasons. He made 11 starts as a senior, authoring eight shutouts with a 0.26 ERA and averaging 1.76 strikeouts per inning with a nearly 7-to-1 strikeouts-to-walks ratio.[4]

In Worrell's senior year, Leonard High was eliminated from the state tournament in a regional playoff game, 1-0 in eight innings, by Douglas High School. Worrell struck out a batter for what would have been the third out in the bottom of the eighth, but a passed ball allowed the only run to score.

Worrell, who also batted .341, was named the 2001 Palm Beach County Player of the Year and the *South Florida Sun-Sentinel* (the primary daily newspaper of Fort Lauderdale and Broward County) Big School Player of the Year.

Major-league scouts were impressed with Worrell's velocity, which was regularly clocked in the 93-94-mph range and topped out at 97 mph.[5] The Los Angeles Dodgers were reportedly set to select him in the third round of the 2001 draft, but Worrell didn't like the Dodgers' offer of a $500,000 signing bonus.[6] The Tampa Bay Devil Rays selected Worrell in the 11th round, but he opted to forgo a professional career and attend college.

Worrell's high-school coach, Tom Evans, offered this scouting report: "He is very competitive. He is like a bulldog going after a wild pig or something. He doesn't let up. When he is focused and goes after it, he gets it. You have to get him

Mark Worrell, St. Louis Cardinals – Courtesy of St. Louis Cardinals

early in the game. Once he establishes tempo, it's rough to knock him out. His future is in his hands."[7]

After graduating from high school, Worrell pitched for the 2001 USA Baseball 18U National Team that played in the COPABE Pan American Junior Championships in Cuba. He pitched six innings, not allowing a hit and recording 13 strikeouts. His teammates included 11 future major leaguers: Matt Chico, Jeff Francoeur, Scott Kazmir, Mike Nickeas, Clint Sammons, Sergio Santos, Zack Segovia, Jeremy Sowers, Denard Span, Huston Street, and B.J. Upton. The United States squad went 9-2, with both losses to Cuba, including 3-2 in the gold-medal game.

Worrell signed a national letter of intent with the University of Florida but never matriculated to Gainesville. Over the next three academic years, he attended three colleges:

- 2001-02: Indian River Community College in Fort Pierce, Florida. Ranked the number-one preseason junior-college pitcher in the country by *Baseball America*, Worrell was a team co-captain and went 4-6 in 14 starts with 77 strikeouts in 77 innings.
- 2002-03: University of Arizona. Worrell appeared in 17 games, all but one in relief, posting a 2-4 record with a 6.75 ERA.
- 2003-04: Florida International University. His record was 2-9, and he topped the team with a 4.25 ERA and 107 strikeouts (11.4 per nine innings).

On June 7, 2004, the St. Louis Cardinals selected Worrell in the 12th round (360th overall pick) of the amateur draft. The 21-year-old subsequently embarked on his professional career with the Johnson City (Tennessee) Cardinals in the rookie-level Appalachian League before being promoted to the Peoria (Illinois) Chiefs of the Class-A Midwest League. He pitched in 29 games combined – all in relief – allowing just 21 hits in 37 innings while striking out 55 batters (13.4 per nine innings) and recording 13 saves.

The 2005 season was a homecoming for Worrell, as he pitched for the Palm Beach Cardinals in the advanced Class-A Florida State League, some 12 miles from his birthplace. In a June 5 article in the *Palm Beach Post*, Worrell said: "I probably have three or four friends a night come, and then my family comes to every game or every other game, so I'm pretty much responsible for the whole crowd every night. Maybe I should get a cut of the attendance."[8]

Worrell enjoyed a tremendous season in 2005. He was chosen for the Florida State League All-Star Game en route to being named the St. Louis Cardinals' Minor League Pitcher of the Year. He also earned the Minor League Baseball Rolaids Relief Man Award after leading all minor leaguers with 35 saves.[9] He amassed 53 strikeouts in 56 innings (8.5 per nine innings), to go with a 2-3 record and 2.25 ERA while holding opponents to a .191 batting average. Nine of his saves came in consecutive appearances between May 16 and June 2. The Cardinals won the Florida State League playoffs over the Detroit Tigers' affiliate in Lakeland, and Worrell earned three saves in the series. He was the winning pitcher in the decisive fifth game.

Worrell spent the offseason in Mexico, where he was 11-for-11 in save opportunities.

Kary Booher of the *Springfield* (Missouri) *News-Leader* interviewed Worrell about his unorthodox delivery in March 2006. "It's always felt natural to me," Worrell said. "Everybody always asks me about the delivery, but I know it's good to be different. I guess I'm just blessed in a sense."[10]

Cardinals pitching coordinator Mark Riggins said: "There are so many things that look awkward. But physically he's had no problems, so we're just letting him ride with it."[11]

As a starting pitcher, Worrell would drop down from the side only with two strikes on right-handed batters. It was when he became a reliever that he went to the side-arm delivery full-time.

"As I became a reliever, it was a little easier for me to adapt with the lower arm angle and recover quicker. I was having success, so I just stuck with it," Worrell said in 2018.[12]

In 2006 Worrell continued his ascent through the minors with the Springfield (Missouri) Cardinals of the Double-A Texas League. Armed with a fastball and slider, he was selected to the All-Star Game and led the league with 27 saves while striking out 75 batters in 61⅔ innings (10.9 per nine innings). He posted a 3-7 record and 4.52 ERA. Worrell was named the Cardinals' Minor League Pitcher of the Month for July after recording a 0.51 ERA (one earned run in 17⅔ innings), with six saves and 22 strikeouts over 13 appearances.

However, on the heels of a rough month of August (12.54 ERA), questions arose about whether skilled batters could adjust to Worrell's Tasmanian Devilish delivery the more they faced him.

"The delivery gets the A-ball hitter out with its deception," Riggins said. "In Double-A, the hitters are more experienced. The hitters aren't going to be scared of that delivery. It is tough to see the ball coming out of it, but he still has to locate."[13]

Nonetheless, Worrell moved up to Triple-A with the Memphis (Tennessee) Redbirds of the Pacific Coast League in 2007, where he went 3-2 with four saves and a 3.09 ERA in 50 games. In 67 innings he allowed 58 hits while striking out 66 batters (8.9 per nine innings). He had another exceptional month of July with a 0.68 ERA (one earned run in 13⅓ innings).

Back with Memphis in 2008, Worrell posted a 1.88 ERA in 21 games – with 38 strikeouts in 24 innings (14.3 per nine innings) – before being called up to the Cardinals on June 2. He made his major-league debut the next night against the Washington Nationals, pitching a scoreless bottom of the ninth inning to close out a 6-1 St. Louis victory.

"It's something you work for your whole life, one of the coolest experiences of my life," Worrell said of his debut. "It was an honor to pitch in the big leagues and something I'll always remember the rest of my life."[14]

Two days later, Worrell entered the second game of a day-night doubleheader at Nationals Park in the fifth inning, with the Cardinals trailing 8-3. He relieved rookie starter Mike Parisi, who like Worrell was drafted in 2004.[15]

Worrell pitched a scoreless fifth inning and then batted in the sixth with two runners on and two outs. On a 3-and-2 fastball from Nationals right-hander Tim Redding, Worrell crushed a three-run home run over the left-field wall to narrow the score to 8-6.

Worrell became the eighth player in Cardinals history to hit a homer in his first at-bat, and the sixth to do so since 2000. The previous ones were pinch-hitter Eddie Morgan (April 14, 1936); center fielder Wally Moon (April 13, 1954); pinch-hitter Keith McDonald (July 4, 2000); left fielder Chris Richard (July 17, 2000); pitcher Gene Stechschulte (April 17, 2001); second baseman Hector Luna (April 8, 2004); and pitcher Adam Wainwright (May 24, 2006).[16] Worrell joined Wainwright in accomplishing the feat as a reliever.

"I was always a good hitter growing up," said Worrell, who had two previous professional at-bats with Memphis in 2007, going 1-for-2 with a double. "I wish I could have got more at-bats, but it's really cool that it happened, and I was really proud of it. It was awesome; that's something you always dream about. I was really, really excited."[17]

The Nationals loaded the bases against Worrell in the bottom of the sixth, but he escaped unscathed. In his two scoreless frames, he allowed two hits and two walks.[18]

Worrell appeared in two more games for the Cardinals, allowing five runs in 2⅔ innings. He was the losing pitcher against the Cincinnati Reds on June 12 and was sent back to Memphis two days later. In his four games with the Cardinals, he had a 7.94 ERA (five earned runs in 5⅔ innings).

Worrell spent the rest of the season with Memphis. He did not get recalled by the Cardinals when rosters were expanded in September, despite finishing the year with a 2.15 ERA and 80 strikeouts in 58⅔ innings (12.3 per nine innings) over 53 games. His five saves for Memphis ranked fourth on the team behind Kelvin Jiménez (12 saves), Chris Perez (11), and Jason Motte (9) – all future major leaguers.

On December 3, 2008, the Cardinals traded Worrell and a player to be named later to the San Diego Padres for shortstop Khalil Greene.[19] Worrell was irritated at being overlooked for a September call-up and said, "I really can't control what those guys do with me. I feel like I have done a great job but obviously the Cardinals don't really respect me. So unless they are going to do a 100 percent change and give me a chance, then I am ready to try somewhere else that will appreciate a guy that puts up good numbers and works hard on and off the field."[20]

Expected to have the opportunity to compete for a bullpen spot with the Padres in 2009, Worrell instead missed the entire season after undergoing surgery in March to repair the ulnar collateral ligament in his right elbow. He became a free agent in December and signed a minor-league contract with the Padres in February 2010.

Worrell began the 2010 season with the Padres' Triple-A farm team, the Portland (Oregon) Beavers of the Pacific Coast League. He appeared in 25 games, allowing 20 earned runs in 33 innings (5.45 ERA), while striking out 34 batters and posting a 1-4 record. Worrell was released on June 23 and signed with the Seattle Mariners on July 5. After pitching just four innings over four appearances for the Triple-A Tacoma (Washington) Rainiers, he was released on July 14.

On February 1, 2011, Worrell signed as a free agent with the Baltimore Orioles. Pitching for the Triple-A Norfolk (Virginia) Tides, he was selected to the International League All-Star team and was subsequently called up by the Orioles on July 18. At the time of his recall, he had 12 saves for the Tides, with a 2.95 ERA and 30 strikeouts in 36⅔ innings.

The same day Worrell joined the Orioles, Baltimore's closer Kevin Gregg began a three-game suspension for a July 8 skirmish with David Ortiz of the Boston Red Sox – creating an opening in the bullpen. In the game that night against Boston at Oriole Park at Camden Yards, the Orioles and Red Sox were tied, 7-7, through seven innings. Worrell entered in the top of the eighth with the bases loaded and one out, becoming the 900th player to take the field in an Orioles uniform. He gave up a two-run double to Dustin Pedroia, walked Adrián González intentionally, and allowed a two-run single to Kevin Youkilis before being removed.[21]

"It's a rough spot, but it's spots [like that] I want to be in, and I feel like I need to succeed in that," Worrell said. "I wouldn't have it any other way. I need to pitch my way out of that.

"All I want to do is do my part and help us win ballgames. I didn't do my part today, and it [stinks]."[22]

Worrell's next two major-league appearances were superior. Called upon with the bases loaded and no outs against Boston on July 20, Worrell struck out Marco Scutaro and Jason Varitek and retired Yamaico Navarro on a fly out to center field. Two days later, he fanned the only batter he faced, Mark Trumbo of the Los Angeles Angels of Anaheim.

"The other day left a bad taste in my mouth," Worrell said about his July 20 outing. "This is what I'm capable of, and I'm ready to go forward from here."[23]

Columnist Kevin Cowherd of the *Baltimore Sun* wrote about Worrell on July 21: "The high point for me [of the previous day's 4-0 Baltimore loss to Boston] was seeing new Orioles reliever Mark Worrell pitch in person for the first time.

"… Have you seen this guy's delivery yet? I'm not quite sure how to describe it.

"OK, let's try this: it's sidearm; it's herky-jerky and then he tumbles off the mound with all the grace of a drunk falling off a stage.

"The guy must drink a pot of coffee in the bullpen before he comes into games, too. He appears to be super-wired and after every pitch, he stomps four or five feet toward the plate to get the catcher's throw before stomping back to the rubber."[24]

On July 24 the Orioles, who were last in the American League East Division with a 40-57 record (20½ games behind the pace-setting Red Sox), trailed the Los Angeles Angels of Anaheim, 3-2, through seven innings at Camden Yards. Worrell entered the game to begin the eighth. He allowed two singles and then after recording an out, surrendered the 19-year-old Mike Trout's first major-league homer – a three-run shot to deep left-center field. One out later, Worrell walked a batter and gave up a two-run homer to Torii Hunter and was replaced.

"Should have been a pretty good spot for [Worrell], but it didn't work out," Orioles manager Buck Showalter said.[25]

Saddled with a 36.00 ERA – after having allowed eight runs on six hits, including two homers, and two walks in two innings spanning four appearances – Worrell was optioned to Norfolk. He would not pitch in the majors again. With Norfolk for the remainder of the season, Worrell pitched in 17 games, earning nine saves with a 4.50 ERA. He was unscored upon in his last 10 appearances.[26] Worrell was granted free agency in November and went on to pitch in five games for the Águilas Cibaeñas of the Dominican Winter League. He pitched professionally for the final time in 2013, appearing in two games in the Mexican League.

For his minor-league career, Worrell recorded 105 saves and a 3.31 ERA, with 399 strikeouts in 370 innings (9.7 per nine innings). His limited major-league experience yielded a 15.26 ERA (13 earned runs in 7⅔ innings).

"This game can humble you very quickly," Worrell said in 2018.[27]

After his playing career, Worrell earned a bachelor of education degree in 2012 and an MBA two years later, both from Florida International University. He went on to earn a PhD in health and physical education/fitness from the University of Texas in 2017. The title of his dissertation was "Former Major League Baseball (MLB) Players and Athletic Identity." In 2024 Worrell was pursuing a doctorate in health-care administration from Oklahoma State University.

From 2014 to 2017, Worrell was a teacher and coordinator for ACE Academy, a private, independent school for gifted students in Austin, Texas, and then worked for Major League Baseball as director of student-athlete education for a year before serving as a minor-league pitching coach and coordinator for the Toronto Blue Jays for two years. He subsequently worked for Amazon as a recruiter (2020-22) and for Cross Country Healthcare as director of premier accounts (2022-24). In February 2024 Worrell joined Locums Choice as director of national accounts. Locums Choice is a health-care staffing agency that specializes in matching physicians and advanced practice providers with health-care organizations to fill critical staffing gaps and deliver high quality patient care.

SOURCES

In addition to the sources cited in the Notes, the author consulted the Baseball-Reference.com and Retrosheet.org websites for pertinent material.

NOTES

1   Through the 2024 season, Trout was a three-time American League Most Valuable Player and 11-time All-Star with 378 career home runs.

2   Derrick Goold, "Cards Notes," *St. Louis Post-Dispatch*, June 3, 2008: D5.

3   Worrell also played basketball for one year at Leonard High School as a point guard.

4   In two of the three games Worrell lost as a senior, his team was shut out.

5   Dave Heeren, "Future in His Hands," *South Florida Sun Sentinel* (Fort Lauderdale), June 8, 2001: 13C.

6   Dave Heeren, "Money Wasn't Right for Wellington's Worrell," *South Florida Sun Sentinel*, June 7, 2001: 5C.

7   "Future in His Hands."

8   Jim Oberdier, "Worrell Right at Home with Palm Beach," *Palm Beach Post*, June 10, 2005: 4C.

9   Worrell's saves total was one shy of the Cardinals' minor-league record and three shy of the Florida State League record.

10 Kary Booher, "'It's Good to Be Different,'" *Springfield* (Missouri) *News-Leader*, March 31, 2006: 1D.

11 "'It's Good to Be Different.'"

12 Eli Fishman interview with Worrell: https://www.youtube.com/watch?v=BueV_SMhoZA.

13 Derrick Goold, "2 Potential Closers; 2 Very Different Delivery Men," *St. Louis Post-Dispatch*, September 1, 2006: D2.

14 Eli Fishman interview.

15 Parisi was selected in the ninth round and made his major-league debut on May 5, 2008.

16 After Worrell and through the 2024 season, two more Cardinals have homered in their first major-league at-bat – Paul DeJong (May 28, 2017) and Lane Thomas (April 19, 2019), both as pinch-hitters.

17 Eli Fishman interview.

18 The Cardinals wound up losing the game, 10-9 in 10 innings.

19 The Cardinals sent minor-league pitcher Luke Gregerson to the Padres on March 23, 2009, to complete the trade.

20 Joe Strauss, "Cards Trade for Greene," *St. Louis Post-Dispatch*, December 5, 2008: D1.

21 The Orioles went on to lose the game, 15-10.

22 Jeff Zrebiec, "Pen Is Punished," *Baltimore Sun*, July 19, 2011: D1.

23 Dan Connolly, "Arrieta's Effort Goes to Waste," *Baltimore Sun*, July 21, 2011: D1.

24 Kevin Cowherd, "In AL East, O's in Beleaguered State of Their Own," *Baltimore Sun*, July 21, 2011: D1.

25 Jeff Zrebiec, "Another Good Start by Guthrie Squandered," *Baltimore Sun*, July 25, 2011: D1.

26 Overall with Norfolk in 2011, Worrell was 1-6 with 21 saves and a 3.42 ERA. He allowed 44 hits and struck out 36 batters in 52⅔ innings.

27 Eli Fishman interview.

DAVE EILAND

BY CRAIG GARRETSON

Dave Eiland holds a unique baseball record: He is the only major-league player to give up a home run to the first batter he faced, and to hit a home run off the first pitcher he faced.

But his contributions to the game go beyond that unusual historical footnote. A "pitch to contact"[1] right-handed pitcher for 10 major-league seasons, after his playing days he served as a pitching coach for three major-league teams. His star pupils included Ian Kennedy, Jacob deGrom, and Yordano Ventura. He also was a "body double" for Kevin Costner in the 1999 baseball film *For Love of the Game*.

David William Eiland was born on July 5, 1966, in Dade City, Florida, the son of Bill and June Eiland. Bill Eiland was the Zephyrhills chief of police from 1961 to 1996.[2]

David attended Zephyrhills High School,[3] also the alma mater of current (as of 2024) relief pitcher Austin Adams[4] and former big-league catcher and then longtime minor-league manager Dave Huppert.[5] The Bulldogs' baseball coach said Eiland "was special – the kind of kid you don't see too often. He could do it all. And he did."[6]

After high school, Eiland attended the University of Florida in 1985 on a football scholarship, but he hurt his shoulder playing football as a freshman.[7] He focused on baseball after that, transferring to the University of South Florida for the 1986 and 1987 seasons. In the summer of 1986, he played for the Falmouth Commodores in the Cape Cod Baseball League.

The New York Yankees drafted the 6-foot-3, 210-pound Eiland in the seventh round (number 185 overall) in 1987. He shot through the Yankees' farm system, going all the way from Low-A to Yankee Stadium in less than two seasons. After a strong debut in 1987 with the Oneonta Yankees in the Low-A New York Penn League (4-0, 1.84 ERA, 0.784 WHIP in 29⅓ innings), Eiland was promoted to Fort Lauderdale in the Florida State League, where he was 5-3 with a 1.88 ERA and 1.043 WHIP in 62⅓ innings of A-ball. He opened the 1988 season with Double-A Albany-Colonie in the Eastern League, where he went 9-5 with a 2.56 ERA and 0.980 WHIP in 119⅓ innings and was named to the Eastern League All-Star team.[8] He made one Triple-A start in Columbus before being called up on August 3 to the pitching-starved Yankees, who had just lost Ron Guidry to a pulled left hamstring.[9]

Eiland's major-league debut that night – 29 days after his 22nd birthday – was an impressive one. Pitching in County Stadium against a Milwaukee Brewers lineup that included future Hall of Famers Paul Molitor and Robin Yount, Eiland allowed just one run on three hits and two walks in seven innings.

Dave Eiland, San Diego Padres – Courtesy of Trading Card Database

"To me, it felt just like any game I'd pitched in the minors," Eiland was quoted as saying in *The Sporting News*. "You can't let all the emotion affect you."[10]

One of those three hits was a home run by Molitor to lead off the bottom of the first inning. It was a hanging slider on a 1-and-2 pitch that Molitor drove over the left-center-field wall. "It was the first batter," Eiland told the *New York Times*. "It only counts for one run."[11]

Eiland threw just 89 pitches, 56 for strikes, but in the sixth inning developed a leg cramp that warranted a mound visit from manager Lou Piniella and trainer Gene Monahan. Still feeling the effects an inning later, Eiland was pulled after the seventh and Piniella summoned closer Dave Righetti to pitch the eighth inning. After the game, Piniella said Eiland would have stayed in if not for the cramping.[12]

Righetti gave up three consecutive singles to open the inning before striking out Jim Gantner. A double by Yount then knocked in two runs, and Greg Brock followed with a two-run single to tie the score at 5-5. Cecilio Guante came in to relieve Righetti, and he gave up a single and a double to plate the go-ahead run before finally getting the final two outs of the inning. The Yankees went down in order in the top of the ninth against Dan Plesac to give the Brewers a 6-5 win.

Back on the mound eight days later, Eiland made his Yankee Stadium debut on August 11 against the Toronto Blue Jays. This time he retired the first batter he faced – Tony Fernández on a bunt scooped up by catcher Don Slaught – but that was followed by back-to-back home runs from Ernie Whitt and Rance Mulliniks to give the Blue Jays a 2-0 lead. The Yankees answered in the home half of the first on Don Mattingly's RBI single, but Whitt's two-out solo home run in the second inning sent Eiland to the clubhouse early. Eiland also hit two batters, Kelly Gruber on the left hand and Fernández on the helmet. Fernández left the game with dizziness but returned the next night; Gruber, although he played all 11 innings in what was an eventual 6-5 Toronto victory, did not start in the following three games.[13]

Eiland was given one more start, on August 17, again at Yankee Stadium, this time against the California Angels. Staked to a first-inning 4-0 lead courtesy of an RBI single by Jack Clark and back-to-back home runs by Dave Winfield and Mike Pagliarulo, Eiland surrendered a second-inning solo home run to Jack Howell and a third-inning solo home run to Wally Joyner. The Yankees added three runs in the fourth, including an RBI double by Rickey Henderson, but Eiland gave up three consecutive singles to open the fifth and was pulled for Steve Shields. The Yankees hung on to win the game, 11-7, but it was Eiland's final start in the majors that season. He returned to Columbus, replaced on the Yankees' roster by Hal Morris. He made three more starts in Triple A that year.

All told, Eiland's eventful 1988 season included a 9-5, 2.56 ERA in 18 starts in Double A; 1-1, 2.59 in four starts in Triple A; and no decisions in three starts, with a 6.39 ERA and six home runs allowed in 12⅔ innings, in the majors.

In 1989 he started in Triple A again, but was called up on June 16 and started the following day against the Texas Rangers. He held the Rangers to three runs over seven innings to record his first major-league win. But he didn't fare as well in his next five starts, going 0-3 with a 6.26 ERA in 27⅓ innings, and was once again returned to Triple A.

Eiland opened the 1990 season in Columbus, and the 23-year-old dominated the competition. He was 16-5 with a 2.87 ERA in 175⅓ innings, and he was named the International League Pitcher of the Year.[14] The Yankees called him up in September, and he went 2-1 with a 3.56 ERA in 30⅓ innings. That offseason, Yankees general manager Gene Michael said Eiland had likely made the Yankees rotation.[15]

And in 1991, for the first time, Eiland was on the Opening Day roster. His first start, on April 11 against the Tigers in Detroit, was a shaky one. He gave up four runs on four hits, a walk, and a hit batter in four innings. Five days later, in Yankee Stadium against the Chicago White Sox, he had a no-decision in

a 4-3 defeat after giving up three runs on six hits and two walks in 5⅓ innings. In his third start, again facing Detroit, Eiland got his first win of the season with seven shutout innings on April 23.

Inconsistent results continued, leaving Eiland 1-3 with a 4.34 ERA on May 27 for a start in the Bronx against the Red Sox. He gave up five runs (four earned) in 4⅓ innings, and then went on the disabled list with a heel injury[16] that was followed by a lengthy rehab in Columbus. He returned August 7, gave up 11 earned runs in 8⅔ innings in his first two starts back, and then was moved to the bullpen for six weeks. He returned to the rotation for the final week of the season, making two starts and giving up just three runs in 12 innings. All told, Eiland was 2-5 with a 5.33 ERA in 72⅔ innings in 1991.

That offseason, the Yankees overhauled the roster, trading Steve Sax to the Chicago White Sox for Mélido Pérez, Bob Wickman, and Domingo Jean, and signing free agents Danny Tartabull and Mike Gallego. They also traded pitching prospect Darrin Chapin to the Philadelphia Phillies for third baseman Charlie Hayes. Needing to clear a spot on the 40-man roster, the club designated Eiland for assignment on January 19, 1992.

"As far as I'm concerned, it was a stupid move on the part of the Yankees and I'm looking forward to leaving," Eiland told the *Tampa Bay Times*. "I've done a lot more for them than some of the people they have kept. I guess I didn't fit into their plans. It doesn't make sense."[17]

Eiland was claimed on waivers by the San Diego Padres, who invited him to spring training as a nonroster invitee. An impressive spring training – three runs and eight hits allowed with 12 strikeouts in 14 innings – earned him the fifth spot in the rotation, beating out Mark Knudson, Mike York, and Frank Seminara.[18]

Facing the Dodgers in the fifth game of the Padres' season on April 10, 1992, Eiland gave up a Darryl Strawberry RBI double in the top of the first inning, and the Padres tied it up in the bottom half of the frame on Gary Sheffield's RBI triple. Eiland set down the Dodgers in order in the top of the second, and in the bottom of the inning he walked up to the plate with Jerald Clark on second base and two out. After four years in the American League, this was not just Eiland's first plate appearance in the major leagues, but in professional baseball – Eiland hadn't batted in the minors either. He later said it was his first at-bat since he played for the University of Southern Florida.[19]

Eiland turned around Bob Ojeda's 2-and-2 offering, hitting a line drive over the 370-foot marker in left field and several rows deep into the bleachers.

"It was a fluke," Eiland said of the home run. (It was the only home run of his career.) "I wish people would talk about my pitching instead of my hitting."[20]

Eiland pitched only four innings in that game. He had a second plate appearance, striking out before being lifted because of a pulled rib cage muscle after the first batter reached in the fifth inning.[21] That season he made seven starts for the Padres, going 0-2 with a 5.67 ERA in 27 innings, while battling back spasms.[22] He spent most of the season with Triple-A Las Vegas, going 4-5 with a 5.23 ERA in 63⅔ innings.

The next season he was back with the Padres, but after going 0-3 with a 5.21 ERA in 48⅓ innings was released on May 27, 1993. Two days later he signed with the Cleveland Indians, who assigned him to their Triple-A team in Charlotte. After two months there, going 1-3 with a 5.30 ERA in 35⅔ innings, Eiland was traded to the Texas Rangers for Gerald Alexander and Allan Anderson. The Rangers assigned him to the Oklahoma City 89ers, where he was 3-1 with a 4.29 ERA in 35⅔ innings.

A free agent again, Eiland returned to the Yankees in 1994 and spent the next two seasons with the Columbus Clippers. He was 9-6 with a 3.58 ERA in 1994 and 8-7 with a 3.14 ERA in 1995. He returned briefly to the majors that season, with one start and three relief appearances. He was 1-1 with a 6.30 ERA in 10 innings.

Eiland signed a minor-league deal with the St. Louis Cardinals, but after a 0-1 mark with a 5.55 ERA in six starts and two relief appearances, was released on June 15, 1996. Three days later he returned to the Yankees organization for a third time, going 8-4 with a 2.92 ERA in 15 starts in Columbus. He spent the final week of the 1996 season on the Yankees' expanded September roster, but did not get into a game.[23]

Eiland returned to the Yankees in 1997 for an injury-plagued season in the minors, battling elbow tendinitis,[24] and went 5-3 with a 6.42 ERA in 81⅓ innings across three levels.

A free agent again, Eiland returned home to Florida in 1998 on a minor-league deal for the inaugural season of the Tampa Bay Devil Rays. A nonroster invitee to spring training, he allowed just one run in seven innings but was sent to Triple A.[25] He had an impressive season with the Durham Bulls, 13-5, 2.99 ERA in 171⅔ innings, and was a September call-up when rosters expanded. He had one appearance, a start on September 25 against the Yankees. In the third-to-last game of the season, Eiland was rocked for six runs on six hits and three walks in 2⅔ innings.

Also in 1998, Eiland appeared on the mound in another capacity. He was cast as the body double for Kevin Costner in the film *For Love of the Game*. He gets a credit as "relief pitcher,"[26] but Eiland's primary purpose on the set was to throw major-league-caliber pitches over the plate. In an interview with the podcast *Breaking Bats*, Eiland said he was asked in October 1998 to appear in the film and was on set at Yankee Stadium for three weeks.

"Any time you saw the ball cross the plate, I probably threw that pitch," Eiland said. He added, "Even though [Costner] says he threw every pitch in that movie, I can tell ya, no he didn't."[27]

Eiland, now 32, returned to the Devil Rays for the 1999 season and again didn't make the team out of spring training. He was called up May 28, replacing Tony Saunders in the rotation, but after just three starts went on the disabled list with back spasms.[28] He returned on June 23 and remained with the Devil Rays the remainder of the season as a swingman, setting career highs in wins, games, starts, and innings, going 4-8 with a 5.60

ERA in 15 starts and six relief appearances. Though he said he had been contemplating retirement since 1997, Eiland returned to the Devil Rays for the 2000 season as a nonroster invitee in spring training. For the first time since 1993, and in his second season with the Padres, he was on the Opening Day roster.[29]

"In those times between 1993 and 1998 I learned a lot about myself, about what type of pitcher I was and what type of competitor I was," he said. "I've gotten better every year. I think that was kind of hard for the decision makers, but just because you've been around for X number of years and just because you get to a certain age doesn't mean you stop improving.

"I kept working and I kept improving. In this game, when you get a label it's hard to shake. Fortunately, they gave me a chance last year. I was able to get my foot in the door, and this spring I just walked right through it, and here I am."[30]

Eiland's first three appearances in 2000, all out of the bullpen, were rough. He was rocked for 10 runs on 10 hits and three walks in 5⅔ innings, a 15.88 ERA. But he didn't give up a run in his next two appearances, and on April 23, he got his first start of the season, against the Anaheim Angels. He threw six scoreless innings, allowing just three hits and two walks. He remained in the rotation for four more starts, allowing 13 earned runs in 14 innings, but left his start on May 23 after facing just one batter. Eiland spent the next 10 weeks on the disabled list with a hip injury.[31] He returned August 9 and pitched six innings, giving up two runs on seven hits to get a no-decision in a 5-4 victory over the Minnesota Twins.

On September 10, 2000, Eiland was summoned to try to keep the Devil Rays in a game they were losing 5-0 in the bottom of the fifth against the Oakland A's. Entering with one out and the bases loaded, Eiland allowed back-to-back hits by Ben Grieve and Adam Piatt to allow two inherited runners to score, but got the final two outs of the inning. In the sixth, he gave up a solo home run to Eric Chávez, and in the seventh, he was pulled after back-to-back walks. No one knew it at the time, but he had thrown his final pitch in the major leagues.

That offseason, Eiland signed a minor-league contract with the Oakland A's, his seventh organization in his 15th year of professional baseball. But elbow pain – reportedly stemming from "arm exercises in the training room" – ended his spring training before it even began.

"What can you do? It's kind of a freaky thing," he said. "I'd like to make an impression, but the most important thing is to get ready for the season, and I'm confident I can do that."[32]

Alas, the elbow pain turned out to be a torn elbow tendon, resulting in Tommy John surgery. Eiland spent the next 10 months rehabbing, returning in time for A's spring training in 2002, only to tear the same tendon after two spring-training games.

"There were no setbacks, no warning signs," Eiland said. "I was throwing the ball as good as I ever had."[33]

At 35 years old, Eiland underwent a second Tommy John surgery, but he didn't attempt another comeback.[34] Instead, he took a position as a pitching coach with the Rookie League Gulf Coast Yankees in 2003, followed by the A-ball Staten Island

Yankees in 2004, the Double-A Trenton Thunder from 2005 to 2006, and the Triple-A Scranton/Wilkes-Barre Yankees in 2007. On October 30, 2008, the Yankees hired Joe Girardi as manager, and on November 20, they announced that Eiland had been hired as the team's pitching coach.[35]

One reason the Yankees wanted Eiland in the position was that he had shepherded the minor-league development of the team's trio of young pitching stars – Joba Chamberlain, Phil Hughes, and Ian Kennedy – but also was a former teammate of veterans Andy Pettitte and Mariano Rivera, giving him an unparalleled level of familiarity as well as trust.[36]

Eiland believed his own struggles as a pitcher helped him be a better coach.

"I didn't have an arm like Phil or Joba; I worked really hard to be mediocre," Eiland said. "But I studied. When I lay my head on my pillow, I'm very satisfied, not so much with my record or my numbers, but I know I gave it everything I had every day."

"I didn't have the God-given ability to get over the hump, so to speak. I kept getting chances because I did my work and I think that helps me in the coaching aspect. I work with guys now who have ability. I can teach them how to work, how to study film, how to read swings, how to attack guys."[37]

Eiland served as Yankees coach for three seasons – including for the Yankees' 27th World Series championship season in 2009 – but his contract was not renewed after the 2010 season. Rumors swirled in the media about why Eiland hadn't been brought back, with the initial speculation that there was a falling-out between Eiland and Girardi.[38] (Eiland said that was "ridiculous and not true."[39]) Most of the speculation centered on Eiland's mysterious three-week hiatus in June,[40] as well as his relationship with struggling free-agent signing A.J. Burnett.[41]

Eiland told ESPN he didn't know why he wasn't brought back and he was "pretty shocked" by the decision. After his last conversation with Girardi, he believed he'd be back with the Yankees in spring training, he said. Yankees general manager Brian Cashman, who had initially called the decision "private and personal," said in response to Eiland's comments: "He knows why. He was given conditions that needed to be followed. So he knows why."[42]

Longtime sportswriter Murray Chass, on his personal website, wrote: "The matter was serious enough that the Yankees told him he could return to his job as long as he didn't resume any of the activities that led to his leave of absence. He didn't adhere to the agreement and was fired. No one has spelled out those activities, and I will refrain from speculating."[43]

Whatever the reason, Eiland wasn't unemployed long. Two months after leaving the Yankees, he was named a special assistant to the Tampa Bay Rays, and then prior to the 2012 season, named pitching coach of the Kansas City Royals. Pitcher Yordano Ventura credited Eiland with helping him improve mechanically as well as psychologically as a pitcher,[44] and Ian Kennedy, the former Yankee, praised the existing relationship he had with Eiland when he signed as a free agent with the Royals.[45] Eiland won a second World Series ring as a pitching coach when the Royals beat the New York Mets in five games in 2015.

Eiland's contract with the Royals was not renewed after the 2017 season,[46] and once again he was not unemployed long, getting hired a month later by the Mets.[47]

As a pitching coach, Eiland was credited with turning Jacob deGrom from a very good pitcher into a star, according to Mike Puma of the *New York Post*. Eiland said he helped deGrom "keep it simple" and focus on his timing. "Get your hand out of your glove, be on time and let your natural abilities take over," Eiland told the *Post*. "And then after that you start talking about pitch sequencing and setting hitters up and how you are going to attack your strengths against his weaknesses and all the other stuff."[48] DeGrom won the National League Cy Young Award in 2018 and 2019.[49]

Eiland also was credited with helping another Mets pitcher, Zack Wheeler, make a change to his mechanics that boosted his velocity as well as his confidence. Lindsey Adler wrote for TheAthletic.com, "The issue Eiland saw was that Wheeler was taking too long getting the ball out of his glove and elongating his windup too much behind him – his 'backstroke,' as the longtime pitching coach said. Eiland, pantomiming the issue, drew his right arm behind him in a ballet-like style, somewhat leisurely and in a sweeping motion. Wheeler, from his perspective, could benefit from sweeping his arm up in a quicker motion, and as his arm reached the top of the arc, it was farther out in front from his body, and generally more in line with what Wheeler's lower half is intended to be doing."[50]

Eiland was fired by the Mets on June 20, 2019.[51] His next stop was as manager of the Eastern Reyes del Tigre in the four-team Constellation Energy League in Texas. The league played a 56-game schedule between July 10 and August 30, 2020.[52] One of his pitchers, 36-year-old Scott Kazmir, went 2-1 with a 4.20 ERA in 15 innings and the following season returned to the major leagues with the San Francisco Giants.[53] Another player, 22-year-old Alec Marsh, was a starting pitcher for the Kansas City Royals as of June 2024.

In 2022 and 2023, Eiland was the pitching coach for the Pensacola Blue Wahoos, then the Double-A affiliate of the Miami Marlins.[54] In 2022 the Blue Wahoos won the Southern League championship.[55]

As of 2024, Eiland was head of baseball for Grand Central Sports, which provides athletes and coaches representation in contract negotiations and other professional matters.[56]

SOURCES

In addition to the sources cited in the Notes, the author consulted sabr.org, baseball-reference.com, and retrosheet.org.

NOTES

1   Pete Young, "From Bulldog to Devil Ray," *Tampa Bay Times*, August 1, 1999. "Eiland relies on multiple pitches and changing speeds to confuse hitters. His tantalizing breaking balls have been clocked at below 70 mph." Eiland said he was primarily a fastball-slider pitcher early in his career who by the end of it had added a curveball and changeup.

2   According to the Zephyrhills 100th-anniversary page, Eiland Boulevard is named in Bill Eiland's honor. http://zephyrhills100.com/2010/02/18/zephyrhills-100th-anniversary-the-naming-of-the-streets.

3   Edward Cifelli, "Pitching in with a Job Close to Home," *Tampa Bay Times*, March 4, 2011. Zephyrhills High School retired Eiland's number 14 in 2008.

4   Austin Lance Adams – not to be confused with Austin David Adams – was an eighth-round pick of the Los Angeles Angels of Anaheim in the 2012 June Amateur Draft out of the University of South Florida. He made his major-league debut on July 15, 2017, for the Washington Nationals, and has since pitched for the Seattle Mariners, San Diego Padres, and Arizona Diamondbacks, and as of 2024 the Oakland Athletics. Adams, who set the modern record (since 1920) with 24 hit batsmen in 2021, signed a one-year contract with the New York Mets on November 30, 2023. Randy Mandhawa, "Adams - in Relief - Sets Season HBP Mark," MLB.com, September 17, 2021. https://www.mlb.com/news/austin-adams-record-for-hit-by-pitches.

5   Dave Huppert appeared in two games as a defensive replacement with the Baltimore Orioles in 1983, but did not bat, and in 15 games with the Milwaukee Brewers in 1985, going 1-for-21. A minor-league player for 10 seasons – including the longest game ever played – Huppert then managed across five minor-league levels for six different organizations between 1986 and 2016. Brian Murphy, "The Longest Baseball Game Took 33 Innings to Win," MLB.com, June 23, 2023. https://www.mlb.com/news/the-longest-professional-baseball-game-ever-played.

6   Tony Castro, "Eiland Resets a Major Goal," *Tampa Bay Times*, July 17, 1997.

7   Natalie Eiland, "Dave Eiland Story," USF Broadcast News, March 18, 2018. https://usfbroadcastnews.wordpress.com/2018/03/18/dave-eiland-story/.

8   "Around the Minors," *The Sporting News*, July 4, 1988: 23.

9   Michael Martinez, "Eiland's Debut Is Ruined as Righetti Blows Lead," *New York Times*, August 4, 1988: 9.

10   "Notebook: A.L. East," *The Sporting News*, August 15, 1988: 12.

11   Martinez.

12   Martinez.

13   "Baseball: A.L. East," *The Sporting News*, August 29, 1988: 19.

14   Cammy Clark, "Yankees' Eiland Ready for Return to Big Show," *Tampa Bay Times*, March 31, 1991. "Eiland was named the International League Pitcher of the Year and tied the league's mark for the most victories in a season, 16, set by Bob Kammeyer in 1979. He also was named the ninth-best major-league prospect in the International League by *Baseball America*."

15   Moss Klein, "A.L. Beat," *The Sporting News*, January 14, 1991: 36.

16   Eiland initially injured his heel May 16 after getting stepped on while covering first base on the first play of the game. He remained in the game for two innings but was on crutches after the game. (Jack Curry, "Sound Heard in the Bronx Was Yanks Going Ker-Plunk," *New York Times*, May 17, 1991: 9). He made his next start on May 21, but was placed on the disabled list after the May 27 start.

17   Jim Carson, "Yankees Drop Local Pitcher from Roster," *Tampa Bay Times*, January 11, 1992. Eiland said the Yankees had offered him a contract that included a raise earlier that offseason. Instead, he was designated for assignment, meaning they had 10 days to release him, trade him, or send him to the minors. Eiland said that if he wasn't traded, he would refuse assignment to Columbus: "There's nothing else for me to do down there -- all you have to do is check my record." He also said his numbers had suffered because he returned from his heel injury too quickly. "You learn by your mistakes," Eiland said. "I was trying to help the team, but I hurt myself. It was my fault. But I finished strong in my last two starts and I was really looking forward to this season."

18   Scott Miller, "Padre Notebook: Eiland Nails Down Fifth Spot in Padres' Starting Rotation," *Los Angeles Times*, April 3, 1992.

19   Tim Kurkjian, "Between the Lines," *Sports Illustrated*, April 20, 1992.

20   Barry Bloom, "Clearing the Bases," *The Sporting News*, April 20, 199: 23.

21   Steve Dilbeck, "Padres Crush Dodgers," *San Bernadino County* (California) *Sun*, April 11, 1992.

22   "San Diego Padres: Fly on the Wall," *The Sporting News*, May 4, 1992: 22.

23   Jason Diamos, "Red Sox and Yankees Wear a Path to Mound," *New York Times*, September 22, 1996: 15. On September 21, the Yankees won a wild 12-11 game that took 4 hours and 45 minutes and featured 15 pitchers throwing a total of 405 pitches. "Had Derek Jeter not driven in the winning run – after the Yankee hitters had gone 3 for their first 18 with runners in scoring position – Torre was prepared to send the 30-year-old Dave Eiland into the game. A journeyman right-hander, Eiland had had his contract purchased by the club yesterday morning. His last appearance in a major league game came in 1995."

24   Rodney Page, "Eiland Makes Most of Minor Moments," *Tampa Bay Times*, May 13, 1998.

25   Page.

26   Dave Eiland's page on the Internet Movie Database: https://www.imdb.com/name/nm0251719/.

27   Breaking Bats. "Episode 109 – 2x World Series Champion Pitching Coach Dave Eiland," February 27, 2024. https://youtu.be/GCd0YVWMkMI?si=8wf7fe4lXRmOY9Qu. According to *The Baseball Filmography, 1915 through 2001* (2nd Edition) by Hal Erickson, some "longshots" of the fictional Billy Chapel, played by Kevin Costner, are actually Eiland. Erickson also reported that the New York Yankees and Detroit Tigers stipulated that anyone wearing their uniforms either be a professional actor or a current or former major leaguer. As a result, other ballplayers in the film were Ricky Ledee, Donzell McDonald, Juan Nieves, and Scott Pose.

28   Marc Topkin and John Romano, "Eiland Gets Through a Long Two Weeks," *Tampa Bay Times*, June 23, 1999.

29   Marc Topkin, "The Once-Lost Eiland Finds Himself on Opening Roster," *Tampa Bay Times*, April 4, 2000. Eiland said he had pain in his elbow and had inquired about a pitching coach position in the Yankee minor leagues, but was told no positions were available.

30 Topkin, "The Once-Lost Eiland Finds Himself on Opening Roster."

31 Bruce Lowitt, "Late for Eiland, but Still a Win," *Tampa Bay Times*, August 10, 2000. The injury was described as "a pinched bursa sac in his left hip."

32 Susan Slusser, "A's Notebook: Frustrating Spring for Eiland," SFGATE, March 10, 2001.

33 "Despite Setback, Eiland Not Ready to Retire," *Tampa Bay Times*, April 12, 2002.

34 "Dave Eiland Hops Into New Job," *New York Daily News*, February 11, 2008. "Eiland says he had the second surgery 'to have a normal life, have a catch. I had it in the back of my mind I'd get into coaching and figured I'd be throwing batting practice for a while.'"

35 "Eiland Named NY Yankees Pitching Coach," MILB.com, November 20, 2007.

36 "Dave Eiland Hops Into New Job," *New York Daily News*, February 11, 2008.

37 "Dave Eiland Hops Into New Job."

38 Andrew Marchand, "Source: Dave Eiland Felt De-emphasized," ESPN.com, October 30, 2010. https://www.espn.com/new-york/mlb/news/story?id=5744816.

39 George A. King III, "Eiland: I Never Feuded With Girardi," *New York Post*, October 31, 2010. "'Joe and I never had a problem, nor do we now,' Eiland said. 'There are no hard feelings in the organization. Joe is a good baseball man, a great manager and one of the best human beings I ever met.'"

40 Mark Viera, "With Eiland Back, a Hope That Burnett Returns to Form," *New York Times*, June 29, 2010. "Eiland, who had been away from the team since June 4, declined to answer questions about why he has been absent, calling it 'a private family matter.'"

41 Steven Marcus, "New and Improved A.J. Burnett?" *New York Newsday*, March 2, 2011. "Burnett may also have had a bit to do with Dave Eiland's firing. If Ireland's [*sic*] unexplained leave of absence was most of the reason, the pitching coach's inability to turn around Burnett was probably at least part of the issue." Burnett signed a five-year, $82.5 million deal with the Yankees on December 12, 2008, but posted a 34-35, 4.79 ERA, 1.447 WHIP in three seasons with the Yankees and was traded before the 2013 season with cash for two minor leaguers. Burnett was 87-76 with a 3.81 ERA and 1.284 WHIP in his 10 seasons before the Yankees and 43-46 with a 3.69 ERA and 1.306 WHIP in his four seasons after.

42 Wallace Matthews, "Dave Eiland 'Pretty Shocked' by Firing," ESPN.com, December 23, 2010. https://www.espn.com/new-york/mlb/news/story?id=5951358.

43 Murray Chass, "Firing of a Different Sort," MurrayChass.com, October 31, 2010. https://www.murraychass.com/?p=2553.

44 Elizabeth Merrill, "How Yordano Ventura Tamed His Temper and Harnessed His Fastball," ESPN.com, October 7, 2015. https://www.espn.com/mlb/story/_/id/13829748/how-kansas-city-royals-yordano-ventura-tamed-temper-harnessed-fastball.

45 Associated Press, "Kennedy Fitting In with World Series Champion Royals," *Arlington Heights* (Illinois) *Daily Herald*, February 20, 2016.

"'Knowing Dave before for me was nice,' Kennedy said. 'It's nice to have that relationship already built.'"

46 Rustin Dodd and Pete Grathoff, "Royals Part Ways with Pitching Coach Dave Eiland, Bench Coach Don Wakamatsu," ESPN.com, October 2, 2017. https://www.kansascity.com/sports/mlb/kansas-city-royals/article176519021.html.

47 Associated Press, "Mets Hire Gary DiSarcina, Dave Eiland, Ruben Amaro Jr. as Coaches," ABC7ny.com, November 15, 2017. https://www.espn.com/mlb/story/_/id/21426295/mets-hire-gary-disarcina-dave-eiland-ruben-amaro-jr-coaches.

48 Mike Puma, "Dave Eiland Tip Led to Jacob deGrom's Mets Star Turn," *New York Post*, March 21, 2021.

49 Jacob deGrom was 45-32 (.584) with a 2.98 ERA (130 ERA+) and 1.122 WHIP before Eiland was hired during the 2017-2018 offseason, and 39-25 (.609) with a 2.08 ERA (191 ERA+) and 0.863 WHIP between 2018 and 2023, though Eiland was fired midway through the 2019 season.

50 Lindsey Adler, "How a Recent Mechanical Change Has Given Zack Wheeler a Significant Jump in His Average Velocity," *The Athletic*, June 27, 2018. Wheeler was 21-23 with a 3.90 ERA and 1.396 WHIP from 2013 to 2017, then 66-40, 3.28 ERA, 1.107 WHIP between 2018 and 2023 after working with Eiland in 2018.

51 Russell Dorsey, "Mets Dismiss Eiland, Name Regan in Interim," MLB.com, June 21, 2019. https://www.mlb.com/news/dave-eiland-dismissed-by-mets. At the time, the Mets ranked 20th in the major leagues with a 4.71 ERA. "The team has finished a season with a higher mark just twice in its history: in 1962, the team's inaugural season, and 2017." Eiland and bullpen coach Chuck Hernandez were replaced by Phil Regan as interim pitching coach, Ricky Bones as interim bullpen coach, and Jeremy Accardo in a newly created role, pitching strategist. "Dave is a tremendous pitching coach. The bottom line is that the results weren't there," Mets manager Mickey Callaway said. "We'll all continue, at all times, to look ourselves in the mirror, try to improve upon our process, and that's the reason we brought in three guys to replace two. Our process is going to get a little more in depth and it's going to take three guys to do it." The Mets improved to an 11th-best 4.24 ERA by the end of the 2019 season.

52 Ryan Dunsmore, "Summer League Announces Team Names and Logos," *Fort Bend* (Texas) *Herald*, July 5, 2020.

53 Kazmir had been out of professional baseball since his release by the Atlanta Braves on March 24, 2018.

54 "Blue Wahoos Announce 2023 Coaching Staff," MILB.com, January 31, 2023. https://www.milb.com/pensacola/news/2023-coaching-staff-x9822.

55 Stephanie Sheehan, "Blue Wahoos Rally Once Again to Win SL Crown," MILB.com, September 29, 2022. https://www.milb.com/news/pensacola-blue-wahoos-win-southern-league-championship.

56 Eiland was listed as head of baseball for Grand Central Sports as of July 25, 2024.

JOHNNIE LEMASTER

BY GISELLE STANCIC

When San Francisco Giants skipper Wes Westrum signaled for Johnnie LeMaster to get into the game, the 21-year-old rookie couldn't find his glove. He had joined the team only a few hours before the afternoon contest on September 2, 1975, in Candlestick Park against the Dodgers.

"A couple of veteran players hid my glove on me," LeMaster said. "My shoes weren't even tied. By the time I found my glove and tied my shoes, the pitcher was ready. I didn't get to warm up defensively."[1]

Probably only a few of the 5,098 spectators that day paid much attention to the third-inning replacement for injured shortstop Chris Speier. But few would ever forget what he did when he came up to the plate in the bottom of the fourth. The right-handed-hitting LeMaster gave them what only two other major leaguers had done before, an inside-the-park home run during his first major-league at-bat.

"We were playing our big rival the (Los Angeles) Dodgers and Don Sutton was on the mound, and he's in the Hall of Fame now. I hit an inside the park home run, the first time I ever stepped to the plate," LeMaster said. "I still pinch myself to see whether it's true or not."[2]

Johnnie Lee LeMaster was born on June 19, 1954, in Portsmouth, Ohio, to John Lowell and Mabel (Fyffe) McMaster.[3] The couple moved to Paintsville, in eastern Kentucky, with their two young sons, Link Bascom and Johnnie Lee, to be closer to family.[4] LeMaster's father worked at the Ashland Oil Catlettsburg refinery.[5] His mother taught at Paintsville Elementary.[6]

Athletic ability ran in the LeMaster family. Johnnie's brother, Link, excelled in golf and baseball,[7] while a cousin, Frank LeMaster, played as a linebacker with the Philadelphia Eagles for nine seasons.[8]

By the eighth grade, Johnnie LeMaster also showed his talent for sports, particularly baseball. So much so that visiting Cincinnati Reds scout Gene Bennett gave the young LeMaster his card.[9]

LeMaster went on to collect 21 varsity letters at Paintsville High School, in football (as the quarterback), basketball (playing center, averaging 21 points per game), golf (high 70s), and baseball (as a pitcher and infielder for the Paintsville High Tigers).[10]

"It was a great memory," LeMaster said. "I wish I could still do it. I played four sports at Paintsville. I would've [run] track, but when I was in high school we didn't have a track team."[11]

Through his high-school years, LeMaster's baseball abilities continued to attract major-league attention. In his senior year, he hit .533. He also pitched, winning four games and saving three.[12]

Johnnie LeMaster, San Francisco Giants — Courtesy of Trading Card Database

"There would be 30 scouts at every game I played," LeMaster said. "They would come knocking on the neighbors' doors wanting to know about me. They would show up at the high school and do eye tests and psychological tests on me."[13]

In the 1973 amateur draft, Kansas City had the ninth pick and wanted to take LeMaster as a pitcher. But the Giants stepped in at number six, slotting him at the shortstop position. "I didn't know that much about the Giants because everyone around here were Reds fans," McMaster said. "I was watching the Big Red Machine in 1973, they were together then, and two years later I was playing against them. It was like a dream come true."[14]

LeMaster was the highest draft pick from Kentucky until Morehead State University pitcher Drew Hall was picked third in 1984. As of 2024 LeMaster still was the highest-selected high schooler from Kentucky. He mostly played shortstop during his 12-year major-league career. He never got the chance to pitch in the majors.[15]

After the draft, the 19-year-old LeMaster spent the summer in the Rookie Pioneer League playing for the Great Falls (Montana) Giants. In 1974 he played on two Giants Class-A teams, the Decatur (Illinois) Commodores (Midwest League) and the Fresno (California) Giants (California League). He was listed at 6-feet-2 but weighed only about 160 pounds. After LeMaster joined the Giants, batting coach Jim Lefebvre said, "Basically he was a defensive hitter. The pitcher could practically knock the bat out of his hands." But he had a good arm and was a better-than-average runner.[16]

In 1975 LeMaster was promoted to the Giants' Triple-A team in Phoenix. He turned 21 in June, and on Monday, September 1, he got the call to join the Giants for the second game of a two-game series in San Francisco against the division rival Los Angeles Dodgers.

LeMaster made it to Candlestick Park just before the 2 P.M. start time on September 2. He didn't expect to play, so he took a seat on the bench during the uncharacteristically balmy (for San Francisco) 82-degree temperature and sunny skies.[17]

But in the second inning, with the Dodgers leading 1-0, Giants shortstop Speier pulled a leg muscle while running out a grounder. To LeMaster's surprise, manager Westrum signaled for him to go in as the replacement. "We had a lot of utility type players on that Giants team in '75 and I thought for sure our manager Wes Westrum wouldn't call on some rookie, but he did," LeMaster said.[18]

Speier's grounder was the third out in the Giants' second. After getting himself together, LeMaster hustled out to the field barely before the Giants' Ed Halicki threw his first pitch of the inning. Halicki retired the Dodgers, and in the bottom of the inning, the Giants scored two runs on a home run by Von Joshua.

In the Giants' fourth, with one out, Sutton walked Gary Matthews. He scored on Willie Montañez's double. With Montañez in scoring position, LeMaster stepped up to the plate for his first major-league at-bat. As LeMaster later recalled, Sutton threw him two curveballs that he missed "by three feet."[19]

The next pitch, however, was a fastball that LeMaster smacked back up the middle. Center fielder John Hale set up to field the ball on one hop and make a play at the plate. Instead, the ball hit a seam in the Candlestick AstroTurf, bounced high over Hale's head, and rolled to the wall.[20] LeMaster flew around the bases during the scramble for the baseball, ending up at home plate on the heels of Montañez.

"You know how a kid would be coming up to the big leagues for the first time, and you're playing your natural rival, and there's 50,000 people in the stands. I hit every base perfect and probably never ran that fast in my life or probably ever again," LeMaster recalled.[21]

LeMaster became the second San Francisco Giants player to hit a first-at-bat home run, after pitcher John Montefusco's two-run homer on September 3, 1974.[22] There have been two since, Will Clark in 1986, and Brett Pill in 2011. Six New York Giants also made the list, before the team moved west in 1958.

LeMaster's new teammates crowded around to congratulate him when he returned to the dugout, and the small crowd gave him a standing ovation. The Giants went on to win the game 7-3. After his big hitting debut, LeMaster had two more plate appearances but didn't get on base. He also had a quiet fielding day at short; no balls were hit his way.

LeMaster played in 21 more Giants games that year. He hit his second major-league home run on September 6 in a 3-2 loss at Cincinnati's Riverfront Stadium, the team he had idolized as a youth. He and Speier, back from the DL, traded off at shortstop the last few games of the season.

The offseason brought changes to the Giants front office after a group of local investors took charge, fending off an eleventh-hour buyout that would have moved the team to Toronto. Called "the greatest save in Giants' history,"[23] the deal to keep the team in San Francisco wasn't inked until well into spring training.

The turmoil at the top had little effect on LeMaster, who was returned to Triple-A Phoenix to start the 1976 season. He had to wait until August to put on a San Francisco uniform again. He made the 1977 Opening Day roster and started the second game of the season. He was back with Phoenix from May 22 to June 20, then returned to San Francisco for the rest of season.

LeMaster filled in at short (Speier was traded on April 27) and as a pinch-hitter in his 68 game appearances with the Giants. Major-league pitching took some getting used to, and LeMaster exited the 1977 season with a .149 batting, 8 RBIs, and no home runs. The legendary Candlestick infield was hard to get a read on, too.

"It was one of the toughest infields that there was to field on," LeMaster said. "They changed the texture of it just about every year. One year, it would be dirt and clay. The next year, it would be pea gravel. The wind would blow the top level of the dirt off by the third inning. If it was pea gravel, it would look like little hand grenades had gone off in it all over the place. But it was home."[24]

The Giants stayed with the young Kentuckian, and he started 1978 with the big-league club. He played in 101 games that year. His numbers improved with the steady work, and he hit .235 in 101 games. He made 14 errors.

In 1979 LeMaster's middling offense and spotty defense began to raise the ire of Giants fans. Along with his individual performance, LeMaster seemed to symbolize everything that was wrong with a team that hadn't placed higher than third in the division since 1971 and was heading back into the cellar. (The Giants ended 1979 in fourth place with a record of 71-91, 19½ games behind division leader Cincinnati.)

"Our record wasn't the greatest the whole time that I played there," LeMaster said. "Maybe they needed somebody to let their frustration out on, or their anger."[25]

Sentiment against LeMaster's presence in the lineup became more vocal, until he was booed by the home crowd at every at-bat. A man with strong Christian beliefs, he turned to his faith as he shouldered the verbal abuse.[26] But the daily drubbing took its toll, until LeMaster's wife, Debbie, came up with an idea to have a little fun with the fans.

"So, I was laying in bed one night and my wife sat up and said, 'You should just change your name to Boo!' I didn't think about it, but a couple days later, I asked our equipment manager to make me up a jersey with "Boo" on the back of it. (And) he did."[27]

LeMaster wore the jersey during the first inning of the July 23, 1979, home game against the Dodgers. "After the half-inning was over, (GM Spec) Richardson was there waiting for me with my normal jersey and he looked mad. 'Put this on right now!' he said."[28]

The accomplice equipment manager was fired on the spot (Richardson rehired him the same night), and LeMaster was fined $500 for being out of uniform. But with his humorous act of defiance, LeMaster turned a corner with the hometown crowd. "I'd have to say it won the fans over and the reporters were all over me about it, because they love a good story. I started getting booed a lot less after that."[29]

Still, the team's playing woes continued. The boos never really went away, and the stress began to change his easy-going personality. Sportswriters learned to leave him alone, and he became a more subdued presence in the clubhouse.[30]

The Giants' downward spiral hit a franchise low of sixth place in 1984, when they finished with a record of 66-96. Manager Frank Robinson was fired in August and coach Danny Ozark finished out the schedule.

At the end of the season, the 30-year-old LeMaster had a .217 batting average, with 98 hits (down from his career high of 128 the year before), and four homers. His fielding percentage of .964 ranked him fifth in the league, and he was fourth in putouts as a shortstop (222). But he committed 23 errors, for the third season in a row.

LeMaster took his regular spot on the field for Giants Opening Day on April 9, 1985, but he played only 11 more games for San Francisco. On May 7 he was traded to the Cleveland Indians for Mike Jeffcoat and Luis Quiñones. On May 8 LeMaster was in Cleveland playing shortstop against the White Sox. On May 30 he was flipped to Pittsburgh for a player to be named later. After playing in only 22 games as a Pirate, LeMaster was released by the organization two days before the start of the 1986 season. He and his wife moved with their two children back to Paintsville to be closer to family while the kids were growing up.[31]

LeMaster signed with Oakland in 1987 as a free agent, but he played only 20 games with the A's. Still, while he was there, he talked with legend Reggie Jackson about the boos he'd endured across the Bay. Jackson told him, "People don't boo nobodies. You're somebody." LeMaster said the comment "made me feel like a million dollars."[32]

After the Athletics released him in July 1987, LeMaster retired from the game. In his 12-year major-league career (including 1975-1985 with the Giants), he played in 1,039 games and batted .222 with 22 home runs and 229 RBIs. He stole 94 bases.

Asked about the biggest regret of his career, LeMaster put old feelings behind him. "My biggest one is never playing in a World Series. It's the pinnacle for every player and what we all dream about. Every player wants that World Series ring. We had great fans in San Francisco and one of the things we always wanted to do was win for them and give them some bragging rights, especially against the Dodgers."[33]

After his retirement, LeMaster played a year of Senior League ball with the Fort Myers Sun Sox. He also became a business owner and coached Little League.[34] In 1994 he was named head baseball coach for the Pikeville College Bears, a position he held until 2006. He was honored as Coach of the Year in the Kentucky Intercollegiate Athletics Conference in 1997, and he led the program to a school-record 40 wins during the 2000 season. To recognize his achievements, the school named the baseball field after him.[35]

LeMaster also coached high-school ball from 2016 to 2019, when his grandsons were attending high school in Ashland, Kentucky.[36] LeMaster became active in church affairs, including teaching Bible-study classes at a nearby prison.[37]

LeMaster was on hand for the final game at Candlestick Park in 1999, and like in the old days, the fans booed him, but with a "gentler" tone.[38] At the new ballpark, there's a plaque commemorating LeMaster's contributions to the team, with a mention of his homer in his first at-bat.[39] The Giants have also held special events in his honor. "They've had two Johnnie LeMaster Nights since I retired," he said. "It's unbelievable how the fans come up to me and say, 'We don't think you were treated right while you were here.'"[40]

There's a fan club, not affiliated with the Giants, called the Sons of Johnnie LeMaster,[41] and you can buy a LeMaster number 10 jersey at the Giants Dugout Store.[42] And by the way, he still has the famous "rogue" uniform from July 1979.

"I still have that 'Boo' jersey and collectors from New York call me all the time wanting to buy it, but I can't part with it," he said.[43]

SOURCES

In addition to the sources cited in the Notes, the author consulted Baseball-Reference.com, Baseball Almanac, and Retrosheet.org for background information on players, teams, and seasons.

NOTES

1   Tom FitzGerald, "Where Are They Now? Catching Up with Former Giants Shortstop Johnnie LeMaster," *San Francisco Chronicle*, September 25, 2019. https://www.sfchronicle.com/sports/article/Where-are-they-now-Catching-up-with-former-14465433.php, accessed May 10, 2024.

2   James Juett, "LeMaster Brings Major League Experience to Ashland," *Huntington* (West Virginia) *Herald-Dispatch*, May 9, 2016, https://www.herald-dispatch.com/sports/lemaster-brings-major-league-experience-to-ashland/article_640d5190-6915-55e5-bdc8-f7d6a7d1c49e.html, accessed May 10, 2024.

3 "John Lowell Lemaster | 1920 - 2013 | Obituary," Jones-Preston Funeral Home, April 29, 2013. https://www.jones-prestonfuneralhome.com/obituary/2077241, accessed May 10, 2024. Mabel's maiden name was Fyffe. https://www.jones-prestonfuneralhome.com/obituary/mabel-lemaster, accessed May 10, 2024. John and Mabel were married 67 years at the time of John's passing in 2013 at the age of 92. Mabel died in 2018 at the age of 95.

4 Trevor Thacker, "Diamond Legend: Johnny LeMaster," *Paintsville* (Kentucky) *Herald*, July 6, 2019. https://www.paintsvilleherald.com/sports/diamond-legend-johnny-lemaster/article_5a09caf8-9f67-11e9-92c0-9772d0b44d6d.html, accessed May 10, 2024.

5 Juett.

6 "Mable Fyffe LeMaster of Paintsville, Kentucky | 1922 - 2018 | Guest Book," April 9, 2018. https://www.jones-prestonfuneralhome.com/guestbook/mabel-lemaster, accessed May 10, 2024.

7 Thacker.

8 Jeff Kerr, "Eagles Great Linebacker Frank Lemaster, Who Was Part of 1980 NFC Championship Team, Dies at Age 71," CBSSports.com, March 25, 2023. https://www.cbssports.com/nfl/news/eagles-great-linebacker-frank-lemaster-who-was-part-of-1980-nfc-championship-team-dies-at-age-71/, accessed May 11, 2024.

9 Thacker.

10 Sam Miller, "They Boo Shortstops, Don't They?" Pebble Hunting, May 10, 2023. https://pebblehunting.substack.com/p/they-boo-shortstops-dont-they, accessed May 10, 2024.

11 Thacker.

12 Miller.

13 Thacker.

14 Thacker.

15 "MLB Draft Database," *Baseball America*, 1973. https://www.baseballamerica.com/draft-history/, accessed May 11, 2024.

16 Miller.

17 "September 2, 1975 Weather History at San Francisco International Airport," Weather Spark. https://weatherspark.com/h/d/145212/1975/9/2/Historical-Weather-on-Tuesday-September-2-1975-at-San-Francisco-International-Airport-California-United-States#metar-04-00, accessed May 10, 2024.

18 Ed Attanasio, "Johnnie LeMaster," This Great Game, https://thisgreatgame.com/johnnie-lemaster/, accessed May 10, 2024.

19 "Giants Belt Dodgers, 7-3," *San Bernardino County* (California) *Sun*, September 3, 1975: 35.

20 FitzGerald.

21 FitzGerald.

22 Chris Mavraedis, "'The Count's Impressive Debut!" Mavo Books, September 3, 2020. https://mavobooks.com/2020/09/the-counts-impressive-debut/, accessed May 10, 2024.

23 Rob Garratt, "San Francisco Giants Team Ownership History," SABR Team Ownership History Project. https://sabr.org/bioproj/topic/san-francisco-giants-team-ownership-history/#_edn47, accessed May 11, 2024.

24 FitzGerald.

25 FitzGerald.

26 FitzGerald.

27 Attanasio.

28 Attanasio.

29 Attanasio.

30 Miller."

31 Thacker.

32 FitzGerald.

33 Attanasio.

34 Thacker.

35 Stacey Walters, "Diamond Memories," *UPIKE Magazine*, Fall/Winter 2020. https://issuu.com/upike/docs/fall_mag_web_final/s/11424714, accessed May 11, 2024.

36 Juett.

37 FitzGerald.

38 FitzGerald.

39 "Johnnie LeMaster San Francisco Giants Wall of Fame," The Historical Marker Database, July 3, 2021. https://www.hmdb.org/m.asp?m=176360, accessed May 10, 2024.

40 FitzGerald.

41 "Sons of Johnnie LeMaster," https://twitter.com/SonsofJohnnieLe, accessed May 11, 2024.

42 "Johnnie LeMaster Jersey," SF Giants Store, "https://www.sfgiantsfansstore.com/Johnnie_Lemaster_Jersey-140, accessed May 11, 2024.

43 Attanasio.

GREG DOBBS

BY BILL PRUDEN

At the peak of a professional baseball career that spanned 11 major-league seasons, Greg Dobbs was recognized as one of the game's best pinch-hitters.[1] Consequently, it is appropriate that Dobbs' membership in the first-at-bat home run club was earned as a pinch-hitter. That home run marked the achievement of his dream to play pro ball, and the start of a career during which he played for teams on both coasts as well as in between. Dobbs also played an important role on the 1980 World Series champion Philadelphia Phillies.

Gregory Stuart Dobbs was born on July 2, 1978, in Los Angeles, the oldest of two sons born to Kenny Dobbs, an auditor for the US Department of Defense, and Monica Dobbs, a vice president at Bank of America. He grew up in Southern California, with the family moving to Burbank, then Valencia, and finally Morena Valley.[2] While his father was not an athlete, he was always supportive of his sports-minded sons, ready to drive them to the game or practice they had on tap after dinner. There was a lot of driving, too, as Dobbs played football and basketball in addition to baseball. He credited his parents for much of his later success, saying they helped instill a sense of discipline in their sons while supporting the boys in every athletic endeavor. There was another distinctive element to the Dobbs household: the boys' maternal grandmother, a native of Lima, Peru, lived with the family. According to one account, Spanish was the family's first language, a skill that undoubtedly would prove valuable in Dobbs' future professional career in the increasingly international world of major-league baseball.[3]

Dobbs initially attended Carlsbad (California) High School before switching to Canyon Springs High School in Moreno, California. He graduated in June 1996. He was drafted by the Seattle Mariners in the 52nd round of the 1996 amateur draft, but opted to attend Riverside (California) Community College. He went on to California State University, Long Beach, and then to the University of Oklahoma. While at Long Beach, he was drafted in the 10th round of the 1999 draft by the Houston Astros, but again decided to remain in school.

Unlike many of his peers at the collegiate level who chose to play in the Cape Cod League in the summer, Dobbs played for the Anchorage Glacier Pilots in the Alaska Baseball League in 2000. He recalled the time as an interesting and distinctive experience, one that left him with many memories and friends with whom he stayed in touch. He added that the diversity of players in the league made for a good preparation for life in professional baseball.[4] But after that summer, Dobbs had his final year in the college ranks, and he made the most of it. In addition to graduating with a degree in sociology from the University of Oklahoma in 2001, after his senior year perfor-

Greg Dobbs, Seattle Mariners – Courtesy of Seattle Mariners

mance he was selected by the National Collegiate Baseball Writers Association as the second team All-American first baseman, the position he played for 21 games before moving to left field for the rest of the season.[5] In his final season at Oklahoma, he hit .428 with 25 doubles, 10 home runs, and 63 RBIs, leading the team in nine offensive categories.[6] Despite his relatively short time playing as a Sooner, Dobbs established himself as one of Oklahoma's most decorated baseball players. In addition to his All-American honors, his postseason accolades included Big 12 Conference Newcomer of the Year award and First Team All-Conference outfielder. He was named to the Phillips 66 Big 12 All-Tournament Team, and the *Dallas Morning News* selected him as the Big 12 Transfer of the Year, as well as a first-team outfielder. He also was named to the American Baseball Coaches Association Midwest All-Region first team. En route to his postseason honors, Dobbs was named conference Player of the Week and National Collegiate Baseball Writers Association National Player of the Week for the week he hit .625 with four home runs in four games.[7] He ultimately signed a free-agent contract with the Seattle Mariners just before the 2001 amateur draft.

With that signing, Dobbs began his professional baseball journey. He started with the Everett AquaSox, the Mariners' affiliate in the short-season Northwest League. In 65 games, Dobbs hit .321 with 80 hits and 41 RBIs. He experienced high-A ball when he was moved up at the end of the season, appearing in three games for the San Bernadino Stampede of the California League. During his short stint on the squad, Dobbs hit .385 (5-for-13), and he drove in three runs.

Dobbs split the 2002 season between the Wisconsin Timber Rattlers of the Class-A Midwest League and the San Antonio Missions of the Double-A Texas League. He hit .275 with the Timber Rattlers in 86 games, driving in 48 runs. In a 27-game stint with San Antonio, Dobbs hit .365 with 15 RBIs.

Unhappily for Dobbs, 2003 was a lost season when, with only two games under his belt, he injured his Achilles tendon and was out for the rest of the season.[8]

Back to health, Dobbs started the 2004 season in San Antonio. After hitting .325 in 51 games, he earned a promotion to Triple-A, the Tacoma Rainiers of the Pacific Coast League. There he hit .271 with 8 home runs and 31 RBIs in 67 games. His performance got him a late-season call-up to the Mariners.

The left-handed-hitting Dobbs made his major-league debut on September 8, 2004, when, with the Mariners trailing the Cleveland Indians 9-4 in the ninth inning at Seattle's Safeco Field, he pinch-hit for shortstop José López. Facing the Indians' veteran right-hander Bob Wickman, Dobbs worked the count to 3-and-2 before jumping on a fastball and driving it deep into the right-field bleachers. The solo shot brought the Seattle crowd to life, but Wickman quickly put a damper on the excitement, retiring the next three batters to seal the Indians' win.

Dobbs' debut home run was the highlight of the 18 games he played in for the Mariners to finish the season. He started 12 games at third base and batted .226, with 12 hits and 9 RBIs. His first-at-bat home run was his sole round-tripper of that abbreviated stay with the team.

With a taste of the big leagues, Dobbs arrived at spring training in February 2005 with high hopes. But when the Mariners headed to Seattle to begin the season, Dobbs was sent back to Tacoma. However, after hitting .321 in 50 games with 27 runs scored and 22 RBIs, he received another call-up, this time leading to appearances in 59 games with the big-league club. He saw time in the field at both first base and third, and he also filled in as a pinch-hitter. Overall, he finished with an average of .247 in 142 at-bats.

During the 2006 season, Dobbs again moved between Tacoma and Seattle. After hitting .314 in 99 games with the Triple-A club, he was a late-season call-up. He played in 23 games in Seattle, putting in time at first, second, and left field. But most of his appearances were as a pinch-hitter. In 27 at-bats he crafted a batting average of .370, scoring four runs and driving in three.

After he appeared in 100 games for the Mariners over three seasons, the club was unable to find a spot for Dobbs on the roster. In January 2007 he was placed on waivers, and on January 15 he was picked up by the Philadelphia Phillies.

For Dobbs, it was a question of events coming full circle. Longtime baseball executive Pat Gillick had been the Mariners general manager when they signed Dobbs. But while Dobbs was working his way through the ranks with the Mariners, in the aftermath of the 2005 season, Gillick assumed the helm of the Phillies. When Dobbs became available, Gillick scooped him up.[9]

The move to the Phillies resulted in more major-league playing time for Dobbs and he took advantage of the opportunity. In 2007 he mainly played in a platooning situation, but over the course of the season he appeared in 142 games, most often at third base, where he started 57 games. He also put in time at first and second as well as in left field and right field. He also began to establish a reputation as an effective and dangerous pinch-hitter. He hit a particularly memorable grand slam against the Mets as the Phillies were barreling toward the playoffs late in the season. They overcame a seven-game Mets lead to win the NL East Division title, but lost to the Colorado Rockies in the Division Series. Still, for Dobbs the season was an undeniable triumph as he recorded personal bests in every major offensive category. Overall, he hit .272 with 10 home runs and 55 RBIs.

Having made the postseason in 2007, especially in such a spectacular way, the Phillies entered the 2008 season with high hopes. Looking back, Dobbs said the 2007 stretch run instilled in the players the belief that they were capable of doing what they needed to get to the top. Their focused effort, he said, was "truly when we became the team."[10] That shared belief was certainly evident in Dobbs' effort.

While still platooning, and playing primarily against right-handed pitchers, Dobbs turned in another strong season. He played in 128 games and batted .301 with 9 home runs and 40 RBIs. While he split time in a number of positions, he made his greatest contributions as a pinch-hitter. Dobbs had studied how his Mariners teammate Dave Hansen made a career for himself as a pinch-hitter: by being prepared, staying engaged in the game, and learning how to anticipate when your time might come up. Dobbs became an important part of the Phillies' offense. Building on his 2007 production of 14 pinch hits and a league-leading 18 pinch-hit RBIs, in 2008 Dobbs hit .355 as a pinch-hitter, and again led the league with 22 pinch hits. His 16 RBIs were second highest among the league's pinch-hitters.

Dobbs' strong postseason helped the Phillies advance through the playoffs and win their first World Series championship since 1980, and the second in their history. He played in every series, appearing in eight games. He had 7 hits in 14 at-bats as the Phillies defeated the Brewers and then the Dodgers on their way to capturing the National League pennant. They faced the Tampa Bay Rays in the World Series, winning in five games.

The next season, neither Dobbs nor the Phillies were able to repeat their 2008 triumph. The Phillies made it back to the World Series but lost to the Yankees in six games. Dobbs was unable to match either his 2007 or 2008 heroics. Splitting time across multiple positions and pinch-hitting duties, he appeared in 97 games, batting .247 with 20 RBIs. While he made appearances in both the Division and League Championship series, he did not see action against the Yankees in the World Series. A bout of the flu did not help his cause.

Dobbs' diminished role on the team became apparent when he started the next season with the Phillies Triple-A International League affiliate, the Lehigh Valley IronPigs. His time with the IronPigs was limited, and after 16 games he was recalled by the Phillies and appeared in 88 games. While he was again shuffled around the field, most of his action came as a pinch-hitter. But after finishing the season with a .196 batting average, on October 28, 2010, Dobbs' time with the Phillies came to an end. He was released, thus beginning the final stage of his baseball career.

In the winter of 2011, Dobbs was signed by the Florida Marlins to a minor-league contract with a spring-training invite. He made the team's major-league roster and appeared regularly in the Marlins' lineup, playing in 134 games with a career-high 411 at-bats. Dobbs achieved a career high in hits with 113, as well as in doubles (23). He finished the season with a .275 batting average, with 49 runs batted in. Back with the newly branded Miami Marlins in 2012, Dobbs' versatility again kept him in the lineup with pinch-hitting and stints at five different positions. He played in 120 games, batting .285 with 91 hits and 39 RBIs. In 2013 he appeared in 114 games for the Marlins, hitting .228. His time continued to be divided among pinch-hitting and multiple positions in the field.

Dobbs started 2014 with the Marlins but on May 6, he was released. He was picked up by the Washington Nationals less than a week later. But his time with the Nationals was short-lived, consisting of only 21 games, during which he hit .214.

Dobbs made his final major-league appearance on June 24, 2014. The Nationals were playing the Brewers in Milwaukee, and in the top of the 15th inning, with the score tied, 2-2, Dobbs pinch-hit for pitcher Drew Storen. Facing Mike Fiers, on a 1-and-2 count, Dobbs flied out to left-center. The at-bat was his last in the majors. The Nationals sent him to Triple-A Syracuse on July 3. Dobbs made 35 appearances there before his professional career came to a close when he decided to retire.

Over 11 seasons of major-league baseball, split among four franchises, Dobbs appeared in 959 games. He batted .261, with 548 hits, 46 of which were home runs, with 274 RBIs – and he has a World Series ring.

Upon retirement, Dobbs considered staying in the game. Becoming an agent was an option – he had negotiated his final two contracts with the Marlins without an agent – and he also contemplated seeking a front-office job. But the thoughtful Dobbs decided to go in another direction. As a player, he seldom read the sports pages or watched major-league baseball; he would rather understand global economics and "how the world really works."[1] His pinch-hitting success was a product of his "strong work ethic [and] obsession with preparation," and he sought a new challenge that would use those same traits in the world

of finance.[12] He joined Parq Advisors as a financial adviser, and in 2018, he moved to UBS in Los Angeles – in his words, "the big leagues of finance."[13] To advance his career, he earned his license in financial advising, passing a range of tests. He studied in the same way he "had prepared every day for the relievers he might face" on any given night.[14] While not directly related to baseball, Dobbs said his daily efforts to serve his clients reflect the same approach he used in baseball.

He explained the connection as "[t]he lessons I learned from baseball and being a good teammate, knowing what teamwork is, being selfless, wanting to help others."[15] He noted, "I had to find ways to add value because I wasn't that everyday guy. I was that complementary 24th, 25th guy. I was guaranteed a roster spot a handful of years. I had to find ways to add value other than on the field, between the lines. I've taken that and I've incorporated that into what I'm doing now with the team that I'm with. It's been incredible. I look back and I'm like, 'Who would've thought?'"[16]

In addition, as he did in his playing days, he became an involved and contributing member of the community. During his days with the Phillies, Dobbs was on the board of trustees for Bancroft Neuro-Health, a nonprofit that serves people with autism and other disabilities. As a Miami Marlin, he started "Lil' Dobbers," a program that benefits children in the Boys and Girls Clubs of Miami-Dade County, by providing youngsters with on-field experiences while stressing the importance of education.

Since retiring and settling back in California, Dobbs has served as co-chair of the West Coast Advisory Board for Team IMPACT, a nonprofit that pairs children facing life-threatening illnesses with NCAA sports teams across the nation. The role is a continuation of his earlier efforts to give back to the community. Dobbs was also recognized in 2008 when the Philadelphia sportswriters voted him the Philadelphia Phillies Good Guy Award, an annual honor bestowed on a player who exemplifies a good-natured personality and professionalism on and off the field.[17]

Dobbs and his wife, Heidi (Reinhardt) Dobbs, whose grandfather was a coach at Glendale College, live in La Cañada, California. They have two daughters.[18]

SOURCES

In addition to the sources cited in the Notes, the author consulted Baseball-Reference.com and baseball-almanac.com.

NOTES

1   Matt Breen, "Greg Dobbs Was Baseball's Best Pinch Hitter. He Uses Those Same Skills in 'the Big Leagues of Finance,'" *Philadelphia Inquirer*, September 21, 2023. https://www.inquirer.com/phillies/greg-dobbs-2008-phillies-world-series-where-are-they-now-20230920.html#:~:text=Greg%20Dobbs%20was%20baseball's%20best,we%20had%20in%20one%20another.%22; accessed on June 2, 2024.

2   John E. Hoover, "Mirror Image," *Tulsa World*, May 16, 2001: 15; Greg's brother, Kenny Jr., was a freshman catcher at Riverside CC when Greg was at Oklahoma. https://www.newspapers.com/image/895643759/?terms=%22greg%20dobbs%22%20peru; accessed June 2, 2024.

3   Hoover.

4   "Greg Dobbs – Anchorage Glacier Pilots – Alumni – 2000 Team," Alaska Baseball League. https://www.youtube.com/watch?v=fZ88F-sp-xgw; accessed on June 2, 2024

5   Athletics Communications, "Dobbs Captures Second All-American Honor," Oklahoma University, June 8, 2001. https://soonersports.com/news/2001/6/8/208402887; accessed on June 2, 2024.

6   "Greg Dobbs," The Baseball Cube; accessed on June 3, 2024.

7   "Dobbs Captures Second All-American Honor."

8   John Sickels, "Prospect Retro: Greg Dobbs," SB Nation, October 8, 2008. https://www.minorleagueball.com/2008/10/8/631018/prospect-retro-greg-dobbs; accessed June 2, 2024.

9   Chuck Hixson, "Who's Greg Dobbs; Why Did the Phils Grab Him?' *Phillies Daily*, January 20, 2007. https://247sports.com/ mlb/phillies/article/whos-greg-dobbs-why-did-the-phils-grab-him-104392874/; accessed June 2, 2024.

10 Breen.

11 Breen.

12 Breen.

13 Breen

14 Breen

15 Breen.

16 Breen.

17 "Greg Dobbs, Financial Advisor," UBS: The Baumgardner Group and Partners. https://advisors.ubs.com/baumgardnergroup/; accessed on June 2, 2024.

18 Seth Amitin, "Family Man in the Big Leagues," *La Cañada Valley Sun*, August 21, 2008. https://www.latimes.com/socal/la-canada-valley-sun/news/tn-vsl-xpm-2008-08-21-lsp-dobbs.0821-story.html; accessed June 2, 2024.

ELIJAH DUKES

BY BARRETT SNYDER

"Dukes can be the proverbial five-tool player. His swing is … I daresay, kind of like Albert Pujols."
– *Joe Maddon, who managed Dukes in 2007 with the Tampa Bay Devil Rays*[1]

"He will snap in a minute."
– *Richie Hebner, who coached Dukes in 2006 with the Durham Bulls*[2]

Hillsborough County in Florida's Tampa Bay area is a renowned breeding ground for professional athletes – especially baseball prodigies. They include Dwight Gooden, Gary Sheffield, Tony La Russa, Steve Garvey, Wade Boggs, and Fred McGriff.

However, amid the abundant talent nurtured within the 813 area code, one individual stands apart: Elijah Dukes. Widely regarded as one of the most naturally gifted athletes ever to emerge from Hillsborough County's sports scene, Dukes was a multisport star in high school and flashed promise in the majors. Yet despite his undeniable natural gifts, his inner struggles transcended his physical prowess. Overhanging his story are off-field behavior and relentless demons. The outfielder's big-league career ended in 2009 after just three seasons; Dukes was only 25 years old. Subsequently, his profoundly sad and harrowing chronicle continued to unfold, marked by a running battle with the law.

Elijah David Dukes was born on June 26, 1984, in Homestead, Florida, a Miami suburb and a major agricultural area. His parents were Elijah Dukes Sr. and Phyllis (Evans) Dukes. Dukes was one of six children. His siblings are Tyrone Joseph Evans, Mary Helen Dukes, Katrina Evans, Rebecca Evans, and Willie Evans.

A formative influence on young Elijah Jr. – for the worse – came after his father shot and killed Kevin Reese in September 1995 outside a bar in Tampa. The motive was that Reese reportedly sold fake crack cocaine to Phyllis. Initially charged with first-degree murder, Dukes Sr. pleaded guilty to second-degree murder with a firearm and was sentenced to 20 years in prison on July 12, 1996.[3] Before Dukes Sr. was imprisoned, his uncle, James Dukes, lobbied the judge for a lighter sentence, suggesting, "If [Dukes Sr.] isn't at home to care for the children, to lead, guide and direct them, I'm almost certain one of them will be standing before you for sentencing … in the near future."[4] Nonetheless, Dukes Sr. received the maximum.

Elijah Jr. and his sisters were in the courtroom as their father was sentenced. Decades later, Katrina recounted how 12-year-old Elijah reached out and tried to touch his dad as the guards led him away in shackles. Phyllis later noted that her kids were really hurt when Dukes Sr. went to prison.[5] Katrina

Elijah Dukes, Tampa Bay Rays – Courtesy of Trading Card Database

remembered that they would return home in the evening to find all the lights turned off and Phyllis alone crying. At that point, young Elijah said, "I'm growing up to be a professional player."[6]

Dukes Sr. was released on November 1, 2009, after serving 14 years. Three weeks after his release, he died of cancer at the age of 43.[7] He never saw his son play in the majors.[8]

While raising her six children, Phyllis received her high-school diploma in 1995 at the age of 34.[9] That accomplishment was important to her. She said, "I needed that, to let [her children] know: If I could, you could." Raised just outside of Miami,

Phyllis was one of eight, and her parents split when she was a child. She had her first child at 20 and Elijah Jr. at 24.[10]

In 1992, after Hurricane Andrew destroyed her family's home in Miami, the family moved to West Tampa. Dukes Sr. stayed in Miami until he and Phyllis were married on January 21, 1994. After that, Dukes Sr. relocated to Tampa and got a job driving trucks. During that time, the family enjoyed many barbecues on Indian Rocks Beach – "good days," as the *Tampa Bay Times* reported.[11]

That changed after Phyllis started purchasing crack in small amounts just to give to a few friends. She subsequently admitted to dealing crack but claimed never to have used it. She later described selling drugs as her biggest mistake.[12] As of 2007, Phyllis worked 12-hour shifts as a complex security guard in Tampa.[13]

Once, in a candid portrayal of her son, Phyllis remarked, "His father and his crack-head mother – it follows him. It brings out his temper. Ever since he was in high school, every little thing he did was in the paper. Nothing good." She admitted that her family never came off well in sound bites.[14]

Despite Dukes' extensive rap sheet and notorious reputation, his sister Katrina made it a point to defend her brother and noted that the public saw only one side of him. "People make Elijah out to be some kind of monster. Like he's not even a person. That's the part that's so tough for our family to deal with," she said. "I'm not saying he hasn't done a lot of things wrong. He has. And he needs to learn from them, not make excuses, but learn from them. He's my brother. It has been hard. It has been hard for all of us."[15]

Elijah Jr.'s own troubles began on September 29, 1997, with an arrest for misdemeanor battery – he was just 13.[16] The following year, he faced another battery charge, but details remained scarce because he was still a juvenile.[17] Dukes attended four high schools, often moving as a result of conflicts with referees, teachers, and coaches.[18] In one school year, Dukes was dismissed from his basketball, baseball, and football teams.[19]

Nonetheless, as a sophomore at Jefferson High School, Dukes gained recognition not only for his emerging baseball talent but also as a skilled linebacker and tailback on the football team. That year, he a second-team All-State linebacker and surpassed 1,000 yards rushing.[20] While at Jefferson, he pitched a no-hitter in baseball.[21] His offensive coordinator at Jefferson, K.R. Lombardia, remarked of Dukes, "He's the best running back I ever coached, and I think the best running back I ever saw in high school ball." On the baseball field, Jefferson coach Pop Cuesta shared a similar sentiment, saying, "Elijah was probably the most gifted athlete I've ever had." (Cuesta dismissed Dukes from the team midway through the season for disciplinary issues.[22])

Dukes later transferred to Hillsborough High School, which boasts alumni such as former major leaguers Carl Everett, Gary Sheffield, and Dwight Gooden. Altogether, Dukes earned varsity letters in four different sports: football, baseball, basketball, and track. He achieved this distinction for four years in football and baseball, and for two years in basketball and track. As a junior he continued to shine as a tailback and middle linebacker, gaining recognition as an All-State linebacker and again rushing for over 1,000 yards. His efforts helped the Hillsborough Terriers reach the state regional football semifinals in his junior year and the quarterfinals in his senior year.[23]

Known for being double-jointed, Dukes was highlighted by *USA Today* in 2002 as the nation's top two-sport athlete. He had excellent size for both baseball and football, standing 6-feet-2 and listed as weighing 225 to 250 pounds. His physique was naturally muscular and imposing. Dukes' former football coach at Hillsborough, Earl Garcia, said in 2007, "Elijah Dukes should be talked about as one of the greatest athletes ever to come from our area. Instead, he's viewed like Dr. Jekyll and Mr. Hyde. You never know what you're going to get." However, Garcia added, "I say that as somebody who never walked in his shoes."[24]

Dukes signed a letter of intent to play linebacker at North Carolina State University. He observed: "I think a lot of the schools backed off because they knew I was interested in baseball. But I didn't want to miss the opportunity of a college scholarship. N.C. State agreed to accommodate my aspirations to play professional baseball and college football. I hope it works out for both."[25]

However, after being selected in the third round (74th overall) of the 2002 amateur draft by the Tampa Bay Devil Rays (as the team was then called), Dukes signed a contract with a bonus of $505,000, officially starting his professional baseball career. He was scouted and signed by Kevin Elfering of the Rays.

Dukes' first assignment was in 2003 with the Charleston RiverDogs of the low Class-A South Atlantic League. He stole 33 bases, the most on the team and the third-most in the organization. His first professional home run, a two-run walk-off, came on May 31 against Savannah. On July 16 Dukes hit two home runs against Hickory. That season, he also struck out 130 times. *Baseball America* named Dukes the organization's best defensive outfielder and the top pure athlete in the Rays system.[26]

Away from the field, Dukes exhibited concerning behavior. On December 8, 2003, the Hillsborough Sheriff's Department responded to an incident at Dukes' residence involving an altercation with his eventual wife and his children's mother, NiShea Gilbert, in which he reportedly threw a remote control at her.[27] Gilbert described Dukes as a "ticking time bomb."[28] The charges eventually were dismissed. Later that month, he was pulled over on suspicion of careless driving. When a Tampa police officer approached his vehicle, he used offensive language toward her, as noted in the arrest report. After he attempted to roll up his window, the officer forcibly removed him from the car, charging him with obstructing an officer without violence. Dukes was later admitted to a misdemeanor intervention program, which led to the dismissal of the charges against him.[29]

In 2004 Dukes returned to Charleston, hitting safely in his first nine games. He soon advanced to the Bakersfield Blaze of the high Class-A California League, where he maintained his impressive performance at the plate. Dukes hit .322 and reached base in 53 of 58 games. His cumulative statistics for that year included a .313 batting average, 117 hits, 70 runs, 10 home runs, 49 RBIs, and 30 stolen bases. Notably, he reduced his strikeouts to 97. His 30 steals ranked third in the organization for that year, and *Baseball America* named him Tampa Bay's sixth-best prospect.

Despite Dukes' on-field success, the year was again marred by numerous off-field incidents. In January Dukes called Hillsborough sheriff's deputies after an altercation with Gilbert. He claimed she sprayed him with an unknown substance from an aerosol can and expressed his intention to document the incident but did not wish to press charges. On April 28 Gilbert sought a domestic-violence injunction against Dukes, citing numerous threatening phone calls and similar threats from his family members. Her request was denied. On October 12 Gilbert reported to deputies that Dukes had thrown a soda can and a candy jar at her. No arrest was made. Three days later, Gilbert filed for another protective order against Dukes, which was granted; it was effective for one year. That same month, Dukes' ex-girlfriend, Carla Bryant, who had previously requested a paternity test proving that Dukes was her child's father, also filed for a protective order. A judge granted her request, issuing a one-year no-contact order against Dukes.[30]

In January 2005, before his assignment to Double-A Montgomery, Dukes' sister Katrina reported to the Tampa police that he had grabbed her by the throat and hit her left arm. Consequently, Dukes faced a battery charge, which he did not contest and resulted in a one-year probation sentence. Just six days later, another former girlfriend, Zanquesha Jefferson, filed a request for prosecution with the Tampa police. She accused Dukes of visiting her home and strangling her.[31] No charges were subsequently filed.

With Montgomery in 2005, Dukes batted .287 with career highs of 128 hits and 18 home runs, and a career-low 83 strike-outs. He was named the Rays' minor-league player of the month for April. On June 19 he hit his first career grand slam in Jacksonville against future major leaguer Chad Billingsley. After the season, he was ranked as the Rays' fifth-best prospect by *Baseball America*.

Also during his time in Montgomery, Dukes learned that he had fathered another child with a different woman, Shantell Mitchell. On June 16 Gilbert gave birth again, with Dukes revealed as the father. Court records indicate that Dukes fathered at least five children with four women between 2003 and 2006.[32] The *Washington Post* reported in 2012 that Dukes by then had six children.[33]

In February 2006, Dukes married NiShea Gilbert. However, by May 1 Gilbert filed for divorce, alleging that Dukes married her to avoid paying child support. Gilbert withdrew the divorce petition in June.[34] On the field, Dukes impressed during his first big-league spring training by hitting .400 (8-for-20) in 14 games, earning the Rays' Al Lopez Award for top rookie in camp. *Baseball America* named him the organization's best athlete and sixth-best prospect, as well as the International League's 11th-best prospect.

Dukes was assigned to the Triple-A Durham Bulls for the 2006 season. In 80 games, he batted .313 with a .401 on-base percentage.

However, the season was marred by suspensions. In June the Rays suspended Dukes following two violent incidents involving hitting coach Richie Hebner and teammate Ryan Knox, whom Dukes choked in a hotel lobby.[35] In August the International League suspended him for five games for misconduct toward an umpire. As his IL suspension was ending, the Rays extended it by 25 games, the remainder of the season. The Rays stated that while no single episode was major, it was the accumulation of small incidents they were addressing.[36]

Post-suspension, Dukes expressed doubt about his baseball career, feeling overwhelmed and frustrated. He said, "I have no idea when or if I'll be back. I packed up all my stuff, and I'm headed home. To be honest, I don't even know about baseball anymore. Everything is just wearing on me, and this year has just been so frustrating. I'm trying to keep my nose clean and keep to myself, but things just keep getting turned around. I'm tired of it."[37] He returned to play in the Arizona Fall League in September but left-knee surgery cut his season short.

In January 2007 Dukes was arrested on a misdemeanor charge of marijuana possession.[38] Police discovered a bag with less than two grams of the substance in his car's center con-sole.[39] On the field, the 22-year-old was poised to make his long-awaited big-league debut, and it began in storybook fashion on April 2. At Yankee Stadium, Dukes hit a fifth-inning home run off Carl Pavano.[40] He became the 98th man to hit a homer in his first at-bat in the majors.[41] (He had walked in his first plate appearance.)

Two days later, an ESPN.com feature on Dukes shed light on the ongoing struggle between his anger management and his five-tool potential. Dukes acknowledged, "The anger would just take over," but he had learned to control it. "Now when something happens," he said, "I can kind of switch sides and think about how the other person is thinking and how I can make it different."[42]

The article also quoted others. Catcher Shawn Riggans defended Dukes, stating, "I love Elijah. He's a great guy. I'd take a bullet for him." The Devil Rays' manager, Joe Maddon, expressed confidence in Dukes by highlighting his five-tool potential while emphasizing the need for self-control. "I think he understands now that he's on a major-league stage where everything is scrutinized even more. I really believe he believes he belongs here. And he wants to stay here, and he understands that it takes a certain decorum in order to do that."[43]

Rays general manager Andrew Friedman acknowledged Dukes' challenging childhood and the importance of focusing on the game. As Dukes spoke, his words appeared genuine and devoid of anger, signifying his determination to harness that emotion and shape a brighter future. But his challenges continued to mount.

On April 26 Dukes was served with a paternity suit by Porcia Reneal Daniels which alleged that he was the father of her son born the previous July.[44] That same month, Dukes barged into Gilbert's classroom at lunch. (She was a middle-school teacher.) He ran to her desk and stated that he was going to beat and kill her. Badly shaken, Gilbert rushed to get the principal and a deputy, who ultimately banned Dukes from the property. Gilbert said she feared for her life and noted that this was the latest in a series of recent outbursts by her husband.[45]

In May Gilbert sought a restraining order against Dukes.[46] She told the court she feared for her life while citing Dukes' death threats, which included sending a photo of a handgun to her phone. On May 30 a Hillsborough County judge granted her a one-year restraining order. He also ordered Dukes to relinquish all firearms and undergo a psychological evaluation before he was allowed to see his children.[47]

On the field, Dukes continued to excel. He set a club record for rookies by hitting seven home runs in May. He led all rookies with nine extra-base hits and 15 RBIs in that month. He hit two first-inning leadoff homers in May, on the 16th against the Texas Rangers and on the 19th vs. the Florida Marlins. As of early June, he had hit 10 home runs.

However, on June 22, Dukes was optioned to the minors and placed on the temporary inactive list as more off-the-field allegations surfaced.

A teenage girl who resided in the foster home of a relative of Dukes told police that Dukes had impregnated her when she was 17. The investigation into the pregnancy concluded that criminal statutes did not apply to consensual sex between a 17-year-old and a 22-year-old. The teenager also alleged that Dukes threw a Gatorade bottle at her.[48]

In August it was reported that Dukes violated Gilbert's restraining order against him by calling her at home and asking to speak to his children.[49] He did not play again in 2007 and finished the season with a .190 batting average and 21 RBIs in 52 games. He returned to action in the Dominican winter league, where he was ejected during one game for bumping an umpire.[50]

The Rays traded Dukes to the Washington Nationals in December for pitching prospect Glenn Gibson.[51] After the trade was announced, his former teammate Riggans noted that if Dukes could focus on the field, there weren't too many other players like him. However, Hebner and Maddon did not mince words. Referring to Dukes' short fuse, Hebner stated, "A new team or a new stadium won't change that." Maddon, who just the previous year had praised Dukes, added about the departure, "It feels a whole lot better here."[52]

Two weeks after acquiring Dukes, the Nationals gave James Williams, a former police officer, the full-time responsibility for overseeing their new player. Throughout spring training, the two were roommates. Dukes affectionately called Williams "Supernanny" and said that Williams played a role akin to a second father.[53]

In 2008 Dukes got into 81 games for Washington and had 334 plate appearances. He made more impact per game than any other player on the roster. He posted a slash line of .264/.386/.478,

walking in 15 percent of his plate appearances. His power was evident with a .231 Isolated Power (ISO). He set personal big-league highs of 13 home runs, 44 runs batted in, and 73 hits. Dukes displayed his defensive abilities at the corner outfield positions with a team-leading nine outfield assists. He accumulated a WAR of 2.9. Although he was a valuable asset, knee surgery sidelined him for a significant portion of July.[54] He also suffered a calf injury in early August, leading to a multi-week stint on the DL.[55]

Dukes embarked on his second big-league season with the Nationals in 2009. In April he was fined $500 by manager Manny Acta for showing up late to the ballpark. Dukes was late, but not for a troubling reason: he was visiting a Little League in Northern Virginia, where he watched a parade, signed autographs, and shared advice with the youngsters. James Mraz, the president of the Great Falls Little League, organized a fundraiser to cover the fine.[56] He noted, "This guy gave back to our community, and now he's in a hard spot. We need to help him. It's not a question of whether this guy can afford the 500 bucks. We're just trying to send a message to our kids: He was here for us. Now we've got to be there for him."[57]

Acta noted, "He was very remorseful about it. He felt bad, but we have to lay down the law. Regardless of who is out there, we are still losing ballgames. We have to change the culture somehow."[58] This was not the first time Acta and Dukes had butted heads. During a game against the Pirates in 2008, they got in a shouting match in the dugout; both men had to be restrained. Dukes then refused to acknowledge Acta during the customary postgame victory handshake line.[59]

Dukes registered career highs in 2009 with 91 hits, 20 doubles, 4 triples, and 58 RBIs in 107 games played. As in the previous season, he was sometimes sidelined by injuries. He went on a minor-league rehab assignment on May 30 and did not return to the Nationals until July 31.

That winter, Dukes returned to the Dominican league and appeared in four games with Tigres del Licey. In spring training 2010, the Nationals let him go abruptly with just 2½ weeks remaining. After the release, he mused, "I don't know what to say. It felt a little funny. I guess I wasn't expecting it. ... That's part of baseball. No big deal, no hard feelings. Just part of the game."[60]

Speculation arose regarding whether Dukes' release stemmed from performance or off-the-field conduct, but Nationals manager Jim Riggleman, general manager Mike Rizzo, and team President Stan Kasten all emphasized that this was a baseball decision and nothing more.[61]

Dukes' big-league career had ended after three seasons. In 240 games played, he hit .242 (199-for-824) with 31 homers and 123 RBIs.

Early in 2010, Dukes was set to play for the Tabasco Olmecas of the Mexican League, but the opportunity fell apart when he failed to show up on the reporting date.[62] Subsequently, Dukes signed with the Newark Bears of the independent Atlantic League, where he batted .366 with 5 homers in 28 games.

During the winter of 2011-12, Dukes rejoined Licey and batted .217 in seven games. That was his last action as a pro ballplayer – he was still just 27.

After his professional career concluded, Dukes openly stated his conviction that he'd been "thrown under the bus" and "blackballed" by Major League Baseball following his disclosures regarding substance abuse among athletes.[63] He claimed players smuggled drugs, including marijuana and cocaine, on planes and used them in hotel rooms.[64] Dukes even admitted to his own marijuana use before home games with the Nationals.[65] MLB denied any claims that Dukes was blackballed.[66]

Dukes briefly pursued a rap music career with the stage name "Fly Eli" in February 2011.[67] That venture didn't pan out, and he continued to tangle with the law. In November 2011 he was incarcerated in Tampa on charges related to failing to pay child support.[68] In 2010 alone, he owed a total of $143,000 in child support and alimony to three women.[69] Previously, in March 2011, Dukes was arrested on charges of aggravated battery against a pregnant woman and driving with a revoked or suspended license.[70] According to a sheriff's office report, Dukes' ex-girlfriend, Mountrail Mounshay Mack, reported that he had slapped her in the face several times.[71] Dukes had also been wanted on a contempt warrant. A month later, on April 25, he was again arrested, this time on charges related to operating a vehicle with a suspended or revoked driver's license.[72]

On Thursday, February 23, 2012, Dukes was pulled over around 1:00 A.M. after committing a traffic violation. The officers noticed a bag of marijuana on his lap; Dukes tried to dispose of it by sticking it in his mouth as if he was going to ingest it. Shortly after being taken into custody, officers noticed a marijuana blunt tucked behind his ear. Dukes was charged with tampering with physical evidence, possession of under 20 grams of marijuana, possession of drug paraphernalia, and driving with a canceled, suspended, or revoked license. He was detained because of two outstanding Hillsborough County warrants related to driving with a suspended license and operating with a suspended or revoked driver's license.[73]

Dukes encountered legal trouble yet again on January 21, 2013, when he was arrested in Tampa for failure to attend court hearings related to various drug and traffic violations.[74] On December 19, 2013, Dukes was arrested in his Brandon home on a warrant charging him with violating his probation.[75]

After being absent from the news for several years, on November 15, 2021, Dukes was arrested on a misdemeanor trespassing charge.[76] As of 2024, he had stayed clear of any further scrapes.

While Elijah Jr. moved on from wearing a baseball uniform, his son, Elijah Dukes III, garnered attention in the Tampa region with success on the diamond. Dukes III graduated from Wharton High School in 2022. A scouting database, Perfect Game USA, recognized him as the eighth-best first baseman in Florida at the time.[77] He then went to San Jacinto College in Texas.

The story of Elijah Dukes Jr., while featuring his remarkable athletic abilities, is ultimately a poignant reminder of the human complexities behind the façade of sports success. His rise and fall serve as a testament to the glory and tragedy that can coexist in this realm.

ACKNOWLEDGMENTS

This biography was reviewed by Rory Costello and Mike Eisenbath, fact-checked by Carl Riechers, and copy-edited by Len Levin.

SOURCES

In addition to the sources cited in the Notes, the author consulted baseball-reference.com, MLB.com, Fangraphs.com, and wilson-funeralhome.com.

NOTES

1   Amy K. Nelson, "Dukes Letting Talent, Not Anger, Take Over," ESPN.com, April 4, 2007. https://www.espn.com/mlb/news/story?id=2823398.

2   "Dukes Letting Talent, Not Anger, Take Over." Farid Rushdi, "Elijah Dukes: Are His Problems the Result of a Bad Man or a Bad Childhood?" *Bleacher Report*, January 16, 2009. https://bleacherreport.com/articles/111960-elijah-dukes-are-his-problems-the-result-of-a-bad-man-or-a-bad-childhood.

3   Katherine Shaver, "Man Sentenced to 20 Years for Cocaine-Sale Killing," *Tampa Bay Times*, July 13, 1996. https://www.tampabay.com/archive/1996/07/13/man-sentenced-to-20-years-for-cocaine-sale-killing/.

4   Joey Johnston, "Since Childhood, Trouble Has Often Shadowed Elijah Dukes," *Tampa Tribune*, May 27, 2007. https://joeyjohnston-communications.com/an-unsettled-life/.

5   Abbie Vansickle, "Dukes Family Pride," *Tampa Bay Times*, June 21, 2007. https://www.tampabay.com/archive/2007/06/21/dukes-family-pride/.

6   Abbie Vansickle, "Mother of Devil Rays' Rookie Slugger Hopes He Will Get Help," *St. Petersburg Times*, June 22, 2007. https://www.theledger.com/story/news/2007/06/22/mother-of-devil-rays-rookie-slugger-hopes-he-will-get-help/25873085007/.

7   Colleen Jenkins, "Mourning Family Questions Care Given in Prison," *Tampa Bay Times*, December 4, 2009. https://www.tampabay.com/archive/2009/12/04/mourning-family-questions-care-given-in-prison/.

8   "Nationals' Dukes Hopes Hard Work Equals Breakout Season." *Lakeland* (Florida) *Ledger*, March 3, 2010. https://www.theledger.com/story/news/2010/03/03/nationals-dukes-hopes-hard-work/8101893007/.

9   Vansickle, "Mother of Devil Rays' Rookie Slugger Hopes He Will Get Help."

10   Vansickle, "Dukes Family Pride."

11   Vansickle, "Dukes Family Pride."

12   Vansickle, "Dukes Family Pride."

13   Vansickle, "Mother of Devil Rays' Rookie Slugger Hopes He Will Get Help."

14   Vansickle, "Mother of Devil Rays' Rookie Slugger Hopes He Will Get Help."

15   Johnston. "Since Childhood, Trouble Has Often Shadowed Elijah Dukes."

16   Chris Jones, "TICK TICK TICK," ESPN.com, May 5, 2008. https://www.espn.com/espnmag/story?id=3382818.

17   "A Decade of Trouble," *Tampa Bay Times*, June 23, 2007. https://www.tampabay.com/archive/2007/06/23/a-decade-of-trouble/.

18   Jones, "TICK TICK TICK."

19   Johnston. "Since Childhood, Trouble Has Often Shadowed Elijah Dukes."

20   Scott Purks, "Two-Sport Prospect Dukes Transfers to Hillsborough." *Tampa Bay Times*, August 8, 2000. https://www.tampabay.com/archive/2000/08/08/two-sport-prospect-dukes-transfers-to-hillsborough/.

21   "Hillsborough County's Legends of the Gridiron," *Big County Preps*. https://bigcountypreps.com/accolades/hillsborough-county-legends/.

22   Johnston. "Since Childhood, Trouble Has Often Shadowed Elijah Dukes."

23   "Hillsborough County's Legends of the Gridiron."

24   Johnston, "Since Childhood, Trouble Has Often Shadowed Elijah Dukes."

25   Scott Purks, "Hillsborough's Dukes Picks Football After All," *Tampa Bay Times*, February 7, 2002. https://www.tampabay.com/archive/2002/02/07/hillsborough-s-dukes-picks-football-after-all/.

26   Jones, "TICK TICK TICK."

27   "A Decade of Trouble."

28   Johnston. "Since Childhood, Trouble Has Often Shadowed Elijah Dukes."

29   "A Decade of Trouble."

30   "A Decade of Trouble."

31   "A Decade of Trouble."

32   "A Decade of Trouble."

33   Matt Brooks, "Report: Elijah Dukes Tried to Eat Bag of Marijuana After Traffic Stop," *Washington Post*, February 23, 2012. https://www.washingtonpost.com/blogs/early-lead/post/report-elijah-dukes-tried-to-eat-bag-of-marijuana-after-traffic-stop/2012/02/23/gIQAF1cVVR_blog.html.

34   "A Decade of Trouble."

35   Jones, "TICK TICK TICK."

36   Marc Topkin, "Suspended Dukes Threatening to Quit," *Tampa Bay Times*, August 2, 2006. https://www.tampabay.com/archive/2006/08/02/suspended-dukes-threatening-to-quit/.

37   Topkin, "Suspended Dukes Threatening to Quit."

38   Marc Topkin, "Rays' Dukes Arrested on Marijuana Charge," *Tampa Bay Times*, January 17, 2007. https://www.tampabay.com/archive/2007/01/17/rays-dukes-arrested-on-marijuana-charge/.

39   Topkin, "Rays' Dukes Arrested on Marijuana Charge."

40   Yankees Beat Rays on Emotional Opening Day," ESPN.com, April 3, 2007. https://www.espn.com/mlb/recap/_/gameId/270402110.

41   "Baseball Feats by Feats," *Baseball Almanac*. https://www.baseball-almanac.com/feats/feats5.shtml.

42   Nelson, "Dukes Letting Talent, Not Anger, Take Over."

43   Nelson, "Dukes Letting Talent, Not Anger, Take Over."

44   "A Decade of Trouble."

45   Eduardo A. Encina, "Ballplayer's Wife: 'He Threatened Me, Kids,'" *Tampa Bay Times*, May 23, 2007.

46   Encina, "Ballplayer's Wife: 'He Threatened Me, Kids.'"

47   Carrie Weimar, "Judge Orders Devil Rays' Elijah Dukes Away From Wife for One Year," Lakeland *Ledger*, May 30, 2007. .https://www.theledger.com/story/news/2007/05/30/judge-orders-devil-rays-elijah-dukes-away-from-wife-for-one-year/25779433007/.

48   Abbie Vansickle, "Former Foster Teen Says She Is Carrying Dukes' Baby," *Tampa Bay Times*, June 13, 2007. https://www.tampabay.com/archive/2007/06/13/former-foster-teen-says-she-is-carrying-dukes-baby/.

49   Jones, "TICK TICK TICK."

50   Jones, "TICK TICK TICK."

51   Jones, "TICK TICK TICK."

52   Rushdi, "Elijah Dukes: Are His Problems the Result of a Bad Man or a Bad Childhood?"

53   Jones, "TICK TICK TICK."

54   "Elijah Dukes' Knee Is Dead, Dawg," NBC Washington, October 20, 2008. https://www.nbcwashington.com/news/sports/fanho-elijah-dukes-knee-is-dead-dawg/1839838/.

55   "Rain in Denver Postpones Nats-Rockies Game," ESPN.com, August 7, 2008. https://www.espn.com/mlb/recap?gameId=280806127.

56   Bill Littlefield, "Elijah Dukes Gives Kids Questionable Advice for $500 a Minute," WBUR, April 23, 2009. https://www.wbur.org/news/2009/04/23/elijah-dukes.

57   Andrew Giermak, "A Good Idea, a Fine, and a Reward," *Suffolk* (Virginia) *News-Herald*, April 21, 2009. https://www.suffolknews-herald.com/2009/04/21/a-good-idea-a-fine-and-a-reward/.

58   Giermak, "A Good Idea, a Fine, and a Reward."

59   "Acta (Defuses) Notion of Bad Blood with Outfielder Dukes," ESPN.com, June 11, 2008. https://www.espn.com/mlb/news/story?id=3438353.

60   "Nats: Dukes Let Go for On-Field Reasons." ESPN.com, May 17, 2010. https://www.espn.com/mlb/spring2010/news/story?id=5002750.

61   "Nats: Dukes Let Go for On-Field Reasons."

62   Nick Cafardo, "Cafardo's Latest: Blue Jays, Dunn, Washburn, Dukes," MLB Trade Rumors, May 2, 2010. https://www.mlbtraderumors.com/2010/05/cafardos-latest-blue-jays-dunn-washburn-dukes.html.

63   Craig Calcaterra. "Elijah Dukes Is Now a Rapper. And He Used to Smoke Weed before Nats Games." NBC Sports, February 11, 2011. https://www.nbcsports.com/mlb/news/elijah-dukes-is-no-a-rapper-and-he-used-to-smoke-weed-before-nats-games.

64   Calcaterra, "Elijah Dukes Is Now a Rapper"; "Elijah Dukes Embarks on Rap Career, Admits to Smoking Weed Before Nats Games. Meet Fly Eli?" *Nats Enquirer*, February 11, 2011. https://www.natsenquirer.com/2011/02/elijah-dukes-embarks-on-a-new-career-as-a-rapper-meet-fly-eli.html.

65   Calcaterra, "Elijah Dukes Is Now a Rapper."

66   Brooks, "Report: Elijah Dukes Tried to Eat Bag of Marijuana After Traffic Stop."

67   "Elijah Dukes Embarks on Rap Career."

68   "Former Major Leaguer Dukes Arrested in Tampa," ESPN. com, November 2, 2010. https://www.espn.com/mlb/news/story?id=5757912.

69   "Drug Charges Send Former Rays Outfielder Elijah Dukes to Jail Again," *Tampa Bay Times*, February 23, 2012. https://www.tampabay.com/news/publicsafety/crime/drug-charges-send-former-rays-outfielder-elijah-dukes-to-jail-again/1216712/.

70   "Elijah Dukes Accused of Slapping Pregnant Ex," ESPN.com, March 3, 2011. https://www.espn.com/espn/wire?section=mlb&id=6177276.

71   "Former Montgomery Biscuit Elijah Dukes Arrested on Aggravated Battery Charge," AL.com, March 3, 2011. https://www.al.com/sports/2011/03/former_montgomery_biscuit_elij.html.

72   Craig Calcaterra, "Shocker: Elijah Dukes Arrested Again," NBC Sports, April 25, 2011. https://www.nbcsports.com/mlb/news/shocker-elijah-dukes-arrested-again.

73   "Drug Charges Send Former Rays Outfielder Elijah Dukes to Jail Again."

74   Laura C. Morel, "Former Rays Player Elijah Dukes Arrested in Tampa," *Tampa Bay Times*, January 22, 2013. https://www.tampabay.com/news/publicsafety/crime/former-rays-player-elijah-dukes-arrested-in-tampa/1271715/.

75   "Former Tampa Bay Rays Player Elijah Dukes Arrested in Brandon," *Tampa Bay Times*, December 20, 2013. https://www.tampabay.com/news/publicsafety/crime/former-ray-elijah-dukes-arrested-on-warrant-in-brandon/2157962/.

76   Search Results for "Elijah Dukes," Florida Arrests.org. https://florida.arrests.org/search.php?minage=&maxage=&sex=&county=&chargecode=&fname=Elijah+&fpartial=True&lname=Dukes&startdate=&enddate=.

77   "Player Profile – Elijah Dukes," Perfect Game.org. https://www.perfectgame.org/players/playerprofile.aspx?ID=714962.

19-YEAR-OLD PROFAR HITS HOME RUN IN INITIAL MAJOR-LEAGUE AT-BAT

September 2, 2012: Texas Rangers 8, Cleveland Indians 3, at Progressive Field, Cleveland

BY PAUL GEISLER

On an overcast Sunday afternoon during the Labor Day weekend – September 2, 2012 – over 19,000 fans gathered at Cleveland's Progressive Field to watch the home team Indians take on the Texas Rangers. The Rangers came in with an American League-best record of 78-54, leading the West Division by three games over the Oakland Athletics. Cleveland (56-77) stood in fourth place in the American League Central Division, 16½ games behind the Chicago White Sox.

Cleveland's starting staff had an ERA well over 6.00, the worst in the majors in the second half and a major reason for the Indians' 12-36 record since the All-Star break.

Each team had won one game of the three-game set. Texas won on Friday, 5-3; Cleveland took Saturday's game, 4-3.

The Indians' starting pitcher, right-hander Zach McAllister (5-5, 3.82 ERA), faced a Texas team averaging over five runs per game in the season so far. McAllister traded shutout innings with the Rangers starter, southpaw Derek Holland (9-6, 4.90), until Jurickson Profar led off the top of the third.

About an hour before game time, All-Star Ian Kinsler reported stiffness in his lower back. Texas manager Ron Washington asked 19-year-old Profar, called up two days earlier from the Rangers' Double-A affiliate in Frisco when team rosters expanded to the 40-man limit, how much second base he had played that season.

Profar answered "15-20 games." (It was 25.) "I was kind of shocked at first," the youngster said when he learned that he would get the start. "But I was ready for it."

The Rangers signed the native of Curaçao in 2009 at the age of 16 as an international free agent. His baseball abilities had drawn notice much earlier. The pitcher-shortstop led his country's Little League team to the world championship at Williamsport, Pennsylvania, in 2004 and back to the title game in 2005.

The newest Ranger became the first player born in 1993 to reach the majors and the youngest position player in the franchise's history.

Profar proved his readiness when he hit the fourth pitch he saw, a fastball from McAllister on a 2-and-1 count, 15 rows deep in the right-field seats, a distance of 388 feet. With that towering

Jurickson Profar, Texas Rangers – Courtesy of Trading Card Database

blast, he became the first batter in a Texas uniform to homer in his first major-league at-bat. Brant Alyea accomplished the feat with the Washington Senators in 1965, before the Senators moved to Texas in 1972.

Profar ranks as the second-youngest to hit a home run in his initial at-bat, joining the New York Giants' Whitey Lockman in 1945 and Cincinnati Reds' Ted Tappe in 1950 as the third teenager to do so.

Elvis Andrus followed Profar at the plate and grounded out to first base, unassisted. Then Michael Young singled and Josh

Hamilton walked. After McAllister struck out Adrian Beltré, Nelson Cruz clubbed a ground-rule double to deep right-center field, scoring Young and moving Hamilton to third. David Murphy followed with a groundball single to the right side of the infield, bringing in both Hamilton and Cruz. The eighth batter of the inning, Mitch Moreland, flied out to deep left field to end the inning with the Rangers leading 4-0.

The Indians' Ezequiel Carrera and Jason Donald grounded out to begin the bottom of the third inning, then Jason Kipnis singled. Holland picked him off first base, but Kipnis ended up on second base anyway, on an error by first baseman Moreland. Next, Carlos Santana turned a full-count pitch from Holland into a line-drive home run to left field, cutting the Rangers lead in half. After Russ Canzler doubled to deep center field, Holland struck out Thomas Neal to end the inning.

Texas threatened again in the top of the fourth inning. After the first batter, Luis Martinez, struck out, Profar doubled on a line drive to deep left field. He reached third base on a single by Andrus, but Young hit into a 4-3 double play.

Cleveland got only a two-out single from Lou Marson in their half of the fourth inning. The Rangers went back to work again in the top of the fifth inning.

Hamilton put the first pitch from McAllister over the right-field wall (his 37th of the season) and Beltré went back-to-back with his 27th, over the left-field wall. On the next pitch, Cruz lined out to deep center field, then Murphy turned his first pitch into the third round-tripper of the inning, a drive to deep right field (his 13th). The Rangers led 7-2.

Martinez followed a Moreland groundout to the pitcher with a single to right field. Up next, Profar did not appear in the on-deck circle, causing some to speculate that perhaps the brand-new Ranger had forgotten it was his turn to hit. "Suddenly," reported the Associated Press, "he grabbed a bat, ran to the plate and flied out on the second pitch,"[2] ending the inning.

In relief of McAllister, Scott Barnes contributed two score-less innings in the sixth and seventh. Facing Frank Herrmann, Cleveland's third pitcher of the day, Profar opened the top of the eighth inning with a fly ball to center field. Andrus singled to center field and Young brought him home with a double to deep right field, stretching the Texas lead to 8-2.

Cleveland rallied in the bottom of the eighth inning. With Mark Lowe pitching in relief of Holland, Santana sandwiched a double between fly outs from Kipnis and Canzler. Neal hit a double and Santana scored the third Cleveland run before Brent Lillibridge lined out to deep center field to end the inning.

Texas went quietly with a three-up three-down top of the ninth inning against Herrmann, leaving the score 8-3 in the Rangers' favor.

Tanner Scheppers became the Rangers' third pitcher of the game. He opened the bottom of the ninth inning with a walk

to Matt LaPorta before retiring the next three batters to seal the win for Texas.

Holland, 10-6 after his third win in a row, gave up two runs on seven hits, with six strikeouts and two walks in his seven innings, as the Rangers took two of three in the series. Texas matched its best record through 133 games, having also gone 79-54 in 1999.

McAllister's record dropped to 5-6, as he completed five innings and surrendered seven runs on 11 hits, with four strike-outs and two walks. All four of the Rangers' home runs came off McAllister. With the loss, he fell to 1-4 with a 6.08 ERA over his last seven starts.

Andrus had three hits in the contest and now had hit in all 29 of his career games against Cleveland.

The Rangers skipper seemed satisfied with the team's convincing 8-3 victory. "That's what we needed," Washington said. "We needed to really break out and show our authority in that ballgame and we certainly did that."[3]

Profar and his first-at-bat home run became the highlight of most of the postgame discussion. "I was thinking, 'Go, go, go, go' after I hit it," remarked Profar, who got the souvenir ball back.[4] "I didn't feel any pressure up there. I got a fastball and put a good swing on it. After the home run, I felt great."[5]

Andrus congratulated the youngster with the customary "pie" of shaving cream in the face. "I guess it's a pretty big thing," Profar said, smiling, with his hair and neck covered in white foam.[6] "After a win, it tastes great."[7]

Washington attributed Profar's delay in getting to the plate in the fifth inning more to nervous excitement than forgetfulness. "Mother Nature called," he said. "He got a couple hits and maybe his stomach realized what was happening."[8]

"We've got to see how he reacts as a young kid sitting on the bench for days and then having to play," mused Washington. "That's not something that's easy to do. But right now, we've got to make sure we keep him focused and ready for another opportunity."[9]

Profar played in eight more games for Texas that September and continued with the Rangers through 2018. He joined the Oakland Athletics for the 2019 campaign, then moved to the San Diego Padres for 2020 through 2022. He began 2023 with the Colorado Rockies and finished that season back with the Padres, with whom he remained active in 2024.

SOURCES

In addition to the sources cited in the Notes, the author consulted Baseball-Reference.com and Retrosheet.org.

https://www.baseball-reference.com/boxes/CLE/CLE201209020.shtml

https://www.retrosheet.org/boxesetc/2012/B09020CLE2012.htm

Profar's home run can be seen on YouTube at: https://www.youtube.com/watch?v=S5ARWCGVrqw

NOTES

1   Drew Davison, "Jurickson Profar Has Blast in Debut with HR in First At-Bat," *Fort Worth Star-Telegram*, September 2, 2012.

2   *Sportsnet*, "Rangers Prospect Profar Homers in 1st At-bat." Accessed May 31, 2024. https://www.sportsnet.ca/baseball/mlb/jurickson-profar-home-run-first-career-at-bat.

3   Davison.

4   Mark Francescutti, "What a Debut! Rangers' Mega Prospect Jurickson Profar Homers in First At-Bat," *Dallas Morning News*, September 2, 2012.

5   Davison.

6   Francescutti.

7   Davison.

8   Francescutti.

9   Davison.

JUNIOR FELIX

BY MALCOLM ALLEN

Speed and power made switch-hitting outfielder Junior Félix a top prospect, but his career was derailed by defensive deficiencies, injuries, and concerns about his real age. Félix was believed to be just 21 when he hit the first pitch that he faced in the majors for a home run in 1989. By 1994, however, when he played his final game at the top level, many suspected that he was already in his mid-30s.

Junior Francisco Félix Sánchez was born in the in the Laguna Salada municipality of the Dominican Republic, about 15 miles south of the Atlantic coast and 40 miles from the country's western border with Haiti. His birth date was recorded as October 3, 1967.

Moneno Félix and Gladys Sánchez were Junior's parents, according to New York's *Impacto* newspaper, which said he had a brother, Génesis, and a sister, Iris Margarita.[1] Another paper said Junior was the youngest of seven.[2] (Félix's personal Facebook page includes a childhood photograph with his parents and five sisters.[3] The same social media platform hosts an account belonging to Genis Feliz (b. 1955), who lists his parents' names as Moneno Féliz and Gladys Estervina Sánchez.[4])

Shortly after Junior was born, his father left the home, so he was raised by his mother while his siblings lived in other places. "He won't say why," reported the *Miami Herald*.[5] Little is known about the family except that they were poor.

By the time Junior entered professional baseball, he was living about 150 miles southeast of Laguna Salada in Yamasá, an hour's drive north of Santo Domingo.[6] Toronto Blue Jays scout Epy Guerrero discovered him in 1983. "I went to the Dominican national track-and-field competition," Guerrero described.[7] "He was running long and he was running short, and he was winning everything. I'd never seen a faster kid. I had to ask him if he played ball, and he said he did when he was a little kid. He said he wasn't sure about the rules."[8]

Félix confirmed that occasional street games – mostly on Sundays – were the extent of his childhood baseball experience.[9] But he insisted that Guerrero's account was embellished. "I was never in an organized track meet in my life," Félix said in 1993. "I was just running with two other guys and Epy just happened to see me. He said I was fast and he told me to try playing baseball. So I did."[10]

"[Félix] didn't have a penny, so he lived in my baseball complex for two years. The Jays gave us money to pay for things for him," Guerrero explained.[11] "We taught him to be a switch-hitter. He showed immediate power for a kid who's not very big."[12]

Félix, listed at 6-feet and 170 pounds, signed with Toronto for $3,000 on September 15, 1985. Until he could give the money to his mother, Félix asked the neighborhood man who had brought

Junior Félix, Toronto Blue Jays – Courtesy of Trading Card Database

him to Guerrero to hold it. "I never get it back," Félix said in 1991. Convinced that involving the police would accomplish nothing, he recalled, "I just let it go. But I told him, if I ever see him and [if] I'm out of baseball after two years, I will go for [after] him."[13]

In 1986, Félix made his professional debut in the rookie-level Pioneer League. "I never even picked up a baseball glove until 1986," he said later. "I didn't even own a real pair of shoes until Epy gave me a pair."[14] Félix batted .285 with a league-leading 37 stolen bases in 67 games for the Medicine Hat (Alberta, Canada) Blue Jays.

Félix advanced to Class A in 1987 and tied for the South Atlantic League lead with nine triples. He batted .290 with 64 steals in 124 games to help the Myrtle Beach (South Carolina) Blue Jays win the championship. Myrtle Beach coach Leroy Stanton acknowledged Félix's propensity to get poor jumps on the basepaths and in the outfield, but noted, "He's so fast that he's been outrunning his mistakes."[15]

Meanwhile, the big-league Blue Jays spent most of the season in first place, led by two Dominican stars. American

League MVP George Bell bopped 47 homers, and Gold Glove shortstop Tony Fernández batted .322. That summer, though, Guerrero predicted, "Junior Félix will be the best player to ever come out of the Dominican… He has unlimited talent. Just wait and see."[16]

Félix made his Dominican League debut that winter with the Santo Domingo-based Leones del Escogido. He earned Rookie of the Year honors by hitting .322 in 47 games. In the circuit's All-Star Game, he went 4-for-4.[17] After winning the championship, Escogido triumphed in the Caribbean Series for the first time in franchise history.[18]

Despite batting just .253 in 1988, Félix stole 40 bases in his 93 games with the Knoxville (Tennessee) Blue Jays and was selected for the Double-A Southern League All-Star Game. When Félix arrived two hours late for Knoxville's first game of the second half, however, he was sent home to the Dominican Republic for insubordination. "It was an accumulation of things, nothing real serious," explained Blue Jays vice president Bobby Mattick. "We think we did it for his own good."[19]

That fall, Toronto added Félix to its 40-man roster. Gord Ash, the club's administrator of player personnel, remarked, "We'll give him a second chance, but I'm not saying we're prepared to give him a third chance."[20] After Knoxville catcher Matt Stark was claimed by the Chicago White Sox in the minor-league draft, he complained, "They [the Blue Jays] protect a guy like Junior Félix, who has the worst attitude in the world. He missed bus rides, was late for games, talked back to coaches."[21]

During the 1988-89 Dominican League winter season, Félix batted .281 with five homers and 10 steals in 57 games. Escogido repeated as champions.

In early 1989, Guerrero reflected on Félix's suspension. "It was the best thing that could have happened to him. He's a completely different guy now. He's matured a lot… I fully expect that he will be the centre fielder this year."[22]

The Blue Jays had another idea. In a National Basketball Association trade just before spring training, former Blue Jay Danny Ainge (a .220 hitter from 1979-1981) went from the contending Boston Celtics to the struggling Sacramento Kings. Toronto GM Pat Gillick called Ainge, suggesting that he quit basketball and return to the Blue Jays. "They always felt like I would be a great defensive centre fielder, even when they signed me as a shortstop they kind of felt that was my future position," Ainge said in 1995. "He felt they had a good young outfielder in Junior Félix but that he didn't have any glove. So the idea was that I would have come into games in late innings, along with [closer Tom] Henke."[23]

Ainge elected to stick with hoops, and Félix opened the season in the Triple-A International League by homering in his first at-bat for the Syracuse (New York) Chiefs.[24] Although he played only 21 games for Syracuse, Félix was named the circuit's most exciting player and best baserunner.[25] On April 30, Toronto traded Jesse Barfield to the New York Yankees. Three nights later, Félix made his big-league debut at Exhibition Stadium by playing the final inning of a Blue Jays victory in right field.

On May 4, Félix started at designated hitter, batting ninth. Leading off the bottom of the third inning, he took the California Angels' Kirk McCaskill deep to right-center field, becoming just the 13th player in history to homer on the first pitch he faced in the majors.[26]

In Boston on June 2, Félix hit the first inside-the-park grand slam by a visiting player at Fenway Park.[27] Despite minor injuries to both ankles, he circled the bases in just 14.9 seconds. "In the Dominican one time, they got me at 13.7," he said.[28] Two days later, Félix smacked a game-winning, two-run homer in the 12th inning.[29] Overall, he collected 11 RBIs during Toronto's three-game sweep, capping an American League Player of the Week performance despite being benched once for disciplinary reasons.[30]

Blue Jays manager Cito Gaston kept him out of the lineup again after Félix ran through a coach's stop sign on June 6 trying (unsuccessfully) to score from first base on a single. On June 10, the *Toronto Star*'s Bob Duff wrote, "Junior Félix is such a miserable person, even George Bell hates him."[31] (Bell had feuded with former Blue Jays' skipper Jimy Williams the previous year and had a reputation for being difficult with reporters.)

But Félix's combination of speed and power was impossible to ignore. His four-hit performance against the Tigers on June 11 featured a home run and two infield singles. In June, his 26 RBIs led all major leaguers.[32] "If he's Junior Félix, I'd like to see Senior Félix," joked Orioles scout Ed Farmer.[33]

Blue Jays pitcher Mike Flanagan observed, "[Félix]'s a very dangerous player. He plays the game with reckless abandon, full speed ahead. It's hard to fault that."[34] Through July 30, Félix had led off 71 of Toronto's last 74 games and was batting .283 with his unusual open batting stance. That afternoon, though, he ran into the wall at Yankee Stadium while pursuing a double and separated his left shoulder.[35]

Félix started fewer than half of Toronto's remaining contests and batted just .183 after returning. "I tried to come back too quickly," he said the following spring.[36] "I was worried about someone maybe taking my job."[37]

In 110 games – mostly playing right field – Félix slashed .258/.315/.395, with eight triples, nine homers and 18 steals. The Blue Jays, in sixth place with a 9-17 record when he joined the team, then went 80-56 – trailing only the Oakland Athletics (84-55).[38] "He came in and really gave us a lift," said Gaston.[39] On the season's final weekend, Toronto edged the Baltimore Orioles to win the AL East. Félix started three ALCS contests against Oakland and went 3-for-11 (.273), but the Blue Jays fell in five games.

Next, Félix helped Escogido claim a third straight Dominican League title. He hit .412 (21-for-51) in 16 regular season contests, and .294 in 23 playoff games. For the second time in three years, Escogido also won the Caribbean Series.

With the Blue Jays in 1990, Félix produced a .284/.359/.488 slash line prior to the All-Star break, with 11 homers and 11 steals. But he tore a right calf muscle in the first game of the second half. After it hemorrhaged overnight, surgery was required to relieve the pressure, and he missed four weeks.[40] He wasn't the same player when he returned, batting .227 with diminished power and speed. Toronto finished two games behind Boston.

Félix exasperated his teammates by repeating correctable mistakes like overthrowing the cutoff man and not hustling after balls. "All you can do is keep talking to him," said Gaston. "You can't take him in a room and beat him up."[41] Félix, however, had reportedly tried to punch Bell in the locker room that summer after the latter accused him of being "very stupid for such an old man" in Spanish.[42] The barb made more sense that fall when Toronto's *Globe and Mail* published comments from Dominican sportswriter Roosevelt Comarazamy. "People who know Félix from his neighborhood say that he is a lot older than he says he is," remarked Comarazamy. "Félix was a weightlifter in men's competitions here a few years before he signed with the Jays. Well, you can't be a 14-year-old kid in those competitions. He had to be a lot older at the time."[43]

The same article confirmed that Félix – who had ostensibly turned 23 on October 3 – was on Toronto's trading block. "He needs to be more dedicated," said Gaston. "He has to want to be better. You have to have that inside of you."[44] On December 2, Félix, infielder Luis Sojo, and a player to be named later (catcher Ken Rivers) were traded to the Angels for center fielder Devon White, and pitchers Willie Fraser and Marcus Moore.

That offseason, Félix married Paula Treadway, a Myrtle Beach native whom he had met in the minors.[45] Félix also helped Escogido reach another Dominican League finals, but they were dethroned by the Tigres del Licey.

During spring training in 1991, veteran Angels outfielders Dave Winfield and Dave Parker sought out Félix to work with him.[46] "I don't like it here. I love the people here," Félix told the *Los Angeles Times.*[47] California made Félix the full-time center fielder, but he batted just .183 in his first 24 games. Nevertheless, Angels manager Doug Rader insisted, "Félix probably has the God-given ability to hit third."[48]

Félix heated up at bat. But on June 1 he strained a muscle in the same calf on which he'd had surgery the previous year. Following a stint on the 15-day disabled list, he aggravated the injury in his third game back and missed more than two months.[49] While Félix was sidelined, he was fined by the Angels' kangaroo court for asking the name of a pitcher (Floyd Bannister) who had been with California all season. When Félix protested that he didn't know the name of reliever Mike Fetters either, he was fined again.[50] Although Félix raised his batting average to .283 with a strong finish, he appeared in only 66 games. "Maybe he didn't care too much to come back," teammate Luis Polonia said later. "You have to push yourself to come back. I know he didn't."[51]

Escogido claimed its fourth Dominican League title in five years in 1991-92. Although Félix hit just .215 in 19 regular-season games, he batted .397 in 15 round-robin playoff contests and .538 (7-for-13) in the finals.

Back in the United States, though, Felix still had his skeptics. During spring training 1992, Angels vice president Whitey

Herzog said of Félix, "He's a dog, always has been. They say he's got talent, but a lot of players have talent."[52] Félix worked on his defense with outfield instructor Sam Suplizio and staved off a challenge from rookie Chad Curtis to retain the center field position. "Last year [Félix] learned a lesson," Polonia observed. "He understands that if he doesn't work, he could lose his job… And he's listening to people for the first time."[53]

Before April was over Rader's successor, Buck Rodgers, said that Félix's bat, glove, and speed had already keyed California victories. "Junior Félix has been a joy," Rodgers said. "Junior Félix is turning into a good, good player. We're seeing some of his overall talent, complete talent."[54]

On May 21, one of the Angels' team buses flipped over on the New Jersey Turnpike. Thirteen members of the traveling party were injured, including Rodgers, who missed more than three months. Félix emerged with a sore knee and back but kept playing.[55] Five nights later, however, he caught his spikes while backpedaling after a ball hit over his head.[56] Félix strained his left groin and wound up on the 15-day disabled list. At the time, he was batting .287 with a team-high 31 RBIs.[57]

Despite Félix's improvement, shortly after he returned to action, the *Los Angeles Times* reported that he had nearly been traded to the Red Sox for 36-year-old designated hitter Jack Clark. The same paper noted that Félix had also been offered to the Cubs for center fielder Jerome Walton, but Chicago's GM wasn't interested.[58] In July, Herzog told a group of Angels boosters that the club couldn't win a pennant with Félix in center field.[59]

California's interim manager, John Wathan, fined Félix multiple times for failing to slide, and said he was tempted to bench him following another baserunning gaffe.[60] That winter Rodgers, who reclaimed the managerial reins on August 28, described how Félix could frustrate teammates. "He was making mistakes that you would expect from a youngster, not from a guy who was over 30… We always suspected that he was 30-plus."[61]

Félix insisted that his graying hair was hereditary. Although he appeared in a career-high 139 games during his "age 24" season and led the fifth-place Angels with 72 RBIs, his batting average dropped to .246, and he struck out 128 times while producing only nine homers and eight steals. Nevertheless, as the fall expansion draft to stock the rosters of two franchises approached, Rodgers said California's 15-player protected list would include Félix if the decision were his to make.[62] But the Angels brass disagreed. On November 17, 1992, the Florida Marlins selected Félix in the third round with the 60th overall pick.

Félix agreed to a one-year, $1.25 million contract and bought his mother a new seven-bedroom home in the Dominican Republic.[63] When *Miami Herald* writer Dan Le Batard contacted her, "She said, in a mysterious voice, that she wasn't really sure how old her son was."[64] Marlins GM Dave Dombrowski said, "We're aware that Junior probably is older than the records say. But it's not a big ordeal for us… He's our right fielder."[65]

For the first time in six years, Félix skipped winter ball, though he sponsored four youth teams in his native country.[66]

He spent the bulk of his offseason in South Carolina, where his wife gave birth to their first child, Junior Félix Jr. Upon joining the Marlins, he reiterated that his listed age was correct – "until someone can prove that I'm not 25" – but said the team's media guide was wrong to report that he had one son. "I have three – with three different women," he clarified.[67]

Rookie Scott Pose had a good spring training and won the starting job in center for Florida. On April 5, 1993, Félix started in right field and batted third when the Marlins made their National League debut, against the Los Angeles Dodgers at Joe Robbie Stadium. He lost the first ball hit his way in the sun and was charged with an error, but he recorded an outfield assist on the same play.[68] Félix went 1-for-4, and Florida won, 6-3.

Félix hit the first grand slam in Marlins' history on April 25, off the Rockies' Scott Aldred at Mile High Stadium with 71,192 in attendance.[69] Félix told the *Globe and Mail* he was more relaxed than ever. "But I'm still learning," he said. "I have a long way to go before I'm an established player."[70]

In the eighth inning of a tie game against the Cubs on May 21, Félix dropped a fly ball that he lost in the lights. He heard about it from Marlins' fans and had a beer thrown at him, but no runs scored. In the bottom of the frame, he clobbered a high fastball on an 0-2 count for what proved to be a game-winning homer. "They were booing him like crazy. Then he gets a standing ovation. That's what the game is all about," said Florida manager Rene Lachemann.[71]

But when Félix earned another standing ovation six night later, it came from the opposing fans in Pittsburgh. He had misplayed three balls, leading to six runs – including an inside-the-park homer by slow-footed catcher Tom Prince. (The previous evening, Pittsburgh had tallied another inside-the-park homer when Marlins right fielder Geronimo Berroa allowed an in-between hop to skip past him.) "Right field for us was like the Bermuda Triangle in this series," said Lachemann. "The problem is you have to catch the ball to play right field."[72]

Marlins coach Vada Pinson, a former Gold Glove outfielder, described hitting balls to rookie center fielder Chuck Carr (who'd claimed that job in mid-April) before one game when Félix approached and said he needed the help more. "When I made eye contact with him, I saw he was sincere. It hurt me," Pinson said.[73]

The Marlins sent Félix down to the Edmonton (Alberta, Canada) Trappers for a defensive refresher in the Triple-A Pacific Coast League, where he played center field. "Playing in center field was a little bit of a joke because center field and right field are completely different," he said upon returning to the majors two weeks later. Lachemann defended Félix's effort and compared him to a former teammate. "He`s a lot like George Hendrick… George often looked like he wasn`t giving 100 percent, but he drove in 100 runs, had a great arm and was a good outfielder."[74]

Félix's return to the Marlins, though, lasted only 13 games. In 57 overall appearances for Florida, he batted .238 with a dismal .940 fielding percentage. Shortly before Félix was designated for assignment on June 25, he responded to a question about which teammates had been the most supportive by saying, "Friends? I don't have any." The *Orlando Sentinel*'s Jorge Milian wrote, "In his short stay with the Marlins, Félix lived up to his reputation as a moody loner."[75]

No other major-league team claimed Félix on waivers.[76] Initially, the Marlins refused to release him, preferring to keep him in Triple-A as insurance. Just four days after he reported to Edmonton, however, Félix was indeed released outright. "The way he responded to being sent down and his attitude complicated things," explained Marlins assistant GM Frank Wren. Trappers manager Sal Rende said, "When a guy doesn't want to be somewhere and shows he doesn't want to put out, it's pretty obvious."[77]

Félix did not catch on with another organization in 1993. In winter ball, he joined Escogido just before the playoffs, but the Leones were eliminated before the finals.

The Detroit Tigers invited Félix to spring training in 1994. "He needs somebody to not only treat him nice, but also to demand out of him what he has to offer," said Tigers skipper Sparky Anderson. "I'm at the stage now, 25 years managing, that I have a luxury other managers don't have. I'm no longer trying to save him for me. I'd like to save him for himself."[78]

Félix made the team but didn't produce much early on. He spent time on the disabled list after straining his left hip flexor by playfully sliding between pitcher Mike Henneman's legs during batting practice on May 6.[79] When Félix returned, though, he went deep four times in the final week of May. In June, he batted .351 with 20 extra-base hits (13 doubles, seven homers) in 27 games. Overall, Félix slashed .306/.372/.525 in 86 games for Detroit before a players' strike ended the season prematurely on August 11.

The labor dispute was not settled until April 1995. Meanwhile, Félix was granted free agency. That June, Félix – described as "a little overweight" by Expos GM Kevin Malone – was still unsigned and working out at Montreal's minor-league spring training facility.[80] Félix joined Montreal's Triple-A affiliate, the Ottawa Lynx, for 51 games but batted only .225 before he was released on August 13.[81]

Félix saw action with four different teams in the Triple-A Mexican League over the next three years: the Broncos de Reynosa in 1996, the Mexico City Reds and Leones de Yucatan in 1997, and the Algodoneros de Unión Laguna in 1998. He went to spring training with the Pirates in 1997 but didn't make the team.[82] Félix finished the '98 campaign with the Seoul-based LG Twins in the Korean Baseball Organization. He returned to that KBO team in 1999 and batted .253 with 13 homers in 97 games.

In 2000, Félix went back to the Mexican League. After 17 games with the Algondoneros, he rejoined to the Leones de Yucatan and helped them claim the South Division title by hitting .294 with a team-high 22 homers in 94 games. "I'm doin' pretty good," he told a *Toronto Star* reporter who tracked him down that June. Félix said he was up to five sons – "all Juniors" – and insisted that his official listed age of 32 was correct.

(Félix's sons with his wife Paula were named Ethan, Deanny and Gabby according to her personal Facebook page.) Regarding the reputation he built for himself over six major-league seasons, he said, "Hey, I was young. I see plenty of guys now just like I was. Hardheads. Can't tell them anything. So I just laugh."[83]

Félix continued to play sporadically in the Dominican Winter League – with Escogido and the Azucareros del Este – until 2000-01. In his native country, he hit .283 with 12 homers and 29 steals in 247 regular season games over 10 seasons, plus .275 with eight homers and 16 steals in 147 playoff contests.

In 2001, Félix played his final 75 games as a professional and slashed .305/.429/.461 for the Leones de Yucatan.

After baseball, Félix divorced, remarried and fathered a daughter, Efraisa. (The name of the woman he identified as his wife in a photo posted to his personal Facebook account in 2011 wasn't specified.) As of 2022, he was the proprietor of Super Colmado Junior Félix, a grocery store that hosted karaoke nights in Santo Domingo.

ACKNOWLEDGMENTS

This biography was reviewed by Rory Costello and David Bilmes and fact-checked by Paul Proia.

The author would like to thank SABR colleague Paul Proia for research assistance.

SOURCES

In addition to sources cited in the Notes, the author consulted www.baseball-reference.com, www.retrosheet.org and https://sabr.org/bioproject.

Junior Félix's Dominican League statistics from https://stats.winterball-data.com/home (Subscription service. Last accessed May 20, 2022.)

NOTES

1   Martin Zapata, "Junior Félix Regala a Su Hermano en Nueva York Automóvil Modelo 1999," *Impacto* (New York, New York), April 13, 1999: 31.

2   Tim Brown, "Former Jay Félix Making Friends with Angels This Year," *Ottawa* (Ontario, Canada) *Citizen*, May 13, 1992: F3.

3   Junior Félix, Facebook post from June 6, 2015, https://www.facebook.com/photo/?fbid=895144307219517&set=ecnf.100001718683320 (last accessed August 27, 2022).

4   Genis Féliz, Facebook post from April 28, 2016, https://www.facebook.com/photo/?fbid=10207214668139131&set=pb.1056309619.-2207520000.., (last accessed August 27, 2022).

5   Dan Le Batard, "Marlins' Félix: Talent with a Question Mark," *Miami Herald*, March 3, 1993: 6D.

6   Junior Félix, 1987 ProCards Myrtle Beach Blue Jays baseball card.

7   Marty York, "Superb Play by Félix May Hasten Trading Bell," *Globe and Mail* (Toronto), May 10, 1989: A15.

8   Marty York, "Speedster Next Jay Superstar," *Globe and Mail*, June 25, 1987: D13.

9   Robyn Norwood, "On Center Stage in Center," *Los Angeles Times*, May 10, 1991: C1.

10   Marty York, "Genuinely Junior Credits Cartoons with Improved Relaxation," *Globe and Mail*, May 14, 1993: C10.

11   York, "Superb Play by Félix May Hasten Trading Bell."

12   York, "Speedster Next Jay Superstar."

13   Norwood, "On Center Stage in Center."

14   York, "Genuinely Junior Credits Cartoons with Improved Relaxation."

15   York, "Speedster Next Jay Superstar."

16   York, "Speedster Next Jay Superstar."

17   Larry Millson, "Draft Halts Jay Effort for Rookie," *Globe and Mail*, December 16, 1987: D3.

18   Gustavo Rodríguez, "Leones Rugen Logran Premera Serie del Caribe 1988," *Hoy* (Dominican Republic), January 19, 2016, https://hoy.com.do/leones-rugen-logran-primera-serie-del-caribe-1988/ (last accessed May 28, 2022).

19   Larry Millson, "Jays Cite Insubordination as Top Farmhand Gets Boot," *Globe and Mail*, August 3, 1988: A15.

20   Larry Millson, "Tenace Hired by Jays as Minor-League Coach," *Globe and Mail*, November 17, 1988: A26.7

21   Larry Millson, "Stark Bitter After Draft and Lashes Out at Jays," *Globe and Mail*, December 6, 1988: A28.

22   Marty York, "Superscout Says Félix Jays' Top Outfielder," *Globe and Mail*, February 1, 1989: A14.

23   Neil A. Campbell, "Ainge Eyes Return to His Diamond Roots," *Globe and Mail*, February 23, 1995: C12.

24   Dave Perkins, "First-toss Homer Old Hat to Félix," *Toronto Star*, May 5, 1989: B5.

25   Neal MacCarl, "Rose Turns Down Cooperstown Trip," *Toronto Star*, July 21, 1989: D2.

26   David Adler, "Players Who Homered on First Career Pitch," MLB.com, April 4, 2021, https://www.mlb.com/news/mlb-rare-feats-home-run-on-1st-career-pitch-c265964496#:~:text=Walter%20Mueller%2C%20Pirates%3A%20May%207%2C%201922%2C%20vs.&text=Mueller%20is%20the%20first%20Major,of%20Famer%20Grover%20Cleveland%20Alexander. (last accessed May 28, 2022).

27   Two Red Sox players had hit inside-the-park grand slams at Fenway Park before Félix: Don Lenhardt on April 19, 1952, and Gary Geiger on August 8, 1961. Associated Press, "Around the Parks," *Globe and Mail*, June 5, 1989: C7.

28   Dave Perkins, "Félix Burns Up the Basepaths in Beantown," *Toronto Star*, June 4, 1989: H3.

29   Mark, Blaudschun, "From 10-nothing to Nothing," *Boston Globe*, June 5, 1989: 35.

30   Bob Duff, "Félix Alienating Own Teammates," *Toronto Star*, June 10, 1989: B3.

31   Duff, "Félix Alienating Own Teammates."

32   Norwood, "On Center Stage in Center."

33   Tim Kurkjian, "Anderson Skips Batting Practice After Undergoing Back Exam," *Baltimore Sun*, June 23, 1989: 3C.

34   Bob Duff, "Félix a Dangerous Player," *Windsor* (Ontario) *Star*, June 12, 1989: C2.

35 Neil A. Campbell, "Jays Reeling After Losing Félix, Game," *Globe and Mail*, July 31, 1989: C1.

36 Tom Laloney, "Félix Flies for the Jays," *Ottawa Citizen*, April 22, 1990: B2.

37 Tom Salter, "A Healthy Félix Resumes Assault on AL Pitchers," *Toronto Star*, April 18, 1990: E3.

38 The National League's best records after May 2 in 1989 belonged to the Chicago Cubs (80-57) and San Francisco Giants (79-57).

39 Larry Millson, "Félix Working Hard on Breaking Ball," *Globe and Mail*, June 28, 1989: A16.

40 Larry Millson, "Félix Rejoins Jays" *Globe and Mail*, August 10, 1990: C12.

41 Larry Millson, "Jays on Rough Road to Recovery," *Globe and Mail*, June 29, 1990: C14.

42 Marty York, "Clubhouse Boxscore: Félix No Hits, Bell No Catches," *Globe and Mail*, December 20, 1990: C12.

43 Marty York, "Jays Have the Not-So-Junior Félix on the Trading Block," *Globe and Mail*, November 7, 1990: C14.

44 York, "Jays Have the Not-So-Junior Félix on the Trading Block."

45 Norwood, "On Center Stage in Center."

46 Marty York, "Jays Look Like Big Losers for Trading Félix," *Globe and Mail*, April 6, 1991: A13.

47 Helene Elliott, "Félix Making a Good Impression," *Los Angeles Times*, March 27, 1991: C4.

48 Norwood, "On Center Stage in Center."

49 "Junior Félix Goes on DL," *Los Angeles Times*, June 26, 1991: C9.

50 Le Batard, "Marlins' Félix: Talent with a Question Mark."

51 Tim Brown, "Former Jay Félix Making Friends with Angels This Year," *Ottawa Citizen*, May 13, 1992: F3.

52 David Cunningham, "Fly on the Wall," *The Sporting News*, May 25, 1992: 25.

53 Brown, "Former Jay Félix Making Friends with Angels This Year."

54 Helene Elliott, "He Can't Serve When He Sits and Waits," *Los Angeles Times*, April 28, 1992: C4.

55 Helene Elliott, "Tree Saved Angels Rodgers Injured in Bus Crash," *Los Angeles Times*, May 22, 1992: 204.

56 Ross Newhan, "Red Sox Dampen Return by Angels," *Los Angeles Times*, May 27, 1992: C1.

57 "Muscle Strain Puts Félix on Disabled List," *Los Angeles Times*, May 29, 1992: OCCC7.

58 Helene Elliott, "Jackie Autry Vetoes Félix for Clark," *Los Angeles Times*, June 18, 1992: C8.

59 Gordon Edes, "On Baseball," *Sun Sentinel* (Fort Lauderdale, Florida), July 26, 1992: 5C.

60 Helene Elliott, "Félix Says He Wants to Be Traded," *Los Angeles Times*, July 29, 1992: C3.

61 Marty York, "Marlins Took the Bait on Not-So-Junior Félix," *Globe and Mail*, January 27, 1993: C8.

62 Helene Elliott, "Rodgers Says Trade Might be Answer," *Los Angeles Times*, October 3, 1992: C4.

63 Le Batard, "Marlins' Félix: Talent with a Question Mark."

64 Dan Le Batard, "Junior Félix? Not Exactly," *Miami Herald*, January 19, 1993: 1D.

65 York, "Marlins Took the Bait on Not-So-Junior Félix."

66 York, "Genuinely Junior Credits Cartoons with Improved Relaxation."

67 York, "Genuinely Junior Credits Cartoons with Improved Relaxation."

68 Gordon Edes, "Day of the Marlin," *Sun Sentinel*, April 6, 1993: 1A.

69 Mike Klis, "Florida Comes Away with First Series of the 'Rivalry,'" *Colorado Springs Gazette-Telegraph*, April 26, 1993: C1.

70 York, "Genuinely Junior Credits Cartoons with Improved Relaxation."

71 Associated Press, "Félix's 2-Run Shot Revives Marlins," *Orlando Sentinel*, May 22, 1993: C1.

72 Gordon Edes, "Marlins a Fright in Right," *Orlando Sentinel*, May 28, 1993: 1C.

73 Amy Niedzielka, "Marlins Call Up Whitmore," *Edmonton* (Alberta, Canada) *Journal*, June 26, 1993: H5.

74 Craig Barnes, "Long Journey Pays Dividend for Félix," *Orlando Sentinel*, June 12, 1993: 5C.

75 Jorge Milian, "Marlins May Tell Félix to Throw in His Cards," *Orlando Sentinel*, June 29, 1993: D1.

76 SouthamStar Network, "No One Wants Junior Félix," *Kitchener-Waterloo* (Ontario, Canada) *Record*, July 5, 1993: C4.

77 Robin Brownlee, "Marlins Cut Junior Loose," *Edmonton Journal*, July 7, 1993: C2.

78 Alan Solomon, "Out to Save a Career, Anderson Goes to Bat for Félix in Field," *Chicago Tribune*, March 27, 1994: 11.

79 Jayson Stark, "Injuries of the Week," *Philadelphia Inquirer*, May 15, 1994: 45

80 Jeff Blair, "Rodriguez Could Be Out for Month," (Montreal) *Gazette*, June 4, 1995: D4.

81 Allen Panzeri, "Missing Lynx," *Ottawa Citizen*, August 14, 1995: D3.

82 "Transactions," *Baltimore Sun*, March 6, 1997: 2C.

83 "A Grown-Up Junior Félix Still Playing a Kid's Game," *Toronto Star*, June 6, 2000: E11.

TOMMY MILONE HITS A 3 RUN HOMER IN HIS PITCHING DEBUT

September 3, 2011: Washington Nationals 8, New York Mets 7, at Nationals Park, Washington DC

BY LAURA H. PEEBLES

It was a beautiful late summer evening for a meeting between two teams that would not sniff the postseason. The Nationals, losers of nine of their last ten games, sat at 63-73, 26 games back of division-leading Philadelphia. The Mets were not much better, 22 games out of first at 67-69. Perhaps attracted by the weather or the post-game concert, 34,821 were in attendance.

Tommy Milone[1] was making his major league pitching debut. Having Jesús Flores behind the plate may have helped steady his nerves: they had worked together in the minors. José Reyes stepped in to face Milone, and grounded the third pitch to Ryan Zimmerman at third. A quick throw across the infield and Milone had his first out. Two fly outs completed Milone's 1-2-3 first inning of work. In the bottom of the inning Dillon Gee (12-5, 4.24 ERA)[2] took the mound for the Mets. Ian Desmond knocked Gee's 2-2 offering into the left field seats to give the Nationals a quick 1-0 lead. Roger Bernadina (recalled the day before after spending a month at AAA Syracuse) grounded out to first. After Zimmerman singled up the middle, Michael Morse struck out waving at a pitch well outside. With Jayson Werth batting, Zimmerman was caught stealing: he was tagged on the sleeve by the second baseman as he slid by. Zimmerman thought he had the base stolen, making faces while lying flat in the dirt touching the bag. There were no replay challenges in 2011, but the video showed that he was indeed tagged.

In the top of the second David Wright popped out to short right. Ángel Pagán was Milone's first strikeout: Pagán swung at a pitch well above the zone. Jason Bay flied out to left to give Milone his second 1-2-3 inning. Werth's at-bat continued in the bottom of the third: he struck out. Espinosa tried to bunt, and was HBP on his back leg.[3] Chris Marrero singled: his bat exploded over the infield, with the ball squirting past a diving Justin Turner. Jesús Flores singled, scoring Espinosa from third. That brought Milone to the plate for his first at-bat. He hit Gee's first pitch into the Nationals' bullpen for a three-run homer, bringing the score to 5-0, Nationals.[4] The relievers were jumping and cheering in the bullpen: one grabbed the historic ball so it could join his first pitch and first strikeout balls.[5] The crowd demanded a curtain call. A grinning Milone made his way back through the dugout, crowded with the September callups, to

Tommy Milone, Washington Nationals – Courtesy of MLB.com

salute the crowd from the dugout steps. Desmond blooped one into right, where it fell in between three Mets defenders. The Nationals threatened to break the game open, but Bernadina grounded into a 4-6-3 double play to end the inning.

In the third Ronny Paulino got the first hit against Milone (a single past a diving Zimmerman), then advanced to second on a sac bunt, but got no further. The Nationals were out 1-2-3.

In the top of the fourth, Justin Turner blooped a single into center. After Lucas Duda lined out to Desmond, Wright bounced one that first hit near the third base line, then bounced into the stands and back out. The umpires did not call fan interference, since the ball was already in the stands when the first fan touched it, so it was a ground rule double advancing

Turner to third. Pagán then singled into the right field gap scoring two for the Mets. With Bay at the plate, Milone tried a pick-off at first: it was close so manager Davey Johnson came out to argue.[6] Pagán managed to time Milone and steal second. He could have stayed on first for all it mattered: After Bay grounded out to third, Nick Evans hit a two-run homer over the visitor's bullpen. A Paulino ground out finished the Mets half of the fourth with the score 5-4, Nationals. In the bottom of the fourth, Danny Espinosa drew a walk. After Marrero was out on a fielder's choice, Flores hit a foul pop near third. There was almost a three-way collision between Bay, Wright, and Reyes, although Bay did manage to catch the ball while falling. Espinosa tagged up and ran to third. Wright, realizing what was going on, grabbed the ball from Bay's glove and threw it in to keep Espinosa from scoring. Milone bounced to short to end the inning.

Gee opened the fifth with a fly out to center. Reyes then hit Milone's first pitch into center for a single. Turner came up to bat, but Johnson pulled Milone after he had made two pick off throws to first (but had thrown no pitches). Milone exited to great applause. Given that Milone had thrown only 74 pitches and could not qualify for the win,[7] fans and commentators were surprised that Johnson pulled him that early. Tom Gorzelanny took over on the mound against Turner and induced two ground outs to first to retire the side. The bottom of the fifth was two strikeouts and a groundout punctuated by Bernadina's solo homer into the visitor's bullpen, bringing the score to 6-4, Nationals.

After Wright grounded out to open the sixth, Pagan bounced a single into left. Bay hit his tenth homer of the year into the Red Porch seats in center, tying the game at 6. Gorzelanny managed to avoid any more damage with a strikeout and a groundout. Pedro Beato took the mound for the Mets. Espinosa grounded back to Beato, who tried to throw to first from his backside—but Espinosa beat the throw. Marrero grounded to the shortstop: Espinosa did a take-out slide into Turner to avoid the double play. A Flores single off the Mets' new pitcher Danny Herrera advanced Marrero to third, but pinch hitter Iván "Pudge" Rodríguez[8] grounded into a 5-4-3 double play to end the inning.

In the seventh, Tyler Clippard took the mound. The Mets took a 7-6 lead on a Duda sac fly scoring Willie Harris. Manny Acosta pitched a 1-2-3 bottom of the seventh for the Mets.

Johnson called on hard-throwing Henry Rodríguez to pitch the eighth. He struck out the three Mets he faced: Bay, Evans, and Paulino, and left to a standing ovation. More than half his pitches were 100-mph or better. Acosta continued pitching for the Mets. After Morse struck out, Werth walked and Espinosa struck out. With Marrero batting, Werth stole second and took third on a throwing error, but was left there when Marrero looked at strike three.

Sean Burnett took the mound for the Nationals in the top of the ninth: A groundout, a fly out, and a strikeout held the deficit at one run. In the bottom of the ninth Bobby Parnell came in for the Mets for the save. Flores opened with a single

to left.[9] Johnson put in Brian Bixler as a pinch runner for Flores. With Jonny Gomes batting, a wild pitch allowed Bixler to take second; Gomes ended up walking. Desmond tried to bunt: On his third try, he succeeded in bunting the runners over. Parnell intentionally walked Bernadina so the bases were loaded with one out for Zimmerman, known as "Mr. Walk-off."[10] The crowd roared as Zimmerman came to the plate, and he rewarded the fans with a broken-bat bloop hit into right field: Duda dove for the ball but couldn't reach it, so two runs scored for the walk-off win.

SOURCES

baseball-reference.com/boxes/WAS/WAS201109030.shtml

retrosheet.org/boxesetc/2011/B09030WAS2011.htm

Video of game: https://www.youtube.com/watch?v=F825YA4ch1c

Game summary video: youtube.com/watch?v=jBQSdXWHgVk

Milone debut highlights: youtube.com/watch?v=DNNwpzEuEzU

AUTHOR'S NOTE

We were in attendance that day. Given the Nationals' relatively mediocre performance to that point in their existence, any memorable event was worth celebrating. Even without knowing the historic background, everyone in the stadium knew that a first pitch homer was a rare occurrence.

NOTES

1   Milone had been a tenth-round pick of the Nationals in 2008.

2   Gee's ERA had been as low as 2.86 in mid-June with a 7-0 record, but his performance went downhill steadily after that.

3   Espinosa was second in MLB in HBP with 17, behind only Carlos Quentin, who had 23.

4   Milone was batting .346 in the minors in 2011. His only extra-base hit was a double. As of 2018, he hadn't hit another home run.

5   The TV broadcast displayed a chart showing that Milone was the eighth pitcher in MLB history to hit a home run on the first pitch he saw. mlb.com/news/mlb-rare-feats-home-run-on-1st-career-pitch/c-265964496. Accessed August 19, 2018.

6   In 2011, only home runs were eligible for replay review, so all Davey could do was argue.

7   Milone earned his first win 12 days later, also against the Mets. Because the Nationals traded him to Oakland over the winter, he didn't earn his second win as a National until August 1, 2018 . . . and yes, it was against the Mets. In the meantime, he had pitched for Oakland, Minneapolis, Milwaukee, and the Mets.

8   This was Pudge's first game back after a six-day rehab assignment.

9   This was Flores' only three-hit game of the year.

10 Dan Steinberg, "How Ryan Zimmerman got his "Mr. Walk-Off" Nickname," *Washington Post*, May 20, 2015, washingtonpost.com/news/dc-sports-bog/wp/2015/05/20/how-ryan-zimmerman-got-his-mr-walk-off-nickname/?utm_term=.f0029ebf521b. Accessed August 19, 2018.

PETE HILL

BY PHIL WILLIAMS

"Pete Hill was the first great outfielder in black baseball history," suggests baseball historian Lawrence Hogan.[1] The left-handed Hill was a five-tool star with several famed independent African-American teams: the Philadelphia Giants (1904 to 1907), Leland Giants (1908 to 1910), and Chicago American Giants (1911 to 1918). He then slugged his way to Ruthian heights as the Detroit Stars' player-manager in 1919, before his professional career wound down in 1925. Crowning recognition of his accomplishments came in 2006, when he was inducted into Baseball's Hall of Fame.

John Preston Hill was born in the Culpeper County, Virginia, hamlet of Buena, on October 12, 1882. Two brothers, Jerome and Walter, preceded him. His parents, "Ike" and Elizabeth "Lizzie" (née Seals) Hill, were Virginia natives. Early in his life, his father seemingly disappeared, with county records suggesting he may have died in 1887. Soon afterwards, his mother boarded a northbound train with her young sons and settled in Pittsburgh.[2]

Hill's professional baseball career is sometimes cited as beginning with the Pittsburgh Keystones in 1899 then, after two years with that squad, moving on for a stint with the famed Cuban X-Giants.[3] This storyline seems questionable. At the time of the 1900 census, the teenager lived with his mother, brothers, and stepfather in Pittsburgh, and worked as a day laborer. He may well have played with the Keystones at some point – the scant coverage the era's newspapers granted Black baseball makes any sweeping conclusions to the contrary ill-advised – but none of the limited references to this team mention a "Hill."[4]

Perhaps his professional debut instead came in 1901. That January a "J.P. Hill" was included in a roster of Black players signed by the Golden Slides club.[5] Yet box scores for the Slides are elusive. The Barnes Colored Americans, organized by Bud Fowler, also debuted in Pittsburgh that season. Although not listed in the squad's opening roster, a "Hill" played left field and homered in their 9-7 loss to a Monaca team on July 1.[6]

Neither the Golden Slides nor the Colored Americans apparently lasted past 1901. Pittsburgh newspapers reference a "Hill" in the Matthews Colored Amateurs' roster in 1902, and the (likely African-American) Iron City's roster in 1903.[7] Again, box scores for either team are elusive. Meanwhile, the "Hill" playing for the X-Giants in this span was infielder Johnny Hill.[8] The X-Giants toured western Pennsylvania twice in 1902 and once in 1903, and quite possibly scouted local teams. But, like so much of Pete Hill's development, this remains a mystery.

Somehow, by the time the 1904 season dawned, Hill had come to the attention of the Philadelphia Giants. Owned by newspaperman H. Walter Schlichter and managed by Sol White, the team's 1903 campaign had culminated with a key series loss to

Pete Hill, 1905 Cuba – SABR-Rucker Archive

the X-Giants. That off-season, the "Phillies" induced several "Cubes" to sign with them: infielder Charlie Grant, outfielder Andrew "Jap" Payne, and pitcher Andrew "Rube" Foster. Hill joined these newcomers in April 1904. He initially played left field and batted in the bottom third of the order. But he soon took over center field and regularly batted third, fourth, or fifth. A season highlight: against a Hoboken team on August 14, Hill contributed four hits and the sole run scored as Foster outdueled semipro ace Ernie Lindemann in a 1-0 thriller.[9] That fall, the Phillies avenged their series loss to the Cubes the year before, taking two of three games in a rematch between the teams. Hill struggled, contributing only one hit in the three contests.[10]

The Phillies again recruited that offseason, adding infielder Grant "Home Run" Johnson and pitchers Emmett Bowman and Dan McClellan. The resulting 1905 squad proved a juggernaut, achieving a 128-23-3 record and earning a place among the finest African-American teams of the Deadball Era, if not all time.[11] Per baseball historian Phil Dixon's research, from the

133 games with box scores (and nine of these lacked summaries detailing extra-base hits and stolen bases), Hill banged out 198 hits, including 37 doubles, 11 triples, and 10 home runs, while stealing 34 bases.[12] Then, concluding a lengthy barnstorming campaign – that for Hill had begun in the Florida Hotel League at the beginning of the year – he finished 1905 as the leading offensive star for an X-Giants squad playing in the Cuban Winter League.[13]

The Phillies remained dominant in 1906, both against other Black teams and White semipro and minor-league competition. That October they met the barnstorming Philadelphia Athletics for two games. The Mackmen took the pair. Facing Eddie Plank and Rube Waddell, Hill contributed three of the Phillies' seven hits in the matches.[14] Per Seamheads' Negro League database, Hill amassed a BA/OBP/SLG line of .327/.417/.423 (and an OPS+ 217) in 31 career games against major-league teams. Moreover, as baseball historian Gary Ashwill illustrates, in Hill's extended play in Cuba (against both Cuban teams and exhibitions against major-league teams), he fared strikingly better than Rafael Almeida and Armando Marsáns, two light-skinned Cubans who went on to play in the majors.[15]

Yet the Phillies' decline seemed inevitable. "The 1905 Philadelphia Giants, for all their impressive firepower, were a precarious financial balancing act;" observes Ashwill, "they were too dominant, and had trouble booking enough truly high-profile games against worthy opponents."[16] Johnson left prior to the 1906 season, and Bill Monroe as it opened. Following that campaign, owner Schlichter cut some salaries, and instituted other cost-saving measures at his players' expense.[17] Foster, seeking a fairer deal, recruited several Phillies that offseason to join him with the Leland Giants, one of Chicago's leading Black teams, owned by ex-player Frank Leland. After another fine campaign with the Phillies in 1907, Hill left to join the Lelands.

For the next 11 seasons, he played for Foster. The pitcher transitioned to a successful magnate role, finding increasing autonomy and profit for his squads. Hill was his captain and, in his absences, the de facto manager.[18] Contrasts distinguished the two. Foster conveyed bravado. Hill was described as "quiet" and "modest."[19] Foster issued sweeping pronouncements regarding the past, present, and future of Black baseball. Hill's press output was crisp and minimal. Foster was physically imposing. Hill stood 5-foot-8 and weighed 170 pounds.[20] Hill was also a family man, having married Gertrude Lawson in either 1906 or 1907. A son, Kenneth, arrived in 1910.

The highlight of the Leland Giants' 1908 season was a planned seven-game series with the Philadelphia Giants. The teams split the first six games, with Hill contributing eight hits, including three doubles and one triple, against his former teammates.[21] The seventh, deciding game never occurred. In 1909 the Lelands easily captured Chicago's semipro City League pennant with a 31-9 record.[22] Hill played in 37 of these matches, hitting .321 and posting a .429 slugging percentage (in both cases, second among Leland regulars).[23] Yet the team lost a three-game rematch against the Phillies that August and a three-game set against the Chicago Cubs in October. In each of these series, Hill collected only two singles.[24]

Leland and Foster split at the end of the 1909 season. Foster retained rights to the team's name and, that offseason, recruited with determination. Catcher Bruce Petway, shortstop John Henry Lloyd, and outfielder Frank Duncan were lifted from the Phillies. Grant Johnson came over from the Brooklyn Royal Giants. Pitcher Frank Wickware was added to the rotation.

With the Phillies, Hill spent stretches in both left and center field. Upon arriving in Chicago, he became Foster's center fielder. Duncan took over left field in 1910; "Jap" Payne remained in right. The trio stayed in place for the next three seasons.

Defensively, Hill impressed onlookers with his heady play and athleticism. In a 1910 match against the semipro Gunthers, "Pete Hill pulled off the unusual trick of dropping an outfield fly purposely with men at first and second in the sixth inning. He picked the ball up and threw to third and the ball was sent back to second for a double play that retired the side."[25] Against the Cuban Stars in 1911, Hill was praised for "cutting off many well-meant hits by sensational running catches."[26] In 1912, against a Tufts-Lyons opponent in Southern California, Ivy Olson took flight from second base on a single to deep center and seemed "a cinch" to score. "Hill, however, upset all calculations with a sensational throw to the plate. His peg came in fast and true, and Petway, throwing himself in front of the sliding Olson, cut him off within a foot of his goal."[27]

Hill prospered from the revitalized lineup. Hitting second or third in the order, and sandwiched between Duncan and Johnson, he enjoyed one of his finest offensive seasons in 1910. By mid-August, per contemporary sources, he had 17 home runs and 16 triples to his credit.[28] Seamheads, from a limited sample of 22 documented games, credits him with a gaudy BA/OBP/SLG line of .511/.540/.830 (and an OPS+ 319).

Foster next partnered with John C. Schorling. For 1911, the squad was renamed the Chicago American Giants and played their home games at Schorling Park. The new field was spacious, with its fences 350 and 360 feet away down the lines and 450 feet away at dead center.[29] Hill's reputation turned from slugger to one of baseball's finest line-drive hitters. In one regular-season stretch during 1911, he reportedly hit safely in 115 of the Americans' 116 games. This seems doubtful: José Méndez alone shut him down twice that summer.[30] But even .400 hitters suffer oh-fers, and this was quite possibly Hill's status at the beginning of the decade.

Like many of his teammates, Hill possessed exceptional speed: at an 1911 "Athletic Field Day" competition, he was timed circling the bases in 14.4 seconds.[31] His ability as a lefthanded batter to drag bunts was heralded.[32] He routinely took extra bases with his aggressiveness, drawing contemporary comparisons to Ty Cobb.[33]

Although the team suffered some setbacks, most notably losing a lengthy series to the New York Lincoln Giants in 1913, they were likely the winningest of major western independent Black teams in this era.[34] At home, the Americans could outdraw the Cubs and White Sox.[35] By 1913, thanks to lengthy West Coast tours, they played over 200 games a year. Beyond this already impressive commitment Hill and several teammates also typically spent a winter month playing hotel ball in Florida.[36]

Challenges towards both Hill's and the Americans' pre-eminence came in mid-decade. A succession of Black outfield standouts – Judy Gans, Spottswood Poles, George Shively, and Cristóbal Torriente – had arrived in the previous half-dozen seasons. But arguably the greatest outfielder in pre-Integration Black baseball history, Oscar Charleston, debuted in 1915. His team, the Indianapolis ABCs, also toppled the Americans that season.

In Chicago, on July 18, a key series opened between the teams. With the affair knotted, 3-3, a "melee" broke out between the squads, and "the umpire and Pete Hill had an argument and the umpire jerks out a gun and hits 'Pete' over the nose."[37] The umpire promptly forfeited the game to Indianapolis. Foster and ABCs manager C.I. Taylor proceeded to squabble in print over what had transpired. But Indianapolis swept the series, despite Hill hitting two home runs in each of the final two matches.[38]

The teams continued to battle over the next several years. In October 1916 Indianapolis claimed "the colored baseball title of America" after winning five of nine games in a contested series with the Chicagoans.[39] In 1917 the Americans dominated their rivals. The next season, although Foster's squad again led the west, the ABCs won two matches, and gained a tie, in a three-game series played versus the Americans in Pittsburgh's Forbes Field. Hill contributed two hits and three runs in the set. Charleston collected six hits and six runs.[40]

If Hill had been a .400 hitter at the beginning of the decade, in his final five years with the Americans, he may have been closer to a .300 hitter.[41] As with the White major leagues – where runs-per-game plummeted from 4.5 in 1911 to 3.6 in 1917 – Black independents also scored less over this span. Data from the Seamheads' database suggest these teams averaged 5.4 runs-per-game in 1911, then 4.1 in 1917.[42] Even more pronounced was the decline for the Americans. After the team averaged 5.7 runs in 1911, they scored only four per game in 1917.[43]

In part, the reasons for the offensive contraction in Black baseball likely paralleled those in the major leagues. For example, in 1942, Hill stated he could have "murdered" that era's live balls, and recalled of the dead balls, "You had to put the wood on it sure enough."[44] But mushy baseballs, doctored pitches, and even park factors may not fully explain the Americans' scoring decline.

The "small ball" that Foster, aided by captain Hill, refined may been motivated as much by the teams' strengths as by necessity. Chicago not only possessed excellent team defense and strong starting pitching, but also a disciplined, speedy offensive attack. Cool Papa Bell, for example, recalled that Foster's "favorite play was the steal and bunt. The runner on first would take off and the batter would bunt the ball so the third baseman had to field it. If he threw to first, the lead runner just kept going to third. If he held the ball, it was runners on first and second. It was a beautiful play and Foster's team made it work over and over

again. To make it work, his guys had to be able to really place their bunts. They used to practice for hours bunting the ball into areas Rube would mark off with chalk."[45]

As the Americans evolved, Foster continued to seek a well-organized and economically viable Black baseball league. Detroit, whose African-American population grew from 5,000 in 1910 to 40,000 in 1920, was a fertile opportunity for such a circuit. Foster parted ways with Hill after the 1918 season, setting him up as manager of the new Detroit Stars, and seeding the new franchise with considerable talent. Chicago mainstays Duncan, Petway, and Wickware accompanied Hill to Detroit. Additionally, two newcomers to the Americans in 1918, first baseman Edgar Wesley and shortstop/pitcher José Méndez, were bequeathed to Hill.[46]

The Stars drew an impressive 3,500 fans on April 20, 1919, for their home debut at Mack Field, as they beat the semipro Maxwells, 8-4. Hill, playing center field and batting third, went 2-for-4.[47] A month into the campaign they remained unbeaten.[48] In mid-June, visiting Schorling Park, Detroit lost three of four against Chicago. Hill contributed four hits and two runs in the series; Foster's new center fielder, Charleston, contributed six hits and six runs.[49] The teams met again in Detroit for a seven-game set a month later. After losing the first two games, the Stars won the remaining five.[50] 10,000 fans attended the second game, at Navin Field. Hill batted 10-for-25 in the series, with a double, two triples, and three home runs.

Such slugging was indicative of Hill's 1919 season. Mack Field possessed a friendly right-field fence that rewarded his left-handed bat.[51] But his homers were often anything but cheap. On April 27, Hill "performed a feat duplicated only once before at Mack Park" since its 1915 opening as he "drove the ball far over the centerfield fence."[52] He repeated the accomplishment on May 18.[53] On June 8, his drive over the right-field fence "was the longest ever seen at Mack Park."[54] Then, on an eastern road trip, "Pete Hill hit the longest home run ever seen in the Atlantic City park" against the Bacharach Giants' Dick Redding on July 16.[55]

Hill finished the campaign with 28 home runs, one less than Babe Ruth hit in his breakthrough final season with the Red Sox.[56] It was his most dominant offensive season since 1910 with the Lelands. The Stars scored 5.6 runs per game, well ahead of the Black independent teams' average of 4.7.[57] Like Ruth, Hill led baseball out of the Deadball Era. Detroit finished alongside Chicago atop the western standings.

In 1920, following years of Foster's efforts to build a Black league, the Negro National League was formed, with the Stars as a charter member. On May 15, Hill homered in his first NNL at-bat against the visiting Cuban Stars, leading Detroit to a 5-2 victory.[58] Yet, for most of the season, teams worked around Hill. "The slugging right fielder of the Stars, P. Hill, was the particular victim of the veteran manager's wiles," a reporter noted of C.I. Taylor's strategy as Indianapolis took a game from Detroit on July 3, "He was given three bases on balls, twice in critical moments when a hit would have meant a run."[59] Analyzing 45 documented games, Seamheads credits

Hill with the same number of hits (38) as walks. He also battled injuries, as did several other key Stars.[60] Although his home run count plummeted, Hill still produced a strong offensive campaign. But in the inaugural NNL pennant race, Chicago comfortably outpaced Detroit.

The Stars raced to the front of the NNL pack to begin the 1921 campaign, compiling a 15-6 league record by early June.[61] But St. Louis took four straight games at Mack Park in early July, and Hill's team then sank further during a lengthy road trip.[62] He again contributed another plus season offensively, yet Detroit finished below .500. Owner Tenny Blount dismissed him at the end of the season.

Hill signed on with Chappie Johnson's semipro Philadelphia Royal Stars for the 1922 season. Johnson, who had been a team-mate of Hill's during his "rookie" year with the Phillies in 1904, named his friend captain. The Royal Stars' lengthy barnstorming tours of the Northeast must have reminded Hill of his Phillies years.[63] He returned to the NNL in 1923 to manage the Milwaukee Bears. The "young and inexperienced" squad finished in last place.[64] "Old timers say Pete was a whale of a player," a correspondent wrote in January 1924, "but newer fans who saw Pete attempt to manage the Milwaukee club, knew his days were about ended as a manager or a player in fast company."[65]

"It is true that I am slowing up as a player," Hill responded, "but I do take exception to being 'through as a manager.'" He added, "I have never knowingly made an enemy in baseball."[66] If so, as he assumed the helm of the Eastern Colored League's Baltimore Black Sox, he would soon find many.

The ECL, founded by Hilldale Club owner Ed Bolden in 1923, reflected Bolden's animosity toward Foster.[67] Eastern raids upon the NNL helped to ensure a successful inaugural campaign for the league. Yet Baltimore finished in the ECL cellar that season, leaving owner Charles Spedden anxious for improvement in 1924. To this end, Hill vigorously raided NNL teams. Most notably, he enticed three ABCs: second baseman Connie Day, third baseman Henry Blackmon, and right fielder Crush Holloway. The NNL reportedly "blackballed Pete Hill from future participation in any league clubs as a result of his actions."[68]

Hill's Black Sox kept the Hilldales at bay until mid-July, when the Philadelphians took over the league lead.[69] Baltimore eventually finished the 1924 season in second, several games behind the Hilldales. Hill, as he had in Milwaukee, came off the bench occasionally for an outfield start, or to pinch hit.

Disappointed with the 1924 finish, Spedden appointed slugger John Beckwith as Black Sox manager that offseason.[70] Hill stayed on as the team's business manager and occasional pinch hitter.[71] In 1925 Baltimore fared little better under Beckwith and Spedden re-appointed Hill skipper in August.[72] The team played poorly the rest of the way, and he was let go.

Hill moved to Buffalo that offseason, rooming with his old friend Grant Johnson.[73] In 1926 they revamped the local Pullman Colored Giants team, calling it Pete Hill's Colored Stars.[74] In 1927, with the Colored Elks, he was still playing semipro ball.[75]

By this time he was likely divorced; Gertrude was in Chicago for the 1930 census.

He spent the remainder of his life in Buffalo, working as a porter on the Delaware, Lackawanna & Western Railroad. Hill died on December 19, 1951, of coronary thrombosis. His son, Kenneth, survived him and arranged for his father to buried in Holy Sepulchre Cemetery in Alsip, Illinois.[76] He rests today under a headstone provided by SABR's Negro Leagues Grave Marker Project.

Months after his passing, Hill was named to the second team of the famed 1952 *Pittsburgh Courier* All-America Baseball Team.[77] Four decades later, baseball historian James Riley argued, "If an all-star team had been picked from the Deadball Era, Cobb and Hill would have flanked Tris Speaker to form the outfield constellation."[78] In 2006 Pete Hill was among 16 men and one woman elected to the Hall of Fame by the Special Committee on the Negro Leagues.

SOURCES

In addition to the sources noted in this biography, the author also accessed Hill's file from the National Baseball Hall of Fame and the following sites:

ancestry.com

digital.chipublib.org/digital/collection/examiner

fultonhistory.com

genealogybank.com

newspapers.com

NOTES

1   Lawrence D. Hogan, *Shades of Glory: The Negro Leagues and the Story of African-American Baseball* (Washington, D.C.: National Geographic, 2006): 108.

2   Upon his induction into the Hall of Fame in 2006, Hill was believed to have been born as Joseph Preston Hill, on October 12, 1880, in Pittsburgh. Soon afterwards Patrick Rock and Gary Ashwill's research suggested Hill's given name, birth year, and birthplace were otherwise. Ashwill contacted Leslie Penn and her cousin Ron Hill (the player's great nephew) with this evidence. Hill then emailed Rob Humphreys, editor of the *Culpeper* (Virginia) *Star-Exponent*. Humphreys assigned the story to local researcher Zann Nelson, who delved into local sources, and produced a revealing three-part story that appeared in December 2009. Hill's Hall of Fame plaque was recast and unveiled on October 12, 2010. For an overview of this tale, see Kevin Kirkland, "Penn Hills Man Wins Battle with Baseball Hall of Fame for his Great-Uncle," *Pittsburgh Post-Gazette*, August 8, 2010, https://tinyurl.com/y4r2oudt. For one of Gary Ashwill's entries, see "Is Pete Hill' Hall of Fame Plaque Wrong?" *Agate Type*, April 20, 2007, https://tinyurl.com/y49x3ve4. For Zann Nelson's *Culpeper Star-Exponent* series, see "Correcting History," December 29, 2009, https://tinyurl.com/y43f32as; "The Mystery Unravels," December 30, 2009, https://tinyurl.com/y6a4x93y; and "Digging Deeper," https://tinyurl.com/y4se5473, December 31, 2009. [All online sources accessed February 20, 2019]

3   The source for this information may have been reporting late in Hill's playing career. See "Black Sox Players, No. 1, Pete Hill, Manager," *Baltimore Afro-American, January 18, 1924. Also, an 1899 debut becomes less plausible once Hill's birth year moved forward two years. Or more – as some of Nelson's sources suggested an 1883 or 1884 date.*

4   See for example the roster within "Afro-American Notes," *Pittsburgh Press*, March 18, 1900.

5   "The Golden Slides Are Ready," *Pittsburgh Post*, January 24, 1901. On the Slides being an African-American team, see "Among the Amateurs," *Pittsburgh Post*, September 14, 1901.

6   "Monaca Wins a Good Game," *Pittsburgh Post*, July 2, 1901. For Colored Americans background, see "Strong Colored Team," *Pittsburgh Post*, April 16, 1901 and "Colored Champion Baseball Team," *Pittsburgh Post*, April 19, 1901.

7   On the Matthews' team, see "Pittsburg's Big Colored Team," *Pittsburgh Post*, March 8, 1902; "Colored Amateurs at Rochester," *Pittsburgh Post*, April 27, 1902; "Colored Amateurs Want Games," *Pittsburgh Post*, June 15, 1902. Iron City: "Amateur Notes," *Pittsburgh Press*, March 29, 1903. On Iron City being an African-American team, see "Amateur Baseball Notes," *Pittsburgh Post*, April 5, 1903.

8   There are 50-100 readily-available box scores for the X-Giants per season from 1900 through 1903. None of them list another "Hill" beyond the weak-hitting Johnny Hill who regularly played short or third.

9   "Hoboken Lost in Record Game," *Jersey Journal*, August 14, 1904.

10 "Phila. Giants Trim Cuban X-Giants, Foster Fanning 18 Men at Plate," *Philadelphia Inquirer*, September 2, 1904; "Cuban X Giants Land 2D Game," *Philadelphia Inquirer*, September 3, 1904; "Phila. Giants Win Championship," *Philadelphia Inquirer*, September 4, 1904.

11 The team's record per Phil S. Dixon, *Phil Dixon's American Baseball Chronicles - Great Teams: The 1905 Philadelphia Giants Volume III* (Xlibris, 2010): 22-23.

12 Ibid., 33, 46-47, 56-57, 232.

13 For a Florida box score, see "A Palm Beach Fan Valentine," *Kentucky Post*, February 14, 1905. For Cuban Winter League statistics, see Seamhards.com.

14 "Athletics Win in Chester," *Camden Daily Courier*, October 13, 1906; "Rube Fans 18 Batsmen," *Camden Post-Telegram*, October 15, 1906.

15 Gary Ashwill, "Fourth of July 1911," *Agate Type*, July 4, 2011, https://tinyurl.com/y3eyrdzl.

16 Gary Ashwill, introduction to *Sol White's Official Base Ball Guide* by Sol White (South Orange, NJ, Summer Game Books, 2014): xvii.

17 Larry Lester, *Rube Foster in his Time: On the Field and in the Papers with Black Baseball's Greatest Visionary* (Jefferson, NC: McFarland, 2004): 29.

18 The earliest mention of Hill as captain identified by the author: Cary B. Lewis, "Baseball Gossip," (Indianapolis) *Freeman*, May 28, 1910.

19 "Baseball," (Chicago) *Suburban Economist*, August 26, 1910; "Scraps of Sport," (Indianapolis) *Freeman*, June 27, 1908.

20 Possibly he was shorter. Late in his career, sportswriters called him "a small man" and "diminutive." See "Briscoes to Play Pair of Games Here," *Jackson* (Michigan) *Citizen Patriot*, August 7, 1921; Herman Appelman, "Amateur Ball," *Detroit Times*, May 3, 1920.

21 "Leland Giants Take Game," *Chicago Tribune*, July 28, 1908; "Get Even with Their Rivals," *Chicago Tribune*, July 29, 1908; "Batting

Rally in the Ninth Gives Leland Giants Game," *Chicago Tribune*, July 29, 1908; "Victory for Leland Giants," *Chicago Tribune*, August 3, 1908; "Trimming for 'Rube' Foster," *Chicago Tribune*, August 7, 1908; "Another Game To Easterners," *Chicago Tribune*, August 8, 1908.

22 "City League Ends Season Schedule," *Chicago Tribune*, October 4, 1909.

23 Lester, *Rube Foster in his Time*, 40.

24 For the Phillies' series, see Lester A. Walton, "In the Sporting World," *New York Age*, August 19, 1909. For the Cubs' series, see "City Champs Win from Lelands, 4-1," *Chicago Tribune*, October 19, 1909; R.W. Lardner, "Foster Argues, Schulte Scores," *Chicago Tribune*, October 22, 1909; R.W. Lardner, "Cubs Trim Giants in Final Game, 1-0," *Chicago Tribune*, October 23, 1909.

25 "Gunthers' Errors and Lelands' 5-1 Win," *Chicago Examiner*, May 16, 1910.

26 "American Giants Are Blanked by Cuban Stars," *Philadelphia Inquirer*, August 30, 1911.

27 "Giants Beat Nagle's Men," *Los Angeles Times*, November 11, 1912.

28 Cary B. Lewis, "Diamond Dashes," (Indianapolis) *Freeman*, August 6, 1910; Cary B. Lewis, "Diamond Dashes," (Indianapolis) *Freeman*, August 20, 1910.

29 Lester, *Rube Foster in his Time*, 56.

30 For Méndez's success versus Hill, see "American Giants Are Blanked by Cuban Stars," *Philadelphia Inquirer*, August 30, 1911; "American Giants Win Then Tie Cuban Stars," *Brooklyn Daily Eagle*, September 11, 1911. For other instances of a Hill oh-fer in 1911, see "Giants Down Cuban Stars, 7-3," *Chicago Tribune*, June 1, 1911; "Lincoln Giants Win Twice at American League Park," *Brooklyn Daily Eagle*, September 5, 1911; "American Giants Lose," *Chicago Inter Ocean*, September 17, 1911.

31 Sylvester Russell, "Athletic Field Day," (Indianapolis) *Freeman*, October 21, 1911.

32 Russell J. Cowans, "Thru the Sport Mirror, *Detroit Tribune*, August 19, 1933.

33 "Bots and Bingles," *Tacoma Daily Ledger*, April 14, 1915.

34 Seamheads' partial season records support such a conclusion.

35 Robert Charles Cottrell, *The Best Pitcher in Baseball: The Life of Rube Foster, Negro League Giant* (New York: New York University Press, 2001): 63.

36 For instances of his Florida play, see "Baseball Season Ends on Florida Fields," *Brooklyn Daily Eagle*, March 18, 1914; "Ball Players Go South," (Indianapolis) *Freeman*, January 16, 1915.

37 "American Giants in Fierce Riot at Hoosier City," *Chicago Defender*, July 24, 1915.

38 Cottrell, *The Best Pitcher in Baseball*: 92-93.

39 "Colored Title Won by A.B.C.s," *Indianapolis Star*, October 30, 1916.

40 "Giants-A.B.C. Deadlocked in Eleven Innings," *Pittsburgh Post*, July 26, 1918; "Colored Series to Close Today," *Pittsburgh Press*, July 27, 1918; "American Giants Go Down to Defeat," *Pittsburgh Press*, July 28, 1918.

41 Seamheads' database, for the available statistics, suggests as much.

42 These counts do not include Seamheads' data of games versus MLB teams in this span.

43 Again, per Seamheads.

44 "Pete Hill, Retired Baseball Player Visits Solider Son," *Chicago Defender*, December 12, 1942.

45 Lester, *Rube Foster in his Time*, 105.

46 Cottrell, *The Best Pitcher in Baseball*: 133-134.

47 "Big Crowd Sees Detroit Stars Lick Maxwells," *Detroit Free Press*, April 21, 1919.

48 "Jackson's Best Tries to Halt Detroit Stars," *Detroit Free Press*, May 25, 1919.

49 "15,000 Fans See American Giants Trim Detroiters," *Chicago Tribune*, June 16, 1919; "Foster's Giants Cop Again," *Chicago Tribune*, June 18, 1919; "American Giants Beat Detroit, 8-5; Hurlers Wild," *Chicago Tribune*, June 19, 1919; "American Giants Lost Final Battle to Detroiters, 5-4," *Chicago Tribune*, June 20, 1919.

50 "American Giants Rally in Ninth to Annex First," *Detroit Free Press*, July 27, 1919 ; "Whitworth is Master Over Blount's Cast," *Detroit Free Press*, July 28, 1919; "Stars Pummel Foster's Club in Third Game," *Detroit Free Press*, July 29, 1919; "Detroit Stars Tie Up Series with Chi Team," *Detroit Free Press*, July 30, 1919; "Five Scores in Fifth Enough to Beat Chicagoans," *Detroit Free Press*, July 31, 1919; "Detroit Stars Take Slugfest From Chi Team," *Detroit Free Press*, August 1, 1919; "Detroit Stars Capture Final Game of Series," *Detroit Free Press*, August 3, 1919.

51 For more on Mack Park, see Gary Ashwill, "Mack Park, 1929," *Agate Type*, April 23, 2010, http://tinyurl.com/yymghtft.

52 "Stars Work Hard Scoring Odd Run on Doyle's Boys," *Detroit Free Press*, April 28, 1919.

53 "Champs Defeated by Colored Team in Good Battle," *Detroit Free Press*, May 19, 1919.

54 "Second Battle Goes Same Way as Initial One," *Detroit Free Press*, June 9, 1919.

55 "Stars Capture First in East," *Detroit Free Press*, July 17, 1919.

56 For more on Hill's 1919 season, see Gary Ashwill, "Pete Hill's Historical Marker, Annotated," *Agate Type*, March 18, 2011, https://tinyurl.com/y5h3vkd8.

57 Again, per Seamheads, with data from games versus MLB teams not included.

58 "Stars Take First from Cuban Team," *Detroit Free Press*, May 16, 1920.

59 "Classy Pitching Wins For A.B.C.s," *Muncie Star Press*, July 4, 1920.

60 "Blount and Hill Ready for Gong," *Chicago Defender*, February 19, 1921.

61 "Monarchs in Second Place," *Kansas City Kansan*, June 9, 1921.

62 "Charleston's Hit is Winning Blow," *Detroit Free Press*, July 6, 1921.

63 For more on the Royal Giants, see Gary Ashwill, "Black Sox Players,' Nos. 1 & 2" *Agate Type*, December 11, 2006, http://tinyurl.com/yyuvt53u; "19 Men Report to Chappie Johnson," *Philadelphia Evening Public Ledger*, April 1, 1922; "Knights Down Chappie's Men," *Schenectady Gazette*, July 19, 1922; "North Phils to Oppose Fletcher," *Philadelphia Evening Public Ledger*, July 31, 1922.

64 William Dismukes, "Winter's Blast and Summer Echoes," *Pittsburgh Courier*, November 24, 1923.

65 "Hilldale Played Only 59 League Games During 1923," *Chicago Defender*, January 12, 1924.

66 "'Not Through as Player and Manager,' Says Pete Hill," *Pittsburgh Courier*, February 23, 1924.

67 For more on this rivalry, see Courtney Michelle Smith, *Ed Bolden and Black Baseball in Philadelphia* (Jefferson, NC: McFarland, 2017): 22-36.

68 "Holloway Better Jumper Than Frog, Hops to Baltimore," *Chicago Defender*, April 24, 1924.

69 "Black Sox Take Lead in Eastern Colored League," *Baltimore Evening Sun*, July 17, 1924; "Baltimore Black Sox Swamped by Hilldale," *Philadelphia Inquirer*, July 25, 1924.

70 "Clubs Forming East and West Remain Intact," *Baltimore Afro-American*, December 20, 1924.

71 G.L. Mackey, "Sports Mirror," *Baltimore Afro-American*, April 18, 1925.

72 "Sox and Giants to Lock Horns Sunday," *Baltimore Afro-American*, August 8, 1925.

73 Ryan Whirty, "Remembering Pete Hill," Hill's Hall of Fame file.

74 "Easter Brands Bow to Colored Giants," *Buffalo Evening News*, May 10, 1926; "County Champs Win, *Fredonia* (New York) *Censor*, July 7, 1926.

75 "Colored Elks to Travel," *Buffalo Evening News*, June 25, 1927.

76 Just as the identification of Hill's birthplace and year has a compelling story of historical research behind it, so does Jeremy Krock's determination of his resting place. See Gary Ashwill, "Found: Pete Hill's Grave," *Agate Type*, November 8, 2010, https://tinyurl.com/yxu4p9q3.

77 "Power, Speed, Skill Make All-America Team Excel," *Pittsburgh Courier*, April 19, 1952.

78 James A. Riley, *The Biographical Encyclopedia of the Negro Baseball Leagues* (Carroll and Graf, New York, 1994): 381.

APPENDIX A: JAPAN

Nippon Professional Baseball

A home run is a cause for celebration in every league. In Japan, home run celebrations on the field can be epic, including props and choreographed team moves. In the stands, Japanese fans show their appreciation by waving flags, singing songs, and showering confetti.

For players hitting a home run on their first at-bat in Japan's Nippon Professional Baseball, surrounded by their excited teammates amid the cheering crowd, the feeling would be unforgettable. That occasion happened for the 67 players on the list below. We would like to gratefully thank our friends in the SABR Tokyo Chapter, especially Yoshihiro Koda, for their invaluable contributions in conducting research for the list below and stories.

Several highlights from this distinguished group of players include Japanese Hall of Famer Morimichi Takagi, "Mr. Grand Slam" Norihiro Komada, and Jon Nunnally, the only player (as of 2023) to hit a home run in his first at-bat in both Major League Baseball and Nippon Professional Baseball. Their accomplishments, along with the other 60 players and those to come, demonstrate the talent, hard work, and joyous spirit that define Japanese baseball.

— Giselle Stancic

	Player	Date	Team	First pitch	Pinch hitter	Grand slam	Opponent	Pitcher	Career HR*
1	Akio Kanemitsu	1944-04-22	Asahi		●		Kyojin	Hideo Fujimoto	2
2	Katsuki Tokura	1950-05-11	Mainichi Orions				Nishitetsu Clippers	Isamu Kinoshita	75
3	Morimichi Shiose	1950-05-11	Tokyu Flyers				Daiei Stars	Koji Himeno	1
4	Morimichi Takagi	1960-05-07	Chunichi Dragons				Taiyo Whales	Kazuyoshi Miyamoto	236
5	Kent Hadley	1962-05-01	Nankai Hawks				Nishitetsu Lions	Junichi Nakajima	131
6	Tadahiro Goto	1962-08-21	Kintetsu Buffaloes				Daimai Orions	Frank Manny	1
7	Susumu Aikawa	1966-09-28	Chunichi Dragons		●		Sankei Swallows	Shiroku Ishido	17
8	Dick Stuart	1967-04-19	Taiyo Whales				Hanshin Tigers	Yutaka Enatsu	49
9	Mitsuo Komuro	1968-08-21	Nishitetsu Lions		●		Kintetsu Buffaloes	Hideo Kato	1
10	Yoshinori Yamamura	1975-05-30	Taiheiyo Lions		●		Lotte Orions	Masaaki Kitaru	70
11	Rafael Batista	1975-06-03	Lotte Orions				Nankai Hawks	Takenori Emoto	3
12	Bobby Mitchell	1976-04-27	Nippon Ham Fighters				Kintetsu Buffaloes	Toshio Kanbe	113
13	Yasuyuki Nakai	1979-04-11	Yomiuri Giants		●		Hanshin Tigers	Kazuyuki Yamamoto	3
14	Nobuyuki Kagawa	1980-07-08	Nankai Hawks				Kintetsu Buffaloes	Takashi Imoto	78
15	Ike Hampton	1981-06-05	Kintetsu Buffaloes				Nippon Ham Fighters	Masami Takahashi	15
16	Norihiro Komada	1983-04-10	Yomiuri Giants			●	Taiyo Whales	Kazuhiko Migita	195
17	Kozo Mori	1984-05-30	Hiroshima Carp	●			Yakult Swalloes	Daisuke Araki	1
18	Keiji Abe	1984-08-08	Hiroshima Carp		●		Yomiuri Giants	Hiromi Makihara	1
19	Shinichi Murakami	1984-08-09	Hankyu Braves		●		Nankai Hawks	Shinichi Kato	18
20	Kenta Aoshima	1985-05-11	Yakult Swallows		●		Hanshin Tigers	Kazuhiko Kudo	2
21	Akira Yonemura	1986-08-23	Chunichi Dragons				Yakult Swallows	Eijiro Ai	1
22	Doug DeCinces	1988-04-08	Yakult Swallows				Yomiuri Giants	Masumi Kuwata	19

	Player	Date	Team	First pitch	Pinch hitter	Grand slam	Opponent	Pitcher	Career HR*
23	Mike Easler	1988-05-19	Nippon Ham Fighters				Lotte Orions	Hiroshi Ogawa	26
24	Ming-Tsu Lu	1988-06-14	Yomiuri Giants				Yakult Swallows	Bob Gibson	18
25	Masutaka Hironaga	1989-04-08	Fukuoka Daiei Hawks		●		Nippon Ham Fighters	Yukihiro Nishizaki	34
26	Benny Distefano	1990-04-07	Chunichi Dragons				Taiyo Whales	Hiroaki Nakayama	5
27	Hiroyasu Hayashi	1990-06-29	Lotte Orions		●		Fukuoka Daiei Hawks	Yuji Inoue	5
28	Hideki Saeki	1990-09-24	Seibu Lions				Nippon Ham Fighters	Hiroaki Matsuura	1
29	Phil Bradley	1991-04-06	Yomiuri Giants				Chunichi Dragons	Tatsuo Komatsu	21
30	Koichi Morita	1991-04-10	Chunichi Dragons				Hiroshima Carp	Kenko Akimura	2
31	Don Schulze	1991-05-29	Orix Blue Wave				Kintetsu Buffaloes	Motoyuki Akahori	1
32	Mike Marshall	1992-04-04	Nippon Ham Fighters				Seibu Lions	Kimiyasu Kudo	9
33	Kevin Mitchell	1995-04-01	Fukuoka Daiei Hawks			●	Seibu Lions	Kuo Tai Yuan	8
34	Atsunori Inaba	1995-06-21	Yakult Swallows				Hiroshima Carp	Makoto Kito	261
35	Yudai Deguchi	1995-09-19	Yomiuri Giants				Chunichi Dragons	Shinji Imanaka	13
36	Kosei Ono	1997-07-20	Yakult Swallows				Yomiuri Giants	Koichi Misawa	16
37	Hiroki Fukutome	1997-09-15	Orix Blue Wave				Seibu Lions	Jun Takeshita	6
38	Frank Bolick	1999-04-14	Chia Lotte Marines				Orix Blue Wave	Satoshi Tokumoto	92
39	Corey Paul	1999-06-25	Seibu Lions				Daiei Hawks	Tomohiro Nagai	16

駒田徳広（巨人）

Norihiro "Mr. Grand Slam" Komada, Yomiuri Giants – Courtesy of Trading Card Database

Munetaka Murakami, Yakult Swallows – Courtesy of Trading Card Database

	Player	Date	Team	First pitch	Pinch hitter	Grand slam	Opponent	Pitcher	Career HR*
40	Koji Hiroike	1999-09-29	Hiroshima Carp				Hanshin Tigers	Toshiyuki Hesaka	1
41	Jon Nunnally	2000-06-28	Orix Blue Wave				Kintetsu Buffaloes	Katsuhiko Maekawa	5
42	Shogo Mori	2001-05-01	Chunichi Dragons				Yomiuri Giants	Sorao Nomura	5
43	Hisao Heiuchi	2002-04-08	Lotte Marines				Nippon Ham Fighters	Chris Seelbach	9
44	Yoshiyuki Noguchi	2002-09-13	Yakult Swallows				Yokohama Baystars	Hideki Chiba	8
45	José Ortiz	2003-03-28	Orix Blue Wave				Kintetsu Buffaloes	Jeremy Powell	135
46	Toshimitsu Higa	2005-09-19	Hiroshima Carp		●		Yokohama Baystars	Mike Holtz	1
47	Ryuichi Kajimae	2008-06-06	Yomiuri Giants				Lotte Marines	Yusuke Kawasaki	2
48	Tony Blanco	2009-04-03	Chunichi Dragons				Yokohama Baystars	Daisuke Miura	181
49	Nobumasa Fukuda	2009-07-07	Chunichi Dragons				Yakult Swallows	Takehiko Oshimoto	84
50	Stephen Randolph	2009-08-16	Yokohama BayStars				Hiroshima Carp	Takeshi Komatsu	1
51	Kazunari Morita	2011-07-26	Hanshin Tigers		●		Chunichi Dragons	Maximo Nelson	1
52	Ryan Mulhern	2011-08-05	Seibu Lions				Softbank Hawks	Sho Iwasaki	1
53	Jose Lopez	2013-03-29	Yomiuri Giants				Hiroshima Carp	Bryan Bullington	198
54	Shohei Kato*	2013-05-12	Lotte Marines				Rakuten Eagles	Rei Nagai	16
55	Naomichi Nishiura*	2014-03-28	Yakult Swallows				DeNA Baystars	Kazuki Mishima	38
56	Ernesto Mejia	2014-05-15	Seibu Lions				Nippon Ham Fighters	Naoyuki Uesawa	142
57	Tomo Otosaka	2014-05-31	DeNA BayStars		●		Lotte Marines	Naoya Masuda	10
58	Félix Pérez	2016-07-12	Rakuten Eagles				Seibu Lions	Felipe Paulino	5
59	Taishi Hirooka*	2016-09-29	Yakult Swallows				DeNA Baystars	Daisuke Miura	28
60	Xavier Batista	2017-06-03	Hiroshima Carp		●		Lotte Marines	Takahiro Matsunaga	62
61	Seiya Hosokawa*	2017-10-03	DeNA BayStars				Chunichi Dragons	Shotaro Kasahara	30
62	Jorge Martinez	2018-07-27	Yomiuri Giants				Chunichi Dragons	Daisuke Yamai	2
63	Yudai Yamamoto*	2018-08-19	DeNA BayStars		●		Hiroshima Carp	Tetsuya Iida	5
64	Munetaka Murakami*	2018-09-16	Yakult Swallows				Hiroshima Carp	Akitake Okada	191
65	Oscar Colás	2019-08-18	Softbank Hawks				Seibu Lions	Ken Togame	1
66	Seiichiro Oshita*	2020-09-15	Orix Buffaloes				Rakuten Eagles	Wataru Karashima	4
67	Ryoto Kita*	2021-07-13	Orix Buffaloes	●			Nippon Ham Fighters	Takahide Ikeda	2

List provided by Yoshihiro Koda.
* Active player in 2024.
** Statistics through 2023 NPB season.

APPENDIX B: KOREA

Korea Baseball Organization

Since the 1982 formation of Korea's first professional baseball league, 20 batters in the Korea Baseball Organization (KBO) have announced themselves with a home run in their first at-bat. In the league's third season, in early April 1984, Seuk-gyu Lee of the Lotte Giants teed up a blast over the wall against Sung-man Jung of the now-defunct Sammi Superstars. The blast came in the second inning in front of the home crowd at Lotte's former home, the Gudeok Baseball Stadium in Busan.

Lee's home run was the only first at-bat homer hit during the 1980s, but a new decade brought an influx of power. In August 1992, Chun Yun of the LG Twins homered in his first time up against the Ssangbangwool Raiders in Jeonju. In 1998 the KBO allowed foreign players into the league for the first time. The first great foreign superstar, Tyrone Woods, a former Montreal Expos prospect who reached Triple A in the United States, presaged his tremendous career in Korea by homering in his first at-bat for the OB Bears (now the Doosan Bears) on Opening Day. That same day, Kyung-hwan Cho of the Lotte Giants also homered in his first at-bat in Daegu. Cho hit eight more home runs in 1998, and he turned into a consistent slugger for the Giants and the SK Wyverns, accumulating 131 homers during his KBO tenure.

In 2000, two more foreign players accomplished the feat when Tom Quinlan, who spent parts of four seasons in the US major leagues, and Jim Tatum, a journeyman who last appeared with the New York Mets, each homered on Opening Day April 5, 2000. Tatum's home run came on the first pitch he ever saw in a Korean regular-season game.

Over the subsequent two decades, the number of first-at-bat home runs grew, with 14 coming between 2001 and 2022. Mendy López of the Samsung Lions in 2004 and Christian Bethancourt of the NC Dinos in 2019 homered upon their arrival in Korea. While López played only a half-season in the KBO, he helped the Samsung Lions to the 2004 Korean Series title by hitting two home runs with a .588 on-base percentage en route to playoff MVP honors. The defense-first catcher Bethancourt, once a highly regarded prospect with the Atlanta Braves, struggled through five seasons in the US major leagues before moving to the KBO for one year. He returned to the major leagues in 2022 with the Oakland A's and began the 2024 season on the Miami Marlins roster.

Bethancourt's home run was one of two in a first at-bat that came off a foreign-born pitcher. The other was hit by then-18-year-old phenom Baek-ho Kang of the KT Wiz against Héctor Noesí in 2018. Arguably the most accomplished Korean player to homer in his first at-bat, Kang hit 29 home runs in his rookie season and hit 95 over his first seven seasons through 2023. Kang also had a robust .302/.382/.479 slash line over that time.

Of the 20 KBO players who homered in their first at-bat, Tyrone Woods went on to hit the most career home runs in the league. Woods' 174 home runs are also the most by any foreign player in KBO history. Kang, who in 2024 was 24 years old and starring for the KT Wiz, could hit more than 174 by the time his career is over, which would make him the career leader for those who started their KBO tenure with a homer. At the other end of the spectrum, two players, Young-jin Kwon and Jae-yong Lee, hit homers in their first at-bat and never hit another in the KBO.

— Zac Petrillo

ACKNOWLEDGMENTS

Special thanks to Jim Bulley and Dan Kurtz for their research support. The author also consulted Baseball-Reference.com, Mykbostats.com, and Statiz.Sporki.com.

	Player	Date	Team	City	Inning	First pitch	Pinch hitter	Opponent	Pitcher	Career HR**
1	Seok-gyu Lee	1984-04-10	Lotte Giants	Busan	2			Sammi Superstars	Sung-man Jung	2
2	Chan Yun	1992-08-23	LG Twins	Seoul	2			Ssangbangwool Raiders	Dong-han Jin	2
3	Kyung-hwan Cho	1998-04-11	Lotte Giants	Busan	2			Samsung Lions	Kye-hyeon Cho	131
4	Tyrone Woods	1998-04-11	OB Bears	Seoul	2			Hatai Tigers	Dae-jin Lee	174
5	Tom Quinlan	2000-04-05	Hyundai Unicorns	Suwon	1			Hanwha Eagles	Yong-duk Han	65
6	Jim Tatum	2000-04-05	LG Twins	Seoul	2	●		Lotte Giants	Hyung-kwang Joo	4
7	Won-guk Song	2001-06-23	Doosan Bears	Seoul	9	●	●	SK Wyverns	Won-hyeong Kim	6
8	Il-sang Heo	2002-04-16	Lotte Giants	Busan	8			Hyundai Unicorns	Jun-ho Jeon	2
9	Mendy López	2004-07-20	Samsung Lions	Daegu	1			Hanwha Eagles	Chang-sik Song	3
10	Jun Heo	2006-10-02	Hyundai Unicorns	Suwon	9		●	Samsung Lions	Byeong-ho Jeon	4
11	Young-jin Kwon	2008-07-08	SK Wyverns	Incheon	8			Samsung Lions	Hyun-keun Cho	1
12	Jeong-lip Hwang	2012-09-14	Kia Tigers	Gwangju	12		●	Lotte Giants	Young-sik Kang	2
13	Sung-woo Jo	2013-03-30	SK Wyverns	Incheon	7		●	LG Twins	Sang-yeol Lee	4
14	Woong-bin Kim*	2016-07-13	Nexen Heroes	Seoul	3			KT Wiz	Si-hwan Jang	19
15	Tae-yeon Kim*	2007-06-21	Hanwha Eagles	Daejeon	2	●		Nexen Heroes	Jae-young Shin	27
16	Baek-ho Kang*	2018-03-24	KT Wiz	Suwon	3			Kia Tigers	Héctor Noesí	121
17	Christian Bethancourt	2019-03-23	NC Dinos	Changwon	1			Samsung Lions	Deck McGuire	8
18	Yoon-hoo Shin*	2019-05-15	Lotte Giants	Busan	8			LG Twins	Jung-rak Shin	4
19	Jae-yong Lee	2022-05-06	NC Dinos	Changwon	5	●		LG Twins	Jin-sung Kim	1
20	Young-woong Kim*	2022-09-13	Samsung Lions	Daegu	3			NC Dinos	Myung-gi Song	31

List provided by Zac Petrillo.
* Active player in 2024.
** Statistics through 2024 KBO season.

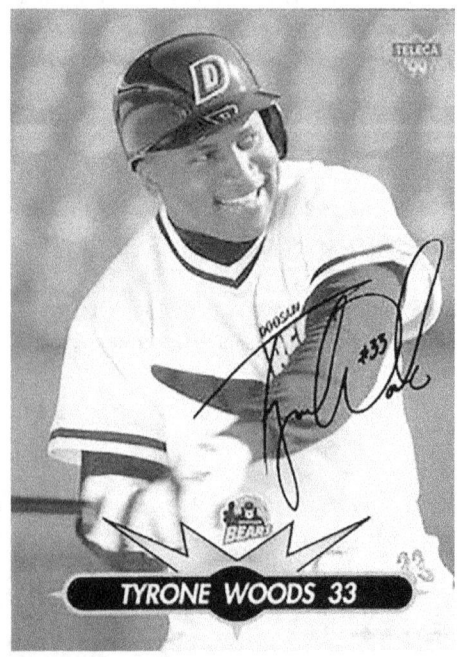

Tyrone Woods, OB Bears – Courtesy of Trading Card Database

Baek-ho Kang, KT Wiz – Courtesy of Trading Card Database

APPENDIX C: PUERTO RICO

Liga de Béisbol Profesional Roberto Clemente

Thanks to Jorge Colón Delgado, SABR member and Official Historian of the Puerto Rico Professional Baseball League, for his valuable contributions in compiling research on first at-bat home runs.

In 1898, the first organized baseball game took place in Puerto Rico, and by 1938, the island's first professional baseball league was established. The league continued to grow in popularity, thanks to the talented players who filled the stands with enthusiastic fans, establishing baseball as one of Puerto Rico's most beloved sports.

The Puerto Rico Baseball League, also known as the *Liga de Béisbol Profesional Roberto Clemente* (LBPRC), includes six teams entering the 2024 season: Criollos de Caguas, Gigantes de Carolina, Indios de Mayagüez, Leones de Ponce, Cangrejeros de Santurce, and RA12. Notably, every team except RA12 (founded in 2020) is represented by at least one player who hit a home

run in their first at-bat. Former league teams Lobos de Arecibo and Vaqueros de Bayamón are also represented on the list below.

The roster of players who hit a home run in their first at-bat highlights Puerto Rican-born athletes like Miguel Negrón and Orlando Cruz, both of whom later played in the US minor leagues. The list also includes Major League Baseball stars like Darryl Strawberry, who participated in the LBPRC during the offseason.

Given the Puerto Rico Baseball League's distinguished history of developing baseball talent, we anticipate more players will join this exclusive list in the years to come. To delve deeper into the rich history of baseball in Puerto Rico, explore the SABR Digital Library publication, *Puerto Rico and Baseball: 60 Biographies*.

— Giselle Stancic

	Player	Date	Team	Opponent	Pitcher
1	Howard Easterling	1940-10-27	Leones de Ponce	Criollos de Caguas	Billy Byrd
2	Jack Harshman	1953-10-10	Senadores de San Juan	Leones de Ponce	Steve Ridzik
3	Bubba Phillips	1955-10-18	Leones de Ponce	Cangrejeros de Santurce	Bill Greason
4	Reggie Smith	1966-10-21	Senadores de San Juan	Indios de Mayagüez	Fritz Fisher
5	Dave Duncan	1967-10-19	Lobos de Arecibo	Senadores de San Juan	James Gillman
6	Bill Kelso	1968-10-17	Leones de Ponce	Indios de Mayagüez	Les Cain
7	Miguel Negrón	1978-10-29	Criollos de Caguas	Leones de Ponce	Luis de León
8	Mark Davis	1988-10-25	Lobos de Arecibo	Leones de Ponce	Ray Krawczyk
9	Joseph Calder	1990-12-30	Senadores de San Juan	Criollos de Caguas	Juan Roberto Rivera
10	John Mabry	1993-11-02	Senadores de San Juan	Cangrejeros de Santurce	Juan Edwin Correa
11	Darryl Strawberry	1995-11-18	Cangrejeros de Santurce	Senadores de San Juan	Anthony Telford
12	Preston Wilson	1998-11-06	Leones de Ponce	Criollos de Caguas	Derrin Ebbert
13	Aubrey Huff	2000-11-10	Cangrejeros de Santurce	Criollos de Caguas	Ismael Villegas
14	Travis Hafner	2000-11-24	Gigantes de Carolina	Indios de Mayagüez	Enrique Calero
15	Scott Podsednik	2001-11-01	Vaqueros de Bayamón	Criollos de Caguas	Ismael Villegas
16	Jeff Inglin	2001-11-09	Leones de Ponce	Gigantes de Carolina	Dickie González
17	Adam LaRoche	2003-11-01	Indios de Mayagüez	Leones de Ponce	Héctor Mercado
18	Orlando Cruz	2005-11-11	Lobos de Arecibo	Atenienses de Manatí	Kasey Olenberger
19	Yasiel Puig	2012-11-17	Indios de Mayagüez	Atenienses de Manatí	Shinya Kayama
20	Jim Haley	2022-01-02	Indios de Mayagüez	RA12	Ricardo Vélez
21	Jerry Downs	2022-11-05	Indios de Mayagüez	Criollos de Caguas	Aneuris Rosario

List provided by Jorge Colón Delgado.
* Statistics through 2023-24 PRBL season.

APPENDIX D: MEXICO

Liga Mexicana del Pacifico

On October 6, 1984 – Opening Day of the 35th season of the *Liga Mexicana del Pacifico* (Mexican Pacific League) – the Mayos of Navojoa hosted the Yaquis of Obregón. Mayos first baseman Larry See homered in his first at-bat against Yaquis pitcher David Franco. Coming to bat again in the fourth inning, See homered in his second at-bat as well. Both were solo home runs and both off Franco. The Mayos beat the Yaquis, 4-3.

That same day, in a strange coincidence, rookie Genaro Rodríguez made his professional debut with the Venados de Mazatlán against the visiting Tomateros de Culiacán. He was called to pinch-hit with the bases loaded, and on the first pitch, Rodríguez hit the ball out of the park for a grand slam and his team beat Culiacán 13-7. The pitcher's name is not known.

Two days later, on October 8, 1984, Venados de Mazatlán opened a series against Algodoneros de Guasave, Venados manager Jorge Calvo called on Rodríguez to pinch-hit again. Facing Hector Serafin, again he homered on the first pitch and thus became, along with Larry See, the first two players to hit home runs in both of their first two at-bats in the league.

On October 12, 2000, the Yaquis of Obregón visited Los Mayos de Navojoa. Alfredo Amézaga, an Obregón native and a US major leaguer for nine years (2002-2011), made his debut as a shortstop. As the Yaquis' leadoff hitter, Amézaga hit the first pitch from Juan Manuel Palafox out of the ballpark in right field. The final score was 6-4 in favor of the Yaquis.

Exactly 16 years later, on October 12, 2016, Obregón hosted Los Naranjeros de Hermosillo in their new stadium, Nuevo Estadio Yaquis Ney. Rolando Valdez was the starter for Obregón. The first batter of the game, Eric Young Jr. of Los Naranjeros, hit a home run to open the game in his first at-bat in the league. It was the first home run hit at the brand-new new stadium as well. Hermosillo won the game, 3-2.

— Carlos Fragoso

	Player	Date	Team	Opponent	Pitcher
1	Larry See	1984-10-06	Mayos de Navojoa	Yaquis de Obregón	David Franco
2	Genaro Rodríguez	1984-10-06	Venados de Mazatlán	Tomateros de Culiacán	n/a
3	Alfredo Amézaga	2000-10-12	Yaquis de Obregón	Mayos de Navojoa	Juan Manuel Palafox
4	Eric Young Jr.	2016-10-12	Naranjeros de Hermosillo	Yaquis de Obregón	Rolando Valdez

List provided by Carlos Fragoso.
Statistics through 2023-24 season.

APPENDIX E: AAGPBL

All-American Girls Professional Baseball League

In addition to major-league baseball players, *Dazzling Debuts: First At-Bat Home Runs* is pleased to highlight players from other professional baseball leagues, including the All-American Girls Professional Baseball League (AAGPBL). Special thanks to Merrie Fidler, official historian of the AAGPBL Players Association, and Dr. Leslie Heaphy and Carol Sheldon, members of the SABR Women in Baseball Research Committee, for their research support and suggestions.

While we did not identify an AAGPBL player who hit a home run in her first at-bat, the research offered valuable insights into how modifications in playing equipment, pitch delivery, and diamond dimensions affected home-run production during the league's 12 years in operation, from 1943 to 1954.

During the early years of the AAGPBL, the league was known to favor pitching over hitting. The baseball was 12 inches in circumference (like a softball), pitchers threw underhand (like in softball), and the distance to home plate was 40 feet (compared to the men's leagues' 60 feet 6 inches). Basepaths were also shorter.[1] Along with strong pitching, the playing field rules typically resulted in team batting averages in the low .200s. Individual players rarely hit more than a few home runs in a season (if any), and team totals were typically less than 10.[2]

Seeking to appeal to a broader fan base, the league began making modifications to the game as early as 1944. The ball gradually became smaller, while the distances between bases and to home plate gradually increased. A major change came in 1948 when the league adopted overhand pitching. Ball size and distance adjustments continued until midseason 1954, when the playing field was nearly identical to the men's game, and the use of a 9-inch baseball was adopted.[3]

The smaller baseball may be more challenging to hit, but when players connected, the ball traveled farther and faster. The statistics reflected this change. For example, in 1954, Joanne Weaver led the league in home runs (29), hits (143), and batting average (.429),[4] numbers that would have been unheard of a decade earlier.

Fans and the press took notice of the offensive surge. The headline in the *South Bend* (Indiana) *Tribune* on July 2, 1954, read, "Smaller Ball Proves Boon to Bat Stars," declaring the dawn of the home-run era for the AAGPBL and highlighting three home runs "smashed" at Playland Park, two of which were hit by Weaver.[5]

One can imagine that if the league had continued past 1954, recruiting more women directly into the more offense-conducive playing conditions, we could be writing about one or more first-at-bat home runs by AAGPBL players. However, we still celebrate the players who had the opportunity to showcase their hitting abilities in this league, especially during its later years.

Visit the AAGPBL Players Association website (aagpbl. org) to learn more about this exciting time in American baseball history. SABR's Women in Baseball Research Committee is another rich resource for the role of women in various aspects of professional baseball.

— Giselle Stancic

NOTES

1   "Rules of Play," All-American Girls Professional Baseball League. https://www.aagpbl.org/history/rules-of-play, accessed June 22, 2024.

2   Traci L. Rucker, *Reconciling Femininity and Athleticism: The All-American Girls Professional Baseball League, 1943-1954* (Indianapolis: ScholarWorks, 2004), 71. https://scholarworks.indianapolis.iu.edu/items/d162b1ac-bcd2-4476-a2d3-8abd4b6b98a3, accessed June 22, 2024.

3   Merrie A. Fidler, *The Origins and History of the All-American Girls Professional Baseball League* (Jefferson, North Carolina: McFarland, 2006), 71.

4   "Joanne Weaver," All-American Girls Professional Baseball League. https://www.aagpbl.org/profiles/joanne-weaver-jo/623, accessed June 22, 2024.

5   "Smaller Ball Proves Boon to Bat Stars," *South Bend Tribune*, July 2, 1954: Section 3, 1.

APPENDIX F: PLAYERS WITH HOME RUN IN FIRST AT-BAT, 1887-2024

	Name	Date	Team	First pitch	Pinch hitter	Grand slam	Opponent	Pitcher	Career HR**
1	George Tebeau	1887-04-16	Cincinnati Red Stockings (AA)				Cleveland Blues	George Pechiney	15
2	Mike Griffin	1887-04-16	Baltimore Orioles (AA)				Philadelphia Athletics	Ed Seward	42
3	Billy Gumbert	1890-06-19	Pittsburgh Alleghenys	●			Cleveland Spiders	Jack Wadsworth	1
4	Joe Harrington	1895-09-10	Boston				St. Louis Browns	Bill Kissinger	3
5	Bill Duggleby	1898-04-21	Philadelphia			●	New York Giants	Cy Seymour	6
6	Johnny Bates	1906-04-12	Boston Beaneaters				Brooklyn Superbas	Harry McIntire	25
7	Pete Hill	1920-05-15	Detroit Stars (NNL)				Cuban Stars	José Leblanc	7
8	Luke Stuart	1921-08-08	St. Louis Browns				Washington Senators	Walter Johnson	1
9	Walter Mueller	1922-05-07	Pittsburgh Pirates	●			Chicago Cubs	Grover Alexander	2
10	Earl Averill	1929-04-16	Cleveland Indians				Detroit Tigers	Earl Whitehill	238
11	Clise Dudley	1929-04-27	Brooklyn Dodgers	●			Philadelphia Phillies	Claude Willoughby	3
12	Gordon Slade	1930-05-24	Brooklyn Dodgers				Boston Braves	Bob Smith	8
13	Eddie Morgan	1936-04-14	St. Louis Cardinals	●	●		Chicago Cubs	Lon Warneke	1
14	Ace Parker	1937-04-30	Philadelphia Athletics		●		Boston Red Sox	Wes Ferrell	2
15	Gene Hasson	1937-09-09	Philadelphia Athletics				Washington Senators	Dick Lanahan	4
16	Ernie Koy	1938-04-19	Brooklyn Dodgers				Philadelphia Phillies	Wayne LaMaster	36
17	Emmett Mueller	1938-04-19	Philadelphia Phillies				Brooklyn Dodgers	Van Mungo	17
18	Bill LeFebvre	1938-06-10	Boston Red Sox	●			Chicago White Sox	Monty Stratton	1
19	Clyde Vollmer	1942-05-31	Cincinnati Reds	●			Pittsburgh Pirates	Max Butcher	69
20	Paul Gillespie	1942-09-11	Chicago Cubs				New York Giants	Harry Feldan	6
21	Buddy Kerr	1943-09-08	New York Giants				Philadelphia Phillies	Bill Lee	31
22	Hack Miller	1944-04-23	Detroit Tigers				Cleveland Indians	Al Smith	1
23	Whitey Lockman	1945-07-05	New York Giants				St. Louis Cardinals	George Dockins	114
24	Eddie Pellagrini	1946-04-22	Boston Red Sox				Washington Senators	Sid Hudson	20
25	Dan Bankhead	1947-08-26	Brooklyn Dodgers				Pittsburgh Pirates	Fritz Ostermueller	1
26	George Vico	1948-04-20	Detroit Tigers	●			Chicago White Sox	Joe Haynes	12
27	Les Layton	1948-05-21	New York Giants		●		Chicago Cubs	Johnny Schmitz	2
28	Ed Sanicki	1949-09-14	Philadelphia Phillies				Pittsburgh Pirates	Rip Sewell	3
29	Ted Tappe	1950-09-14	Cincinnati Reds		●		Brooklyn Dodgers	Erv Palica	5
30	Bob Nieman	1951-09-14	St. Louis Browns				Boston Red Sox	Mickey McDermott	125
31	Hoyt Wilhelm	1952-04-23	New York Giants				Boston Braves	Dick Hoover	1
32	Wally Moon	1954-04-13	St. Louis Cardinals				Chicago Cubs	Paul Minner	142
33	Chuck Tanner	1955-04-12	Milwaukee Braves	●	●		Redlegs	Gerry Staley	21

	Name	Date	Team	First pitch	Pinch hitter	Grand slam	Opponent	Pitcher	Career HR**
34	Bill White	1956-05-07	New York Giants				St. Louis Cardinals	Ben Flowers	202
35	Frank Ernaga	1957-05-24	Chicago Cubs				Milwaukee Braves	Warren Spahn	2
36	Don Leppert	1961-06-18	Pittsburgh Pirates				St. Lous Cardinals	Curt Simmons	15
37	Cuno Barragan	1961-09-01	Chicago Cubs				San Francisco Giants	Dick LeMay	1
38	Bob Tillman	1962-05-19	Boston Red Sox				Los Angeles Angels	Ted Bowsfield	79
39	John Kennedy	1962-09-05	Washington Senators		●		Minnesota Twins	Dick Stigman	32
40	Buster Narum	1963-05-03	Baltimore Orioles				Detroit Tigers	Don Mossi	3
41	Gates Brown	1963-06-19	Detroit Tigers		●		Boston Red Sox	Bob Heffner	84
42	Bert Campaneris	1964-07-23	Kansas City Athletics	●			Minnesota Twins	Jim Kaat	79
43	Bill Roman	1964-09-30	Detroit Tigers		●		New York Yankees	Jim Bouton	1
44	Brant Alyea	1965-09-12	Washington Senators	●	●		California Angels	Rudy May	38
45	John Miller	1966-09-11	New York Yankees				Boston Red Sox	Lee Stange	2
46	Rick Renick	1968-07-11	Minnesota Twins				Detroit Tigers	Mickey Lolich	20
47	Joe Keough	1968-08-07	Oakland Athletics		●		New York Yankees	Lindy McDaniel	9
48	Gene Lamont	1970-09-02	Detroit Tigers				Boston Red Sox	Cal Koonce	4
49	Don Rose	1972-05-24	California Angels	●			Oakland Athletics	Diego Seguí	1
50	Benny Ayala	1974-08-27	New York Mets				Houston Astros	Tom Griffin	38
51	Reggie Sanders	1974-09-01	Detroit Tigers				Oakland Athletics	Catfish Hunter	3
52	John Montefusco	1974-09-03	San Francisco Giants				Los Angeles Dodgers	Charlie Hough	4
53	José Sosa	1975-07-30	Houston Astros				San Diego Padres	Danny Frisella	1
54	Dave McKay	1975-08-22	Minnesota Twins				Detroit Tigers	Vern Ruhle	21
55	Johnnie LeMaster	1975-09-02	San Francisco Giants				Los Angeles Dodgers	Don Sutton	22
56	Al Woods	1977-04-07	Toronto Blue Jays	●	●		Chicago White Sox	Francisco Barrios	35
57	Dave Machemer	1978-06-21	California Angels				Minnesota Twins	Geoff Zahn	1
58	Tim Wallach	1980-09-06	Montreal Expos				San Francisco Giants	Phil Nastu	260
59	Gary Gaetti	1981-09-20	Minnesota Twins				Texas Rangers	Charlie Hough	360
60	Carmelo Martínez	1983-08-22	Chicago Cubs				Cincinnati Reds	Frank Pastore	108
61	Mike Fitzgerald	1983-09-13	New York Mets				Philadelphia Phillies	Tony Ghelfi	48
62	Andre David	1984-06-29	Minnesota Twins				Detroit Tigers	Jack Morris	1
63	Will Clark	1986-04-08	San Francisco Giants				Houston Astros	Nolan Ryan	284
64	Terry Steinbach	1986-09-12	Oakland Athletics				Cleveland Indians	Greg Swindell	162
65	Jay Bell	1986-09-29	Cleveland Indians	●			Minnesota Twins	Bert Blyleven	195
66	Ricky Jordan	1988-07-17	Philadelphia Phillies				Houston Astros	Bob Knepper	55
67	Junior Félix	1989-05-04	Toronto Blue Jays	●			California Angels	Kirk McCaskill	55
68	José Offerman	1990-08-19	Los Angeles Dodgers				Montreal Expos	Ramón Martínez	57
69	Dave Eiland	1992-04-10	San Diego Padres				Los Angeles Dodgers	Bob Ojeda	1
70	Jim Bullinger	1992-06-08	Chicago Cubs	●			St. Louis Cardinals	Rhéal Cormier	4
71	Jay Gainer	1993-05-14	Colorado Rockies	●			Cincinnati Reds	Tim Pugh	3
72	Mitch Lyden	1993-06-16	Florida Marlins				Chicago Cubs	José Bautista	1
73	Garey Ingram	1994-05-19	Los Angeles Dodgers		●		Colorado Rockies	Mike Munoz	3

	Name	Date	Team	First pitch	Pinch hitter	Grand slam	Opponent	Pitcher	Career HR**
74	Jon Nunnally	1995-04-29	Kansas City Royals				New York Yankees	Mélido Pérez	42
75	Jermaine Dye	1996-05-17	Atlanta Braves				Cincinnati Reds	Marcus Moore	325
76	Dustin Hermanson	1997-04-16	Montreal Expos				Houston Astros	Shane Reynolds	2
77	Brad Fullmer	1997-09-02	Montreal Expos		●		Boston Red Sox	Bret Saberhagen	114
78	Marlon Anderson	1998-09-08	Philadelphia Phillies		●		New York Mets	Mel Rojas	63
79	Carlos Lee	1999-05-07	Chicago White Sox				Oakland Athletics	Tom Candiotti	358
80	Guillermo Mota	1999-06-09	Montreal Expos				Boston Red Sox	Mark Guthrie	2
81	Esteban Yan	2000-06-04	Tampa Bay Devil Rays	●			New York Mets	Bobby Jones	1
82	Álex Cabrera	2000-06-26	Arizona Diamondbacks		●		Houston Astros	Yorkis Pérez	5
83	Keith McDonald	2000-07-04	St. Louis Cardinals		●		Cincinnati Reds	Andy Larkin	3
84	Chris Richard	2000-07-17	St. Louis Cardinals	●			Minnesota Twins	Mike Lincoln	34
85	Gene Stechschulte	2001-04-17	St. Louis Cardinals	●	●		Arizona Diamondbacks	Armando Reynoso	1
86	Marcus Thames	2002-06-10	New York Yankees	●			Arizona Diamondbacks	Randy Johnson	115
87	Miguel Olivo	2002-09-15	Chicago White Sox				New York Yankees	Andy Pettitte	145
88	Dave Matranga	2003-06-27	Houston Astros		●		Texas Rangers	Joaquín Benoit	1
89	Kaz Matsui	2004-04-06	New York Mets	●			Atlanta Braves	Russ Ortiz	32
90	Héctor Luna	2004-04-08	St. Louis Cardinals				Milwaukee Brewers	Chris Capuano	15
91	Greg Dobbs	2004-09-08	Seattle Mariners		●		Cleveland Indians	Bob Wickman	46
92	Andy Phillips	2004-09-26	New York Yankees	●	●		Boston Red Sox	Terry Adams	14
93	Mike Jacobs	2005-08-21	New York Mets		●		Washington Nationals	Esteban Loaiza	100
94	Jeremy Hermida	2005-08-31	Florida Marlins		●	●	St. Louis Cardinals	Alberto Reyes	65
95	Mike Napoli	2006-05-04	Los Angeles Angels				Detroit Tigers	Justin Verlander	267
96	Adam Wainwright	2006-05-24	St. Louis Cardinals	●			San Francisco Giants	Noah Lowry	10
97	Kevin Kouzmanoff	2006-09-02	Cleveland Indians	●		●	Texas Rangers	Edinson Vólquez	87
98	Charlton Jimerson	2006-09-04	Houston Astros		●		Philadelphia Phillies	Cole Hamels	2
99	Josh Fields	2006-09-18	Chicago White Sox		●		Detroit Tigers	Jamie Walker	34
100	Elijah Dukes	2007-04-02	Tampa Bay Devil Rays				New York Yankees	Carl Pavano	31
101	Mark Worrell	2008-06-05	St. Louis Cardinals				Washington Nationals	Tim Redding	1
102	Luis Montañez	2008-08-06	Baltimore Orioles				Anaheim Angels	Ervin Santana	5
103	Mark Saccomanno	2008-09-08	Houston Astros	●	●		Pittsburgh Pirates	Ian Snell	1
104	Jordan Schafer	2009-04-05	Atlanta Braves				Philadelphia Phillies	Brett Myers	12
105	Gerardo Parra	2009-05-13	Arizona Diamondbacks				Cincinnati Reds	Johnny Cueto	90
106	John Hester	2009-08-28	Arizona Diamondbacks		●		Houston Astros	Wilton López	6
107	Jason Heyward*	2010-04-05	Atlanta Braves				Chicago Cubs	Carlos Zambrano	184
108	Luke Hughes	2010-04-28	Minnesota Twins				Detroit Tigers	Max Scherzer	8
109	Starlin Castro	2010-05-07	Chicago Cubs				Cincinnati Reds	Homer Bailey	138
110	Daniel Nava	2010-06-12	Boston Red Sox	●		●	Philadelphia Phillies	Joe Blanton	29

	Name	Date	Team	First pitch	Pinch hitter	Grand slam	Opponent	Pitcher	Career HR**
111	J.P. Arencibia	2010-08-07	Toronto Blue Jays	●			Tampa Bay Rays	James Shields	80
112	Brandon Guyer	2011-05-06	Tampa Bay Rays				Baltimore Orioles	Zack Britton	32
113	Tommy Milone*	2011-09-03	Washington Nationals	●			New York Mets	Dillon Gee	1
114	Brett Pill	2011-09-06	San Francisco Giants				San Diego Padres	Wade LeBlanc	9
115	Starling Marte*	2012-07-26	Pittsburgh Pirates	●			Houston Astros	Dallas Keuchel	154
116	Eddy Rodríguez	2012-08-02	San Diego Padres				Cincinnati Reds	Johnny Cueto	1
117	Jurickson Profar*	2012-09-02	Texas Rangers				Cleveland Indians	Zach McAllister	111
118	Jorge Soler*	2014-08-27	Chicago Cubs				Cincinnati Reds	Mat Latos	191
119	Eddie Rosario*	2015-05-06	Minnesota Twins	●			Oakland A's	Scott Kazmir	169
120	Daniel Norris*	2015-08-19	Detroit Tigers				Chicago Cubs	Jon Lester	1
121	Willson Contreras*	2016-06-19	Chicago Cubs	●	●		Pittsburgh Pirates	A.J. Schugel	152
122	Aaron Judge*	2016-08-13	New York Yankees				Tampa Bay Rays	Matt Andriese	315
123	Tyler Austin	2016-08-13	New York Yankees				Tampa Bay Rays	Matt Andriese	33
124	Paul DeJong*	2017-05-28	St. Louis Cardinals		●		Colorado Rockies	Greg Holland	140
125	Lane Thomas*	2019-04-19	St. Louis Cardinals		●		New York Mets	Seth Lugo	72
126	Zack Collins*	2019-06-21	Chicago White Sox				Texas Rangers	Ariel Jurado	11
127	Tyler Stephenson*	2020-07-27	Cincinnati Reds				Chicago Cubs	Duane Underwood Jr.	50
128	Keibert Ruiz*	2020-08-16	Los Angeles Dodgers				Anaheim Angels	Julio Teheran	42
129	Sergio Alcántara*	2020-09-06	Detroit Tigers				Minnesota Twins	Rich Hill	12
130	Akil Baddoo*	2021-04-04	Detroit Tigers	●			Cleveland Indians	Aaron Civale	28
131	Seth Beer*	2021-09-10	Arizona Diamondbacks				Seattle Mariners	Diego Castillo	2
132	Joe Dunand*	2022-05-07	Miami Marlins				San Diego Padres	Sean Manaea	1
133	Christopher Morel*	2022-05-17	Chicago Cubs		●		Pittsburgh Pirates	Chase De Jong	63
134	James Outman*	2022-07-31	Los Angeles Dodgers		●		Colorado Rockies	Germán Márquez	28
135	Brett Baty*	2022-08-17	New York Mets				Atlanta Braves	Jake Odorizzi	15
136	Spencer Steer*	2022-09-02	Cincinnati Reds				Colorado Rockies	Kyle Freeland	45
137	Josh Jung*	2022-09-09	Texas Rangers				Toronto Blue Jays	Ross Stripling	35
138	Davis Schneider*	2023-08-04	Toronto Blue Jays				Boston Red Sox	James Paxton	21
139	Weston Wilson*	2023-08-09	Philadelphia Phillies				Washington Nationals	MacKenzie Gore	4
140	Jasson Domínguez*	2023-09-01	New York Yankees				Houston Astros	Justin Verlander	6
141	Jhonkensy Noel*	2024-06-26	Cleveland Guardians				Baltimore Orioles	Grayson Rodriguez	13

* Active in 2024
** Statistics through 2024 MLB season

CONTRIBUTORS

JOE ADONA is on the board of directors of SABR's Rocky Mountain Chapter. A New Jersey native and a lifelong Mets fan, he retired from his career as a technology VP for an investment bank in New York City and moved out to the mountains of Colorado in 2021. A passionate baseball fan and avid traveler, Joe has attended well over 2,000 major-league games, including at least one in every ballpark. He maintains a blog at My7thInningStretch.com with reviews and ratings of each park he's visited.

Originally from Baltimore, **MALCOLM ALLEN** manages a production warehouse in Brooklyn, New York, where he lives with his wife, Sara, and their two daughters. He saw Luis Montáñez play at Yankee Stadium and witnessed Junior Félix in action at both Oriole Park at Camden Yards and Memorial Stadium. Outside the latter ballpark, Félix signed a cracked bat for him.

JORGE COLÓN DELGADO has been a member of SABR since 1999 and has spent the last 25 years researching Puerto Rican baseball history. In 2003 he was named the official historian of the Puerto Rico Professional Baseball League and received a lifetime pass to the National Baseball Hall of Fame in Cooperstown for his tireless efforts to preserve baseball history. He is the editor of beisbol101.com and negroleaguerspuertorico.com, as well as the author of seven books and a short film. In October 2022 he was named general coordinator of the Puerto Rico Professional Baseball Hall of Fame.

MIKE COONEY earned a master's degree in journalism and worked for more than 50 years in the automotive industry. Being a diehard baseball fan, he became a SABR member in 1999 and wrote and edited biographies. He was also an adjunct professor at Ivy Tech Community College in Indiana, where he taught English composition for 10 years. As a hobby, he has written over 500 "A Stones Throw" columns for his local newspaper. Now retired for the fifth time, he lives with his wife, Jade, and two rescue German shepherds on a bluff overlooking the Ohio River.

RORY COSTELLO is co-chair and chief editor of the SABR BioProject. He lives in Brooklyn, New York, with his wife, Noriko, and son, Kai.

RICHARD CUICCHI joined SABR in 1983 and is an active member of the Schott-Pelican Chapter. Since his retirement as an information technology executive, Richard authored *Family Ties: A Comprehensive Collection of Facts and Trivia about Baseball's Relatives*. He has contributed to numerous SABR BioProject and Games Project publications. He does freelance writing and blogging about a variety of baseball topics on his website, TheTenthInning.com. Richard is a regular contributor to CrescentCitySports.com, where he writes about New Orleans baseball history. Richard lives in New Orleans with his wife, Mary.

JOSEPH "JOEY" ELLEDGE is the chair of the business department and an associate professor of sport management at Erskine College. As an avid baseball fan, Joey is a lifelong Chicago Cubs fan and a big supporter of minor-league baseball. He became a baseball fan by attending games of the Capital City Bombers (former Single-A affiliate for the New York Mets) with his family, and holds partial season tickets to minor-league games in Columbia, South Carolina, with his mother, sisters, and his wife. He works with the Lexington County Blowfish (Coastal Plain League) in sales. He is a new contributor to SABR projects and studies the business side of baseball in his free time. Joey resides in Lexington, South Carolina, with his wife, Katie, and three dogs, Cookie, Sammy (named after Sammy Sosa), and Boone.

CARLOS FRAGOSO is a Mexican native and retired chemical engineer and now a freelancer consultant on environmental matters. A SABR member since 2000, he has contributed to fellow members in books like Bill Nowlin's *The Kid: Ted Williams in San Diego*, Ron Anderson's book *Long Ball a Baseball Biography of George Scott*, and many specific requests regarding Mexican baseball. He is also a former Red Sox Special Assignment Scout for Mexico in 1999-2002 under Lee Sigman and Ray Poitevint being instrumental in the signing of Luis Mendoza and Mauricio Lara. A baseball lover for life as amateur player, Little Leagues and national teams manager, and former Mexican Baseball Federation Officer.

JOHN FREDLAND is an attorney and retired Air Force officer. As an undergraduate at Rice University, he covered Rice's nationally ranked baseball teams for the school newspaper, the *Rice Thresher*. John received his law degree at Vanderbilt University, then served as an active-duty attorney in the Air Force's Judge Advocate General's Corps for 20 years. He lives in San Antonio, Texas, and chairs SABR's Baseball Games Project Research Committee.

DAVID GAGNON contributed his bio of Gates Brown to the SABR book *Sock It To 'Em Tigers!* At the time, he wrote that he "splits his time between running a small accounting firm and being a baseball fanatic. While completing 1040 returns, he's got a headset on listening to the Tigers in his office. He had to cut short one client consultation to watch the Tigers play the Yankees in the 2006 ALDS."

As a teenage New York Yankees fan, **CRAIG GARRETSON** was confident that Dave Eiland, Kevin Maas, and Wade Taylor were the foundations of the next pinstripe dynasty. A member of SABR since 2019, he has contributed to a number of SABR publications including *Yankee Stadium 1923-2008: America's First Modern Ballpark* (2023). Craig lives in New Jersey with his wife and two daughters.

PAUL GEISLER JR. grew up in San Antonio, Texas, and served as a Lutheran pastor for 45 years. He lives in Lake Jackson, Texas, with his wife Susan; they have three grown children: Sarah, Brydon, and Johanna. Now retired, Paul writes a weekly column for his local newspaper. He loves anything baseball—playing, watching, coaching, researching, and writing.

NELSON "CHIP" GREENE, a longtime contributor to SABR's Biography Project, is the grandson of Nelson Greene, who pitched in 15 games in the 1920s for the Brooklyn Robins. Chip and his wife, Elaine, reside in Waynesboro, Pennsylvania.

YOSHIHIRO KODA was born in Kobe, Japan, and has lived more than 30 years in Tokyo. His first time visiting an American ballpark was Yankee Stadium in 1982. He joined SABR in 1996. As a member of the Business of Baseball Committee, he has noted the differences between Japan and USA baseball in the committee's bulletin.

SEAN KOLODZIEJ, a SABR member since 2018, is a lifelong Cubs fan. He was born, raised, and still lives in Joliet, Illinois, with his wife, Amy. His greatest moment at Wrigley Field was watching Glenallen Hill hit a home run onto the rooftop of a building on Waveland Avenue.

TARA KRIEGER drove in a run in her first middle school at-bat, which she's pretty sure was a 4-3 ground out. She culminated her high school softball career with a grand slam, which she's pretty sure was her only home run. She's also pretty sure she's better at writing sports than at playing them. She currently works as an attorney for the City of New York and was previously on the editorial staff at *Newsday* and MLB Advanced Media. A member of SABR since 2005, she has participated in the publication of several SABR books, most recently editing *Yankee Stadium 1923-2008: America's First Modern Ballpark.*

JUSTIN KRUEGER is an assistant professor of social studies education at Delta State University in Cleveland, Mississippi, and was a 2023 Mississippi Humanities Council teacher of the year recipient. He enjoys listening to baseball games on the radio.

BRYAN LAKE is an attorney in Minneapolis who likes writing about ballplayers he watched while growing up. He dislikes the designated hitter and the expanded playoff format, but he has grudgingly accepted interleague play.

LEN LEVIN is a longtime newspaper editor in New England, now retired. He lives in Providence with his wife, Linda, and an overachieving orange cat. He now (Len, not the cat) is the grammarian for the Rhode Island Supreme Court and edits its decisions. He also copy-edits many SABR books, including this one. He is just down the interstate from Fenway Park, where he has spent many happy (and some not-so-happy) hours.

BILL NOWLIN is a Boston native and Red Sox fan, author of the recent memoir *Bitten by the Red Sox Baseball Bug* (Summer Game Books). The first time he played in a major-league ball-park (Fenway Park) was in a charity game. He popped up to the shortstop. Two at-bats later, he hit a ball to left that one-hopped the wall. One of the founders of Rounder Records, he has enjoyed writing and editing for SABR.

LAURA H. PEEBLES is a retired CPA, now an Associate Editor for the SABR Baseball Games Project. Besides writing and fact-checking stories, she puts her rhyming ability to work summarizing games and writing baseball parodies of holiday songs. She grew up with the Oakland A's, but has been a Washington Nationals fan since 2010. She lives in Arlington, Virginia with her wife, two cats, and an extensive collection of baseballs.

ZAC PETRILLO holds a bachelor of arts from Hunter College and a master of fine arts from Chapman University's Dodge College of Film and Media Arts. His experience spans directing multiple short films and producing content for networks like Comedy Central and TruTV. In 2016 Zac played a pivotal role in the launch of Vice Media's 24/7 cable network, Vice TV. As an active SABR member, he dedicates his research to exploring the realm of post-1980s baseball, particularly examining its intersection with the media industry. Currently, he serves as the director of technical operations at A+E Networks and imparts his knowledge in television studies as a lecturer at Marymount Manhattan College.

JACOB POMRENKE is SABR's director of editorial content and chair of the Black Sox Scandal Research Committee. He is the editor of *Scandal on the South Side: The 1919 Chicago White Sox* (2015) and *Joe Jackson vs. Chicago American League Baseball Club: The Never-Before-Seen Trial Transcript* (2023). He lives in Chicago with his wife, Tracy Greer, and their cat, Nixey Callahan.

BILL PRUDEN has been a teacher of American History and Government for almost 40 years. A SABR member for over two decades, he has contributed to SABR's Bio and Games projects as well as some book projects. He has also written on a range of American history subjects, an interest undoubtedly fueled by the fact that as a 7-year-old he was at Yankee Stadium to witness Roger Maris's historic 61st home run.

CARL RIECHERS retired from United Parcel Service in 2012 after 35 years of service. With more free time, he became a SABR member that same year. Born and raised in the suburbs of St. Louis, he became a big fan of the Cardinals. He and his wife, Janet, have three children and he is the proud grandpa of two.

TOM SCHOTT joined SABR in 2020 and has written for the BioProject and Games Project. He got his start in sports journalism at age 12 when he cofounded his own magazine called *The Redbird Chirps*, interviewing nearly 100 major-league players, managers, coaches, and broadcasters from 1981 to 1986. A native of St. Louis, Schott has been a contributing writer for the Cardinals' media guide, Hall of Fame induction program, magazine, and website (Cardinals.com). He is coauthor of *The Giants Encyclopedia* and *The Giants Encyclopedia: Second Edition* – the definitive history of the New York and San Francisco Giants franchise. He also has written for the Giants website (SFGiants.com), the Atlanta Braves media guide and website (Braves.com), and the National Baseball Hall of Fame and Museum website (BaseballHall.org). Schott resides in West Lafayette, Indiana, with his wife, Jane. They have two sons, August and Sam.

BARRETT SNYDER holds a master's degree in sports management and a Master of Business Administration from Drexel University. He is currently enrolled at West Chester University studying exercise science with a concentration in sports psychology.

GISELLE STANCIC grew up a Kansas City Royals fan and now cheers for the San Francisco Giants. She enjoys writing baseball player biographies and telling their stories of dedication, humor, and love for the game. Giselle lives in the Bay Area, where she's a technical writer and the author of two mystery novels.

STEW THORNLEY has been a SABR member since 1979. He is a proud member of the Halsey Hall Chapter (Where the Action Is!), the oldest and most active chapter in SABR. He is married to Brenda Himrich, also a SABR member.

MICHAEL TRZINSKI is retired but works part-time on a cranberry marsh. He lives in Port Edwards, Wisconsin, and has been married to Kelli since 2001. Michael has three children (Corey, Bronson, and Emily) and nine grandchildren. He also has a cat (Hudson) and grandpup (Ellie). Michael has written about a dozen SABR bios, and this is his third contribution to SABR books. He looks forward to writing many more.

JOSEPH WANCHO has contributed to 48 SABR publications as a result of his work with the BioProject and Games Project and *The National Pastime*. These days he catalogs back issues of *Baseball Digest* for the Baseball Index Project and, when needed, he assists with fact-checking for the Games Project. A SABR member since 2005, he resides in Westlake, Ohio.

BOB WEBSTER grew up in northwestern Indiana and has been a Cubs fan since 1963. Bob moved to Portland, Oregon, in 1980 and now works on baseball research and writing and contributes to various SABR projects. Bob is the VP of the Pacific Northwest Chapter of SABR and VP of the Old-Timers Baseball Association of Portland.

PHIL WILLIAMS lives in Oreland, Pennsylvania, and has been a SABR member since 2007. He has contributed numerous articles to SABR's BioProject and is working on a book on Philadelphia baseball during the Deadball Era.

One-Win Wonders

ISBN 9978-1-960819-13-0 $39.95 paperback

ISBN 9978-1-960819-12-3 $9.99 ebook

Biographies of 78 players whose entire major-league pitching record consisted of just one win: from the tragic, like Nick Adenhart, an Angels rookie who was killed by a drunk driver, to the improbable, like catcher Brent Mayne, who was the last player left on the Colorado Rockies bench in an extra inning game after the final bullpen pitcher was ejected.

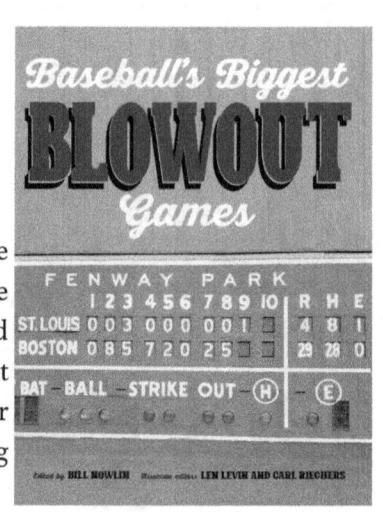

One-Hit Wonders

ISBN 978-1-9701-5956-1 $32.95 paperback

ISBN 978-1-9701-5957-8 $9.99 ebook

The stories of 70 players who got exactly one hit in the majors. Some, like pitcher Arthur Rhodes, were in the big leagues a long time. Rhodes appeared in 900 games but only notched one base hit. Others, like Dan Ardell, had only a cup of coffee. When asked if he thought his story wouldn't have been as interesting if he'd had TWO hits, Ardell replied, "I think that's exactly true."

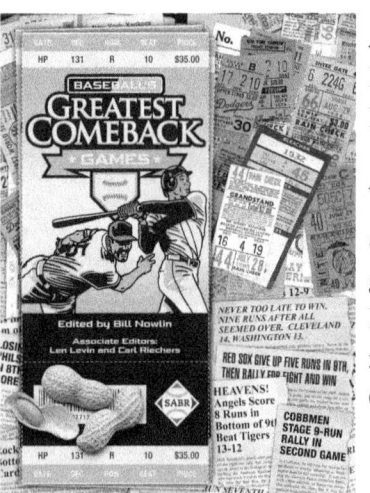

Baseball's Greatest Comeback Games

ISBN 978-1-9701-5946-2, $9.99 ebook

ISBN 978-1-9701-5947-9, $29.95 paperback

What are Major League Baseball's greatest comeback games? Retrosheet ranked a master list of 630 games and we include the top 64, plus seven postseason games in this volume. In the end, every major-league team is represented. The Phillies lead the list with six comeback wins in the top 64. Tied for second for most comebacks are four American League teams: the Boston Red Sox, Cleveland Indians/Guardians, Detroit Tigers, and New York Yankees.

Baseball's Biggest Blowout Games

ISBN 978-1-9701-5943-1, $24.95 paperback

ISBN 978-1-9701-5942-4, $9.99 ebook

The most lopsided games in major-league baseball history. Since 1901, the biggest blowout game in major-league history was on August 22, 2007, when the Texas Rangers beat the Baltimore Orioles, 30-3—a 27-run difference. It eclipsed the 25 runs between the Red Sox and Browns on June 8, 1950, 29-4, a game that followed a 20-4 blowout the day before! We've included the top four games for each franchise so every fan can have a chance to read about their team winning big, plus the six biggest blowouts from the postseason.

The SABR Digital Library

•••

Print & Ebooks

SABR.ORG
OR
WHEREVER
BOOKS ARE
SOLD

The Stars Shone on Philadelphia: The 1934 Phila. Stars
ISBN 978-1-960819-04-8 $9.99 ebook
ISBN 978-1-960819-05-5 $29.95 paperback
Biographies of Ed Bolden's 1934 Negro National
League champions, including Biz Mackie and Jud
Wilson.

Yankee Stadium: America's First Modern Ballpark
ISBN 978-1-960819-16-8 $9.99 ebook
ISBN 978-1-960819-21-5 $39.95 paperback
Essays about the history of Yankee Stadium and
recaps of over 50 historic games and other events
there, including papal visits, football, and more.

*Ebbets Field: Great, Historic, and Memorable Games at
Brooklyn's Lost Ballpark*
ISBN 978-1-960819-16-1 $9.99 ebook
ISBN 978-1-960819-17-8 $39.95 paperback
Relive Jackie Robinson's and Sandy Koufax's debuts,
and over 90 other heartbreaks and triumphs in
Brooklyn, plus essays on the ballpark.

Nichibei Yakyu: Volume II: 1960-2019
ISBN 978-1-960819-14-7 $9.99 ebook
ISBN 978-1-960819-15-4 $34.95 paperback
Fascinating recaps of the exhibition tours and
MLB games by US baseball teams in Japan.

Sox Bid Curse Farewell: The 2004 Boston Red Sox
ISBN 978-1-960819-18-5 $9.99 ebook
ISBN 978-1-960819-19-2 $34.95 paperback
Biographies of every player and coach on the 2004
World Championship team, as well as essays about
the season, effects of the win on fans, and more.

Dodger Stadium: Blue Heaven on Earth
ISBN 978-1-960819-20-8 $9.99 ebook
ISBN 978-1-960819-21-5 $29.95 paperback
Essays about the history of Dodger Stadium and
recaps of over 50 historic games there, from
Fernandomania to Vin Scully's bow.

One-Win Wonders
ISBN 978-1-960819-13-0 $39.95 paperback
ISBN 978-1-960819-12-3 $9.99 ebook
Biographies of 78 players whose entire major league
pitching record consisted of just one win, from the
tragic, like Nick Adenhart, to the improbable, like
catcher Brent Mayne.

Willie Mays: Five Tools
ISBN 978-1-960819-02-4 $9.99 ebook
ISBN 978-1-960819-03-1 $29.95 paperback
Twenty essays on Mays' life and career, plus
recaps of 30 historic games.

www.ingramcontent.com/pod-product-compliance
Lightning Source LLC
Chambersburg PA
CBHW080957120626
46546CB00010B/2936